Also by John Watt

The District Magistrate in Late Imperial China

Health Care and National Development in China, 1950-2000

Public Medicine in Wartime China, 1931-1945

Saving Lives in Wartime China, 1928-1945

The WISDOM of the COVENANTS and Their RELEVANCE to OUR TIMES

John Watt

authorHOUSE

AuthorHouse™
1663 Liberty Drive
Bloomington, IN 47403
www.authorhouse.com
Phone: 1 (800) 839-8640

© *2019 John Watt. All rights reserved.*

No part of this book may be reproduced, stored in a retrieval system, or transmitted by any means without the written permission of the author.

The KJV is public domain in the United States.

Holy Bible, New Living Translation, copyright © *1996, 2004, 2015 by Tyndale House Foundation. Used by permission of Tyndale House Publishers, Inc., Carol Stream, Illinois 60188. All rights reserved.*

The Jerusalem Bible © *1966 by Darton Longman & Todd Ltd and Doubleday and Company Ltd.*

Published by AuthorHouse 01/04/2019

ISBN: 978-1-5462-7396-7 (sc)
ISBN: 978-1-5462-7397-4 (hc)
ISBN: 978-1-5462-7409-4 (e)

Library of Congress Control Number: 2018915253

Print information available on the last page.

Any people depicted in stock imagery provided by Getty Images are models, and such images are being used for illustrative purposes only.
Certain stock imagery © *Getty Images.*

This book is printed on acid-free paper.

Because of the dynamic nature of the Internet, any web addresses or links contained in this book may have changed since publication and may no longer be valid. The views expressed in this work are solely those of the author and do not necessarily reflect the views of the publisher, and the publisher hereby disclaims any responsibility for them.

For Alison, Duncan, Fiona, Jennifer

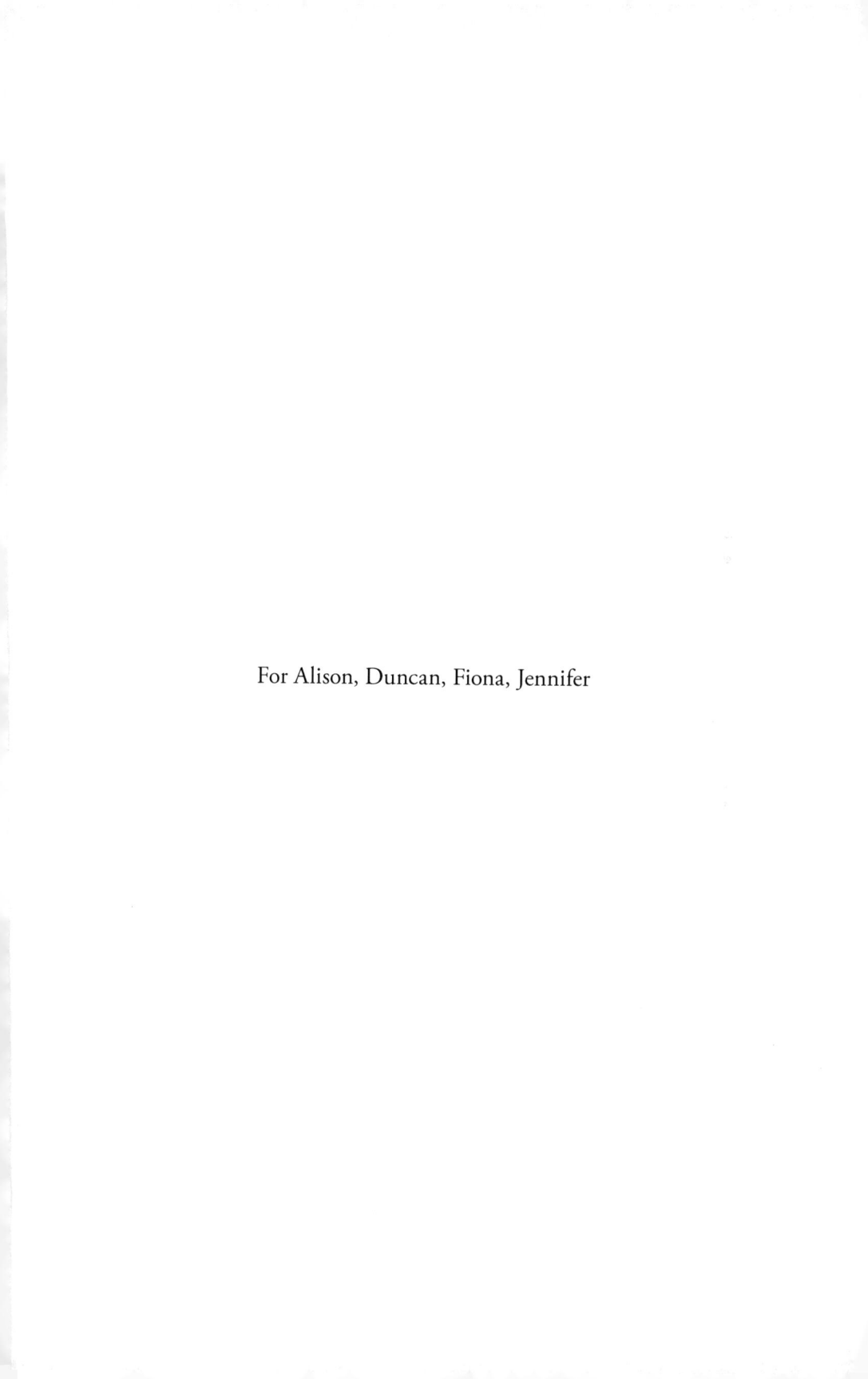

CONTENTS

Acknowledgements ix

I   Covenants and the Bible 1

Chapter 1   Covenants as a Guide to Ethical Conduct 3
Chapter 2   The Hebrew Scriptures: A Brief Outline 23
Chapter 3   The Christian Context 38
Chapter 4   Reading the Bible in a Materialist Age 55

II   In Search of the Covenants 69

Chapter 5   Adam and Eve and The Creation Covenant 71
Chapter 6   Moses and the Sinai Covenant 83
Chapter 7   Covenant Guardians: The Isaiah Prophecies 107
Chapter 8   The Individual and Covenant in the Psalms 128
Chapter 9   Covenant in the Wisdom Tradition 148
Chapter 10   Jesus and the Covenant of Redemption 174
Chapter 11   Paul and the Covenant of Redemption 192

III   Covenants and Contemporary Problems 211

Chapter 12   Covenant and Management of Androcentric Power 213
Chapter 13   The Strange Fate of Women in the Covenantal World .. 236
Chapter 14   Marriage as Sacramental Covenant 267
Chapter 15   The Covenant and Economic Justice 292

Chapter 16 The Relevance of Covenant to the Natural World..........312
Chapter 17 Covenant as the Key to Justice and Mercy.................... 336
Chapter 18 Conclusion: The Two Ways... 358

Author Description 383

ACKNOWLEDGEMENTS

This book was precipitated by my anxieties about the state of moral ethics in our times. My thinking about it grew out of a seminar on Bible study that I was invited to lead at the Friends Meeting House in Purchase, N.Y. in 1988. I am indebted to Rabbi Edward Schechter of Temple Beth-Shalom in Hastings on Hudson for recommending me for that project, and to Rabbi Schechter and other members of Temple Beth-Shalom for inviting me to participate in their study classes.

My interest in the Bible and its values has been at various times encouraged by my father and my brother Robin, both of whom were active in the Church of Scotland. While my father never actively discussed the life of the spirit, he certainly did his best to live it. As for my brother, he revived my interest in the Bible at a time when I was feeling uncertain about my future.

I am also grateful to other friends and spiritual communicants, among them Rev. Jerry and Meredith Morgan, Rev. Helen Beasley, Charles Aschmann, and members of my choir at North Yonkers Community Church. Others who have played an important part in developing my perspectives include Elizabeth Armstrong, Woody Bliss, Doug Bowman, Frank and Harriet Blume, Judith Chasin, Tenzing Chhodak, Zhu Fang, Jerry and Judy Grant, Robin and Edie Hartshorne, Peter and Jean Jones, Charles Kessler, Jane and Jeremy Knowles, Father Roland LaJoie, Dave and Sue Lawrence, Rachel and Mark Macke, Mary and Jesse McKinney, Kim Nadler, Joe and Janis Nicolosi, Laura Nurse, Bill Porter, David Riesman, Pat Roth, Lobsang Sangay, Susanna Wolfe, a number of friends encountered through the Kripalu Center, Landmark Education, and Vermont Music and Arts, and various members of the Weston United Church of Christ.

Several people have reviewed the text, among them Elaine

McGillicuddy, Lisa Forberg, Douglas Bowman, Bill McDonald, Helen Beasley, Bill Porter, and Woody Bliss. I'm especially grateful to Doug for providing me with the text from Black Elk and introducing me to the writings of Dietrich Bonhoeffer. A conversation over 30 years ago with Father Thomas Berry put me in possession of some of his writings, which have helped to inspire the theme and perspective of this work.

Especially I want to thank my spouse Anne (to whom I dedicated a previous book) and our living children Alison, Fiona and Jennifer, for encouraging me in one way or another to persevere with this twenty-year enterprise. I've written this book as a tribute to friends, but especially to our offspring, to whom I dedicate it. They have each supported me in innumerable ways. I could not have come to where I am without their love and friendship.

I must also express my gratitude to the authors whose works are listed in the appendix on further reading. I have relied on their work and ideas extensively, especially for interpretation of Biblical texts. As this is intentionally not a scholastic study there are very few footnotes or citations, but those who know this literature will recognize how much I have depended on it. There are a few authors whom I particularly want to recognize. It was Elizabeth Schussler-Fiorenza's study In Memory of Her, which introduced me to the powerful and essential perspective of women theologians. It is not too much to say that only this perspective can restore the submerged dimension in Christianity, namely the central role of women in giving rise to this world-wide spiritual and moral path.

I am also grateful to the authors of Back to the Sources: Reading the Classic Jewish Texts for writing with such enthusiasm and clarity about this great religious literature. Brian Peckham's History and Prophecy: The Development of Late Judean Traditions proved an amazingly valuable guide. Another work that has maintained my interest for many years is Matthew Fox's study of Hildegard of Bingen.

Finally, I should thank the editors of the Jerusalem Bible for coming up with a version of the Bible and formatting it in a way that made sense to me, especially in bringing out the poetic passages. My copy of this Bible is scored with pencil marks; I hope they will consider this an act of respect, even if I do not precisely follow the theological stance of this translation. It goes without saying that any mistakes or misunderstandings in this book are mine.

    Lincoln, MA, 2018

I

Covenants and the Bible

CHAPTER 1

Covenants as a Guide to Ethical Conduct

Do not be afraid, for I am with you.

—Isaiah 41:10

Love one another, as I have loved you.

—John 15:12

Covenants and the Biblical Context

This book is designed to offer ethical guidance for dealing with today's problems. It addresses this subject from the perspective of biblical covenants and is written primarily for individuals born into Judeo-Christian spiritual traditions. For people who may be disenchanted with formal religion yet are unsatisfied with a purely secular existence, my aim is to examine the relevance of biblical covenants to our times. I will draw attention to the central value of biblical teachings about justice and mercy and the covenantal context in which they are presented. While I understand the views of people who question the relevance of the Bible to contemporary life, there is no other text as strongly positioned to provide ethical guidance to people living in the Western world. For people whose outlook is based on Judeo-Christian traditions, the Bible remains the fundamental source to guide us in meeting life's challenges.

What then are biblical covenants, and why are they central to the establishment of what the Bible defines as justice and mercy on this earth?

Covenants, also known as testaments, are agreements reached between humans that lay out the mutual obligations of the contracting parties. In the Bible, the idea of covenant is applied to the relationship between certain human beings and the God Yahweh. From the earliest recorded times, the Jewish people were in search of the divine. They met around the context of covenant. The very first story in the Bible about Adam and Eve is built around a prototypical covenant with Yahweh, which the humans then proceeded to break. Covenants were also made between Yahweh and Noah, Abraham, Jacob, Moses, Joshua, and David. The Christian testament is also covenantal in the understandings reached between Jesus and his followers. Covenants generally involve change of place or circumstance and basic changes in human consciousness. By far the most elaborate and formal covenant was made with Moses and the children of Israel during their escape from Egypt; it is described in chapter 6 of this book. This covenant has set its stamp on the entire Bible. It is the one that tells us in the greatest detail what covenanting is all about and why covenants are so important.

The fact that covenants are biblical documents makes it necessary to begin by reviewing the biblical context, especially as it applies to our times. Almost forty years ago, the American theologian Thomas Berry wrote an essay arguing that "we are in between stories. The Old Story—the account of how the world came to be and how we fit into it—is not functioning properly, and we have not learned the new story." His analysis referred primarily to conditions of thought in the late twentieth-century West, especially in the United States. Berry argued that ever since the fourteenth-century Black Death plague had ravaged Europe, destroying much of its population, the survivors responded in two distinctly different ways. The believing Christian community developed a modified version of the old story of creation that had guided it over the previous millennium. The Black Death had generated a vision of the cosmos as pervaded by evil, from which only a redemptive spirituality could save humankind from the ravages of the material world. With the onset of the Reformation, the saving grace of Jesus and the kingdom of heaven became for Christians the focus of this redemptive spirituality.

On the other hand, an emerging scientific community of Renaissance Europe focused on understanding what Berry called the "earth process." This included the workings of the cosmos, creation, the rise of humanity, the story of human evolution, and the emergence of a conception of humanity as the life-form through which the universe "became conscious of itself." As one scientific discovery led to another, creation and the world order became the domain of the secular, leaving redemption and salvation to the domain of an increasingly sectarian spirituality, particularly in the United States. Despite this radical divergence and the increasing secularization of the scientific worldview, people of goodwill on both sides were willing to remain committed to the Bible as a source of values that could undergird each position. But no sustaining values emerged to hold the basic story together. The result, Berry concluded, was that both traditions became trivialized.

This trivialization is apparent in the declining interest of many educated people in reading the Bible and attending church services. In my experience, such people regard reading the Bible as possibly helpful to a person's private life but not germane to the problems of our times. For people who hold this perspective, our times are postbiblical in that they are governed by complex economic, political, and military rivalries far beyond the reach of biblical experience. Reading the Bible could not help us draw back from two bloodthirsty world wars or from the arms race characterizing the Cold War era. It has not helped Americans tread warily before getting engaged in the problems of the contemporary Middle East or think carefully before making decisions about "aliens in our midst." The fact that the Roman Catholic Church has lost much of its ability to guide public morality is indicative of the trivialization of biblical experience to which Berry drew attention.

Yet there are ways in which the Bible can still be made accessible, regardless of one's stance toward competing definitions of creation, evolution, and redemption (i.e., the basic story). To illustrate this point, I've chosen as a chapter heading a text from the book of Isaiah. This text expresses the biblical conviction of the divine as a spiritually sheltering power here on this earth, no matter what our views of creation or redemption may be. This idea is proclaimed several times in Isaiah and in other texts, such as the psalms, the book of Job, and the New Testament. What these texts affirm is a conviction of the divine as Immanuel, meaning not necessarily out there somewhere in space or some other invisible dimension but here in this life on earth with us. These texts are saying that to be alive on this earth is to be in the presence of an immanent (indwelling) power called divine, and this power is available to support us as we live out our lives.

Such a conviction addresses the basic fear of spiritual abandonment of the sort experienced by Job, as well as the incapacitation caused by fear of danger. Fear of physical and spiritual isolation can block one's ability to deal with challenges, experience the fullness of life, and find ways to act with integrity. But it is also the essence of an awakening spiritual consciousness to experience a long, dark time of doubt and anxiety during which one is prey to every fear. Sometimes these long, dark times can be a collective experience signaling the transition to a new collective consciousness. It is in such situations that recognition of divine power as being here with us can make all the difference to our integrity. For human experience has repeatedly shown that when one aligns with that power, it is possible to find the courage to act.

I've also included a text that addresses the idea of love in a simple but universal way. Typically, we are conditioned to think of love as something that applies to people with whom we have intimate relationships. Hopefully, one loves one's spouses, children, parents, close relatives and special friends. But after that, love tends to peter out. Can one really love anyone? Indeed, how do we love anyone? How, for example, is it possible to love a neighbor?

The key, from a biblical perspective, lies in the meaning of the word love, and a clue to that lies in the words "as I have loved you." Jesus, to whom this text is applied, was able to love people, such as those to whom he brought a transformative renewal of health, without having to seek them within familiar contexts or know them on a mundane level. This capacity is true of all great spiritual leaders. They radiate spiritual vitality without restricting this power by gender, ethnicity, class, nationalism, age, language, or any of the other categories that divide us from each other. Such love is openhearted. The American poet Edwin Markham addressed this theme when he wrote,

> He drew a circle that shut me out—
> Heretic, rebel, a thing to flout.
> But Love and I had the wit to win:
> We drew a circle that took him in.

Drawing a circle that takes people in is one of the great challenges and opportunities of our times. Despite the trend toward economic globalization and the rise of global climatic and health problems, we live in a world still separated by nationalisms, ideologies and frontiers, and inhabited by well over 7 billion strangers. How can we possibly open ourselves to all those people, especially when some of them evidently would like to get rid of us and others would like to have our jobs? Why, one might also ask, should they be willing to open themselves to us? The cultures and institutions that separate us still control our lives to a far greater extent than the challenges, some of them huge, that we face in common.

No less problematic are the divisions that exist within nations and systems of faith. As predicted by Berry and others, the so-called culture wars that have risen within the United States can divide us politically, culturally, and religiously. Even the Bible is not immune to these divisions.

Yet there are powers that can draw us together, that transcend all these artificial barriers, and that allow the selfless love that the Greeks call agape to take root in our lives. That, as we shall see, is one of the basic messages of the Bible. Every day that we live affords us the opportunity to enter and take part in this world of spiritual freedom and grace, provided we open our eyes to its existence. Now more than ever this opportunity is upon us. But before getting to that point we should acknowledge some of the barriers standing in our way.

The Bible and the Culture Wars

In recent years the Bible has been used to play a quite visible role in shaping political advocacy in the United States, particularly among individuals adhering to certain Christian evangelical and fundamentalist perspectives. According to these perspectives, various texts in both Testaments of the Christian Bible proclaim an end-time "eschatological" future, in which an endless struggle of good versus evil will move into a series of decisive phases, triggered by an anticipated reappearance of the risen Christ Jesus. Those who proclaim Jesus as Lord will be rescued from earthly destruction through a process known as "rapture", while those who fail to do so will be condemned when the final "second coming" happens.

Among secular circles there has been a tendency to discount this kind of thinking as a relic of a pre-Enlightenment past, when faith (representing the traditional story) carried more weight than reason (representing the evolutionary story). If this is your viewpoint, the Berry argument helps to explain why Christian fundamentalists have, during recent years, become a rising spiritual and political force in the United States. They have staked out a leading position on the redemptive side of the "old story." Authors of the "Left Behind" books, who are enthusiastic advocates of the rapture theory, have reportedly sold well over 60 million copies. Leaders of this fundamentalist tide have been able to exert a powerful influence on public policy. As their leaders point out, this kind of advocacy is part of the democratic process. If liberals can lobby for what they regard as progressive and/or scientific causes, conservative fundamentalists can lobby for what they regard as redemption and the sanctity of life. And they have been actively doing so.

The only remarkable aspect of this dramatic rise in fundamentalist power is its seeming suddenness. Yet the growing influence of fundamentalism and end-time perspectives, based on what is seen as Biblical teaching, has been developing over the last two centuries, at the very same time that Enlightenment thought, industrialization, and scientific discovery were revolutionizing Western society and creating the basis for modern science-based theories of evolution and creation. One could attribute this advance of opposing perspectives, in part at least, to the social and philosophic upheavals caused by the nineteenth century industrial and scientific revolutions in Britain and other Western countries and the waves of population increase and migration that accompanied them. These radical changes opened so many new doorways to scientific and economic development while at the same time severely challenging the lives of people thrust into disease-ridden urban environments in search of employment and survival. It was evangelical Christianity, with its focus on personal redemption, which came to the rescue of countless urban and transnational migrants.

Twentieth century crises widened the gulf between the spiritual and secular domains. Enlightenment doctrines anticipating progressive advancement and liberalization of the human condition were challenged by world wars and genocides, conducted with extreme brutality and destructiveness and demonstrating a terrifying human attraction to cultures of oppression and death. The fact that the Second World War became (at least for the victorious allies) a war of life versus death and good versus evil could not hide the terrible destructiveness of secular science and material power, as witnessed by both the efficient mass-killing gas chambers of the Holocaust and the effect of the atomic bombs dropped on Hiroshima and Nagasaki.

The Cold War also became defined, on both sides, as a struggle of good versus evil. But it is better seen as the era in which mass annihilation of life on our planet earth became an increasing possibility, thanks to the spread of science-based weapons of mass destruction. Climate change is another product of the Cold War era, resulting principally from an increasingly massive combustion of fossil fuels. In short, the scientific method that redefined global creation has now also redefined and made possible global annihilation.

Meanwhile many fundamentalist upholders of the spiritual old story are seeking to escape from this earth through rapture rather than continue to puzzle out how to survive and live on it. The short-lived post-Cold War era has now given way to another rising tide of good versus evil, in which evil has been defined in the United States and elsewhere in the West as 'terrorism' but applied principally to forces of "Islamist" extremism, while the "Islamist" enemy in turn proclaims the same language of good versus evil against its Christian and Jewish counterparts, led by the United States (the so-called "Great Satan") and Israel.

Within this new terrorism-defined global political order, other shifts in social and political conditions have occurred that are reason for uneasiness. To individuals who adhere to the redemptive values of the old story, globalism, liberalism, sexual permissiveness, and especially abortion and homosexuality, seem to tear at the traditional fabric of social bonds, such as marriage, family, work and worship. They connote, from this perspective, a license to think and do whatever seems desirable, or is legitimized by Hollywood and other networks of modern mass culture, without regard to their impact on traditional values and the security or sanctity of life and livelihood. It is not hard to find in Biblical history examples of the social and political breakdown that can occur when societies depart from agreed-on value systems or covenants designed to sustain life. Biblical writers attributed the destruction by the Assyrians of the ancient kingdom of Israel to the negative results of moral and spiritual unraveling. Some of those writers viewed the Babylonian invasion of Judah and destruction of the Jerusalem temple in the same way. Indeed, much of Jewish and Christian biblical teaching warns vehemently of the ill consequences of societal breakdown resulting from disregard of basic covenants for supporting life.

But evidence of societal stress does not mean that one can solve it by reverting to prior formulas. Each time that ancient Israel transformed itself from a subjugated people to a tribal confederation, to a kingdom, to feuding kingdoms, to a remnant in exile, to a succession of post-exilic colonial dependencies, the Bible was reedited or expanded to take account of the changing circumstances and challenges of the times. Unlike the Quran, the Bible is not a text that was created in one short burst of illumination. It reflects the human necessity to reformulate public ethics every step of the way.

The counterpoint between Biblical teaching and the straining of social covenants over the last three centuries, beginning with the Industrial and French revolutions, can be seen at work in the rise of fundamentalism and the shrinking of mainline religious practice. Fundamentalism, in its primary meaning of adherence to certain basic religious values, expresses a well-founded fear of what can happen when normative expectations are threatened and traditional Bible-based teaching about values—particularly those associated with redemption—is subjected to challenge and rejection. The rise of fundamentalism, even though appearing to liberals as anti-democratic and anti-Enlightenment, cannot be brushed aside as a product of Bible mania. It grows out of a fear that life on our planet is threatened by dangerous and demonic forces, some of them located within the United States. Campaigns to promote 'Intelligent Design' and the sanctity of Christmas, as well as attacks on the Devil, are part of a widespread effort to revalidate the redemptive side of the old story, as well as to reestablish a claim over teaching about divine creation, with which the redemptive story begins. Meanwhile mainline religious denominations have been striving with much less popular impact to reevaluate from their perspectives the basic myths on which we depend for meaning.

Factoring in Contemporary Dangers

Events since the destruction of New York's World Trade Towers on September 11, 2001, and the loss of around three thousand lives, have lent force to the fundamentalist perspective. Although in the grand scheme of world-wide slaughter 3,000 is a pretty small number, every one of those lives matters, whether they are American, Russian, Jewish, Indian, Chinese, Syrian, or some other identity. Meanwhile human life continues to be in many places quite insecure and in some places subject to far greater loss of life than occurred in the US on nine-eleven. Natural catastrophes, such as famines, droughts, epidemic diseases, tsunamis, hurricanes and earthquakes, and the growing threat of climate change, are compounded by numerous brutal civil wars and the rising tide of a terrorism driven by fanaticism and bigotry.

The frequency of the natural catastrophes should be reason enough to make us wonder about where we are headed. As all creation stories remind us, planet Earth and the entire surrounding cosmos are integral to the meaning and actuality of creation. Without the Earth and its complex web of life there can be no human society, no history, no culture, no economy, no politics, no cities and nations, no food or shelter, in fact no human existence or consciousness. Our dependence for our lives and material welfare on the proper functioning of our planetary life systems is unequivocal. We may not notice this on a day-to-day basis, but natural disasters make our dependence self-evident. If the air, water and earth turn foul or overly warm and dry—as is already happening in too many places—we are in trouble.

Some voices in the fundamentalist world have taken the provocative view that the world is there for our use, as implied, for instance, in the first chapter of Genesis. An alternative and more recent evangelical view holds that the universe is itself a mode of divine communication, and the diversity and fecundity of our planet is our most precious endowment. Meditation on the natural world in all its diversity is an act of meditation on the divine, as is illustrated in numerous biblical passages, particularly in the Psalms. From this humbler perspective, systemic natural hazards and calamities are ways of letting us know that the natural world is in disorder—in fact dangerously so.

Despite the urgency of natural disorder, it is the human disorder characterizing the twentieth century and our present times that must be our immediate concern. Even with the baleful lessons of a century of mass slaughter behind us, it is still far too easy for humans to turn against each other. Fellow humans are suddenly attacked, opponents become enemies, and enemies demonize and plot destruction against their foes. God is invoked as the ultimate sanction of violence, and terrorism and refugee crises became the great issues of the day. Parents, children and friends now must grieve the victims of this aggression, which until recent economic meltdowns came to dominate public policy. Such violence and chaos occur somewhere nearly every day. From time to time there is mention of Armageddon—the war between civilizations or religions. Perhaps we are already on a march towards a fateful destiny.

Before that happens, do we really need to fear and hate each other so much that this kind of outcome becomes justifiable? If we were to stay on this course, we could be leading ourselves down a road towards a conflagration that would cause untold destruction on its way to victory. While our minds are preoccupied with economic crisis, such a contingency may seem remote. And yet it is no longer implausible that an expanding trans-national violence lies ahead of us. For example: if the fighting in the Middle East and Central Asia continues for any extended period, it could reawaken the centuries-long conflict between Christianity and Islam. These are dangerous currents to get caught in. "Islamists" who have been beheading Americans and others as infidels in Iraq and killing and terrorizing women, children, teachers and aid workers in Afghanistan, Beslan, Mumbai, Paris, West Africa and increasingly in Pakistan, should get wise to the fact that crusaders once used that term 'infidel' against all Moslems and could easily do so again. In 1099 invading Frankish Christian crusaders attacked Palestine and slaughtered every Moslem and Jewish 'infidel' they could find in the streets of Jerusalem, on the grounds that the latter were desecrating Christian territory. For taking on that bloodthirsty task those crusaders were promised salvation, just as are today's Islamist suicide killers. Not so long ago, Serbian Christians were slaughtering Moslems in Bosnia and Kosovo. There are deep, irrational forces in every one of us that could be rekindled if this kind of fanatical targeting continues. The race hatred unleashed by Nazi leaders should remind us of that danger.

It is my strong impression that the general public in the Western democracies is not yet ready to face this kind of end-time possibility, let alone know how to counteract it. So many Americans and Europeans of Christian heritage do not read the Bible critically, do not attend church in a serious way, do not think much about God or salvation, and do not feel comfortable in the presence of Christian witness in any shape or form. Many are still unfamiliar with the rising tide of Christian fundamentalism and the end-time, eschatological thinking espoused by so-called dispensationalist and Pentecostal congregations and widely popularized in the "Left Behind" publications.

This is not surprising. Most Americans living outside the Christian fundamentalist orbit lack the language and ideology with which to reflect about end-times. Basically, they are secular or mildly religious people focused on bread and butter issues of home, work and income. Such people, among whom I have for years included myself, are content to leave end-times decision- making to the government, the policy elites, and the religious fundamentalists. So long as we have a home, a family, and a promising career, we are doing well enough. With good fortune, such as a major promotion or an unexpected inheritance, we are doing even better.

But this kind of thinking no longer suffices to deal with the world today. In a time when normal assumptions about security are under attack, those of us inhabiting a 'live and let live' culture need to reflect more actively about our purposes in life as individuals, and as members of communities, nations and religious groups. What are we here for? What do we hope to accomplish during our lives on earth? What are our missions as individuals and group members? What are we willing to entrust to our leaders? What do we value most and why? How do we function as moral and spiritual agents, and for what purpose? What will give us the greatest feeling of accomplishment and fulfillment? And what are we supposed to do when these values and missions, and our very lives and bodies, come under assault from extremists for whom destruction or rejection comes with an anticipated entrance to higher life?

It is an irony of our times that extremists appear to have given more thought to these questions of spiritual direction than so many people living in the centers of cultures and civilizations. Extremists who go on suicide missions are likely to have answers to such questions. Some of their answers may appear superficial and absurd, yet they are answers. Often these people are following leaders who have deeply studied religious texts and are familiar with the recent histories of their cultures and times. If these leaders are of Islamist persuasion, for example, they are certainly familiar with the teachings of the Quran and likely to be familiar with the history of Western colonialism and its impact on their countries. If they are of Christian fundamentalist persuasion, they are likely to know the relevant texts and strategies from the Bible by heart.

In addition, a growing number of Islamist leaders are regarded by their followers as martyrs, who died fighting for their co-religionists. Traditional definitions of martyrdom did not call for killing enemies in the process of sacrificing one's own life. Martyr, literally meaning 'witness', once meant someone willing to confess faith at the cost of suffering death. In the twentieth century such heroes as Mahatma Gandhi, Martin Luther King, Oscar Romero, and Dietrich Bonhoeffer, manifested this kind of confessional, love-inspired, non-violent martyrdom. But now it is the suicide bomber who has become for so many people, especially in the world of Islam, the standard-bearer of martyrdom. Warrior martyrdom has edged out confessional martyrdom.

One of the many unanticipated consequences of the Israeli-Palestine conflict has been its capacity to generate warrior martyrdom. Islamist warrior martyrdom can be found in anti-colonialist struggles (e.g. in Chechnya or Afghanistan) and in struggles by organizations such as the Muslim Brotherhood and ISIL against the secular leadership of various Muslim countries. The United States, its armed forces and overseas employees and allies, have provided a rich new target for Islamist revenge and warrior martyrdom. Islamists, notably in Central Asia and Nigeria, are targeting women and girls for daring to seek education and challenge male leadership. Yet this Islamist martyrdom is highly effective in attracting sympathizers, particularly from among young and impressionable boys.

So long as Western politics is guided by a secularist center, the strongest ideological forces that Westerners have been able to employ to counteract Islamist warrior martyrdom are political freedom and the trappings of democracy, backed up by a nationalistic patriotism. However admirable these values may be, they will never inspire the ardor that comes from a fervent trust in religious authority. The history of the United States offers plentiful evidence of the power of religious values.

Meantime in 2008 the global economy was battered by financial meltdowns affecting almost all people of limited means, and especially children and poor people in countries dependent on marginal economies. People living in affluent countries must face the fact that deregulated financial systems and their operators somehow brought us to this pass, and that millions of privileged people looked the other way while this crisis built up. It is hard to escape the conclusion that a systemic worldwide weakening of moral values facilitated this economic crisis as well as other crises eroding our health systems, liberties, athletic standards, global environment, and our concern for less fortunate people.[1] To expect financial and political leaders to put all these pieces back together is unreasonable, when the troubles we face extend far beyond the financial and political arenas. Since this passage was drafted, new fissures have emerged in public discourse in The United States and elsewhere about climate change, national priorities, and health delivery, and these fissures show little sign of diminishing.

What Biblical Covenants Ask and Offer

For anyone concerned about the moral equivocation all around us, the Bible is available to help us navigate through such difficult times. Far from being merely a backstop for fundamentalist thinking or a warning to the wealthy, the Bible contains a tremendous literature covering manifold aspects of human experience of the divine and explaining why that experience is significant for our lives and our world. For people living

---

[1] The New York Times op-ed articles of Nicholas Kristof have been particularly helpful in drawing attention to the acute problems faced by children and pregnant women in marginal countries and regions.

in the West, it is by far the most important text dealing with human spiritual growth, ethical conduct, and divine revelation and guidance. For Jewish people it contains the earliest written sources about Jewish salvation history, particularly the crucial covenants with the God Yahweh and the prophetic tradition that upheld them. It is also the primary source for the powerful wisdom tradition, exemplified in such writings as the Psalms, the Book of Job, and the Book of Proverbs. For Christians it contains what one needs to know about those same covenants, as well as about the kingdom of heaven on earth and the practice of love and forgiveness. Specifically, the Bible teaches about service to other people, and about living in a state of grace with the source of life and the planet on which we depend for our existence. As far as I am concerned, there is not a human being alive who would not benefit in some personal way by developing a critical understanding of these teachings. Armed with such teachings, one can live intentionally—even if only seeing through a glass darkly, as the apostle Paul put it—without feeling that one has no choice left in these days of danger but to zone out or get ready for more difficulties.

But if we are to live intentionally, the Biblical covenants, in both Hebrew and Christian testaments, do ask us to open our lives to two great ways of being in the world. The first is the way of unequivocally loving, or at least living in awe of, that power that makes possible the life-giving world in which we all live, and the human lives on which we depend for love, friendship and guidance. This means, in the manner of the Psalms, getting up every day and praising the source of life for the life we have. Call it what you like, then get up and praise that power for the life you and I have been given. It means, as in Psalm 100, being joyful in the presence of life, or expressing—as in Psalm 104—wonder and awe over how it all came into being. It means recognizing, as in Psalm 111, the wisdom of honoring creation, or as in Psalm 139, understanding that our own presence in this life-giving arena is graced and matters. It would certainly benefit our planet and all of us living on it if we were to try to follow such a way of life, indeed if we were even to follow the Hippocratic oath first to do no harm. But at present the fact is that most of us are not sufficiently living by either message. Too often we either damage ourselves or accommodate to harm done by others to the planetary systems on which we depend for our lives.

The second critical covenantal undertaking is to love our neighbors as ourselves. This undertaking is a logical extension of the first one. It expresses our realization that life in all its manifestations—including all its human manifestations—is part of the great cosmic undertaking of life on earth and in this universe. It means that unless we want to live in a universe of one, we need to get used to getting along with neighbors wherever and whoever they are, indeed to loving and respecting them as ourselves. Now that the world's human population is well over seven billion and increasing by tens of millions every year, this is easier said than done. But the alternative of either killing large numbers, or letting millions starve to death or be killed or maimed by others, is a violation of these covenantal undertakings, which call on us to love, not merely tolerate, others. We need to recognize this call to love, especially love of neighbors, and that includes what the Bible calls aliens in our midst. They too are children of this earth, and in spiritual terms they too are children of the power that made living, rather than mere subsistence on this earth, possible.

It has taken me a lifetime to understand these teachings, much less practice them. For example, I have personally spent a good deal of time despising and resenting some of my 'neighbors.' During the Second World War I hated all Germans indiscriminately, without once stopping to think about how many of them were suffering just as much as I was or much more; and I've spent a good deal of time since then hating or despising various individual neighbors. Several of them were my teachers and superiors. This time spent on hating and resenting neighbors has all been wasted and is an abuse of my limited energy and time on earth. There are times when one cannot help hating or resenting some people, but it is best to get over those times as quickly as possible and think about how one might learn to coexist with those neighbors and even like them.

But the Bible dares to ask us to love, not just coexist. It calls on us to participate in the great work of creation, not merely to be its beneficiaries. Traditionally these two undertakings to love have been presented as commandments—in other words, do them "or else"—as when a parent may call on a child to love a sibling, when resentment or covetousness may be the preferred reaction. But commandments, defined as orders, will not enable us to assume the humanness, of which a capacity to love and serve others is the fullest expression. To get to that point there are many doubts and fears to overcome, beginning with the difficulties that stand in the way of loving oneself. The Bible is a powerful source through which one can learn how to address such fears and difficulties and open one's mind to engagement in the work of creation through generosity of spirit towards others.

It is my fervent hope that people will take these teachings to heart and learn to live by them and make them come alive. Loving the source of life and loving our neighbors as ourselves (no matter how hostile or unpleasant they may seem), is vital to our survival and wellbeing and that of our planetary home. That is the fundamental teaching of Jewish salvation history, and its adoption by Christianity, as I will indicate in the chapters that follow. Love, as the apostle Paul emphasized, is the essence of life. The consequences of depending for survival essentially on our material strength are not pleasant to contemplate. In an earlier age the great native American leader Black Elk acknowledged that "when I look back from the high hill of my old age, I can see that something else died there in the bloody mud [of Wounded Knee] … A people's dream died there. You see me now a pitiful old man who has done nothing, for the nation's hoop is broken and scattered. There is no center any longer, and the sacred tree is dead." [2]

If we are not to turn into pitiful old people who have done nothing except survive and make some money, we should take these words to heart. We should do whatever we can to preserve the nation's hoop, cherish the center, and at all costs strive to keep the people's dream and the sacred tree alive. In Judeo-Christian terms that means living covenantally, cherishing and preserving the resources given to us through the great gift of life, including the air we breathe and the land and water we live on, and learning to inspire the dreams of ourselves and our neighbors. Of course, we could put all that on the back burner and prepare instead for 'rapture' or Armageddon. Indeed, in terms of armaments and military readiness we Americans are well prepared for so-called times of tribulation. But this is a very dangerous course to take, particularly if that is what we concentrate our energy and vision on.

By comparison, our readiness to participate in the great work of nurturing neighbors and preserving the planet we live on is still, for most of us, half-hearted. Yet if we are willing to open our minds to this work, the manual on how to do it is within our grasp. All we need to do to get

---

[2] Reference courtesy of Douglas Bowman.

started is to read the manual and find a way to meet some of the people who practice what it preaches, so that we too can engage in the work of sustaining life.

Reviving the Sacred World

As Black Elk warns us, keeping the "sacred tree" alive is easier said than done. The center of our culture, even in the Christian-oriented United States, has to a remarkable extent let go of serious, critical study of the Bible by the public, without coming up with a convincing alternative text or set of agreed-on values or basic story line to take its place. One could blame secularization (i.e. growth of materialism and worldliness) for this development, and this study will seek to explore this theme. Secularization has diluted understanding of the sacred, whether by polluting or destroying sacred spaces, diminishing the credibility of guardians of the sacred, or abusing sacred values to achieve materialistic goals. Even some professional guardians of the sacred (e.g. priests) have contrived to undermine and destroy sacred values. The relentless pressures of materialism and cynicism have taken a heavy toll on the capacity of modern people to comprehend the meaning of sacredness and its claim on our lives.

But blaming abstractions such as secularization, materialism or cynicism does not resolve the problem. During the Twentieth Century people in the centers of great cultures had to live through overwhelming experiences of catastrophe and madness just as much as those on the cultural wings. Every one of us must deal with the terrible lessons of the twentieth century, no matter where we are on the political spectrum.

This is not just a matter of owning up to the Holocaust and its Nazi perpetrators. That is one particularly virulent aspect of a very much larger problem, which we need to see in its full dimensions. Europeans must admit to the terrible carnage that they inflicted on each other during two world wars. How could this have happened, and how is this appalling self-destruction to be purged from our hearts and minds? Russians need to own up to the monstrous famines, mass killings and slavery unleashed by Soviet Communism. Chinese need to come to terms with the worst human-induced famine in world history (it occurred from 1959-1962), and with all the chaos and bloodshed precipitated by the Cultural Revolution of 1966-1976. Japanese need to face up to the military atrocities committed before and during World War II (a few brave writers in that country have done so). People living on the Indian sub-continent need to acknowledge the religious hatred and killing fomented by both Muslim and Hindu extremists. White Americans need to fully own up to the accumulated savagery of slavery and racism. One of the worst atrocities of the twentieth century occurred in the once benign and beautiful country of Cambodia. Beyond such human atrocities, we all need to take account of the grave damage we are doing every day to the planet and biosphere on which we depend for life.

These acts of mass destruction, occurring in the heartlands of so-called civilization, constitute extended frontal assaults on the sacredness of life. How could these and so many other atrocities have happened? How did we go wrong? How could 'civilization' have taken such disastrous turns in so many countries, and why is it still doing so? Modern secularized thinking is far from comprehending this on-going worldwide catastrophe. But how could it, when secularization is itself in so many respects an assault on the sacredness of life and creation? If we want to find paradigms that empower us to examine this century of mass slaughter and destruction and move beyond it, without simply sliding from one world crisis into another, we must begin by restoring an awareness of the profound sacredness of life. For most of us, immersed as we are in a culture of materialism, this will not be a simple task. We will, as Berry put it, need a new story, or a new vision of the old one; and we will need help in finding it. If paradigms of sacredness exist in the Bible—and they do—it is time to reawaken ourselves to them. [3]

The organization of this book is designed to introduce Biblical covenantal ideas to secular readers, or to those with religious affiliations who want to reflect more on its teachings about creation, love, sacredness, protection of life, and in especially justice, mercy, and service to others. The first part of this book deals with how the Bible is organized and what is its basic literary content and structure. It includes a chapter on how to read the Bible in our materialist and violence-prone age. I assume here that many educated and busy people are not especially familiar with the

---

[3] Anyone seeking a broad and detailed discussion of the scope of 20th century atrocities could consult Niall Ferguson, The War of the World: Twentieth Century Conflict and the Descent of the West, New York: Penguin Books, 2006.

structure of the Bible and may have had no formal education in how to read it. Many people may have had some Sunday school training in Bible study. But this does not mean that they are in touch with contemporary Biblical scholarship and its profound reconsideration of how to interpret this text (or set of texts) and related non-Biblical texts. Nor does it mean that one is practiced in applying Biblical thinking to the problems of our times or to our personal situations. If the Bible is to serve us today, we need to think about how to understand and apply it today.

The second part explores the meanings of covenant and revelation as they take shape in the Hebrew and Christian scriptures. My focus is on the Sinai covenant (as described in the Book of Exodus) and its working out in various Biblical traditions, including those of the Christian scriptures. The Sinai covenant is far from being the only covenant recorded in the Bible, but it is the most detailed one, and the ethical and sacred core of the Bible grows out of that covenant. From a Christian perspective, this is a way of recognizing that contemporary Christian writing is much more mindful, than was the case in previous ages, of Christianity's ongoing inheritance from Jewish history and theology.

Much of what is contained in this part, especially the material in the Torah (meaning in this context the first five books of the Bible), derives from traditions that rely on myth to establish a structure of meaning. This is not surprising once one discards the popular and trivialized meaning of myth as non-factual fantasy and understands myth instead as sacred story incorporating central beliefs and traditions of a culture. From this perspective, the Bible is grounded on a powerful mythic structure, and this structure is used by subsequent Biblical traditions, such as the historical, prophetic and wisdom literatures, as a basis for interpreting and finding solutions to the problems of their times. Consequently, any time we look for what the Bible has to say about ethical and spiritual conduct, we find that time and again the Sinai covenant is taken as a basic frame of reference.

The third part of this book applies Biblical witness about covenantal ethics and revelation to problems of our times. My aim is to show that problems we face today, such as those dealing with gender identity and roles, marriage, work, protection of the earth, justice, and love of others, are not beyond the realm of Biblical consciousness. Far from it: to the extent that such problems result from loss or confusion of ethical and spiritual direction, they can be illuminated by examination from a Biblical perspective. As argued earlier, some of these problems are so urgent that it is mandatory to address them from the perspective of our most central beliefs and values. We cannot do this if we are out of touch with—or insufficiently challenged to think about—what those values are, and how they apply to our daily lives.

Before moving on, I should clarify that this book will argue that Biblical covenantal teaching is essentially inclusive, not exclusive, and directed to maintenance of life here on this earth, not life in some sky-bound rapture or alternative dimension for saved people. While there are texts, e.g. in the book of Revelation, that could be used to support an exclusivist and otherworldly position, these are not normative to covenantal teaching, which is about how to live in this world in relation to the divine, as well as to the needs and concerns of our fellow humans and the planet that supports us.

We will also be looking to see how the sacred can appear in our own personal lives. This is something to which the Torah, the Psalms and the Christian gospels pay special attention; but the sacred can be broadly accessed through Biblical texts, once one perceives that it is all around us. Another way of saying this is that the sacred is not something that we have to hope and pray will appear sometime in our lifetimes, in the manner of the so-called second coming or the return of the messiah. Nor is it up in the sky or in another world accessible only after death. Wherever there is love of the source of life and love of neighbor here on earth, the sacred is immanent.

CHAPTER 2

The Hebrew Scriptures: A Brief Outline

> That which is hateful to you
> Do not do to your neighbor.
> This is the entire Torah; the rest is commentary.
> Go and learn it.
> Hillel, Babylonian Talmud, Shabbat 31a

Bibles and Testaments

The Bible is a work of universal relevance developed by Jewish civilization. Of course, the Christian Bible is the fundamental text of Christianity, but the Old Testament of the Christian Bible is the Hebrew Bible, although in a significantly different arrangement; and the New Testament is so leavened by ideas, values and prophetic declarations drawn from the Hebrew Bible, that it is itself a product of Jewish thought and action. There are strong Hellenistic overtones in parts of the New Testament, but most of the critical ideas come from Jewish salvation history.

Three versions of the Bible are in common circulation: the Jewish Bible (the Tanakh) and two versions of the much more widely circulated Christian Bible. The word tanakh refers to the three divisions of the Jewish Bible into torah, prophetic books, and writings. Decisions about which books to include in the Tanakh were determined by Pharisee teachers and scholars during the first century CE. This version of the Jewish Bible survived the catastrophe of the mid-first century Jewish rebellion against

Roman occupation of Judea; it became the orthodox Bible text adopted by Rabbinic Judaism. The text—though not the order of the books—was taken over by Roman Christians and incorporated into the orthodox Latin Bible (the Vulgate) and subsequent Christian versions.

The Christian Bible consists of two parts, commonly referred to as the Old Testament and the New Testament. 'Testament' is a synonym for covenant. Roman Catholic Bibles contain an additional 'Deuterocanonical' section, consisting of certain secondary (deutero) texts included in pre-Christian Greek versions the Tanakh translated by Hellenistic Jews, but which are for various reasons not included in the Rabbinic Bible or in Protestant versions of the Old Testament.

What, then, are the Old and New Testaments of the Christian Bible, and what is the significance of 'old' and 'new'? The Old Testament contains the same books as the Tanakh but in a different order and set of subdivisions, and with some different book titles. The New Testament consists of certain Christian texts authorized by early Christian councils as the legitimate expression of the early Christian covenant. Christians refer to these two Testaments as 'old' and 'new' on the grounds that the 'old' one represents the Biblical God Yahweh's covenants with Moses and the ancient Israelites and the witness of Yahweh's presence in human affairs prior to the advent of Jesus. The 'new' one was established by the mission and sacrificial death of Jesus and his believed resurrection as the risen Christ or Messiah. After the Roman destruction of the Jerusalem Temple in 70 CE, this covenant took precedence in the minds of early Christians over the existing Judaic covenant and sacrificial cult (using 'cult' here to mean system of religious practice).[4]

One can compare this use of 'old' and 'new' to the use of 'old world' and 'new world' which used to characterize American and Eurocentric thinking about the world until quite recently, when the convergence of world development and modern revolution made this approach redundant. Application of the terms 'old' and 'new' to the Biblical Testaments reflects divisions that erupted between Rabbinic Judaism and Christianity in the earliest years of these movements. The Jewish or Hebrew Bible may be older

---

[4] In his book Christ Actually, James Carroll clarifies how the Roman suppression of Jewish revolt in the first and second centuries CE drove an inescapable wedge between the Rabbinic and early Christian communities.

in the chronology of its subject matter and the dates of its composition, but as a spiritual and ethical text it has its own distinctive history and is the living text of contemporary Judaism. To refer to the Biblical testament of Judaism nowadays as 'old' is an antiquarian appellation.

Let us clear our minds, then, of this early, traditional Christian concept of 'Old Testament' and use a title more appropriate to our times, such as the Hebrew Scriptures. What do they consist of, and how were they put together?

First Five Books

The Bible begins with five books, referred to in Greek as Pentateuch (five scrolls) and in Hebrew as Chumash (also a name for five scrolls) or more significantly as Torah (narrowly 'learning', broadly 'revelation'). In English they are traditionally called the five books of Moses. These books provide the core texts and teaching of Rabbinic Judaism and are regarded by Jewish theologians as embodying the "spirit and destiny" of the Jewish people. It is for this reason, rather than for their chronological antiquity, that they are placed at the beginning of the Bible.

The book of Genesis contains stories about the creation of the world (which give the book its non-Hebraic and Hebraic titles). The book includes ancient myths (sacred stories incorporating central values), such as the stories about Noah's Ark and the great flood, the covenant reached with Noah after the flood subsided, and the Tower of Babel. A large central section records the covenants of the God Yahweh with Abraham and Sarah and the experiences of the patriarchs Isaac and Jacob, and their extended families. During this time the cult is not focused exclusively on Yahweh but continues to recognize the ancient Canaanite deity El. What seems to distinguish Yahweh is his generally (but not exclusively) male identity, his familiarity with and closeness to the patriarchs, and his interest in human affairs.

Then follows the fascinating story of Joseph, the favored son of Jacob and his beloved spouse Rachel, who was sold by his brothers into slavery in Egypt but rose through his psychic and managerial powers to become grand vizier, 'father of Pharaoh', and protector against famine. Because of Joseph's intervention the grateful Pharaoh invited his relatives into Egypt, where they settled, according to the Bible, for four generations. This sets the stage for the unfolding of Jewish salvation history, which is the central theme of the Hebrew scriptures.

The next book is Exodus. This is one of the world's most influential and ethically defining texts. It recounts the early life and upbringing of Moses as an Egyptian prince, and the liberation of the children of Israel from enslavement in Egypt. It contains the triumphant story of the Passover, still celebrated every year by Jewish people in the 'Pass-over' Seder, the escape through the sea of 'Reeds', the beginnings of the long march through the arid desert to encounter Yahweh, and the forging of the great covenant at Mount Sinai. Yahweh is here characterized as a demanding tribal overlord but does not yet express the exclusive divine power that would become the hallmark of Yahwism. Exodus contains crucial texts establishing the Yahwist covenant, among them the Ten Commandments, the so-called Book of the Covenant, an alternative, ceremonial covenant contained in chapter 34, and records relating to construction of the Ark and the Tabernacle.

While Moses is on top of the mountain 'receiving' these decrees, everything nearly goes wrong when the impatient Israelites, under the leadership of Moses' brother Aaron, construct a golden calf as a representation of divinity. This apostasy from the emergent but not yet established Yahwist cult is rigorously suppressed. The sacred structures and their furnishings are assembled, and the cult is brought into being.

Exodus is followed by Leviticus. This book sets out sacrificial, dietary and conjugal regulations governing the existence of the children of Israel and defining them as a distinctive ethnic and religious group. Much of the text is heavy reading for those not brought up in the Jewish tradition, particularly the passages describing the complex procedures for sacrificing animals. But it is central to an understanding of the meaning of holiness and the idea of Israel as a holy nation. It also establishes a radical separation of that which is holy from that which pollutes. There is a remarkable passage describing the investiture of Aaron and his sons as priests, and a fatal mistake made by two of the four sons very shortly thereafter. The sacred rituals, one learns, are to be carried out with extreme reverence for sacral objects and dread towards the law-giving Deity. The text contains vital regulations defining purity and laying out procedures for purification.

A core passage, known as the holiness code, sets out an ethical framework for those living in relationship with Yahweh, the God of Israel. It includes the unequivocal injunctions to love neighbors and aliens (strangers living in your land) as yourself.

The next book, Numbers, records information about the tribal configuration and demographic size of the children of Israel and provides more regulations and codes of conduct. The Hebrew title "In the Wilderness" emphasizes this long and puzzling stage in the formation of the children of Israel by giving further accounts of their wanderings through the Sinai wilderness and their efforts to enter the "promised land" of Canaan. The puzzle is that the trek through the wilderness is taking much longer than expected. Several rebellions break out, which are suppressed by means of plagues, serpents, and landslides, and an attempt to enter the promised land from the south is repulsed. Although Moses generally intercedes eloquently on behalf of his rebellious followers, on one fatal occasion he loses his patience and is informed by Yahweh that he and his brother Aaron will not be permitted to lead the people into the promised land.

Years pass, the tribes remain stuck in the wilderness, and Aaron and his sister Miriam die. Finally, the children of Israel decide to approach the promised land from the East. Balaam and his famous donkey make their appearance. The donkey satirizes human blindness, while Balaam warns the king of Moab not to resist Yahweh and his followers. Hardened by decades in the desert, and organized into tribal and military configurations, a new generation of Israelites, led not by the elderly Moses but by one of their own (Joshua), prepares to carry out a holy war against their opponents.

The fifth of the 5 books, Deuteronomy, meaning second law, is in some ways the most challenging. The product of a reformist wing of the Israelite cult, the core text was 'discovered' in the temple of Jerusalem in the late 7th century BCE. In language burning with conviction Deuteronomy summons the people to renew their covenantal faith in Yahweh, the God of Israel, and terminate allegiance to all other gods. The text takes a militant stance against polytheism and insists that monotheism is essential to cultural survival. The bulk of Deuteronomy is a code of ethical conduct designed to embody the practice of the covenantal faith. The book continues with a section of blessings and curses, characteristic of covenant format, large parts of which reflect the destruction of the northern and southern kingdoms (of Israel and Judah) and which were compiled during the tragic experience of exile during the Babylonian captivity. It concludes with impassioned exhortations attributed to Moses and culminates in a powerful ode cursing the people for their infidelity but promising renewal after suffering. Finally, blessings are bestowed on each of the tribes and the death of Moses is recorded.

There has been much debate about the intensity of this text, and the incongruence between the impassioned belief in Yahweh's love on the one hand and the expression of divine rage and malediction against inconstancy on the other. Is the God of Deuteronomy loving or punitive? For the authors of the received version the question is rather focused on human behavior. Are human beings—and especially those buying into a covenant with the Deity—to live by ethical and spiritual standards, or is an indiscriminate polytheism of conflicting norms to govern religious identity? What accounts for the seductive attraction of polytheism? With the kingdom of Israel destroyed, and conquest by Babylon looming over the remaining Yahwist kingdom of Judah, this had become an urgent question.

The experience of exile intensified the problem. The choice is ours, claimed the text, but for Deuteronomy the choice is clear. "Hear, O Israel! Yahweh alone is our God." "You shall love the Lord your God (Yahweh) with all your heart, and with all your soul, and with all your strength!" Later we find Moses spelling out the consequences of death and life and in an impassioned summation urging the people to "choose life!" These texts have reverberated down through the ages and are part of what gives Deuteronomy its special force. The message is clear: adhere to Yahweh's covenant; imprint it on your heart; or else—like the people of the ancient kingdom of Israel—face cultural and ethnic extinction.

As a group of texts, the Torah has several identifying themes. One is creation: the creation of the world, the tribal origins associated with the patriarchs, and especially the creation of the people of Israel as a political and cultic entity, achieved through the powerful leadership of Moses, who is their foundational prophet and lawgiver. Another is the establishment of revealed law or teaching (torah) as the foundation of moral existence. Many of the regulations set out in the covenantal codes, and inserted into the Exodus account, are still widely observed in contemporary Judaism, as are the cultic festivals. Indeed, study and observance of Torah remains at the heart of Jewish worship and its search to comprehend and uphold divine authority.

The central and unique theme in the Torah is the association of ethnic identity with an invisible Deity, who makes divine allegiance the central focus of tribal and cultic life. The justification for this allegiance is the intervention of the Deity into human history as liberator of the captive Israelites in Egypt and as guarantor of their spiritual and tribal freedom. The Torah is about liberation of both the individual and the group, encompassed through the life and work of its central personality, Moses. His struggles, and his insistence on calling the people of Israel into a covenantal, i.e. declaratory and binding, relationship with the liberating Deity, are what make the Torah such a compelling text for generations of Jewish and non-Jewish people.

The Torah texts were written in a patriarchal age and reflect the male-dominant and warrior values of tribal patriarchalism. According to the texts, the liberation of the Israelites was accomplished at the expense of numerous other ethnic groups. Some of these peoples lived in more materially advanced cultures than that of the semi-pastoral Hebrew tribes. Certain tribal groups who worshiped other deities were placed under a ban and sentenced to extermination. Goddess-centered religions were denounced, witches condemned, and women's lives strictly regulated to serve the interests of tribal and religious identity.

Many people are bothered by this aspect of the Torah. The Torah is not a manual of non-violent pacifism, or of recognition of earth-centered divinity. It is concerned with the survival of nomadic people and their redefinition as a political and cultic community with a sense of destiny and an ability to survive in a politically volatile region. That destiny is to be attained through a binding agreement with an irascible yet merciful Deity, who resists Moses' request for a name and answers only "I am that I am." In the cultic and militarized environment of the times, such a concept required a new understanding of divinity as a power accessible through present time rather than place, as befitted the needs of migrating Hebrew tribes.

This shift in divine-human relations from place to time is one of the critical innovations of Jewish religious history. The Torah expresses the nature of the Divine-human relationship, as it applied to the circumstances of the migrating Hebrew tribes. But the shift from place to time is very difficult to maintain, as is evident from the constant human tendency to relocate the Deity in specific placements (e.g. the temple, or any one of millions of churches and synagogues), rather than in the consciousness of the eternal present. According to the Torah, consciousness of divinity as 'Yahweh'—the liberator and protector of the Jewish people—as opposed to all other cultic divinities and mythologies, is achieved only through intense struggle, such as was experienced by both Abraham and Moses, and for their followers through adherence to complex ethical rules and sacrificial rituals. Torah insistence on imageless monotheism, essential to a time-present and therefore constantly changing ontology, was particularly subject to abuse. Thus, the Torah is a record of human failure as well as achievement. Yet, whether treated as a document of its times, a national declaration, a blueprint of covenantal discipline, or a manual of political survival, the Torah has become one of the great defining expressions of human experience. As such, it is about who and what we are as inheritors of Biblical religion.

This point may trouble people who have turned their backs on organized religion. They may wonder why we should concern ourselves with the religious needs of ancient generations. The answer has to do with the power that myth, as representation of spiritual power, exerts over human imagination. As this study will argue, we continue to be influenced in innumerable ways by Biblical myths. Our views about guilt and innocence, gender attitudes, creation and the natural order, the education of children, war and peace, vengeance and forgiveness, are all heavily influenced by myths in the Hebrew scriptures and the Bible as a whole. The better we understand these myths and sacred texts, the better we can discern their relevance today.

It is also appropriate to notice ways in which Jewish sages have interpreted this seminal text. One such was Hillel, an earlier contemporary of Jesus and a famous sage in Jewish history, whose views are summarized at the top of this chapter. All of Torah, he argues, boils down to the following: do not do to your neighbor that which is hateful to you. That is the essence of Torah; everything else is commentary. "Hateful" is a strong word. We are asked to ponder anything that would make us feel hateful if someone did it to us, and then make sure we do not do it to someone else. What are the actions that have made me feel resentful and hateful? Figure them out and don't let them control your dealings with others. Purge whatever is hateful to you from your repertoire of motives. Everything else in the Torah is commentary. That means it is what happened, but not the essence of Torah as moral and spiritual teaching.

Textual Traditions

One of the great contributions of nineteenth and twentieth century biblical scholarship has been to discern the existence of several distinctive textual traditions within the Torah as a whole. These can be noted in the two very differing creation accounts with which Genesis begins, and two parallel accounts of the story of Noah's Ark, which have been ingeniously conflated. Many of the most fascinating stories in the Torah, beginning with the story of Adam and Eve, derive from the tradition known by scholars as J, standing for the Germanic form of Yahweh or Jehovah and reflecting J's use of that term for the divine name. The J account is regarded by scholars in this field as the oldest textual layer of the Torah. It has a storyteller's interest in human narrative, an eye for character, and a grasp of the ambiguous aspects of human-divine relations. It incorporates ideas from other middle-eastern creation myths but interprets them in its own way. J provides the basic story line about the development of the Yahwist covenant from Genesis 2 through the end of Numbers (excluding Leviticus), which other traditions sought to modify and reshape. It is the bedrock text of the Hebrew Bible. Its myths shaped the Hebrew imagination and continue to reverberate in our time.

The J text was assembled sometime during the middle years of the kingdom of Judah; some scholars date it as early as the reign of the apostate king Rehoboam (late 10th century BCE), whose tyranny had resulted in the loss of the northern territories to non-Davidic upstarts and the fateful division of the kingdom bequeathed by the founding monarchs David and Solomon. In that sense the J text can be read (as it is by contemporary commentators such as Harold Bloom) as an oblique commentary on the Davidic and post-Davidic kingdoms.

A second Torah tradition, P (for Priestly), gives a more organizational and liturgical view of the relationship of human beings with the Divine than that supplied by the myth-laden J text. It is P that supplies many of the genealogies and censuses, in other words the historicity of the tradition, as well as the information concerning the sanctuary and its ceremonial usage. Among its most arresting passages are the seven-day Creation story, the longer version of the story of Noah, the description of the Passover ceremony, and accounts of the construction of the tabernacle. Priestly sources account for the book of Leviticus. Emergence of the P tradition has been associated with the 8th century BCE reform era of King Hezekiah of Judah or with the next half century. It favors the Aaronite priesthood and may have been compiled in part to counteract anti-Aaronic and anti-priestly elements in other texts.

Another important tradition, known as E, because of its use of the older term Elohim to refer to the divinity, overlaps and in certain ways modifies J's accounts of the patriarchs and the Exodus. The E tradition is a strong advocate of Moses, particularly in his role as lawgiver. It features prominently in Exodus, where it emphasizes the divine revelations experienced by Moses, the enigmatic naming of the Deity, the handing down of the book of laws, and the contrarian incident of the golden calf. E's vision of human order is prophetic and theocratic. Textual analysis has suggested to modern scholars that E was the product of an anti-monarchical priestly tradition in the northern kingdom of Israel, for which Moses and Joshua were the heroic archetypes. It is believed to have been brought south to Judah after the collapse of the kingdom of Israel.

Deuteronomic Tradition

The remaining source is known as D (for Deuteronomy). This source, as we have seen, has its own separate book within the Torah. Recent scholarship suggests that the Deuteronomic view may be the main source for the reshaping of the covenantal narratives in the first four Torah books to give primacy to the role of Moses. It is also generally regarded by textual scholars as the editorial force shaping the early prophetic or historical writings from Joshua through Kings. These books, known as the Earlier Prophets in the Hebrew Bible, tell of the conquest and settlement of the Promised Land, the renewal of the covenant by Joshua and its betrayal by subsequent generations, the emergence of Israelite state systems and the establishment of the Davidic monarchy, followed by the division of the kingdom into northern and southern parts (Israel and Judah) and their gradual political and moral decline. In the late 8th century BCE the northern kingdom of Israel was swallowed up by Assyria. Its people were deported and disappeared from history. The southern kingdom of Judah, around Jerusalem, struggled on until captured by Babylonian forces early in the 6th century BCE and a sizable portion of its people carried off into exile.

The dominant figure in the post-Mosaic portion of the Hebrew Bible is king David. David led a charmed existence and was beloved of Yahweh. As a youth he destroyed the tyrant Goliath. He served king Saul, evaded his wrath, and was anointed by the prophet Samuel to succeed Saul as king. He was one of the world's most ardent lovers, and it is this capacity that seems to have made him graced by Yahweh. Most importantly, he was the beneficiary of a special divine covenant that promised the kingship to his descendants for all time. It was through this covenant that the rulers of the southern kingdom of Judah claimed their legitimacy. It was also this covenant that gave force to the much later Jewish messianic tradition, and which made certain early Christians pay attention to the descent of Jesus from the Davidic line. At the same time, David as king made personal and political choices which would have implications, not all of them beneficial, for the future of the people of the covenant. The Deuteronomists would try to make sense of those implications.

The revival of Jewish life in Judah is recorded in the books of Ezra and Nehemiah. These books recount the rebuilding of Jerusalem and the temple under the dispensation of the Persian empire. The priest Ezra produced a Torah scroll and read it to the assembled people, while priests went around explaining the text. Urgent efforts were made to reinstate the sabbath and to enforce ethnic solidarity. These and other measures established the foundations for the development of modern Judaism.

Prophetic and Wisdom Literature

The prophetic and wisdom books include some of the Bible's most familiar literature, including the book of Psalms (spiritual songs), prophetic texts such as Isaiah and Jeremiah, and that most 'modern' of Biblical texts, the book of Job. Job is said to have lived in Uz, east of the river Jordan, while the book of Ruth is about a woman who came from the neighboring country of Moab. This is a reminder that as religious and cultural literature the Hebrew scriptures are not exclusively drawn from Jewish sources, even though the Hebrew scriptures are definitively Jewish in how they view human existence.

The prophets served as guardians of the covenantal tradition They warned rulers of Israel and Judah of forthcoming disaster, denounced them for apostasy, and fumed at the inconstancy of human behavior. More broadly, they criticized the Yahwist cult with its emphasis on sacrificial liturgies and accommodating policies towards non-Yahwist cults. The prophets want to replace the cultic worship of Yahweh with a vision of human-divine relations that is monotheistic and ethical. In their time the smaller cultic societies were being swallowed up by the emergent empires of Assyria and Babylon. The kingdom of Israel was captured by Assyria and repopulated by strangers. It appeared as if the kingdom of Judah would collapse in a similar manner. The prophets felt that the survival of Yahwism as a source of human order was at stake and that it was of paramount importance to get rid of cultism. That is why most of their energy goes into strident attacks on idolatry and cultic sacrifice and dire warnings of political disasters lying ahead. Thus, there is an often downbeat and negative tenor to prophetic writing that makes it difficult to absorb in large quantities.

The prophetic texts are also the source of much of the most powerful visionary and healing literature to be found in the Bible. They anticipate not only the breakdown of the old cultic definition of Yahwism but its replacement by one built on an ethical foundation of justice and mercy. The new age visions in the books of Isaiah and Ezekiel describe dramatic and intensely imaged accounts of this new monotheistic order. They refuse to accept that the material reality of corruption and conquest is the only reality accessible to human beings and instead challenge their contemporaries to visualize alternative 'powers' and principalities with entirely new ways of interacting with human existence. Some of the most powerful prophetic visions emerged during the exile in Babylon, when the Jewish exiles were cut off from their cultic centers. The revisioning of

Yahwism that took place during this time was essential not only to preserve Jewish identity but also to make Yahweh-worship a source of renewed strength to individuals experiencing prolonged upheaval and catastrophe. The prophets came up with some of the most profoundly healing images in the Bible. It is in their writings that the belief in redemption is spelled out. Examples of healing images include the Prince of Peace in Isaiah, a passage set to inspirational music by Handel in his oratorio the Messiah. Another famous image, also from Isaiah, is of the chosen servant, the image of a being who took on the sins of others and bore them as a sacrifice. That one also evoked some of Handel's most inspired artistry. Naturally this image has been universally subsumed by Christians as a foreshadowing, or prophetic visualization, of the crucified Jesus.

For readers with a special interest in spiritual life there is no better text than the book of Psalms. Every human emotion is on display here, from unbounded joy to anguish, guilt, and hatred. The writers of the Psalms understood the experience of doubt and failure that so inevitably accompanies the life of the spirit. They recognized the human desire to flee from the divine as well as the anguished calls for help. The arena of spiritual life is depicted as one of conflict, subversion and danger. To be sure, this is also true of the secular world. But the psalms describe life as lived with consciousness of divine presence. There are wonderful epiphanic passages that describe what it feels like to experience divine power. It is this quality which gives the psalms their power to sustain the human spirit. The faith of the Psalms extends beyond daily life and holds out the possibility of living with integrity in a time of chaos.

The wisdom books also address the spiritual needs of individuals. At a symbolic level, the book of Proverbs sets out for the reader the image of a tree of life, at the apex of which resides Wisdom (Hochmah), a vibrant feminine power, existent before the world was made and the soul's pathway to life. An opposing force also exists—the 'strange woman'—which lures the unwary fool to death and dissolution. Faced with this contingent dualism the book becomes an urgent cry to avoid the latter and adhere at all costs to the former. Fear of Yahweh, it insists (as do other wisdom texts), is the beginning of wisdom.

Another idea about wisdom, which would enter Christian theology, is that it is beyond the comprehension of every living thing, unknown and unknowable. In later wisdom literature the conception of wisdom would be elevated to a manifestation of divine power: "pure emanation of the glory of the Almighty", as the Jerusalem Bible puts it. (Wisdom 7, 25). In this manner wisdom theology would play a vital part in the development by Gospel writers of an understanding of the nature of Jesus.

To a certain extent the prophets combine elements of the wisdom tradition, since they incorporate the same belief in the wisdom of humility and fear of the God Yahweh. The prophets, however, are principally concerned with covenantal crisis, that is, with the collective fate of the people. The wisdom literature is concerned more with individual consciousness and behavior. It reflects the emergence of individual consciousness separate and apart from tribal or covenantal identity. In this respect the wisdom literature is highly relevant to the individualism and spiritual deconstruction widespread in contemporary life.

Endings

The standard Hebrew Bible (Tanakh) ends with another historical text, known as Chronicles. This document focuses on the history and temple worship of the kingdom of Judah. It describes its patriarchal genealogy, the establishment of the Israelite monarchy by David and Solomon, the evolution of the southern kingdom of Judah under David's descendants, and its eventual degradation and the destruction of the kingdom and temple by Babylon. There is the barest mention of the Babylonian captivity, and the text ends with the promise of the reconstruction of the temple by the Persian king Cyrus. The account focuses on the association of the Davidic monarchy with the Temple and the preservation of the Yahwist cult. It brings the Hebrew Bible to an end on the promising note of the reconstruction of the temple and the revival of covenantal worship.

For Christian editors this was not an appropriate terminal point for the Hebrew scriptures. Their version (the 'Old Testament') ends with the brief and apocalyptic prophecy of Malachi, the 'Messenger'. This castigates the people of Israel for apostasy and anticipates the faithful worship of the God of all nations by non-Jewish Gentiles. The text warns Israelites to return to the true faith and announces that a new Elijah will be sent

The Wisdom of the Covenants and Their Relevance to Our Times

prior to the coming of the final judgment day. Early Christians took this as pointing the way to John the Baptist (or Baptizer) and the proclamation of the Christian covenant, which would in their view bring to fulfillment the prophetic Hebrew scriptures.

CHAPTER 3

The Christian Context

> Thy name, O Jesus, be forever blest
> Alleluya, Alleluya
> from William Walton How, "For All the Saints"

Significance of the Gospels

After that brief introduction to the Hebrew scriptures, we now move on to the covenant of Jesus. In its focus on one unique life and one covenant the New Testament is quite different from the Hebrew scriptures. That is why I've chosen as text heading a confession of faith from one of modern Christianity's great hymns. The Victorian author, Bishop William Walton How, believed fervently in the mission of Jesus and spent a lifetime in service to poor people and children. The hymn is based on a covenantal text from Jeremiah and the Book of Hebrews promising divine redemption. When sung to the inspiring music of Ralph Vaughan Williams it becomes a proclamation of joy.

Christians have from the earliest times called the Christian section of the Bible the 'New' Testament - i.e. new covenant - to distinguish it from the pre-Christian, Hebrew Covenants. Today it could also be referred to as the Christian Testament. It consists of four sections: Gospels, Acts of the Apostles, Letters or Epistles, and the Book of Revelation (or Apocalypse). These sections parallel the Christian division of the Hebrew scriptures into the five books of (or more accurately about) Moses, the histories, confessional and wisdom literature, and prophecy, through which the Old Testament is projected by its Christian editors as a foretelling of the New.

Here again the basic vocabulary involves religious terminology. 'Gospel' or 'good news,' denotes what are now widely recognized by scholars to be accounts reconstructed along mythic lines—using 'mythic', as before, to refer to sacred story incorporating central values—about the life and work of Jesus of Nazareth. There are four in the standard Christian Bible, associated with the names of Matthew, Mark, Luke and John. The Good News named for Mark, although second in order of sequence in the Bible, is the earliest of the four gospel texts and is the paradigm for this form of literature. It was written not long after the Roman military destruction of Jerusalem and its people in CE 70 and reflects the impact of that earth-shattering event.

The Good News associated with the names of Matthew and Luke incorporate significant amounts of the Mark gospel, while each uses alternative accounts and traditions. The most well researched among the latter has been reconstructed by scholars as the so-called 'Sayings Gospel' (commonly identified as Q for Quelle or 'source', because of its original identification by German scholars). Contemporary specialists view this as a multi-layered text, the earliest strata of which give us the earliest insight into the goals and mores of a community of Jesus followers. These three gospels are known as the 'synoptic' (similar vision) gospels, because of certain similarities in material and story line. But they are not similar in either their vision of Jesus or their concept of the Jesus mission.

The Mark gospel is the earliest to provide a cohesive depiction of Jesus. It describes an authoritative missionary and martyr for the kingdom of God, whose work survived the attacks of Jewish opponents, while the temple in Jerusalem was destroyed. The gospel has no interest in infancy traditions or Messiah genealogies (the Roman military destruction of Jerusalem, the core of the Jewish world, may have made them seem irrelevant). Its birthing story is about spiritual awakening. It identifies Jesus as Son of God, baptized through a sacred ritual by John the Baptist and blessed and confirmed by the Holy Spirit. It then launches him into a 40-day (i.e. prolonged) struggle in the desert wilderness with the Satan, the contest with which his mission opens. It is this wilderness experience that gives birth to the prophetic voice proclaiming reconnection with divine power.[5]

The gospel sets up the mission of Jesus as a struggle between two forces: one dedicated to the repair of damaged human lives, the other to achieving human destruction and chaos. This division between a life-supporting cosmos and a life-dissolving chaos is reflected in the creation stories in Isaiah, Job and the Psalms with their emphasis on the struggle required to assert divine order over chaos. The oppressiveness of Roman military rule over Palestine and the Roman destruction of Jerusalem, its temple and its inhabitants in 70 CE provided shocking immediacy to this struggle. Christianity took shape in the context of this life and death struggle, and the Mark gospel focuses on this visceral theme. Its Jesus appears as a shaman-like healer who takes on the prince of devils, casts out demons and unclean spirits, and cures people with polluting disabilities. In turn the Satan puts together a successful campaign to get Jesus betrayed to the authorities and crucified (the Roman method for getting rid of trouble-makers)—but not before Jesus had enlisted male and female followers who would carry on his anti-demonic, life-preserving work on earth.

This emphasis in Mark on confrontation with the demonic world alerts us to the radical challenge of Jesus' effort (and that of his Marcan followers) to claim the kingdom of God as an alternative to the turmoil and destruction occurring in Roman-occupied Judea. It is a battle fought over the bodies of ordinary, vulnerable human beings; but the battle rages both between Roman paganism and the religious mores of Judaism, and unfortunately also within Judaism between the emerging culture of the Rabbinic synagogue and the mixed Jewish-Gentile communities of Jesus followers.

The society depicted in the gospel is obsessed by demonic forces opposed to Jewish religious practice and social order. The purpose of its early passages is to demonstrate the anti-demonic authority of Jesus. Unclean spirits that can defile and destroy ordinary humans are said to quail

---

[5] I am indebted for this insight to John P. Keenan, The Gospel of Mark: A Mahayana Reading. New York: Maryknoll, 1995. Readers interested in wilderness and soul awakening can find out more about it through the writings of Bill Plotkin, e.g. Soulcraft: Crossing into the Mysteries of Nature and Psyche, Novato, CA: New World Library, 2003.

in the presence of Jesus, because they—unlike the human opponents of Jesus—recognize him as the 'Holy One of God.'[6] Sick and maimed people regard Jesus as healer, despite their impurity (as defined in covenantal law) and consequent rejection by normal society. This is an illustration of the capacity of seriously diseased people, some of whom may be rejected as social outcasts, to experience a transformation in spiritual perception, a theme developed so eloquently in the Book of Job. Their faith in Jesus is contrasted with the malevolence attributed to Jesus' synagogue-centered opponents and the ignorance and wrong-headedness of some of his leading male followers.

The community of Jesus followers reflected in the gospel appears to have once been close to the culture of Jewish synagogues in and around Galilee. But a bitter conflict over adherence to purity codes had arisen between the Marcan community and the Pharisees, necessitating that the Marcan community develop its own scriptural justification and means of survival. The synagogue was emerging as a focal point for the allegiance of Jewish communities disoriented by the Roman destruction of Jerusalem and the temple. The Mark gospel thought it mandatory to attack the authority of the synagogue and reinforce that of the Marcan community. Consequently, the gospel incorporates miracles that resonate with the earlier missions of Moses and Elijah, thus adding to the authority of Jesus and placing his mission within the context of Hebrew salvation history. It also proclaims the capacity of gentiles to recognize Jesus as Son of God—an indication that the community included gentile adherents.

A critical feature of this gospel, which puts it into a different category from collections of Jesus sayings, lies in its incorporation of the Jerusalem-based Christ-as-martyr story (associated with the Jerusalem leadership and the disciple Peter) into accounts about Jesus and the kingdom of God focused on the mission in Galilee. Midway through the gospel the itinerant missionary for the kingdom of God is repositioned as a Messianic martyr-king, whose martyrdom and resurrection provide a freely offered covenant of redemption for his followers. As contemporary scholars have shown, the authority of the Galilean miracle worker is infused with the

---

[6] Readers wishing to follow this theme in detail should consult Elaine Pagels, The Origin of Satan, (New York: Vintage Books, 1996).

authority of the Messiah and that of the virtuous Son of God found in wisdom literature.

This repositioning is signaled by an event known as the Transfiguration, in which Jesus, accompanied by the 'three pillars' of the Jerusalem community, goes up a high mountain and appears with Elijah and Moses. The account is modeled on the highly charged mountain epiphany in the Sinai story. It signals the enlarged role claimed for Jesus as redeemer and fulfiller of the divine salvation plan, while acknowledging a special if flawed status enjoyed by the Jerusalem community leaders reported as accompanying Jesus.

But this Jesus is going to follow a different script from previous messiahs who had arisen and failed as anti-Roman rebels. The crucifixion event, through which Jesus as Christ/Messiah is betrayed and sacrificed to the demonic powers of darkness headquartered in Jerusalem, and the resurrection— demonstrating the capacity of the divine to survive earthly dissolution—initiate the process. The coming persecutions of Jesus followers, the Roman destruction of the Temple and the population of Jerusalem, and the anticipated triumphal return of the resurrected Son of Man, are then unfolded as sequential manifestations of that script. The anti-demonic struggle continues, but the source of life now operates from beyond the reach of demonic power.

This story line sets out the Marcan community's case for Jesus as Christ/Messiah and for his Marcan followers as inheritors of the Yahwist covenant. The fighting spirit of messiah mythology is retained by positioning Jesus as an anti-demonic warrior. But from a Marcan perspective, the significance of the claim for Jesus as the Messiah/Christ is that it turns on its head the old and damaged ethnocentric model of messiah as liberator of Jerusalem from Roman domination. With Jerusalem destroyed by Roman legions and the temple and its mystique in ruins, a radically new conception of a messiah liberated from Jerusalem becomes a possibility. Thus, the original text of the gospel ends by reclaiming the Messiah Jesus for the Galilean mission and removing him from Jerusalem, once his role as Messiah has been scripturally fulfilled.

The gospel associated with the name of Matthew was written for Jewish Christians several years after the destruction of Jerusalem in 70 CE and the rapid breakdown of relations between the Rabbinic communities and those Jews and gentiles who became followers of Jesus. This gospel goes to much greater lengths than that of Mark to situate the Jesus mission in the theological history of Judaism. It begins with a genealogy linking Jesus to the founding father Abraham and his descendant King David, founder of the earthly kingdom and the messianic tradition. This is followed by an account of the visit by the Magi (wise men from communities not subject to Jewish or Roman authority). The arrival of the Magi signals a shift in the ordering of human affairs. According to the gospel, Herod king of Judea attempted to prevent this shift by ordering the massacre of male children up to the age of two in and around Bethlehem. Warned by a dream, the Holy family left hurriedly for Egypt, where they stayed until Herod was dead. The account draws on themes associated with the birth of Moses. We know nothing from this gospel about how the family got on in Egypt, only that Jesus' life was from the outset in danger from Jewish authority. After Herod's death the family returns and settles in Nazareth, and nothing more is reported until Jesus is baptized and undergoes his preparatory ordeals in the desert.

Given that Moses spent some 60 years in eclipse as a Midianite sheep farmer, we should not cavil too much that the gospel writer has nothing to say about the roughly 30 years between the birth of Jesus and his emergence as a prophetic voice. After all, this text is a spiritual discourse, not a biography. There is the birth, that picks up the lineage from Abraham through David, and the hint of a dangerous prophetic calling; then there is the spiritual preparation, initiated by the Baptist and the Satan and presided over by the Heavenly powers. From a prophetic perspective, a new and sanctified voice has arisen to challenge the dangerous earthly authority of the times. The people who live in darkness are about to see a new light.

The theme of preaching in the face of Jewish opposition is then dramatically explored in several extended tableaux of narrative and discourse, predicating events of the Jesus mission as fulfillment of earlier Biblical prophecy. The shamanic demon-combatant, portrayed in the early pages of Mark, is toned down and transformed into an eloquent teacher who has come to fulfill the Torah and make the kingdom of Heaven tangible to people living on earth. To emphasize this critical change in strategy, the gospel begins its account of the Jesus mission with the justly famous 'Sermon on the Mount', a distillation of sayings from the Q tradition. These sayings describe the nature of the kingdom of heaven and the ways of life that make it accessible. As will be discussed in chapter 10, the sayings include a prayer universally known to those practicing Christianity, which includes key features of the Jesus covenant. The sermon is laced with Biblical quotations, principally from Isaiah and the Psalms. It concludes with a pointed meditation on the Deuteronomic theme of the two ways of life and death, which had concluded Moses' great peroration to the Children of Israel as recorded in the book of Deuteronomy.

Several tableaux describing the Jesus mission form the main body of the Gospel and the source of its message about the kingdom of Heaven. As contemporary scholars have pointed out, the key to the gospel lies in its determination to establish the Jesus mission and its non-Jewish as well as Jewish converts as fulfillment of the Hebrew epic. It also establishes parameters for how that mission is to function. A core passage (in chapter 18) teaches that the true source of righteousness in the new community of Jesus followers consists in adopting the humility of childhood rather than the entitlement of authority, and in forgiving one's companions at all costs—up to seventy times seven if necessary.[7] The passage also records the memorable observation attributed to Jesus, that "when two or three are gathered together in my name, I shall be in the midst of them.[8]" Incorporated into liturgy, this promise has resonated through the ages as an expression of Jesus as a resurrected life force.

After a series of confrontations with opponents, the tableaux build up to a powerful, harrowing eschatological (end-time) discourse. This 'predicts' the destruction of the temple (it had already happened by the time the gospel was written), along with wars, famines, earthquakes and great distress unparalleled since the world began. This is a pretty viable description of the appalling conditions of life in Judea during and after the Roman destruction of Jerusalem and its people. Then the Son of Man will return to preside over a Day of Judgment by which the sheep of purity, who are Jesus practitioners, and the goats of sin, who disown him,

---

[7] Sometimes translated as seventy-seven times, but the thrust of the argument supports the larger number. I am indebted to the writings of Raymond E. Brown for insight into this passage.

[8] St. John Crysostom, a fourth century Archbishop of Constantinople, incorporated this passage into a liturgical prayer commonly recited in Anglican episcopal services.

are conclusively separated and the latter cast into eternal fire. In short, the lines between supporters and opponents of Jesus are irrevocably drawn.

The gospel concludes with a passion account, which contrasts Jewish denunciation with Roman recognition of Jesus' divinity. This is a vital shift in the anguished story of how the Jesus mission brought about the revival of an oppressed group of people. Although the Roman military are by far the chief oppressors of the population of Roman-occupied Judea, it is the Jewish opponents of Jesus that the gospel most bitterly condemns. Modern readers will appreciate that we are caught up here in conflicts about how best to react to Roman domination. In rejecting rebellion as the way to beat off Rome, Matthew's Jesus parted company with a powerful strain of messianic rebellion, which kept surfacing in Judea right up to the middle of the second century of the Common Era. He paid heavily for this decision, and the gospel does not mince words in denouncing Jews who turned on him and his followers. This not so subtle account of Jewish rejection of Jesus, foreshadowed by the Herodian massacre of the innocents, is now complete. The old Mosaic covenant, seen as adrift with the destruction of Jerusalem and the temple in 70 CE, has its successor in the new Jesus covenant of redemption. The apostles are sent out to bring that good news to peoples of all nations.

The Luke gospel, part 1 of an account of the origins and development of the Christian movement, is written for a non-Jewish constituency and draws on elements in Jewish theology and myth that point to its universalism. The gospel contains a strong component intended to allay Roman fears that Christians were a subversive religious sect. Like Matthew it weaves elements of historicity into the story of Jesus, providing not only a genealogy going back to Adam as son of God and primal father of all, but also a scheme for dating the Jesus mission in a manner comprehensible to Roman readers.

In contrast to Matthew, this gospel provides an Isaian vision of the Jesus covenant as proclaiming justice and mercy to the poor and to neighbors in need of help. The idea of Jesus as Redeemer for all people is introduced in the infancy narrative, which avoids the persecution and terror in Matthew's account and instead proclaims in highly poetic language the advent of salvation and joy to the humble people of this earth. It is this Lucan poetry, most of it drawn from, or modeled on, passages in the Hebrew scriptures, that has inspired the reverence associated by many people with the festival of Christmas and the birth of this world-wide way of life.

This gospel is the only one to give us a tantalizing glimpse into the life of Jesus during the thirty years prior to the assumption of his public mission. At the age of twelve he is found lingering in Jerusalem after a Passover visit, engaging in discourse with the teachers in the temple. Already a sophisticated mind is at work, and when discovered by his parents Jesus told his mother that he wanted to be in his 'father's' house. Did his thirst for religious learning only manifest this once? It seems unlikely, particularly since the text tells us that he grew in wisdom and stature. But there is no further information about the education that he must have received. Instead the boy Jesus dutifully returns home with his parents, and the text moves on to the appearance of John the Baptist, the baptism, and the struggle with the Satan in preparation for launching his mission.

The account of Jesus's mission to poor and oppressed people, announced through an Isaian text, adopts the Marcan 'biographic' outline by proceeding in stages from Galilee to the denouement in Jerusalem, the holy city and source of both Jewish travail and divine redemption. On the way the Satan is observed falling like lightning from Heaven (defeated even as he contrives the betrayal of his opponent), and the followers of Jesus experience the power to trample on serpents and overcome the whole strength of the enemy. Empowerment through redemption is the critical theme of the Luke message, spelled out in memorable parables and human encounters. How different this is from the disempowerment and frustration attributed to the Jerusalem-based disciples in the Mark gospel.

There is also a tragic lament in the account of this journey to Jerusalem, and that is over what happens to those who fail to repent. As Jesus and his associates approach Jerusalem, the city and its inhabitants, doomed to face a time of terrifying destruction, become the focus of that lament. This perspective on the Crucifixion story is very different from that taken by the Matthew gospel. Jesus must first face his own personal day of anguish; but the faith of the disciples and the intervention of an angel strengthen him in his hour of crisis. The crucifixion and resurrection events become the consummation of the covenant of redemption, which is to be communicated throughout the world beginning from the ruins of Jerusalem. In short, Christianity as a religion of redemption is already on the march.

In its continuation, as the Book of Acts, the Luke account describes the work of the Spirit of God in inspiring the apostles, led by Peter, to extend the Jesus mission through the Roman empire and create early Christian communities, for the successors to which this gospel was written. Here again, if the Christian scriptures were rearranged to put Luke and Acts together as a composite and seamless text, we would see more clearly the emergence of an account about how a vision of redemption takes hold of and transforms human community. The fact that Christianity emerged in one of the most battered regions of the Roman empire would become clearer to us, as would the significance of a religion of the oppressed infiltrating—and in due course capturing—the headquarters of the Mediterranean world's pagan imperialism. The implications of that achievement and their ensuing problems would then resonate much more loudly today.

We would also notice that the Luke gospel (if defined to include both the gospel itself and the Acts of the Apostles) is very directly about the impact of the Christ story, as reported in this gospel, on the nascent world of Christ followers. It is a resurrection story, filled with speeches about the meaning of the Christ events (trial, crucifixion and resurrection) for those who had lived through them. This is a new motif in gospel writing, inasmuch as the intention is to script both the life force of the redeemer Christ and its expression in ordinary mortals through the agency of the Holy Spirit.

An aspect of this gospel teased out by contemporary scholars is that it strongly favors the apostolic mission of Peter. It also favors Peter over the woman friend and apostle who was closest to Jesus, namely Mary Magdalene. A study by Anne Graham Brock spells out this argument in detail and follows its implications through subsequent texts. The elevation of Peter and of the male apostles generally over Mary and other women apostles is part of a broader trend, that picked up speed in the second and third centuries of the common era, towards the emergence of Christianity as a patriarchal religion. I will discuss this controversial topic and its fundamental significance and problematic for the future of Christianity in later chapters dealing with the apostle Paul and with women in Christianity. What is significant here is that the move in the direction of patriarchal leadership and dominance is already apparent in the Luke gospel, whereas it is less overt in the other three gospels.

The Good News of John, compiled around the year 100, takes us into another distinct community of Jesus followers with its own leadership, traditions and assumptions about the significance of Jesus and his mission. This gospel draws on early traditions about the life and death of Jesus, around which it weaves a theology of redemption. The basic symbolism, voiced by John the Baptist, is of Jesus as the Lamb of God (agnus dei) that takes away the sins of the world. His incarnation is directly from the divine Father and is the manifestation of divine love for the created world. Although Mary is acknowledged as the mother of Jesus, it is Jesus' relationship as son to God the father that is transcendent. From this perspective, Joseph as human father and descendant of King David is irrelevant, as there is no interest in an earthly genealogy linking Jesus to the messianic inheritance. His manifestation in this gospel is directly from the originating divine Word.

On this theology of Word made flesh is overlaid a symbolism of light and darkness. Jesus as son represents the forces of light in arduous struggle with the forces of darkness. This battle formation echoes the Marcan demonic struggle but is configured at a cosmic level and embraces all of humanity. Drawing on Torah and prophetic symbolism, the gospel represents Jesus much as depicted in the texts of deutero-Isaiah about the servant-son beloved of Yahweh. His mission reaches its climax and crowning fulfillment in the crucifixion and resurrection, through which Jesus is first treated like a lamb led to the slaughterhouse and then raised up as the assurance for all believers of spiritual protection from the forces of annihilation. The crucifixion is envisioned as an act of glory through the transformative power of bodily sacrifice.

For early Christians experiencing denunciation from Jewish and death from Roman opponents, as well as disagreement and conflict within their own ranks, this vivid message of redemption was of tremendous importance. Even today it helps to explain the unusually powerful claim that the John gospel and the Johannine epistles have exercised over the Christian imagination. The John gospel argues that Jesus is divine beyond all time— and specifically before and beyond Abraham and therefore pre-Judaic— thereby raising the transformative power of the Son and producing what scholars call a "high Christology." Those who believe in this manifestation of divine as human are reborn by that belief and their spirits, if not their bodies, are saved. Depictions of this Johannine Jesus, such as those in the gripping Isenheim altarpiece painted by Matthias Grunewald in the early sixteenth century, may show the Baptist at the Crucifixion scene (even though his execution predated it). This differentiates the divine-as-human savior-king from a human prophet-messiah. It also specifically establishes Jesus as the lamb of God through the experience of crucifixion. It intensifies the significance of the divine in human flesh and establishes a vital connection between human suffering and divine glory.

In addition to its focus on the divine redeeming power of Jesus as son, lord, and friend, the gospel provides details about the lives of the 'three' Marys (Mary the mother of Jesus, Mary of Bethany, and Mary Magdalene) not found in the other gospels, which give evidence pointing to their special significance in the life and mission of Jesus. Another unique feature of this gospel is its reference to an unknown community leader as the 'beloved' disciple, the male companion who was closest to, and most befriended by, Jesus. Indeed, the gospel can be read as a meditation on the spiritual power and collective force of friendship—a theme that was unfolding in the remarkable life stories of early Christian martyrs.

The gospel also goes furthest in separating Christian witness and friendship from synagogue Judaism. As many scholars have pointed out, the high Christology that assigned divine status to Jesus would have been quite unacceptable to synagogue leaders. Consequently, synagogue Jews emerge as a focal opposition to the Johannine community. This point is driven home in the gospel's account of the pre-Crucifixion trial, which contrasts the hostility ascribed to the temple leadership with the attitudes of respect for Jesus attributed to the harsh and cynical Roman governor Pontius Pilate.

Problems of Interpretation

The gospels pose several problems of theological and historical interpretation. Apart from brief bits of data in other passages of the Christian Testament, they are the only texts authorized by the early Church as recounting the life and teaching of Jesus; and only marginal references to his existence have been found outside of texts deriving from the Christian tradition. So Christian texts, whether orthodox or outside the Biblical canon (of which there are several), are the only written sources that tell us anything material about Jesus' life and work.

A problem for believers and skeptics consists in the mythic structure of the gospel accounts. Recognition of the gospel texts as myth rather than fact is necessary to access the power that resides in myth. To illustrate this point: the fact that the great German theologian Dietrich Bonhoefer and his friends and relatives were hanged by members of the Nazi SS in 1945 is an abomination of the sort practiced universally by Nazis against Jews and anyone else they disliked. The idea that Bonhoefer chose to risk and sacrifice his life in Hitler's Germany as witness to the power of Christian redemption is amazing and something to cherish deeply when viewed as an act of faith and love. This is an example of how mythic power, with its access to the sacred, transcends factual power. It is this message that gave Bonhoefer and his friends, and numerous other witnesses for divine love, the courage to do what they did. Through their faith they transformed misery into glory.

Another problem for many readers is that the gospels strike an avowedly anti-Jewish tone. The Matthew gospel is the most critical of 'the Jews' (i.e. those Jews who are reported to have denounced other Jews who became followers of Jesus); and it is a major source for the patristic and medieval canard that the Jews, as an entire ethnic identity, were guilty of deicide, a charge that survived, with genocidal consequences, to the present day. Hatred of Jews among modern Aryan extremist groups, while drawing heavily on historically recent Aryan racist dogma, has benefited hugely from this anti-Semitic strain in Christian scripture. The gospels are angry and critical towards leading religious elements of Jewish life of that time, principally certain Pharisees and Scribes, and the Chief Priests, who managed the all-important temple cult. Ironically the Pharisees represented an important reform movement. Hillel, for example, who is one of the greatest sages of rabbinic Judaism, was a Pharisee. It was Pharisees who preserved Judaism from collapse after the Roman destruction of Jerusalem and the second Temple in 70 CE. The apostle Paul himself started his adult life as a Pharisee and retained a very strong orientation towards the Hebrew scriptures - not surprisingly, since those Hebrew scriptures were his Bible.

The gospels, however, were concerned that after the destruction of Jerusalem, the Pharisees provided the main momentum within Jewish religious life for opposition to the early Christian sects. As a result, they include polemical and frequently harsh anti-Pharisee passages. There is no overt mention in them anywhere of the profoundly devout Hillel and only the scantiest mention in Acts of another distinguished Pharisee leader, Rabban Gamaliel. In certain key passages the Pharisees of the Gospels are depicted as untrustworthy, hypocritical people who ganged up on Jesus and plotted his downfall. The chief priests are also, with much better reason, portrayed in a negative light. As political appointees who viewed Jesus as a contender against the temple power structure from which they benefited, they were strongly in favor of getting rid of him.

Individual Romans, by contrast, appear in the Christian gospels, and even more in Acts, as more tolerant and open to conversion. It is not obvious from a surface reading of the gospels that it was these same Romans who were responsible for the destruction of the Temple in 70 CE, the savage slaughter of the people of Jerusalem and other Jewish communities, and the ruthless suppression of Jewish independence. All this was going on before, during, and after the composition of the gospels. The crucifixion accounts in the gospels do provide a flavor of the cruelty of the Roman soldiery but focus that cruelty almost exclusively on the suffering of Jesus. Their portrayal of Pilate as honest broker is at odds with the harsh cynic reported by the Jewish historian Josephus. Thus, a colonial occupation, that brutally oppressed Jewish people over a long time period, is treated with circumspection, while forces such as the Pharisees and Rabbinic Judaism, which struggled against Roman oppression, are denounced.

There are accounts of the life and sayings of Jesus and his early Christian followers outside of the four gospels. The most well-known is the gospel of Thomas, a collection of sayings preserved in Coptic script, which were authenticated during the 1950s. Some of these sayings are also recorded in the Q tradition. Other sources belong to what became labeled as 'heretical' traditions. Some of these texts, e.g. the Gospel of Mary, counterpoised prophetic revelation to the principle of male apostolic succession, or put forward doctrines of spiritual growth and salvation in conflict with crucifixion or apocalyptic theologies. Such texts were barred from the patriarchal canon, and those labeled Gnostic were as rigorously attacked by orthodox Christianity as was Rabbinic Judaism. What emerged in their place was the New Testament canon, the Nicene Creed, and what the theologian Karen King deservedly calls "the master story" of Christianity.

The World of Early Christians

There were a substantial number of apostle-missionaries who spread the 'good news' about redemption into the Hellenistic and specifically Roman worlds. Yet there is one personality that dominates these sections of the Bible, and that is the apostle Paul. Paul played a crucial role in the formation of Christianity as an organized religion, transforming it from an unknown and largely Jewish sect into one that embraced non-Jewish 'Gentile' adherents, thus making it accessible to populations throughout the Roman empire.

As a Jew who was a Greek-speaking Roman citizen, Paul's energies could not be contained by Jewish sectarian definitions of Christianity. His triumphant belief in the universality of Christian doctrine, his theological sophistication and his unflagging leadership, won over people who could never have embraced an ethnically circumscribed faith, and carried it all the way to the capital of the Roman empire. It was substantially through Paul's missionary activities that Christianity took root in the Roman empire, became the dominant European religion, and so was carried into the rest of the world principally by European and later North American missionaries. Paul literally put Christianity on the map and did everything in his power to ensure that it stayed there.

And the powers at his disposal were considerable. As a Pharisee and a Rabbi Paul was well educated—and an avid believer—in Biblical teaching. A native of Asia Minor, he was bilingual and moved freely and easily between Jewish and Greek speaking society. He was competent at making a living and did so throughout his travels. He was a natural public speaker and an eloquent and persuasive writer.

Above all, he had a commanding personality and a zealous belief in his convictions. This made him fearless and a natural leader of others. He was also at times intemperate and unwilling to accept opposition from peers. Paul had to have his own way, even if that meant breaking with friends, disrupting meetings, or risking his life and that of his companions. Much of the time he was anguished and guilt-driven. He experienced sin with a depth of feeling beyond any encountered elsewhere in the Christian scriptures. He interpreted the Christ Jesus as the power that redeemed him from sin and guilt. At his insistence this 'good news' about Jesus as redeemer was tirelessly conveyed to Jews and non-Jews in Asia Minor and Southeastern Europe. He set up communities of believers and kept in close touch with them. The church-as-mission grew out of his active and lengthy ministry.

All this is reported in the Acts of the Apostles, and by Paul himself, or by other close companions or followers, in letters to the Christian communities that he had set up. These documents provide a basic answer to the question how did Christianity get started? Given the impact that Christianity has had on world history, this is a question well worth considering. The question becomes particularly sensitive when applied to letters, such as those to the Pauline communities in Ephesus and Colossus, which although associated with Paul were for various reasons written later and are regarded by many scholars as 'deutero-Pauline', i.e. written by associates or followers and representing a post-apostolic stage in the development of early Christian communities. There are passages in these letters, particularly regarding the role of women in Christian community, which appear to be at odds with both the practice of Jesus himself as described in gospel passages and the teaching of Paul as preserved in early Pauline letters such as those to the Corinthians. Yet the influence on Christian practice of the thinking reflected in these later Pauline letters has been, and still is, profound (see chapter 11).

The Christian Testament ends with the Book of Revelation, a surrealist vision drawing heavily on apocalyptic prophecy in the Hebrew scriptures. The immediate context of this vision is provided by the persecution and temptations experienced by Christian communities in Asia Minor. Rome had by this time turned against the Christian believers, and the temptation to yield to apostasy was intense. The hope of deliverance from Roman persecution arose from belief in Messianic resurrection and return. This belief predicted an 'end time,' in which the forces of good and evil would battle for the souls of humans. After a period of intense tribulation, reminiscent of the plagues suffered by ancient Egypt at the time of the

Exodus, the powers of evil would be vanquished, and the Devil chained up for a thousand years. A second conflict would be necessary before the final victory of the forces of righteousness. Then the Day of Judgment would take place and the new Jerusalem descend and occupy the earth.

This famous 'eschatological' (end-time) vision has exerted a huge influence over Christian thinking. It is the inspiration of powerful religious poems and some of the most famous Christian graphic art. For millennialists it is the principal script of the 'end time'. It may therefore come as a surprise—and it certainly did to this writer—to discover that the Book of Revelation is also a major source of inspiration for the liberation theology and base communities scattered throughout Latin America. This is because of the text's insistence on the just cause of the oppressed Christian communities and the deliverance that they will finally enjoy from the Roman imperial forces oppressing them. This theme of justice for the oppressed and punishment for the oppressor is emphasized throughout Revelation and has inspired millennialist movements throughout history.

Yet the powerful political influence of the book of Revelation should not detract from its theocratic and visionary stance. The text envisions for its oppressed audiences a brilliant and regal heavenly court, intended to far surpass in glory and majesty anything that Rome could dream up, in which the Redeemer Lamb of God will be glorified. It is this conception that the 18th century composer Georg Friedrich Handel captured so brilliantly in his epic Hallelujah Chorus and in the equally epic and monumental choruses "Worthy is the Lamb" and "Amen", with which his great oratorio The Messiah concludes. These visions, and the vision of a new Jerusalem, with its sacred river of life and trees of nourishment and healing, coming down to earth and taking their place among humans, give the text an especially powerful emotional impact. In that time, it proclaims that God will wipe away all tears, and there shall be no more death or sorrow, or crying or pain. For generations of Christian converts facing Roman martyrdom, this text must have been especially inspiring. And for the rest of us—what a grand conception! Deep in our hearts, don't we all long for such a time?

CHAPTER 4

Reading the Bible in a Materialist Age

> We have a wisdom to offer those who have reached maturity—
> not a philosophy of our age, it is true.
> We teach ... things beyond the mind of man.
> Paul, first Letter to Corinthians, chapter 2

Materialist Criteria

Now that we have briefly reviewed what is in the Bible, the question is how to deal with it. Why study the Bible covenants? Or conversely, why not? It is the same kind of question that faced the apostle Paul, when he arrived in Corinth nearly two thousand years ago.

The question turns on one's interest in applying ethical and spiritual energy to the challenges of our times. And this is where the trouble begins. Since World War II there has been a growing interest in the West in the possibilities of reviving ethical and spiritual practice. But most of us bring to these possibilities accumulated layers of conditioning focused on material existence. Almost all the big institutional structures of human existence, and almost all our conversations and reading, are devoted to advancing materialist agendas. Unless—like some Tibetan monks or desert recluses—we are capable of living for long stretches in the wild, we must operate in the organized, material world in order to survive or prosper.

Yet the material world is intrinsically fascinating and empowering. The possibilities for accumulating material power and wealth are endless. The material world can stimulate the mind and unleash one's creative powers. It provides relationships, it is the source of experience, and it is immediately present during all one's waking hours. It is the arena in which we all operate, and the school in which we learn about life.

But such wellbeing is usually bought at a price. It needs to be defended, yet even with a strong military defense or system of law and order, the security of material existence can never be guaranteed. In an expansionary era, the economy prospers; in a recession it declines, and so do material expectations. In the present era we need to modify our thinking about materialism to take account of problems affecting employability, race relations, health care, health insurance, home heating, urban unrest, the environment, the international order, in fact the entire 'global village'. Prosperity in one country or one social layer is no longer a guarantee of security, if other countries or other layers of society are experiencing violence and social disintegration.

And that is the situation we face today. Until the end of the Cold War the so-called 'Western' world could construct secular ideologies to justify its materialist prosperity and to counterattack the materialist ideology of its Marxist opponents. With the decline of the Communist world order and the end of the Cold War, that strategy has run its course. Now what we see is booming capitalism in the Pacific Rim, China, and various OPEC countries, but elsewhere problems of economic reorganization, the decay of towns and cities, abuses of the environment and its non-human inhabitants, desertification and spread of famine and AIDS across large parts of Africa, and eruption of ethnic violence and hatred, e.g. in the Balkans, the Middle East, Central and West Africa, and various countries of the former Soviet Union. Recently a radical Islamist fundamentalism has arisen to challenge the West and its materialism. Even more recently a global economic meltdown burst upon us. People who examine these problems honestly know that they could get worse before they get better. In various parts of the world - e.g. Dafur, Syria, Yemen, Somalia, Haiti, The Congo, Libya, and southern Sudan - the materialist order has been collapsing before our eyes, and we who live by materialism appear often unable to respond.

I am proposing that the rationalist modalities—especially confidence in materialist development and progress—that have dominated Western thinking ever since the 18th century Enlightenment era, are beginning to run short of credibility. Irrational, destructive and terrorist forces are on the march. Materialist strategies are proving unable to control them, for the good reason that these forces are often indifferent to materialist values. Destruction of towns and villages, and the uprooting, rape and murder of their populations, have suddenly become quite commonplace, as witnessed most recently in Syria and Yemen. The technological forces that governments array against such disorder become the immediate cause of it once they fall into opposing hands. In addition, materialist strategies are themselves undergoing profound and unpredictable change, as national and multi-national economies are forced to respond to changes and advances in global production, technology, communications systems and climatic threats.

Materialism, in short, is on trial. Its visions of progress that have benefited so many millions of middle-class people in the West and East Asia are surrounded by problems that show no signs of going away. For millions living close to the margin, these problems appear to be deepening. It is time, consequently, to face the possibility that the current materialist vision of existence may be reaching its limits as an ideological propellant, and that it will not be indefinitely sustainable through technological ingenuity or political rhetoric.

We are of course debating the issue here at a high level of abstraction. On a personal level, disaster in Afghanistan, Bosnia or Syria, famine in Somalia, Yemen or Nigeria, or economic and ethnic breakdown in various countries of the former Soviet Union or among peoples living in what were former European colonies in the African continent, remain a conceptual problem for people living elsewhere. People still living in moderate degrees of affluence may be aware that we are existing on borrowed time. But are we facing systemic breakdown? The affluent mind rejects such a thought (or did before 2008). Prosperity still exists and in large areas of the West and Asia is still on the rise. Materialism has not yet run out of steam, though its dangers are increasingly apparent.

The fact that Biblical covenants have much to say about achieving balance between the spiritual and material domains may not yet be enough for many people in the West to revert to them in search of guidance on public policy. For the time being we may have to continue to approach the Bible and its covenants from the perspective of our personal lives.

Personal Criteria

Here we enter the sensitive domain of the making of an individual life. How are we to construct our lives, determine success, face danger, or cope with misfortune and failure? When my son died of cancer when I was 31, I sought to compensate by pursuing materialist priorities. Three years later I had a PhD, a fascinating job with all kinds of prospects, a book in the press, and two houses, three cars, and a swimming pool. Not to mention the fact that I was married and had three other children. Job himself could not have done much better. My 'assets' were growing, and my career seemed to be all set.

It was 13 years after the death of my son that I began truly to mourn his life and death and to admit my feelings of loss and incapacitation. By that time my life situation had changed dramatically. The swimming pool and the big cars were gone, my career was off track, and I was, to put it kindly, 'underemployed'. My marriage was in difficulties and my future looked unattractive.

I mention these personal details only to illustrate the unpredictability of individual existence and the possibility for chaos to break out at any moment, no matter where one lives or how much wealth and power one may have acquired. At a macro-social level society may be progressing, the GDP and the stock market climbing upwards, wealth increasing, and new inventions revolutionizing science and technology. To those on the make this is good news and reason to feel one is living the good life. But to the individual in a state of chaos it is dust and ashes. When personal chaos arises the rewards of materialism dissolve. Food, drink, drugs, sex, and travel may provide temporary distraction. But they can never resolve emotional or spiritual disorder.

Traditionally in Western cultures it was the church and the Bible which took on this task. In the modern secular culture, psychiatry and other science-based therapies have arisen to cope with individual emotional problems. More recently a growing ambivalence towards science has led individuals in search of yet other strategies. In a striking echo of 19th century Western missionary expansion, Eastern philosophies and religions, which are less influenced by modern rationalist science, have come westwards to assist individuals in search of meaning beyond everyday life.

We are now in a situation where there is an astounding profusion of strategies available to individuals in the West who are seeking to strengthen the ethical and spiritual dimension of their lives. In my opinion this is largely to the good. It demonstrates the crucial point that human beings, as the Bible puts it, cannot live by bread alone. We all have experiences in life that transcend materialism and require non-materialist interpretation.

Many people therefore prefer to define themselves through religious or denominational labels. A person might be Hindu first and Indian second; or Muslim first, Lebanese or Afghani second; or Catholic or Protestant first, and Irish second. But these religious labels, which once designated pathways to spiritual progression, have themselves become captured by materialist agendas. One may want to capture a territory, another a temple, a third a human following. The life of the individual is not to be satisfied by such goals.

The reason is that spiritual life brings into play not just an institutional structure for achieving certain earthly goals but the existence of the divine and the eternal. For a mind grounded in materialism this is an enormously difficult concept to embrace. What, one may ask, exists beyond the material? If I am the chairman of a corporation, or if I am merely a lowly employee, I have got to contribute to the wellbeing of the organization. I may prefer my hobbies or avocations; I may be hurting inside, my marriage may be on the rocks, my children may distrust me, I may be drinking and consuming too much, but I cannot let go of my material world without facing the possibility of unemployment and economic ruin. Why speak to me of 'God' when I am trying to make a profit, or balance a budget, or keep my job or career on track? I may not even have much time for 'God' any longer or have much of an idea of who or what 'God' is.

To this one may reply, why not speak about it? Why assume that 'God' is interested only in prayer and worship and indifferent to budgets and jobs? Why not bring the divine into our lives? It is precisely here that the potential of the divine confronts the individual. Why should we assume that the spiritual dimension of life has nothing to do with budget balancing and job creation, when it might in fact change our whole approach to budgeting and jobs, and everything else requiring our engagement as human beings? Why should we assume that emotional distress cannot be alleviated by spiritual care? Why should we assume that spiritual life has no bearing on our work in this world? Why not assume—or consider the possibility of—the opposite?

And if secular or mildly religious people today are interested in strengthening their spiritual lives, why not examine the covenants so onerously developed in the Bible? Spiritual and ethical life is what the Bible is all about. Admittedly the Bible is not an easy text to digest. It is not an ideal subject for Sunday School, and it is not even easy for adults to take in. It requires an openness of heart, as well as a tolerance for ancient Jewish history, to comprehend what it is saying. In short, spiritual study generally requires, as the apostle Paul indicates, a certain level of maturity. Yet the Bible is readily accessible. In one form or another it is within reach of most people. And it illustrates, as no other text in the Western tradition has done before or since, the interaction of the spiritual and the material dimensions of human existence.

To place the relationship of these dimensions in a more graphic and immediate perspective, let me describe a scene in which I once participated. Picture a large room at a spiritual retreat center containing 150 people of widely differing ages. Outside that room these people are corporate executives, bankers, professors, architects, government employees, writers, therapists, in short people with jobs, careers and materialist expectations. Inside it, however, they are individual human beings struggling to deal with deep emotional problems and to find some spiritual focus in their lives.

The noise in that room full of highly educated and well-positioned people is at times deafening. There are cries of anguish and rage, and everywhere groaning and whimpering. These are the sounds of long suppressed pain and grief erupting to the surface. As one occupant said to me later, this is how purgatory must sound. It is not pretty, but it is real. This is a part of the reality underlying the mask that goes to work every day.

To participate in such purgatory is an awesome experience. We are looking at people struggling to heal their emotional wounds and to regain the consciousness in their lives of deeply felt love and centeredness. We are in the presence of people struggling to recover the sense of who they truly are. And we find that in this moment of truth it is not materialism, in such forms as food, money and possessions, which sustains and nourishes the human being. It is the presence of other human beings and a comprehension that we exist most fully and with the greatest emotional integrity when we are in a relationship of openness and trust towards others. This is what the Biblical scholar James Breech has called a "free and voluntary willingness to engage with the freedom of the other." Let us call that engagement having an open heart and recognize its spontaneous and combustive force. It can achieve miracles. It can heal the sick and the wounded. It can reach across barriers. It can enable those who are living half-lives behind masks to reorganize and transform their existence. It can open pathways to deep relationships. Above all, it can open the individual to an awareness of the vital forces underlying human and natural life.

I realize that for many people this last statement may be admissible only as an act of faith. The power of materialist consciousness can be overwhelming. The materialist consciousness prefers proof to experience. It is cerebral, analytic and skeptical. It seeks mastery of physical reality. The attributes necessary for such a search require arduous development, and their relative success over the last two hundred years in mastering the material universe have placed a premium on their development. This is one reason why education systems in materialistically dominant cultures place so much emphasis on development of the intellect and facility with words and numbers and pay less and less attention to development of ethical, emotional and spiritual integrity. Their job, after all, is to inculcate skills that will promote mastery of the material order. Emotional or spiritual education is left to the family or churches, sto be picked up on a catch-as-can basis.

But skills that apply to the material order do not necessarily apply to other realities. Mathematics can measure the physical universe; it cannot measure love or pain. Those are attributes that can only be felt or experienced. One cannot prove the existence of the spirit, because it is not experienced cerebrally. It is experienced through spiritual exercises, such as heart-centered breathing, meditation, prayer, or liturgical practice, or through spiritual practice in the form of acts of service to others.

With rare exceptions, very little of this curriculum so vital to our personal welfare is part of any formal academic enterprise. Some spiritual exercises are taught in a very modest way through religious institutions such as churches and church schools, but generally they are only taught systematically to various professionals. The general public receives little in the way of basic, much less comprehensive and ongoing, training in spiritual exercises. And even in churches meditation and prayer are infrequently taught or practiced in depth. So many people go through life without any exposure to training in what is ultimately the vital dimension of human existence.

The Bible as Spiritual Guide

The Biblical covenants are about how to live with integrity in this world, and how to discern its pitfalls. The central motif of the Exodus is the coming of the God Yahweh into the consciousness of the Hebrew tribes escaping from Egypt. Moses is the prophetic witness and intermediary through whom this happens. Moses is also the stern lawgiver who defines the distinction between life and death. Choose life, he insists, otherwise you die!

In the Christian gospels Jesus also teaches the way of life, basing his teaching on the Mosaic Torah. The circumstances are different. Moses is leading the Hebrew tribes towards a life of freedom in what they come to regard as the 'Promised Land'. In the world of the Roman Empire Jesus can offer no promised land or political freedom, only the spiritual freedom of the 'Kingdom of Heaven.' But both seek transformation of subject peoples from materialist oppression to spirit-centered freedom.

The world at the beginning of the 21st century is itself in bondage to materialism. In the United States this bondage manifests itself in struggles to accumulate income and personal property, and in the dawning fear among affluent people that even with governments friendly to materialist values, this strategy may no longer suffice to maintain global cohesion or pay our personal and national debts. In various other parts of the world the bondage is manifest in deadly famine and disease and in brutal conflicts over possession of land and human bodies.

Are such strategies able to carry us into a brighter and more uplifting New World Order? To ask the question is to answer it. When have materialist strategies ever advanced spiritual and ethical wellbeing? If we think about it for long, we can hardly avoid the conclusion that to achieve and survive in any New World Order worth the candle, we need some other approach than the strategies of materialist accumulation and physical violence so aggressively pursued in the last two centuries. The arms race may have helped to expose the limits of materialist power, but that cannot by itself lead to the dawning of spiritual and ethical reawakening. To move in that direction requires the adoption of other means.

In short, with ideologies of materialism already overturned or under stress, and with dangers and uncertainties all around us, the time may have come to reconsider practices, such as prayer and meditation, and texts, such as the Biblical covenants, that can enable us to face the future strong in heart and spirit, and with a modicum of what the Hebrew scriptures call wisdom.

Reading the Bible

Before proceeding on, let me offer a few suggestions about how to read the Bible. First, I recommend that the English language reader have access to a contemporary translation as well as the King James Bible. Translations are cultural artifacts that embody the prevailing assumptions and language of their times. The King James Bible is unparalleled in the English language for its eloquence and sacredness. It is also a product of early 17th century royalist England and reflects the political priorities of that age. In its version of the gospels, recognition of the Roman colonialist occupation of Palestine is muted and in key places missing. Passages sounding the doom of Jerusalem sound strangely eschatological and a-historical, rather than the urgent predictions or posthumous judgments about a political-military explosion that happened. One needs to be reading translations that reflect the remarkable findings of recent scholarship and that can apply contemporary research to problems encountered in the texts. That is why this study uses texts from both the King James Bible and the much more recent Jerusalem Bible. The latter draws on contemporary scholarship. It is laid out in a way that distinguishes prose and poetry and provides clear thematic guidance. While preserving all the traditional (but not original) verse and chapter numbers, it organizes the text into paragraphs and thematic sequences that help greatly to clarify the meaning.

Furthermore, personal transformation from the way of violence to the 'Kingdom of Heaven' is not a luxury to be considered over time but a matter of the utmost urgency, if human and other biological life is to be sustained in our ethically and politically compromised era. Similarly, the work of the life-sustaining human spirit is not something to be regarded as a minor option, suitable for consideration during ancient annual festivals such as Easter and Christmas or comparable Jewish holidays, when archaic language and customs seem less intrusive. Unless that consciousness is part of one's daily life, it can hardly work through the individual towards the transformation of society. The bifurcated world of religious practice on weekends for some, and secular practice during weekdays by virtually everyone, can hardly bring about transformation, even in those who participate in Sunday religion. It would be better to throw oneself at the mercy of secular power, which is what nearly all of us do, rather than engage in such self-defeating dualism.

Secondly, there is much to be said for reading the Bible thematically, and with the aid of a contemporary commentary (one written within the last twenty years), that can help in interpreting the text. For people of Christian background or commitment, I recommend a reading of some contemporary Jewish interpretations of the Hebrew scriptures. (See further reading list for examples). If one's interest is in development of spiritual energy, the wisdom literature and the psalms have much to offer. For an understanding of divine revelation, the Torah remains a unique document. It must be interpreted by each generation and each reader, but that is part of the challenge of living fully. For insight into political downfall and spiritual revival, the prophetic literature is unbeatable. It challenges us to look at our own situation honestly and to redefine our own spiritual and ethical consciousness in the light of the problems we face individually and collectively. Is our ability to deceive ourselves all that different from that of our predecessors? The prophetic literature, as we shall see, is also emphatic in insisting that truly spiritual experience is to be found in service to poor and disadvantaged people.

For witness about the non-violent Kingdom of Heaven, the Christian gospels remain the primary texts for those following a Christian path. Here too there is an equation of divine healing with service to poor and outcast people. For insight into spiritual consciousness, one can turn to the psalms, or the prophetic literature, or the Book of Revelation. For awareness of love one could turn to the Books of Ruth or Hosea, or the Song of Songs. Among the gospels, that of John especially treats this theme. For a sense of spiritual community, Acts or the letters of Paul would be a starting point for readers wanting to know more about how the early communities of Jesus followers were formed. For a grasp of the experience of repentance and conversion, Christian readers need go no further than the early letters of Paul, in which he describes repeatedly how conversion changed his whole outlook on life. Paul in turn drew tremendous strength from the Isaiah text.

Another point, often emphasized by Eastern teachers, is to approach spiritual education on how to live in this world with what is called beginner's mind. That means a mind uncluttered by preconceptions and anxieties, that can approach whatever is experienced in an open, non-judgmental, 'witness' manner, as if for the first time. Another metaphor for this concept is 'child's mind'. That again means a mind that is basically non-judgmental and non-comparing, and more broadly non ego-centered.

The ego is the main barrier in the way of gaining the emotional and spiritual growth necessary to function fully and properly in this world. We all have egos, erected to look out for our own interests and to protect us from abuse and harm. There is so much of the latter around, confronting the growing human being every step of the way, that it is not surprising that ego development is the most characteristic attribute of human existence today, particularly in cultures defined by materialist agendas. The adult mind in such cultures is normally ego-centered, distrustful, suspicious of anything that seems to threaten its security, and cynical about human motivation and about possibilities outside the mundane, material world. To ask such an adult mind to adopt child mind is like asking it to give up everything that it has done to make itself adult. "Look," one can hear the ego mind protesting, "I have struggled to survive and get ahead, and you're asking me to give that up? Who needs that advice?"

As I said earlier, if that is your view of the world, this book may not be for you. I am assuming that you have already sensed that ego mind has its own limitations; that while ego mind may be necessary to survive in the external world, it is not able to ensure you a life of inner peace and vitality that will enable you to "engage with the freedom of the other." For that to happen a transformation of consciousness is needed, and one way to begin to make that happen is to re-adopt beginner or child's mind. Christians sometimes refer to this shift of consciousness in theological terms as 'repentance' or being 'born again'. A parallel term in Jewish literature is teshuvah. By such terms Christians mean our acknowledgement of our ego-centered mind and a willingness to take on the teaching of Jesus as a spiritual guide.

For some people that is the quickest way to obtain that shift in consciousness away from ego-centeredness towards recognition of the divine as the wellspring of wisdom and compassion and the source of inner freedom. For others that transition constitutes too radical a change. If you are in this latter category, adoption of child's or beginner's mind is a non-judgmental first step towards letting go of the distrustful ego mind and opening yourself to the insights and possibilities that exist for non-ego-centered awareness. It does not require you to be non-distrustful in all contexts, only to let yourself be open to sources, such as the Bible, that are able to nurture your spiritual and ethical existence.

Another point, increasingly mentioned by wisdom texts and teachers, is to allow one's mind to concentrate on the present, that is this moment right now, so that one can engage in conversation with a person or a text knowing that one is only alive in the present. We may live for the future, but we do not live in it. We live now, moment by moment, and we can be most engaged when we are mindful of that. Conversing mindfully is to express one's life power through words. Conversing in the now of this moment gives one the possibility to access that power unimpeded by anxieties about the past or the future. Bringing this kind of mindset to conversing with a person or reading a text, permits a mindfulness beyond what is possible when half our mind is thinking about something else, or one has one eye on the clock or some other distraction.

An approach that I use in this book is to access sacred values in the Bible through music, art and poetry. I personally find music very energizing in opening the door to consciousness of the sacred. Some people climb mountains, go on walks, do gardening, visit sacred places, conduct ceremonials, engage in prayer or service to others, or meditate on ancient texts that have survived through time. The world is full of pathways that can open one's mind to consciousness of the sacred. The important point is to lift one's mind away from the material world long enough to become present to the values of the non-material world all around us.

Finally, there is much to be said for studying the Bible in a group or work-related setting. Group consciousness generally builds on individual understanding and almost always produces more powerful results. The Bible also needs to be read both critically and meditatively. Critically, because the texts are themselves cultural artifacts, mediated through layers of interpretation and translation. This is where adult mind (rid of defensiveness) can be of real assistance. Meditatively, because if the Bible is to function as a pathway to the spirit, it can only do so through meditative awareness. Criticism is a necessary first step, but it is meditation that opens the door.

II

In Search of the Covenants

CHAPTER 5

Adam and Eve and The Creation Covenant

> And the Lord God commanded the man, saying,
> "Of every tree of the garden thou mayest freely eat:
> But of the tree of the knowledge of good and evil,
> Thou shalt not eat of it:
> For in the day that thou eatest thereof
> Thou shalt surely die."
> Genesis, chapter 2, King James text

Covenant and Moral Edge

We now review in more detail some key Biblical texts about covenant. The creation covenant is generally viewed as a mythical story about Adam and Eve. But it is constructed as a covenantal document and inserted in the Bible right after the priestly account of the formation of the world. The big difference between the two creation accounts lies in the moral edge in the mythical story. This story is not just about creation. It establishes the point, affirmed repeatedly in the histories of the kingdoms of Israel and Judah, that knowledge of good and evil is the critical variable in human existence. That is the reason for presenting this knowledge as a covenantal issue and introducing it into the sacred narrative as early as possible.

Images of Creation

Let us first see how this beguiling but ominous myth has been treated by Christian cultures over the centuries. The most famous Western image of the Creation story was made by Michelangelo on the ceiling of the Sistine Chapel. The picture shows the images of God and Adam reaching out to touch each other. Adam, a handsome youth, reclines naked on the ground. He leans up and stretches out his arm and fingers towards the Creator. He is man in all his phallic beauty, awaiting only the spark of life from the divine, and he stares longingly at the Creator. And God is a bearded patriarch, sailing by in a huge cape, surrounded by angels, with the image of Eve crooked in his arm. God pauses and stretches out a hand, whose finger almost touches the male creature.

It is an electrifying moment in art and in time. For we are in the early 16th century Renaissance era, when European men rediscover their capacity to enjoy the material and physical world. Michelangelo's Adam and his statue of David are the quintessential expressions of that renaissance. A new youth of physical beauty is being born, and a God more tolerant of human flesh than was his medieval manifestation is doing the birthing. God moves dynamically through the heavens and reaches out to bring a human being to life. Their relationship creates human life in a scene that combines the majesty of the Creator with the yearning of the created youth. Michelangelo surrounded this vision with images of young naked virile men and with female oracles proclaiming the new order. Human beauty and yearning for the divine spark is the central achievement of the Creator and of the renaissance mind.

The image picks up on the patriarchal emphasis of the myth by focusing attention on the male creature. As it happens, Eve is also portrayed in the moment of human creation—which is more than can be said for the myth—emerging from behind the Creator God and resting on the divine arm. Despite the artist's predilection for male youth, he implies that female creation is co-temporal with male, as indicated in the priestly creation myth in Genesis chapter 1. This is a departure from earlier depictions of Adam and Eve. We shall have more to say in chapter 13 about the patriarchal aspect of this myth, and more about its satirical intent in chapter 16.

An entirely different image of the Creation was created by the eighteenth century British artist-poet William Blake. In Blake's conception God is a giant brooding force hovering over the earth, held aloft by vast wings. Beneath the Creator and lying supine on the ground is an inert, sexually indeterminate human body, in cruciform position, around whose leg is coiled a large and menacing snake. It is an image born of the Industrial Revolution, whose "dark, satanic mills" (Blake's words) were already invading the English countryside and portending for unprivileged rural people a short life marred by hardship and disease. No wonder the sun is overcast in Blake's vision by dark, dreary clouds. The shadow of death is present in the act of creation.

It would be hard to imagine two more different views of the Creation. Yet both enable us to see the power of the original story. For this is a story designed to express how relationship, and thus covenant, between human beings and the Deity came into being. If we concentrate on the imagery it may help to set aside the distracting debate between Evolutionists and Creationists, which treats creation as a historical event, and instead focus on perceptions of the relationship evoked between matter and spirit, human and divine, memory and imagination. A relationship moved by erotic love, or ominous fate, or what?

A mid to late twentieth century perception of the scene might depict God and humans wandering in search of each other. From the perspective of 20th century war, revolution and mass murder, one might envision God, wounded and even done in by decades of evil and destruction (as intimated by Elie Wiesel in his chilling personal account of life in Auschwitz), searching vainly for life amidst the rubble of a self-immolating human order. Or one might envision the human being, as did the Psalmist (Psalm 139), hiding from the divine, irresolute, afraid, caught up in the emptiness of ego-driven existence, and shunning questions posed by the possibility of non-material, spiritual consciousness. Such a human being would be preoccupied with its fate and fearful to be called out of a materialistic womb into a spiritual affinity.

Yet another image, from Psalms 77-78, envisages a distraught human being stretching out hands to the divine and like Job finding nothing there. Has the divine lost power, or is it—terrible thought—that the creator God is rejecting the human? Perhaps God is thinking—as in the time of Noah—enough already. Sick and tired of the people's inconstancy, God has condemned them to the sword and let their young men, in the words of the psalmist, "be burned to death" and their brides "widowed."

The Genesis Stories

It says much for the power of the Eden myth that it contains within it such scope for defining the divine-human relationship. The story, found in Genesis chapters 2 to 3, invites us to ask how does a relationship between the divine and the human come into being. How am I touched by the divine? How do I reach out and contact divineness? What happens in the experience of contact? Why would it ever happen? What are its consequences if it does happen? Does it mean that I might be facing fear of the unknown? Can it explain my personal predicament? If one hasn't had the opportunity to meditate on such questions, the Genesis story invites one to do so: to step out of one's mundane world for a while and imagine what it might be like to connect with a higher will for existence, and for what purpose.

But first we should go back to Genesis chapter 1, because there are two creation stories in Genesis. The first one, written from the Priestly tradition and drawing on ancient pre-Israelite myth, envisions the Deity as a cosmic architect, through whose indomitable will order is created out of chaos. In a series of titanic acts of will the Creator-God creates the cosmic order that we know, overarches chaos with structure and emptiness with form. God speaks; and from the divine words come light, goodness and meaning. The division of light from darkness is the very first act of creation. It results in day, which is the time of light and is good, and night, which is the time of darkness. Thence follow heaven and earth, the stars, the sun and moon, the creatures and birds, the animals and creeping things. After the living things have been created and blessed God creates man and woman in the divine image and gives plants to sustain life. When all this labor is finished, and the universe has come into being, God rests.

It is a priestly vision, infused with a sense of ceremonial and reverence. All initiation proceeds from the divine. Each act of creation is assigned a day. Words are spoken and with them form is brought into being and blessed. The profound struggle of the religious act is recognized. God's creation is not a casual, mundane affair but a sustained willing of a universal order, created and upheld by divine power, in which the basic division is light from darkness. The final act of rest is the assurance of order and the fulfillment of the creative will. In rest the power of God can be observed and experienced.

To get the benefit of this vision it is best if the reader can experience the account through its religious power. This is easier said than done. Religion begins when humans begin a relationship with the divine. Of course, relationship here means not a casual affair or temporary interest but a sustained bonding, on the order of marriage as it was meant to be, or any such long-term sacramental union. For many people that could be a barrier. They might say, "how can I enter into a long-term union with an entity, whose existence means nothing to me?"

In that case, let us focus on the word 'enter', for this is what is proposed: an entering into a state of mind that will suspend for the time being the doubts and anxieties of day to day living in the material world. This should not be so difficult. For most of us, temporary suspension of anxiety is an almost daily activity. All that is suggested here is that the same suspension of anxiety be applied to the reading of the Creation story: to let its values, which are essentially relational, take hold of you, rather than your values take hold of it. To imagine it to be a myth designed to embody the wonder and awe of being alive in this world, which you are telling yourself as you learned it from others. To let yourself be touched by the vision that emerges from the printed words.

If one can enter into a world in which the divine is embodied as life-creating force, one has taken the first step along the road taken by those who delineated the creation story and those such as Michelangelo and Blake, who visualized it. This is not an unworthy road on which to travel. Along the way lie the Sistine Chapel in Rome, Milton's Paradise Lost, innumerable psalms, poems and meditations, quiet places, alternative visions by which to organize and imagine one's life and the lives of people around us. Along this way are special people, some famous but most unknown although just around the corner from where each of us lives, who will be encountered because they are on this way. All this experience of life, which could be so enriching to the heart and spirit, can be set in motion by one first step.

Suppose that we have allowed ourselves to be drawn into the context of creation as presented in Genesis 1. Now we can go back to the story in chapters 2 and 3 and imagine what it might be like to be formed in the likeness of the divine.

We have seen how Michelangelo and Blake addressed this experience, so it is appropriate to let the story speak for itself. The basic story comes from the J tradition, which focuses on the relationship between human beings and the God Yahweh. The tradition presents the relationship through a series of colorful, intimate, and almost tactile accounts. In this first story, God moves from the creation of heaven and earth right into the creation of man. Like a potter God scrapes up dust from the barren ground, molds a human image and breathes life and spirit into its nostrils. Other creation stories are also imaged in this way. Infused with God's breath a man comes alive, for yes—this is a story about a time when the creation of man is envisioned as having primacy over the creation of woman.

Straight away God plants the famous garden of Eden. Trees and shrubs grow, including the famous trees of life and of knowledge of good and evil, and rivers emerge to provide water. What a delightful environment: pleasant to look at, good for food, and wonderful for enjoyment and pleasure. God puts the new creature into the garden to till it and keep it. Man takes on God's gardening proclivities. But part of the garden—that part containing the two famous trees—is put off limits. Man is warned not to eat their fruit, or he will die. Such are the stated terms of this creational covenant between the Divine and the human.

Fearing that the man-creature might be lonely, God now makes animals and birds to keep it company. Despite all the living things the man yearns for something more than a barnyard. God the surgeon puts him to sleep, carves out a lung, repairs the cavity, and transforms the lung into a woman. Woman is made from a piece of man's breathing apparatus. Breath is spirit, so in that way the woman is equipped with spirit as well as flesh and is created fully human. The experiment succeeds. The man and the woman live together naked and without shame.

There is a dreamlike quality to the story. The innocent delight in the experience of life seems remote from the everyday 'real' world of sacrifice, pain and death. This is an imagined world of domestic and spiritual happiness. It is a world free from guilt and shame—yet not from sanctions. In the sacred space of Eden, the humans are warned not to trespass on what is God's. Creation of life, and understanding of good and evil, are God's domain and out of bounds for humans. For humans this is a childlike world, in which there is no sin or death and no moral awareness of the consequences of action.

The grace of innocence cannot last, but there is no harm in savoring it. The story presents an image in which nakedness is not shameful and proximity to God a source of delight. It is the image conveyed by Michelangelo of humans made joyful by the work of the creator.

But there is a downside to the story, the side visualized by Blake. It is the side in which appears the serpent—the symbol of earth deity and of deceit—coiled around the tree of knowledge, as in traditional visualizations, or around the human's legs as in Blake's. The serpent tempts, the humans eat the forbidden fruit. Immediately they are transformed by self-consciousness. They become ashamed of their nakedness. They sow fig leaves to cover their sexuality, and they hide. But Yahweh God finds them, and their cover is quickly blown away.

Now comes a lamentable scene in which each creature vainly tries to blame the other. In the original J version of this story Yahweh God informs unseen companions that the man (Adam) has attempted to claim divine knowledge of good and evil by picking fruit from the tree with that attribute. To prevent him from attaining the other divine attribute of eternal life Yahweh God expels the man from the garden to till the earth from which he had been made. It would seem, according to this version, that an act of idolatry, involving the cultic religious power of trees and serpents, has been responsible for the man's ejection from Eden.

The revised, Deuteronomic version, looking back in exile on the lamentable misconduct of the covenantal people, sees a crime with deeper consequences at issue. It brings down on its perpetrators the language of curses and condemnations associated, as we shall see, with breach of covenant. Yahweh God becomes judge and executioner. God condemns the guilty creatures not just to till the earth but to live lives of pain and sorrow, banishes them from Eden, and guards the way back with cherubim armed with flaming swords.

Christian Interpretations

So, the beautiful childlike dream turns into a historicized nightmare. Humans cannot live in paradise so easily. Christianity took on and amplified this view. According to traditional Christian theology, beginning with Paul and amplified by Augustine, human nature is sinful. Through the sin of the first humans all subsequent humans fall from grace and continue to fall to the present day. They are driven from the garden, and a mighty barrier is erected to prevent their return. What a terrible denouement! This scene is compellingly visualized by the 15th century Florentine painter Masaccio, who shows Adam and Eve, downcast and crying, being driven from Paradise. Adam has his hands over his face, Eve has hers over her sexuality. Vines furl around their naked bodies. An angel hovers over them. Those guilty of breach of covenant have no place in Eden. Nor can such guilty people survive in many a community. Expulsion, banning, and physical punishment, are familiar themes in human experience, especially when such breaches take place in a close-knit community. Who, indeed, has not at one time or another slunk shamefaced and crying from a scene of confrontation and punishment? The delineators of the Eden tradition were on firm ground in putting guilt and punishment at the core of the human predicament.

Michelangelo agrees with this perspective, while carrying it further. In his hands it is a lusting Adam who grabs the tree and reaches for the fruit, while Eve reclines her neck on his naked thigh and plays with the outstretched arm of a serpentine woman coiled around the tree. It is a last moment for the unbridled sexuality of youth. Once they have taken the bait and are exposed, it is all over. The two penitents, equally at fault, have aged mightily. They depart naked and cringing across an empty plain, while the avenging angel's sword drives them away.

Yet there are other ways of interpreting this story. Take, for example, the view of the twelfth century German mystic Hildegard of Bingen. This remarkable woman was once unknown except to a few faithful adherents. Fortunately, her writings, as well as her art and music, have survived. They reveal a creative as well as subtle and intuitive mind. In her view the temptation and Fall represent a struggle of consciousness as well as of moral judgment. Eden is a beautiful land of flowers and bushes, above which glow the star-filled heavens. Adam lies naked on the ground as if in a trance. Eve's body rises out of him in the form of a life-manifesting, star-studded and beautiful shell. Above and to the left of them, out of a deep pit, rears up a huge dark shadow in the form of a tree. From it protrudes a menacing serpent, whose tongues reach out and touch the shell of life symbolizing Eve, which is joined in life to the supine Adam. The infection of Eve flows, at both the biological and symbolic levels, directly into Adam.

This dark shadow strikes into the simple-hearted humans who until then have known only trust and happiness. They have been invaded by the realm of darkness, which is shown to be a force of terrifying, inescapable power. Humanity is frail but not evil of itself, for it was made by God in an act of love. Eden was also made in love, but it has been invaded by darkness—something not clear in the mythic story. The struggle between the Creator God and the power of darkness has entered the unconscious and biological realms of humanity. Humans must live with the infection of the shadow and act out, in their own lives, this cosmic struggle.

This vision maintains the fault-lines of consciousness constantly before human beings. Instead of one single forbidden fruit on an innocent-looking but snake-encoiled tree, one sees an intrinsic ambiguity confronting human consciousness. Eden and the shadow both confront us. We cannot see Eden without acknowledging the shadow.

Indeed, if we follow Hildegard, we see that humans cannot exist in any fully realized way without comprehending the shadow aspect of human existence and engaging with it. Human darkness is not just a matter of the historical deviations of specific individuals (such as those constituting the power structures in the kingdoms of Israel and Judah), or the tyrannies committed by people in power. It arises out of the structure of moral consciousness. It is only with moral consciousness that awareness of darkness arises. According to the Creation account, the struggle for human beings is to recover a sense of the divine plan through restoring the relationship of human body and soul with the design of the Creator. The Bible and its covenants were recorded to define what that entails.

Fall Out: Cain and Abel

We will return in later chapters to this powerful myth, which has so profoundly influenced the formation of Western consciousness. But before leaving it now, we should look briefly at its Deuteronomic development in the story of Cain and Abel.

The Deuteronomic redaction of the myth of Eden does not end with the expulsion of Adam and Eve from Eden. Adam must till the soil to keep them alive, and Eve must bear and raise children. Two sons grow up—Cain and Abel. A family emerges, and trouble breaks out. Cain follows Adam as a tiller of the soil, while Abel becomes what Adam would have been had he remained in Eden, namely a shepherd.

An acute dichotomy between the two is thereby established. Cain offers produce of the soil to Yahweh, while Abel offers the first born of his flock and some of their fat. Yahweh, not surprisingly, prefers the latter, for this is the myth of a pastoral tradition and culture, at odds with the settled land-cultivators of Canaan. Cain is angry and is rebuked by Yahweh. Rejecting Yahweh's rebuke, he entices Abel into the countryside and slaughters him. In Rembrandt's chilling depiction, Cain knocks Abel to the ground, kneels over his cowering victim and prepares to crush his skull with a blunt instrument. In the background Cain's dog devours Abel's offerings. So much for the fat of the lamb and its naive purveyor.

All at once we are plunged from creation and expulsion into a mad world of apostasy and fratricide. Adam and Eve are nowhere to be found. Only Yahweh is there to confront the killer. And the payment, as might be expected from a covenantal writer, is intense. The defiant Cain is cursed. The land will no longer support him. He is to become a fugitive and wanderer and a marked man. Worse, he is driven from the presence of Yahweh and his descendants are ejected from the sacred narrative. But Abel, though blessed of Yahweh, fares no better. He becomes the unrequited victim. His blood cries out from beneath the earth. He is left without descendants.

Why does the story take this savage turn? Evidently the redactors, confronted by the frequency of fratricide and tribal warfare in the history of the kingdoms of Israel and Judah, came to view fratricide as an archetypal pattern. In this pattern self represents the subject matter of history. Other is that which opposes identity and is to be rejected from tribal consciousness. Within the Yahwist narrative there is to be only one inheritor.

But in the fratricidal archetype the inheritor is neither Cain nor Abel. The killer is ejected from the sacred story, but the victim dies without issue. Neither stance suffices to inherit the covenant with Yahweh. The fate of the archetypal victim is noteworthy in the light of the later history of the two successor kingdoms of the Davidic monarchy. A stance of victimhood cannot carry the narrative forward any more than can that of a defiant killer. A new descendant must be supplied that could "invoke the name of Yahweh." (Jerusalem Bible)

Turning back to the archetypal family, we cannot but be impressed by the motifs of light and darkness that the story incorporates. In the original J story of Adam and Eve, a balance is maintained between the light and the shadow aspects of the story. Michelangelo illustrates the breaking and dawning of light in the act of creation, while Masaccio and Blake focus on the shadow aspects of the story. But we can see that the latter two artists have depicted the revisionist Deuteronomic vision amplified by Augustine, which in contrast to the basic J myth is more pessimistic and judgmental. In the Deuteronomic version there is a breach of trust between the humans and the divine, in which the woman plays a profoundly consequential role. The myth of Eve as a dark force in the consciousness of patriarchy (precisely the danger that Hildegard of Bingen tried to deflect) develops out of this vision.

The Deuteronomic account carries the shadow aspect further into the story of the primeval fratricide. We can acknowledge that sibling rivalry is a given, so that we would hardly recognize as plausible any mythic story that depicted the two brothers as devoted companions, in the manner—for example—of David and Jonathan. But was it necessary to establish fraternity within a template of murder? Here we must note that it occurs in the context of relationship with the divine. This killing is not over a minor matter but over the fundamental question of our attitude towards the Deity. And the crux of the matter lies in the conduct of Cain. If Cain takes his initial reprimand in good spirits, why should he not hold up his head? But as the text has Yahweh say, "if you are ill disposed, is not sin at the door like a crouching beast hungering for you, which you must master?" (Jerusalem Bible)

This powerful metaphor—of sin at the door as a crouching beast hungering for each one of us, which we must either master or it will master us—takes us away from the dreamland of Eden and into a tormenting reality that we must all confront. In the story of Cain, we see the stark options that face us so powerfully (particularly if we are males) in the world of spiritual consciousness. As the Deuteronomists were to put it again, in the great summation attributed to Moses at the end of the Book of Deuteronomy, we have the option to hold up our heads and choose life or succumb to the hungering of the crouching beast at the door and choose death. Cain chooses the latter. How often has that choice been repeated!

The consequences of such a choice are so critical for upholding the sacredness of life, that the Deuteronomists thought it appropriate to get this message into the text at the earliest possible point, into the life of the first person born, as it were, outside of Eden. Cain represents the archetype that confronts all males when they come to deal directly with the divine. At any point on the road—and not infrequently several times a day—we have the choice: to hold up our heads or give in to the hungering beast at the door. And the choice that we make matters.

In its application of curses to the denunciation of the crime committed by Cain, the story signals that Cain had committed a fundamental breach of covenant. As we can surmise, it is the breach of the commandment against killing. Whereas Adam and Eve can be seen (from a Deuteronomic perspective) to have breached the commandment to have no other gods except Yahweh, Cain's sins are that he dishonors father and mother, murders his brother, and lies about it. These crimes matter, and their ominous consequences need to be learned. That is the Deuteronomic and covenantal perspective.

CHAPTER 6

Moses and the Sinai Covenant

> I call heaven and earth to witness against you today:
> I set before you life and death, blessing or curse.
> Choose life then, so that you and your descendants may live
> In the love of Yahweh your God … for in this your life consists.
> Deuteronomy: Last Discourse of Moses
> From the Jerusalem Bible

Moses

The first journey of faith recorded in the Bible happened when Abraham left the great city of Ur to settle in the Canaanite hill country. He had heard the call of the God Yahweh to leave the urbane polytheistic culture of Mesopotamia in order to forge in the wilderness a monotheistic culture—the first of its kind. He obeyed that call, and in return Yahweh promised to make out of him a great nation. Out of this exchange grew the idea of a covenantal relationship between the God Yahweh and Yahweh's human followers. We shall explore the nature of Abraham's faith in a later chapter. Through the further journeys of Jacob and Joseph, Abraham's descendants through Jacob/Israel made their way south, in time of famine, to Egypt, where they were hospitably received by the reigning dynasts.

Then another Pharaoh came into power, enslaved the 'children of Israel' and set them to work making bricks. During that time the prophet Moses was born. Because the Israelites were increasing in numbers, Pharaoh decreed that all new-born boys should be thrown into the river. Moses' mother hid her baby boy for three months, then put him in a basket at the river's edge. When the daughter of Pharaoh found the abandoned child, she adopted him and brought him up as an Egyptian prince.

One day Moses, now a young and princely man, saw an Egyptian overseer abusing a Hebrew laborer. Enraged, he killed and buried the overseer but was spotted doing so by one of his countrymen. To save himself from Pharaoh's wrath, Moses fled into the Negev desert, to the land of Midian. There he married the daughter of a priest and they had a son. Moses settled down in Midian and spent the next fifty or more years herding sheep and growing old.

Then one day, while roaming the foothills of Mt. Horeb, he stumbled upon a bush that burned without burning. It was a searing and transforming moment. It was also a moment that continues, over three thousand years later, to define the world we live in, as almost any news from the Middle East reminds us. A voice from within the bush told Moses to go down to Egypt and lead his people out of captivity. The former Egyptian prince was to become the leader of the children of Israel. The old man protested, claiming a speech defect, but in vain. He was instructed what to say and do and equipped with a magical staff and magical hands. A brother, Aaron, arrived to help in mediating his speech impediment. They made their way with difficulty back to Egypt to confront the Pharaoh and demand the liberation of their people.

It is a mysterious story, highly charged with mythic detail and lacking corroboration in non-Biblical sources. But the books of Exodus, Leviticus, Numbers and Deuteronomy, are all about Moses and the extraordinary leadership that he supplied at a critical moment to the Hebrew tribes living in Egypt. The tradition is so strong, and it animates the Bible to such a degree, that it is inconceivable that some such leader and some such transforming mission did not occur. One can recognize certain aspects, such as the details of Moses' birth, as occurring to other leaders of mythic proportions, without that invalidating the overall story and its significance for later generations.

That is why it is essential that people today have some understanding of the Exodus story. This story tells about the origins of the Jewish people and how they came to acknowledge the divine. It reminds us how deeply rooted and significant is the history of separation of the Jewish people from other Middle Eastern peoples. Jewish history is made possible through deliverance from oppression in Egypt, and by victory over opponents in Canaan designated for the children of Israel as the "promised land." In this respect it is not unlike the American political story-line. But this is not merely a political construct. It embraces a challenge in how to live with moral and spiritual consciousness, and it spells out the harsh consequences whenever that challenge is abandoned.

The story of Moses and his people can be divided into three stages: The departure (Exodus) from Egypt; the establishment of the covenant at Mt. Sinai (or Horeb); and the period, recorded as almost 40 years, of wandering in the desert wilderness. A fourth stage, the entry into the promised land, was accomplished under Moses' successor Joshua. The details of this epic and convoluted journey are provided in the books of Exodus and Numbers. The covenant is in Exodus and recapitulated in Deuteronomy, with large tracts of law-giving from various traditions preserved in Exodus, Leviticus and Numbers, and again in Deuteronomy. The terrible period of wandering in the hot and arid desert is recorded in the book of Numbers. The entry into the promised land is recorded in the book of Joshua.

The Exodus

The story of the Exodus itself, as combined in the Torah from various sources, is one of the most dramatic in world history. A stuttering old man confronts the Pharaoh and insists that the captive Hebrews must leave Egypt to offer sacrifices in the wilderness. But Yahweh, for unexplained reasons, hardens the Pharaoh's heart, so that he rejects this demand. Ten plagues now reportedly fall on Egypt. Water turns into blood, killing off fish and creating a foul odor. Frogs swarm throughout the land. Mosquitoes attack the people and their animals, followed by a huge swarm of gnats. The livestock are killed by a deadly plague. Then the Egyptian people and their remaining animals are struck with boils. A hailstorm fells crops and trees, and after that a plague of locusts consumes everything left. None of these calamities can persuade the Pharaoh to release the captive Israelites. Then darkness falls on the land for three days; and that doom-laden period is followed by a dreaded plague, which carries off all the first-born Egyptian children and animals.

As this denouement is building up, the Israelites are instructed to prepare a hasty feast and to smear the lintels of their dwellings with the blood of the sacrificed animals. In this way they would be protected from the avenging God and the angel of death, who would pass by overhead. This feast, said Moses, was to be commemorated for evermore, and succeeding generations of children were to be instructed as to its purpose. The annual Passover Seder, to this day, recalls these memorable and deadly circumstances.

A distraught Pharaoh urges the Israelites to get out of his country. They do so, taking their possessions with them and a horde of Egyptian jewelry. But the ruler has second thoughts and sends an expeditionary force after them. By this time the Israelites, led by Yahweh in the form of a pillar of cloud by day and of fire by night, have reached the edge of the Sea of Reeds. The waters part, and they pass through. Then the waters flood back and overwhelm the pursuers. The women, led by Aaron's sister Miriam, sing a triumphant song.

So far (from the Hebrew perspective) so good. Yahweh has emerged as a protector capable of neutralizing the power of the greatest human empire. The Israelites have won their freedom from Egypt and are ready to form their own community.

But now challenges of a more debilitating nature arise. In the desert the people are assailed by thirst and hunger. As a seasoned desert dweller, Moses finds various ways to produce drinkable water. But production of food for so many people is beyond his means. Fortunately, quail fly in, supplying meat, and in the morning dew the people collect a powdery substance tasting like honey wafers, which they call manna. It is on this meager diet, provided by Yahweh, that they will subsist for the next 'forty' years.

Now the forging of a community with its own distinctive laws and ceremonies begins. The people learn to abstain from work every seventh day. They survive their first test in battle with the Amalekites. Then Moses, aided by his visiting father-in-law, chooses capable men to serve as judges and arbitrators. Thus strengthened, they move on to Mount Sinai, to which the God Yahweh had called them.

The Mount Sinai Covenant

Covenantal usage in the Hebrew Bible has been extensively researched. Scholars have identified two different types of covenant: covenants of grace (unconditional), such as those pertaining to Noah and David, in which promises are made under oath by the covenanting Deity; and covenants of obligation (conditional), demanding obligations and oaths from the subordinate people, of which the covenant at Mt. Sinai is the prime example. Much of the covenant typology and format, including recitation of antecedent history and the use of oaths, blessings and curses, is taken from secular covenants imposed by sovereign rulers on vassals. The significance of Bible covenants lies in the application of this type of treaty bonding to the development of the relationship between the God of Israel—Yahweh—and the various peoples and camp followers who came to form the Israelite tribal confederation. So far as is known, this is the first comprehensive covenant in history drawn up with a protector deity.

Another factor complicating our understanding of what happened at Sinai is the different approach taken by the various textual sources towards the form and meaning of the covenant. The basic narrative accounts are supplied by the J and E traditions. These emphasize the direct dealing between Yahweh and Moses and stress Yahweh's commitment to the successful conquest and occupation of the promised land. On the other hand, they vary in important respects as to content, particularly as regards their differing emphasis on covenant (J) and covenantal law (E).

The most famous text of Exodus—the ten commandments (Decalogue)—appears to be superimposed on the ancient narrative, which records its own covenant, inscribed on stone, later in the text. The book of Deuteronomy, however, puts the Decalogue, and the overall accomplishment of Moses, into covenant format. This account is more specifically retrospective, in that it treats Moses as emissary rather than negotiator, includes policy on later matters not found in the shorter accounts (such as on the role of kings, and the centralization of sacrifice), and contains a unique emphasis on the need for the people to commit heart and soul to the service of the God Yahweh. This is not overt in the other textual traditions, but it is stressed in prophetic denunciation of Israelite apostasy, particularly by Jeremiah.

Finally, there is the very important Priestly account. The main intent of this account is to weave a genealogical canvass and liturgical structure around the covenantal process, and to place the priesthood rather than the prophetic function at the center of the Divine-human relationship.

While these overlapping and differing traditions exist, they have been woven by editors and redactors (redaction is the emending and combining of literary traditions to produce a composite account) into a consolidated narration of a single, critical event. Reading the texts in the Torah one often has a sense of looking at each event from different angles. Yet it is the same event, and the same covenantal idea about how to define the relationship between Yahweh and the Hebrew tribes. The fact that Yahweh and Moses insisted on an exclusive relationship carried huge implications, given the polytheistic world that the Israelites were experiencing. The Sinai covenant incorporates the processes through which that relationship was sorted out.

The narrative accounts in J and E emphasize the setting in which the covenant took place. The people assemble before the mountain. Moses is summoned up the mountain and receives a conditional promise, that if the people obey the covenant, they will become Yahweh's chosen people, a "kingdom of priests" and a "holy nation". (These ideas have reverberated with later reformers). They are instructed to cleanse themselves over a three-day period in order to become ritually pure. On the third day the heavens erupt in thunder and lightning, trumpets blast, and a dense cloud descends. The mountain is enveloped in smoke and shakes violently. The trumpet blasts grow longer and louder. Moses calls out and Yahweh replies through the thunder. The trembling people are warned to stay at the bottom, for the mountain is sacred, and dangerous in the extreme. Then Moses descends to speak to them.

It is at this intensely dramatic moment that the Ten Commandments are presented. "And God spake all these words, saying, 'I am the Lord thy God, which have brought thee out of the Land of Egypt, out of the house of bondage. Thou shalt have no other gods before me.'" (King James text). This is the core text of the Sinai covenant. In covenantal language the God Yahweh claims credit for emancipating the Hebrew people from Egypt and Pharaoh-worship and demands in return their unconditional loyalty. Other gods exist, but they are outside the covenant and may not be recognized or served by the covenanting humans. What is happening here is the application of a human political institution to a divine-human relationship. Yahweh as overlord intends to participate in human affairs not by maintaining a geo-animist environment (as with divinity tied to a territorial domain) but by specifically intervening in human affairs. The divine in human space is to give way to the divine in human time.

The Decalogue (ten commandments) demands no worship of graven images (the God of time is imageless), no abuse of Yahweh's name, and no abuse of the Sabbath. Rest is integral to this new vision. The remaining commandments are ethical and community-building. Honor your parents. Don't kill. Don't commit adultery. Don't steal. Don't bear false witness. Don't covet what belongs to your neighbor.

As if to intensify these exhortations, the thunder peals, the lightning flashes, the trumpets blast. The people quake with fear and are barely reassured by Moses. They stand far off, while Moses approaches the thick darkness, where the God Yahweh was.

Now comes a text drawn mainly from the E tradition, which provides specific laws to govern the lives of the people. Much of this legislation amplifies the commandments by stipulating sanctions for breaking them. Sacrifice to other gods is punishable by death. So is murder, abuse of parents, or intercourse with an animal. The commandment, 'thou shalt not suffer a witch to live', would inaugurate a reign of terror in early modern Europe, through which unknown thousands of women and thousands of men would be burned alive or hanged.

The legislation also emphasizes controls on slavery—paramount for a group who came from servitude—as well as on restitution of property, assistance to enemies, and defense of the innocent. It is strongly protective of aliens, widows, orphans, borrowers, and poor people generally. Demanding interest from the poor, for example, is prohibited. The passage concludes with the demand that the three great agricultural feasts be celebrated in Yahweh's honor, along with a promise to destroy the enemy in the promised land, conditional on obedience to Yahweh.

After receiving these instructions Moses reports them to the people, who promise to obey. He writes them down, offers sacrifices and reads the text that he has written. The people again promise to obey. Moses then sprinkles them with sacrificial blood, to confirm the covenant. Then he and his brother Aaron, his brother's two eldest sons, and seventy elders, proceed up the mountain and receive a theophanic (God manifesting) vision, after which they eat a ceremonial meal. But Yahweh wants to give Moses a divinely inscribed text of the Decalogue. Moses goes again up the mountain, accompanied only by his servant Joshua, and stays there for forty days.

At this point (Chapter 25) in the Book of Exodus we are introduced to the sanctuary and the ark of the covenant. Here we enter the Priestly realm. The passage begins with elaborate instructions for the erection of a sanctuary, including the ark (a wooden cabinet) to contain the text of the Decalogue; the sacred throne with its winged cherubim; the tabernacle, or tent, to be the Lord's dwelling, housing the ark and throne; the furnishings, altars, priestly clothing, and rituals of consecration. These descriptions are considerably more elaborate than the accounts of the ark and the tent of meeting preserved in the J and E traditions, and they belong to the later history of the cult. But they are incorporated here because of the connection of the sacrificial cult and its rituals of atonement and cleansing with the covenant itself. There is a special section on observance of the sabbath, profanation of which is punishable by death. Then Yahweh hands over the two tablets of stone, with the Decalogue inscribed on them by Yahweh's hand.

While all this is going on, the people down below are getting restive. Moses appears to have gone for good. The people demand from Aaron a tangible expression of deity. In a quandary, Aaron collects all their earrings and fashions a golden calf. The Israelites recognize this as an image of their God, so Aaron builds an altar to the image. The following day they conduct sacrifices before it and eat and make merry. Contemporary scholars regard this story as a reworking by the E text of the cult of the golden calves or bulls, created by the schismatic king Jereboam I to establish Dan and Bethel as alternative holy places to Jerusalem. This was a violation of the covenantal stipulation, found in the early text of D that sacrifices and sacrificial meals occur only where determined by Yahweh, i.e. Jerusalem. More broadly, it was a defiance of Jerusalem and the temple as the sole custodian of the Yahwist cult. According to advocates of the Yahwist covenant, it set the kingdom of Israel off on the wrong course, which would lead in due course to the destruction of the northern kingdom. Also, the bull image, although possibly intended only as an attribute of Yahweh, was also an attribute of the Canaanite god Baal, thus condemned for inviting apostacy.

The Aaronite calf described by E also constituted a wrong course. However, the consequences, although grave, were less severe. The association of the calf with Aaron mitigated its enormity as an act of apostasy—it could hardly be claimed that Aaron was an intentional apostate. Nevertheless, the creation of the calf was antipathetic to Yahwist leadership and covenantal law. As such it must be destroyed, and those who worshiped it punished, before any further damage is done. One might comment that the experience of the Israelites, from this point on to the Babylonian exile in the 6th century BCE, is defined in the Bible, particularly in the Deuteronomic accounts, as a tension or polarization between the claims of the Canaanite and Yahwist cults.

But that is to anticipate events. Up on the mountain an enraged Yahweh threatens to destroy the people and make a new nation out of the descendants of Moses. But the latter intercedes, and Yahweh relents. It is now Moses' turn to lose his patience. He storms down the mountain, smashes the sacred tablets (symbolically abrogating the covenant), grinds the golden calf to dust, and forces the revelers to drink it. (Requiring one's people to eat the ground-up remains of the enemy's body is a not uncommon way of completing the destruction of a mythic enemy. There are at least two ancient Chinese myths that employ this stratagem).

This time it is Aaron's turn to intercede. But Moses is unyielding. "Who is for Yahweh?" he cries out. "Let him come to me!" The sons of Levi (kinsmen of Moses and foes of the Bethel sanctuary) respond and are dispatched to kill the apostates. That day about three thousand people perish. Aaron (ancestor of the Yahwist priesthood) is excluded from this bloodletting. A plague sent by Yahweh carries off further apostates.

Moses intercedes with Yahweh, who orders him to lead the Israelites towards the promised land and threatens further punishment. Tiring of such inconstant followers, Yahweh refuses to accompany them. An angel will lead the way in Yahweh's place. The people strip off their ornaments and go into mourning. Following divine guidance is not easy—then or now.

The text that follows contains various inconsistencies, suggestive of the crisis between Yahweh and the children of Israel. Moses speaks with Yahweh "face to face" at the tent of meeting outside the main camp. He now begs Yahweh to continue accompanying them, implying that the people dare not move without Yahweh's presence. Yahweh grudgingly agrees, but Moses presses further. "Show me thy glory," he pleads. The Lord Yahweh, who has previously been meeting Moses face to face, now refuses to do so. Moses is to stand among some rocks, while Yahweh covers his face. Moses is only permitted to see Yahweh's back.

Moses is now ordered to cut two more tablets, to replace those that he had smashed, and proceed once more up the mountain. Yahweh descends in the cloud and passes before his faithful emissary. There is a revelation, as Yahweh proclaims, "The Lord, The Lord God, merciful and gracious, long suffering, and abundant in goodness and truth, keeping mercy for thousands", while visiting iniquity on delinquents and their offspring. (The repetition of the words 'The Lord, the Lord' has been the subject of intense Rabbinic interpretation).

A renewed covenant is now announced, with a list of cultic commandments. Yahweh will drive out the idol worshipers occupying the promised land; the covenanting people, for their part, must smash the holy places of such idols. They are to make no deals with the occupants, lest they be seduced into idolatry. They must not make divine images of metal. They must celebrate the feasts and observe the sabbath. They must offer and redeem all first-born creatures (but only the animals are to be sacrificed), for the first-born are pristine and belong to Yahweh. All men must present themselves before Yahweh three times a year. There are several other ceremonial stipulations, for this is a covenant whose every purpose is to bind the people to Yahweh, in preparation for the assault on idolatry that lies ahead. Moses tarries on the mountain another forty days, eating and drinking nothing. He inscribes the tablets with this covenant. Then he emerges from the mountain, his face radiant, and passes on the divine instructions. Henceforth Moses wears a veil, except when speaking with Yahweh and communicating Yahweh's orders.

The Book of Exodus finishes with another long passage concerning the sanctuary and the ark of the covenant. It includes a mandate about the sabbath, and a description of the construction and consecration of the sanctuary, with its tabernacle, surrounding courtyard, altars and furnishings. Materials are provided, and skilled craftsmen are summoned to assemble the necessary furnishings. A veil is installed in the tabernacle, separating the holy of holies, containing the ark and throne, from an entry chamber furnished with a lamp-stand, an incense altar and a gold-plated table. After this has been accomplished, the cloud covers the tabernacle and the glory of Yahweh takes possession. As a prophetic rather than priestly leader, Moses is now excluded from the tabernacle, which is henceforth to be the domain of the ceremonially consecrated priesthood of Aaron and his descendants. The cloud remains with the tabernacle. If the cloud rises, the tabernacle and its contents are packed up and the journey proceeds; if the cloud stays put, so do the people. At night it shines like a fire, so that all the people can see it.

The book of Exodus ends at this point. The Israelite people have been liberated and brought out of Egypt to Sinai. Moses has established himself as their leader and as intercessor with the liberating God Yahweh. The core texts of the covenant have been handed down and inscribed. Moses has read them to the people and ratified them in a formal sacrificial ceremony. A sanctuary has been designed, a cultic act of defiance punished, and the sanctuary and its furnishings constructed. The priesthood, neglected in the J and E texts, has established its centrality in the covenantal order. The history and theology of the Yahwist cult is in the making.

Establishment of Cultic Regulations

The Book of Leviticus (primarily a priestly text) begins with the words "Yahweh called", which is the Hebrew title for this book. It provides regulations on rituals for sacrifice, investiture of priests, and maintenance of purification and holiness. As with other covenant legislation, it ends with a detailed section of blessings and curses, and a promise by the covenanting Lord not to disown the people completely. The Lord will remember earlier covenants of grace with the patriarchs, remember the desolated land, and remember the covenant with the first generations brought out of the land of Egypt. As this phraseology indicates, the promise here is conceived to cover conditions in which the children of Israel had fallen away from Yahweh and been carried into captivity in enemy land.

There is also an undercurrent emphasizing atonement. The people must make amends for their iniquity, because, says Yahweh, "they despised my judgments, and because their soul(s) abhorred my statutes." Much of the legislation has to do with sacrifices for sin, avoidance of uncleanliness and ritual purification. There is a special section dealing with the Day of Atonement, during which purification ceremonies are performed on behalf of both individual members and the community. Uncleanliness is of special concern. When an individual does something that is personally defiling and "abominable", that person must be cut off by death or exile from the people. When a people become unclean, the land itself is stained and must "vomit" out its inhabitants. Even unintentional defilement triggers a period of uncleanliness, which must be terminated by ritual cleansing. Idolatry is the most serious abomination, since it defiles the sanctuary and profanes Yahweh's holy name. Those individuals who commit such abominations must be put to death; otherwise much worse consequences for the people will ensue. In short, sacredness must be protected at all costs from defilement.

Such legislation seems remote from our times, when acts of defilement, so abhorred in Leviticus, have become commonplace. If death were to be exacted today on all those who cursed their parents, committed adultery, or abused the sabbath, we would suffer a precipitous decline in population. Similarly, it is hard to imagine anyone any longer carrying out all the detailed rituals of sacrifice required in Leviticus. Since the fat of sacrificial animals, as well as the blood, belonged to Yahweh, there are specific instructions as to how, and from where, the fat is to be removed, as well as what is to do with the carcass and entrails. In addition, it would be necessary to maintain a vast pastoral culture of sheep, goats, rams and bulls, in order to observe all the sacrifices required in Leviticus and Numbers. Today that is no longer realistic.

The legislation also defines clean and unclean animals and their capacity to defile. Except for locusts, creatures that creep upon the ground were an abomination and must not be eaten. Jewish people belonging to orthodox or conservative persuasions, who follow the 'kosher' prescriptions, still carefully observe the regulations regarding clean and unclean animals. They must not eat pork or shellfish and should not eat any animal flesh not properly prepared, or even use utensils that have been in contact with unclean food. According to Leviticus, eating of blood (the life force which belongs to Yahweh) was punished by banishment.

Other statutes dealt with bodily defilement. Childbirth resulted in defilement (longer for a girl than a boy, because of menstruation) and required a period for purification of the mother's blood, followed by presentation of a burnt offering. Those who developed skin rashes diagnosed as leprosy were required to tear their clothing, cover their upper lips, go around crying "unclean, unclean", and live outside the camp. Housing and clothing of lepers had to be disinfected and if needed destroyed. Bodily discharges, e.g. of blood or semen, required short periods of purification and cleansing of contaminated objects.

The Book of Leviticus emphasizes the establishment and maintenance of holiness. The regulations call on Moses to tell the community, "ye shall be holy, for I the Lord your God am holy." The people are called on to fear (or revere) their parents, keep the sabbath, abandon idolatry, and offer sacrifices of peace offerings in an acceptable manner. More generally, holiness extends to respect for the rights of the poor, of neighbors and of resident aliens, as well as for produce of the land. One must love neighbors and aliens as oneself. All these aspects make this difficult and remote text central to our understanding of what holy means in the Jewish religious context.

Such a broad definition of holiness is hard to imagine today, when we are living in a highly secularized environment. But in one respect we should not consider our situation to be so different from that of the children of Israel. Where we are surrounded by secularism, they were surrounded by the claims of other cultures and deities. Monotheism was not yet well established, and sacrifice to other gods, especially those with well-established territorial claims, continued to be a part of cultic life. Implicit in this juxtaposition of cultic practice is an understanding of the ambiguity of the human-divine relationship, in that it combines intimate closeness with radical separation. Even the many and explicit regulations of Leviticus could not efface the existence of this ambiguity at the heart of the cultic practice and sense of holiness of the individual and the people. They could only devise ways to reconcile Yahweh and Yahweh's people through liturgical practice.

An important aspect of the cultic legislation in Leviticus is that the land itself was holy and belonged to Yahweh. The land was entitled to a sabbatical year of rest, during which it must not be sown or harvested. The fiftieth, or Jubilee, year was a time for special veneration of the land. It is necessary to put these prescriptions in the past tense, as they have been so abandoned by the contemporary world, which has yet to find the will to protect the land and earth from abuse. In this respect it appears that Leviticus, along with other early mythic systems, was in touch with a sense of the ceremonial sanctity of land that we have yet to recover. The attempt in Leviticus to legislate protection of the land appears way ahead of its time—and ours.

There is much else of interest in this extraordinary document. This is the locus classicus for the 'scapegoat', that benighted animal that will carry the sins of the community away into the desert wilderness, where they can be discarded. But the focus for the contemporary reader should be not on the customs of a distant era but on mediation of the relationship between humans and the wholly differentiated divine power. Leviticus establishes ways of doing this effective for its time and place. Much of the specific legislation, such as that dealing with animal sacrifice or human sexuality, was of its time and does not work for our age. Other Levitical principles, such as love of neighbors and aliens and respect for the land, apply acutely to today's world. The document reminds us that such precepts are part of the matrix of covenant and Torah, teaching us how to function in a constantly shifting historical and time-based world.

In the Wilderness

Following the order of books in the Bible, we now move on to the book of Numbers, known in the Hebrew scriptures as 'In the Wilderness'. These words set the stage for the next phase in the journey of Moses and his people.

Before the Israelites are ready to leave Mt. Sinai, further organization is required. A census is taken, producing a substantial force of reportedly over 600,000 fighting men. From this and other censuses we get the name of the Book of 'Numbers' by which the text is designated in Christian Bibles. The tribes are given their marching orders; the tribe of Levi is responsible for moving the entire tent of meeting (or sanctuary) and its sacred contents, after the latter have been properly covered and equipped with carrying poles by the priests. Taxes and offerings are collected to support the Tabernacle and its guardians, and all the able-bodied Levites go through a ceremony of purification. Trumpets sound the order to break camp. At last, after staying almost a year at Mt. Sinai, the huge encampment is ready to move on.

After three days the people stop for a pause, and the first of several mutinies breaks out. We should picture the aridity of the environment, the burning sun in the heat of the day, the lack of creature comforts, fear of isolation in the desert wastes. The people are tired and hungry. Some of them fantasize about the fish, the cucumbers, melons, leeks, onions, and garlic left behind in Egypt. They begin to cry and moan. The aging Moses can hardly bear the noise, let alone all the burdens of leadership. An angry Yahweh agrees to the appointment of seventy elders to share the leadership burden, and arranges for a surfeit of quails to fly in. The people choke on quail meat, and many of them die.

In due course the chastened community moves on. At the next encampment Miriam and Aaron complain against Moses. The pretext is that Moses has married a Cushite (Ethiopian) woman, elsewhere identified as Zipporah, one of the seven daughters of the Midianite priest Jethro (or Reuel). Whether or not this is the same person, the problem is that Moses has married outside the tribal boundaries. In addition, Moses is still identified with his Midianite in-laws, amongst whom he had lived for so long. Earlier, as we have seen, he relied on his father-in-law Jethro to help in solving a leadership problem. More recently he had begged his brother-in-law Hobab to help in guiding the Israelites through the wilderness.

Evidently his natal brother and sister feel left out of Moses' inner councils. "Hath the Lord indeed spoken only by Moses?" they protest. This disloyalty to the divinely chosen leader enrages Yahweh, who strikes Miriam with leprosy. Aaron begs Moses to intervene with Yahweh, and Moses does so. Miriam's punishment is to be banned from the camp for seven days. This is the second time that Aaron is reported as challenging the leadership of Moses and yet escaping without personal harm.

After that unhappy incident, the people proceed on to the wilderness of Paran, where worse things will happen. At Yahweh's bidding, Moses sends out spies to reconnoiter the land of Canaan. They return after 40 days bearing grapes, pomegranates and figs. But disagreement breaks out. Caleb and Joshua describe a rich and fertile land, ready for the taking. The rest depict a frightening land of giants who devour its inhabitants. An ugly murmur swells up against Moses and Aaron. There is talk of stoning them and appointing a leader who will take them back to Egypt. This is too much for Yahweh, who prepares to wipe out the rebels with a plague. Moses again intercedes, and Yahweh relents. But now the rebel generation is condemned to stay in the wilderness for forty years until they die out. It is only their children, who have no nostalgia for life in Egypt, who will inherit the land. The rebellious spies are struck dead. Reluctant to accept this judgment, some of the people set off to fight the Canaanites and Amalekites. Lacking Yahweh's help, they are defeated and sent fleeing.

At this point some cultic legislation is inserted into the account, as if to relieve the impact of the sentence that has just been announced. The regulations here have to do with provision of offerings of flour and bread, and with ritually approved methods of atonement for sins of omission. Those who despise the Lord's commandments and sin willfully are to be banished. A man who broke the sabbath is stoned to death outside the camp. The people are ordered to wear tassels on their garments, as a reminder to be faithful to Yahweh's commands.

Despite these caveats, another dangerous rebellion erupts. The account in fact conflates two rebellions into one. The issue is again over Moses' leadership. The man described as the humblest of men is accused by some Levites of usurping for himself and Aaron a consecrated status that should belong to all. The rebels demand equal rights of access to the tabernacle and contemptuously reject Moses' orders. But they and their families are swallowed up in a landslide, and a fire comes down from Yahweh that destroys their followers. Hardly has that event gone by when yet another rebellion breaks out. Knowing that intercession is useless, Moses tells Aaron to perform the rite of atonement. By the time this has been completed, over 14,000 people have died of a plague.

The accounts of these incidents focus on the sacred properties of the tabernacle and the rights and duties that inhere to the priests and Levites. Abuse of the tabernacle and its sacred objects is deadly dangerous. The idea of holiness as being dangerous had, until recently, been virtually expunged from modern consciousness. Indeed, to the modern mind such an idea may well seem absurd. One recalls Stalin's disdainful inquiry as to how many military divisions the Pope had at his disposal.

Yet the Hebrew scriptures are adamant that what is sacred must not be violated. Those who improperly touch what is holy are destroyed by it. Yahweh may be merciful, but Yahweh is never to be presumed upon. In part we are seeing here an effort by the priesthood to establish the ascendancy of Yahweh over all other deities. The household and community gods could never muster such awesome power as was consistently wielded by the God of Israel.

But this is not a mere propaganda effort on behalf of a specific deity. The texts insist on the sacredness and ineffability of the divine order and everything associated with it, including the liturgical rites, the sabbath, and by extension the whole of the created order. What is sacred is pristine and must never be polluted. The problem is that the human order, with its blood and semen and disease, pollutes. Thus, the coexistence in history of God and humans is inherently problematical. What is noteworthy about the world which produced the Torah is its effort to produce a structure of thought and action, which could mediate and unite divine and human under the changing circumstances of human existence, and thus preserve the power of the divine on behalf of an otherwise alienated humanity.

So important is the issue of pollution that the Book of Numbers introduces a special ceremony for producing ritually clean water, which can then be used to cleanse ritually polluted individuals and objects. Death is especially polluting. Those who are in any way contaminated by contact with corpses must be ritually cleansed over a seven-day period. Otherwise they defile the tabernacle and must be banished. Objects in contact with the dead person must also be cleansed. The text states that this is to be a perpetual law. This legislation is as close as the text comes to discussing burial rituals. Given the centrality of burial rites in Pharonic religion, their absence from the legislation of the covenanting God is not surprising. The Biblical covenant is about how to live on this earth.

The encampment now moves on to Kadesh, still in the Negev wilderness and in enemy (Amalekite) territory. Here the unfortunate Miriam dies and is buried. Then a very inauspicious event takes place. Lacking water, the people cry out against Moses and Aaron for bringing them to such a parched and desolate spot. In a fit of pique, Moses strikes the rock to make water flow, but he does so without proclaiming the majesty of Yahweh. The rock delivers water, but Yahweh's holiness has been slighted. Yahweh informs Moses and Aaron that they will not be the ones to lead the Israelites into the promised land. The community is refused passage through Edom and is obliged to make a long detour. During the journey Aaron dies and is mourned for 30 days.

Forty years have now passed since the Israelites left Egypt. After further vicissitudes the people summon their strength, destroy various tribal forces in battle, and arrive at the borders of Moab, on the east of the Dead Sea.

Here the account pauses to relate several remarkable stories. Alarmed by the approach of the Israelite forces, the king of Moab summons Balaam, a well-known seer, to come and curse them. After considerable pressure the seer finally agrees, but after setting off with the Moabite chieftains his donkey lies down in a narrow defile. Angry and humiliated, the seer beats his animal, only to discover that it has stopped before the angel of the Lord. The journey proves a fiasco. Each time the king of Moab requests a curse against the Israelites, Balaam delivers a blessing. The doom of the Moabites and other tribal enemies of Israel is pronounced.

Meantime, the pleasures of life in Moab prove too much for the Israelites, who have known nothing for years but camp life. Men go off whoring with Moabite women and fall into worshiping their gods. According to a later text, they accepted the yoke of the god and ate sacrifices to the dead. To avert Yahweh's anger, the ringleaders are killed, and their heads are impaled. Then an Israelite—apparently one of many—comes back to camp with a Midianite woman. To the Priestly tradition, from which this story comes, this is an act of blatant defilement—or perhaps too blatant a reminder of Moses' Midianite associations. The priest Phineas (grandson of Aaron) slaughters the two offenders, and plague carries off twenty-four thousand others. Phineas and his descendants are rewarded with a covenant of eternal priesthood.

Thus, even as the new generation is on the verge of leaving the wilderness, deadly trouble breaks out. To bring the people back to their senses, more ritual organization is enacted. There is another census, more counting of Levites, and considerably more demand for sacrificial offerings. Laws are passed concerning vows and pledges. Then, according to the

Priestly text, Yahweh insists on declaring a holy war on Midian, the land that had sheltered Moses for half a lifetime. The men are slaughtered but the women and children spared. Moses is reportedly enraged by this soft-heartedness. The women are held accountable for the recent defilement of the Israelite camp. Those women who have slept with a man, and the male children, must be destroyed. Those who kill them must be ritually cleansed. Then a huge booty of livestock and jewelry is distributed. This is a foretaste of the holy wars that lie ahead. It is also a way of separating Moses once and for all from the people of Midian, with whom he had once been so closely identified. The past must be excised, whether it involves Egypt or Midian.

The boundaries of Israel and Israelite Transjordan are now determined. Towns are allocated to Levites. Six cities are set aside as sanctuaries for unintentional killers, and laws are passed regarding inheritance of tribal land. On this legislative note the Book of Numbers, and the story of the wilderness experience, draws to a close.

The Deuteronomic Synthesis

In following the Torah accounts of Moses and the children of Israel we have taken a primarily narrative and documentary approach. That is, we have been attempting to summarize the Torah narrative of the Exodus as a record of transition from captivity to freedom, which incorporates the development of a new, monotheistic and imageless religious cult.

We have also identified the various documentary traditions that make up the material of the books of Exodus, Leviticus and Numbers, and showing some of the ways in which these traditions influence the interpretation of what happened. For example, the Priestly account is strongly supportive of the role of Aaron and the priesthood and makes their function central to both the historical and religious experience. The E account, by contrast, is a protagonist of Moses the lawgiver, whom it describes more than once as communicating with the Lord Yahweh on an intimate basis. These differences derive from the traditions of different cultic centers. They remind us of the extent to which differing traditions are embedded in the Torah account as we now have it.

We have not yet attempted to view the story from the perspective of religious, as opposed to cultic, consciousness. This perspective requires that we ask the text not what it tells us about the evolution of events and relationships but what it tells us about humans in relationship to the divine. We have, of course, noted many examples of that relationship, but not in such a way as to inform us why the Exodus happened, and why Moses was so convinced that the enigmatic and often terrifying God Yahweh constituted the only true means to the achievement of human freedom. Nor have we read the text from a meditative perspective, as have generations of Rabbinic scholars, pausing over each line and datum to meditate on what it tells us about the meaning of the divine and its function in human existence.

Yet we cannot leave the Exodus story without attempting to grapple with its meaning as a specifically religious and epiphanic experience. This event is, after all, the foundation stone of Jewish and Christian religious life. It is the bedrock of our religious and covenantal consciousness; and that is the case whether we happen to be involved in religious practice or not. How, then, can we set about interpreting the religious meaning of what happened?

One place to start is with the highly charged Book of Deuteronomy. As we have seen in chapter 2, Deuteronomy redefines the nexus of human-divine relations. In place of the emphasis on cultic sacrifices and oblations, Deuteronomy (that is, original source and exilic revision) calls for commitment of heart and soul to the love of Yahweh. In long speeches, attributed to Moses, it reviews the exodus from Egypt, the experience at Sinai, the apostasies, and the tribulations experienced by the people in the wilderness. Their survival and success are the achievement of Yahweh, not of themselves, not even of Moses. If they are to survive, it can only be by loving Yahweh with heart and soul, and by teaching their children to do the same.

The Deuteronomic explanation was based on understanding the political and cultural precariousness of Israelite existence. In the volatile power politics of the prophetic era, the Deuteronomists believed that the only thing that could save the Jewish people from going under was a resolute and binding monotheism, defining the people by internalized belief rather than by exterior observance. Their texts are considered so germane to the survival of the Israelite tradition that they continue to provide the core of Jewish worship. One cannot read Deuteronomy without being tremendously moved by its centering of religious consciousness on heart and soul.

It is Deuteronomy that declares all-out war on idolatry. In the Deuteronomic recounting of the Exodus, towns practicing idolatry are placed under the ban, which means that its citizens old and young are to be put to the sword. This is not because they happen to be in the way of an army on the warpath; it is because their practices were abhorrent and would undermine the coherence and survival of a consecrated people. These abhorrent practices included immolation of small children by fire, and use of cultic prostitutes, both male and female.

Abhorrence towards spiritual pollution permeates Deuteronomy and is the inspiration of the terrible curses, which appear both in treaty format and in the famous song of Moses. From this derives the stark description of two ways with which the text reaches its culmination: on the one hand life and goodness—and survival, based on recognition of the covenant; on the other, evil and death—and destruction, resulting from disobedience and sin. One may not like the options to be stated in such a stark manner, but at least Deuteronomy is quite clear about the choices.

Of all the books dealing with the Exodus, Deuteronomy is by far the most centered on Moses. In Deuteronomy Aaron and the priesthood are relegated to a footnote. Cultic practice is entirely secondary to historical and prophetic consciousness. The book is organized into speeches and poems by Moses, uttered at a time when all challengers to the leadership of Moses have died off and the children of Israel are about to enter the promised land and achieve their inheritance. Moses, we might assume, has achieved all his objectives and is at the pinnacle of success. No one can contest his judgment. What an opportunity for idolization! But the text is not interested in substituting one human power system for another. It reiterates, in the words of Moses himself, that he is a mere mortal, who has made his own mistakes and is himself the object of Yahweh's judgment. He cannot be the one to lead the Israelites across the Jordan. He is merely permitted to view the inheritance from a mountain top, before he dies.

Instead, the task of Moses at this juncture is to teach the Israelites that they are a people consecrated to the Lord Yahweh. That requires not just cultic practice but loving Yahweh with all one's heart and soul, and teaching this to one's children. One should wear these words on one's hand and forehead, write them on one's doorpost, and have them constantly in mind. It means, in a characteristically Deuteronomic and male-oriented phrase, 'circumcising one's heart'. That, in turn, means fearing, loving and serving the God Yahweh with all one's heart and soul, and keeping the laws and commandments set out in the covenant.

We may view the idea of heart circumcision as a transfer of the practice of covenantal consecration from the realization of phallic energy, with its focus on human bonding and creation of physical life (an element in the covenants with Abraham), to the conception and realization of emotional energy, with its focus on love as the source and expression of Divine power. The idea of consecration of heart and soul to Yahweh is central to Deuteronomy as well as to the prophetic book of Jeremiah. It is the Deuteronomic solution to the relentless problem of diffusion of cultural identity through idolatry, conceived here as adulation of the corporeal body and of physical consciousness, in short, an ego identity that centers existence and consciousness on myself or on the tribe or kingdom as collective identity. In place of this tribal and narcissistic consciousness, Deuteronomy insists on a Yahweh consciousness, centered on the God Yahweh as Lord of lords, world creator, lover, and source of justice and mercy. This is the meaning of the Deuteronomic choice, one a blessing and the other a curse. To love Yahweh with heart and soul brings blessing; to love human consciousness expressed in cultic and idolatrous observance brings disaster. With an intensity driven by fear of collective disaster, Deuteronomy insists on the heart-centered path.

Although this covenantal imagery is essentially symbolic, it is trying to tell us something about the evolution of spiritual values, a subject explored intensely by medieval Jewish kabbalistic thinkers. The covenant with Abraham, with its attention to phallic values, referred to the procreative power of the divine world order and its relevance to the creation of ongoing human generations. The Sinai covenant tells us much more about what kabbalists identified as the majesty and the endurance of the divine and the way to represent those values in human conduct on this earth. It places the divine at the center of human consciousness and intention. The Deuteronomists went further, seeking to introduce the energies of the heart into the structure of covenant. Prophetic vision, as we shall see, emphasizes the values of justice and mercy in the process of covenant-building. Throughout this evolution of covenantal consciousness, all traditions agree that Moses was the first prophet to cultivate and nourish such a tree of life.

After voicing these teachings Moses died in Moab. Thirty days of mourning took place, then the Israelites moved on and launched the assault into Canaan, leaving their great prophet in an unknown grave. The Yahwist faith does not idolize human beings. Nor does it flatter the consecrated people. But after occupying the land for which they had sacrificed so much, the people gradually allowed idolatry to make its way back into their lives. Thus perverted, the Israelites were well on the rocky road towards capture and oblivion before the Deuteronomic texts surfaced into history. But it was in those circumstances that the story of Moses, as remembered by later writers and prophets, began to make its mark on human memory.

Deuteronomy ends with the reflection that there has never since been a prophet in Israel to match Moses, "whom the Lord knew face to face." Few would question this judgment. The stamp of an indomitable will lies behind the Sinai covenant and the journey that it entailed. Can one imagine such an extraordinary journey succeeding without a framework of faith with which to give it meaning? For this is not just a journey of survival through a hostile and killing environment. It is also a journey of faith, from captivity of body and spirit to a heart-centered freedom. By signing on to the covenant, the Israelite confederation had opted for freedom to stand on their own feet versus an oppressive if comfortable slavery. That is how the Torah of Moses, as redacted by the Deuteronomists, presents the matter. Theologically the Exodus is presented as a journey from a culture oriented to management of death and the afterlife, to one focused on the meaning of being alive on this earth in the present. The covenant and law are redefined as the road to life, refracting the physical transition from Egypt to the promised land.

The Exodus journey reminds us that the freedom to choose life, earned by virtue of the covenant, can be won and sustained only through intense conviction and struggle. Even so, the survival of this choice depends on eternal vigilance, since opportunities abound for regressing back into a state of idolatry. According to the Torah, regression to non-covenantal, cultic and a-historical consciousness, expressed as idolatry, is the norm of human conduct—a norm not limited to ancient Israel. It is also the road to ruin and destruction, as revealed in the demise of the kingdoms of Israel and Judah. If the Torah redaction told us nothing else, at least it drives home that point. Whenever abandonment of covenantal law and justice occurs, it is time to watch out, then and now.

The Exodus story also insists that freedom is at core a spiritual value, founded on mutual love between humans and a merciful God, "gracious, longsuffering, and abundant in mercy and truth." The idea of basing life on love of God and love of neighbor was new, alien, and fearful in respect to the unconditional love that it demanded. Three thousand years later that idea is still widely regarded as unrealistic, until we stop to consider the alternatives.

CHAPTER 7

Covenant Guardians: The Isaiah Prophecies

> Then I heard Yahweh's voice saying
> "Whom shall I send?
> Who will go on our behalf?"
> I said, "here am I! Send me."
> Isaiah chapter 6

Prophecy in the Context of Covenant

If Torah is the heart of Judaic religion, prophecy is its conscience. Where Torah seeks to bind humans with the divine, prophecy points out what separates them. The biblical prophet emerges as an existential critic, thundering against abuse of the covenant and recalling human attention to the justice and mercy of the covenanting God. Prophecy is particularly about the use and abuse of power. The prophets deride material power as corrupting and transient and invoke divine power as the only source of salvation. In short, prophetic writing is the record of the covenant in action—a running commentary on how Yahweh's people are doing in upholding their part of the bargain.

Since the time of the Deuteronomic reform the Judaic tradition has recognized Moses as the originating and preeminent prophet. This is a way of saying that prophetic consciousness begins with the establishment of the covenant itself and is built into the enactment of the covenant and the study of Torah. Why, then, separate prophecy from Torah? One reply might be that this separation is less apparent in the Hebrew than in the Christian Bible. In the former, the five books of Torah are followed by the Deuteronomic histories, which are designated as the 'Earlier Prophets'. This signals that the books of the earlier prophets are the books of the covenant in action. It also calls our attention to the centrality of the prophetic role in covenantal history, as compared with executive power such as that of the judges and kings, or the ceremonial power of the ritually consecrated priests. The latter represent foci of human authority; the prophet, as we have seen in the case of Moses, derives authority as direct mediator with, or emissary of, the divine. Thus, the prophetic books constitute the record of the presence of the God Yahweh in the evolution of human life.

The books of the earlier prophets are followed by the books of the later prophets, which offer more extended profiles of the prophet in action. These later prophetic books are the ones that both Jewish and Christian bibles recognize as prophetic. The book of the Isaiah prophecies is placed first among the later prophetic books. Chronologically the text includes writings from several different eras. As the sum of its parts it is the longest text in the prophetic literature. It also embraces the broadest range of prophetic utterance.

The later prophets arrive on the scene in the middle of the 8th century BCE, at a time when the rising power of Assyria had begun to dominate and overwhelm its neighboring kingdoms. Small states such as Damascus, Tyre and Sidon, and Israel, proved no match for the Assyrian war machine. First, they were forced to pay tribute. Then they were overrun, and their populations displaced.

This breakdown of civil society threw the existing structures of divine-human relations into question. Although the small kingdom of Judah survived the Assyrian onslaught, it faced a future fraught with danger and uncertainty. Responses among the peoples of the Yahwist kingdoms ranged from frantic diplomatic maneuverings to renewed appeals and sacrifices to cultic gods, to a cynical hedonism, to a radical rethinking of Yahweh's role in human affairs. The later prophets were those people who set out to redefine the covenantal relationship in the light of the vast material power accumulated by the new middle-eastern empires (Assyria and Egypt, then later Babylon and Persia).

The prophetic analysis of the problems affecting Israel and Judah accepts the reality of the covenant but seeks to redefine the powers and responsibilities of the contracting parties. The magnification of secular power leads to a similar magnification of Yahweh's power, to the point where the physical power of the new empires is seen as a mere instrumentality of Yahweh's will, acting in response to human corruption. If Yahweh is going to punish Israelites for apostasy, why not through the medium of Assyrian warfare? Could there, indeed, be any other source for such overwhelming military power? This thinking reminds one of the association of divine power with success in warfare. The Lord of Hosts had demonstrated military power during the Exodus and the occupation of the promised land, and much later during the campaigns of king David. Yahweh was known to withhold power from unrighteous forces and campaigns; Yahweh might, like any other overlord, use enemy forces to punish a corrupted people who had betrayed the covenant.

But prophecy would not have achieved lasting influence as a strategic studies discipline. The prophets had to struggle to redefine Yahwism as a religious experience and as a guide to human order. This required them to turn their backs on the cultic, and in certain respects pagan, concept of religion as a way of mediating with the divine through ceremonial sacrifice. It is probably hard for us now to appreciate what a radical break in religious consciousness was needed to replace a religion focused on cultic sacrifice with a religion focused on ethical conduct derived from direct individual experience of the divine. Yet this is the revolution in consciousness that the later prophets ushered in. This is not to say that ethical comprehension had not been important in earlier Yahwism; what the later prophets did, however, was to make it the principal attribute of Yahwist practice.

Since the idea of prophecy is so commonly associated with forecasting the future, it is as well to note that this is not the principal function of biblical prophecy. Its principal purpose is to speak on behalf of the divine (the literal meaning of the word prophet), criticize conduct that falls away from the covenant, and urge the authorities and the people to recommit to Yahweh as the only source of existential security. In seeking to reinforce allegiance to Yahweh the prophet functions in a political capacity, sometimes as adviser to rulers (for example the prophets Samuel, Nathan,

Isaiah), sometimes as unflinching critic (e.g. Elijah, Hosea, Jeremiah). The prophet may, like Isaiah the man, combine both these political roles.

Part of this political function consists in warning human power structures, and specifically the states of Israel and Judah, of the prospects that will follow from abandonment of the Yahwist covenant—an act of rebellion—in favor of treaties with human power systems (or those of other 'gods'). It is this function that has commonly associated prophecy with forecasting. The reason is that much of prophetic literature consists in denunciation of political misconduct and warnings of the terrifying fate that lies ahead for rulers and peoples who abuse their authority, or who specifically recognize the authority of other powers at the expense of Yahweh's.

When we examine this phenomenon from a covenantal perspective, however, it transpires that prophetic warning is a logical consequence of a breach of contract. Such a breach triggers the curses and maledictions that are part of the covenant itself, and that are the means by which the covenanting lord—in this case the God Yahweh—ensures the allegiance of the signatories—in this case the Israelite people of the kingdoms of Israel and Judah. Prophetic doom and gloom do no more than remind Yahweh's people of consequences already built into the structure of the covenant. It interprets covenant terms to account for the problems of the times.

Since it is a human failing to neglect the small print, we might conclude that the prophet is functioning in a legalistic manner to ensure that rulers and peoples understand the consequences of their actions. But in representing Yahweh, the prophet reminds all willing to listen that the invisible God of Israel is part of human existence and intervenes in the human world to achieve divine objectives. The God Yahweh intervened to bring the children of Israel out of Egypt. Yahweh will also intervene to uphold the integrity of the covenant, even if that means punishing rebel rulers and populations. If the rebels act in a way that seriously compromises their God, they can be sure that the latter will retaliate. If needed Yahweh will repudiate the rebels and overthrow their regime. In this respect divine covenantal history is no different from secular. A breach of covenant is always a very consequential and dangerous act—especially when the mysterious power of Yahweh is at stake.

The Sinai covenant is unique because it is with a divine, not a secular, lord. It therefore conveys assurances of safety that go far beyond earthbound guarantees. For a small nation (the kingdom of Judah), caught between the competing superpowers of Egypt, Assyria and Babylon, this should have been no slight consideration. According to covenantal ideology, Yahweh had already shown superior force and wisdom in dealing with the forces of the Egyptian Pharaoh. There was nothing to suggest that Yahweh could not continue to protect the Israelite people, so long as they remained true to the Yahwist covenant. But the covenant is not merely a source of physical salvation; it is also a moral and sacred bond. It represents the power of Yahweh acting to secure a just and well-regulated human society. Indeed, as depicted by the later prophets, achievement of justice is the overriding goal of covenantal history. Consequently, the covenant with Yahweh is always to be preferred to any other contractual relationship, either with other gods or with human powers. Such relationships cannot guarantee either salvation or justice; and by breaching the only one that can, they merely result in disaster.

We can conclude from this that the prophetic function of forecasting the future derives both from an understanding of how covenants work, and from an understanding of the unique power and earthly agenda of the covenanting God. That power embraces both life and death. The Israelites, as Yahweh's chosen people, always have the option of choosing one or the other. As they choose, so it will be done.

Unfortunately, the breaching of the Sinai covenant began before the ink was barely dry. Relationship with the covenanting Lord Yahweh does not come naturally. Human imagination is too limited, and other forces are often more immediately apparent. Thus, another critical feature of Israelite history is its pervasive idolatry. Cults of other gods either were already present in the land occupied by the Israelites or were brought in by intermarriage. The Deuteronomic histories (the books of Joshua through Kings) document the existence and location of these cults and their propensity to intrude on, or even displace, the Yahwist cult. Their existence challenged allegiance to Yahweh, undermining the covenant and its ethical-religious foundation.

To the modern mind idolatry may once have seemed a problem of primitive or unenlightened peoples, who had no rational or ethical understanding of how the universe works. From this perspective, the history of the Israelites could be viewed as the history of the gradual elimination of idolatry in favor of allegiance to the one true and dependable God. History, in other words, is progressive, and the progression is from cultic idolatry rooted in myth to ethical monotheism rooted in history. To a certain extent this is the case; but this view has always overlooked the continuing influence of cultic idolatry on human imagination and existence. More generally it fails to recognize the limitations of monotheistic worship and ethics in its patriarchal embodiment. Additionally, it fails to recognize the aspect of idolatry that is the consequence of human corruption and self-indulgence. Histories could equally well be written describing the huge and ongoing influence exerted by idolatries resulting from corruption of the divine-human bond. Indeed, corruption and its resulting idolatries are fundamental to human experience. In any case, since the 20th century's two world wars and subsequent Cold War it is now perhaps more widely recognized that modern society is itself idolatrous, and far more dangerously so than any primitive culture.

This realization should have revived interest in the prophetic insistence on returning, for salvation's sake, to the covenant of the God of Israel. At least we should recognize the agonizing efforts by the prophets to recall the people to their God. The covenant with Yahweh alone provided the foundation for ethical and sacred order. Without this bond, as the prophets would argue, there is no hope for a life of integrity; with it, one can yet hope for the restoration of justice and peace. Yahweh is a merciful God, slow to anger and quick to redeem. Redemption is as important to the prophetic tradition as criticism and doom-saying, since it is this aspect of prophecy which points to Yahweh as merciful and just towards earthbound humans. Without the message of redemption, there would be no difference between Isaiah or Jeremiah forecasting doom for Jerusalem and Cassandra doing the same for Troy. In either case no one would listen, and the prophecy would very likely become self-fulfilling. But the redemptive aspect of prophecy always recalls the power of the God of Israel to intervene and transform history. Even if the rebellious people fall utterly away from Yahweh, this redemptive power will suffice to preserve at least a "remnant", so that a just, covenantal relationship can continue.

From this position came the view, developed during the 6th century Babylonian exile, that the covenantal bond is an intentional act by Yahweh to assure justice and peace on earth. We will see this idea more fully developed in the later exilic and post-exilic portions of Isaiah, but it is explicit from the beginning of prophecy, as the Torah tradition makes clear. Where the prophets excel is in the visionary power with which they proclaim the triumphant return of Yahweh. Prophetic utterance provides us with a vitally needed understanding of the saving power of the God of Israel. No source has proclaimed this with more conviction than the book of Isaiah.

The Isaiah Prophecies

Biblical scholarship has long identified more than one voice in the book bearing the name of Isaiah. There is the prophet himself, identified by name and ancestry, and active in Jerusalem in the later 8th century BCE. His utterances provide the basic substrate of the material collected in chapters 1 to 30 of the book of Isaiah. Recent scholarship identifies detailed commentary by later Isaian writers throughout this section of the text. Chapters 40-55 constitute a relatively integrated prophetic perspective of the Lord Yahweh as redeemer. This material deals with events at the end of the Babylonian captivity in the later 6th century BCE. There is no way of identifying the voices, but the ideas belong to the Isaian tradition, therefore the core material of this component is generally referred to as deutero-Isaiah (Second Isaiah).

There are also eleven chapters at the end of the book, and other chapters and extended passages throughout the rest of the text, for the most part dating either from the exile or the period of the revival of the Temple, and therefore quite late. These passages, which include descriptions of the 'remnant' who survived exile, as well as several powerful visionary prophecies, also resonate with the ideas of the prophet and belong to the Isaian tradition. Since Isaiah the prophet had disciples, there is no reason why some of the latter—or their successors—would not have contributed to the tradition, particularly as the historical predicament of Yahweh's people unfolded from invasion to exile to restoration.

The prophet Isaiah himself lived in or around Jerusalem. His oracles focus on the failure of Yahweh's people to uphold the covenant to which they were sworn. According to the Isaian tradition he received his call in

740 BCE, during the last year of the leprous king Uzziah, while meditating in the Temple. The prophet identifies leprosy as a symptom of spiritual pollution, not just of the king but of the people, including Isaiah himself. Aghast at his uncleanliness he cries out in distress, for he has looked upon the true and holy king—Yahweh Lord of Hosts. His lips are cleansed by a seraph and his sin is purged. He hears the voice saying, "whom shall I send?" and he calls out, "here am I! Send me." This is a powerful Biblical example of how individual consciousness is transformed and activated through surrender to divine power. But then, according to the tradition, he received a grim assignment: to speak to a people who would neither listen nor accept what he said, until the kingdom had been destroyed and the Lord Yahweh had driven the people far away.

Two events precipitated Isaiah's prophecies: an invasion of Judah launched by the kings of Syria and Israel (Ephraim) around 735 BCE, and the siege of Jerusalem by the forces of the Assyrian ruler Sennacherib at the end of the 8th century BCE. These events are interpreted in the text not as mere political developments, but as signs of Judah's perdition. Judah is "a sinful nation, a people laden with iniquity." Its religion is hypocritical and sickening. Its business is corrupted with greed and bribery; its hands are covered with the blood of the oppressed. Anarchy has taken over, and Yahweh is angry. "What mean ye that ye beat my people to pieces and grind the faces of the poor?" says Yahweh, the God of Hosts. While the poor are being oppressed and trampled on, Yahweh is watching and observing it all. A day of reckoning is coming, when Yahweh will judge the people who have plundered the Lord's vineyard and filled their houses with the "spoil of the poor." On that day the arrogance of the men will be humbled, and their idols destroyed. Their women will be stripped naked, their men fall by the sword, and the gates of the city "shall lament and mourn."

Is this prophetic gobbledygook, or is it trying to tell us humans something about the consequences of our actions? Is it trying, for example, to tell us something about the meaning of justice? The Isaian prophets yearn for the restoration of a just society. "Learn to do well," the text exhorts; "seek judgment (justice) and relieve the oppressed." Zion will be redeemed by justice. The text envisages an end time when the great Temple will be exalted above all. Nations will flow to it, and out of Zion will go forth the law. The Lord shall uphold justice among the nations, and they shall beat their swords into ploughshares. But in the meantime, the vengeance of Yahweh is kindled. Terrifying forces are on the march, and around the land there is nothing but darkness and sorrow. This sounds more like the human condition.

The invasion of Judah by Syria and Israel precipitated a crisis requiring a more immediate response. According to the Isaian tradition Yahweh sends Isaiah with his son Shear-jashub ("A Remnant Will Return") to meet the beleaguered king Ahaz. He tries to inspire the king with confidence in Yahweh. But Ahaz is an idolater who has already burned his son to appease a false god. He prefers to appeal to the powerful Assyrian monarch Tiglath-Pileser. The latter obliges by invading Syria, capturing Damascus and destroying its king. Not long after that, Assyrian forces invade Israel and deport its population. Ahaz becomes an Assyrian vassal and sets up an idolatrous altar in Yahweh's temple.

For Isaiah these developments are the result of wrongdoing and therefore the work of Yahweh. He warns Ahaz of trouble brewing elsewhere. A son will be born, named Immanuel (God with us). Before he comes of age, Syria and Israel will be gone, and Assyrian aggression will flow on and inundate Judah. But it is Yahweh, Lord God of Hosts, whom you must fear and dread, he warns the king. Isaiah's wife, also a prophet, gives birth to another son, whom they name Maher-shalal-hash-baz (Speed-Spoil-Hurry-Plunder). The God Yahweh is turning away from the House of Jacob.

Yet in this moment of descending gloom the text reveals another vision of a great light shining. A son will be born to the throne of David. The government shall be upon his shoulder, and his name shall be called "Wonderful, Counselor, The mighty God, The everlasting Father, the Prince of Peace." With Yahweh's help he will bring in a reign of peace and justice that will last forever. The titles, though imposing, are not new; even the vision of a ruler working hand in hand with Yahweh harks back to king David. But the idea that such an alliance could usher in peace and justice forever is prophetic. Indeed, later generations took it to be messianic. As the King James Bible so effusively comments, "what joy shall be in the midst of afflictions, by the kingdom and birth of Christ." Handel composed one of his most inspired Messiah choruses to this text, and one can hardly sing or hear this chorus without experiencing the imaginative and redemptive power underlying the words.

But—as so often in this portion of the text—the future gives way to the present. Yahweh is getting ready to destroy Israel. Yahweh is also fulminating against the arrogance of the Assyrian monarch. Zion, it becomes clear, need not fear Assyria. Another vision emerges of a descendant of David, on whom the spirit of the Lord shall rest. "With righteousness shall he judge (bring justice to) the poor … and with the breath of his lips shall he slay the wicked." The wolf shall dwell with the lamb and the leopard with the kid. "They shall not hurt nor destroy in all my holy mountain: for the earth shall be full of the knowledge of the Lord, as the waters cover the sea." This visionary text introduces a new motif: that the earth too will benefit from the renewal of justice. Holiness will replace barbarity. Peace will descend. All will be well with life on earth.

Before that can happen, Judah must withstand a terrifying invasion by a huge Assyrian force. Awaiting this event, the prophet feels an unbearable oppressiveness. He has taken off his mourning dress of sackcloth and shoes and for three years has walked around naked. Judah is searching for help from Egypt. This will do no good, warns Yahweh. The king of Assyria will seize Egyptians and lead them away "young and old, naked and barefoot, even with their buttocks uncovered, to the shame of Egypt."

Jerusalem is attempting to strengthen its defenses. That will do no good either, for nemesis has seized the inhabitants. "Let us eat and drink," they exclaim, "for tomorrow we die." Dazed with alcohol, the priests and false prophets stagger around, pausing only to cover the tables with vomit. 'Experts' deride Isaiah and drunkenly mock his speech. "We have made a covenant with the underworld," they scoff. "The scourge will not catch us, for we have protected ourselves with lies and falsehood!" One can almost hear the drunken, mocking laughter. Horrified by this reckless abandon, the prophet warns that hail and flood will sweep away their cover. Jerusalem will be besieged and blockaded, and the covenant with 'death' torn apart. But his scoffers are beyond caring. Their eyes glaze over; they are stupefied with sleep.

And yet, all is not yet lost. There is a new king in Judah, Hezekiah, and he becomes a Yahwist reformer. With the aid of Levites, he cleans up the temple and rebels against Assyria. The Assyrians send a huge army

The Wisdom of the Covenants and Their Relevance to Our Times

that captures the fortified towns of Judah. Hezekiah attempts to buy off the Assyrian ruler Sennacherib and dispatches messengers to implore help from Egypt. Sennacherib sends a large force to demand the capitulation of Jerusalem. Frantic with worry, the king sends his officials to consult with Isaiah. The latter is untroubled. Assyria despises Zion, but she has blasphemed against Zion's God, and this will be her undoing. During the campaign the Assyrian army is struck by a withering plague. The survivors retreat to Nineveh, and shortly thereafter the Assyrian monarch is assassinated by his sons. This, however, is punishment of Assyria, not vindication of Judah. Judah remains a rebellious people, whose defenses are about to come "crashing down."

Before long, Jerusalem receives a visit from a Babylonian embassy. Hezekiah attempts to placate the unwanted guests. He shows them all his possessions. Hearing of this, Isaiah caustically 'predicts' to the king that Babylon will one day seize everything from his successors. Hezekiah heaves a sigh of relief. "Après moi le deluge," he thinks to himself, and so it proved.

As a final testament Isaiah left a warning, to be inscribed in a book, that the people who rejected Yahweh were living on borrowed time. Their world would soon come crashing down around them, destroyed like a crumbling wall or smashed like an earthen pot. Those who fled would be run down, and hardly a sign would be left of their once great world.

With that ominous forecast we must leave the great prophet. Hezekiah was succeeded by an idolatrous king, by whom—according to one tradition—Isaiah was killed. This would not be surprising. Prophecy is dangerous business, and Isaiah was outspoken. The kingdom of Judah survived until the early 6th century, thanks in part to the reforms of the great king Josiah. But in the early 6th century BCE Jerusalem, its capital, was twice captured by Babylonian forces. The temple was ravaged and most of the inhabitants hauled off into captivity. For sixty years they would endure misery and humiliation until Babylon, too, met its destiny.

Deutero-Isaiah

Towards the end of the Babylonian captivity a prophetic voice arose, with a new vision of the covenantal relationship. There is no way of knowing whose voice it was, but there is no doubt about its eloquence and insight. The prophet's vision exerted profound influence over the lives and teaching of both John the Baptist and Jesus and consequently over the development of Christian doctrine. Large passages of chapters 40 and 53 were incorporated into the text of Handel's Messiah, as a result of which they have become recognizable to millions of people.

The deutero-Isaiah texts advance an image of Yahweh as comforter and redeemer, a shepherd who consoles, revives, and brings renewed joy to an errant flock, a king who will lead the captive people back to the promised land. As Lord of history the God Yahweh operates through human agency. To break the power of Babylon Yahweh raises up the Persian king Cyrus, who liberates Babylon and allows the captive Israelites to return home. But it is Yahweh alone who levels the hills, makes a pathway through the wilderness and leads the people rejoicing back to the city of Zion.

But this Yahweh is not just God of the Israelite people. The text proclaims Yahweh to be the great God of creation, Lord over all from beginning to end and from first to last. This Yahweh formed the light and created darkness. The hand of Yahweh laid the foundations of the earth and spanned the heavens, made the earth and created humanity upon it. The God Yahweh split apart Rahab (the demon of water and chaos), dried the sea, and made the depths of the sea a way for the ransomed to pass over. From a Bible-reading perspective this is Genesis and Exodus all over again, but with the difference that this is not the liturgical seven-day work of a Divine architect but the exertion of an irresistible creative drive that underlies and makes possible life on this earth. The same creator who forms light and creates darkness also makes peace and creates evil (woe/calamity). "I the Lord do all these things!" Yahweh, in other words, is beginning to be perceived as the power in charge of the cosmos.

As well as being the universal creator-destroyer, Yahweh is upheld as the one and only God. This is one of the most striking themes in this portion of the Isaiah text. There are no other gods. There are only idols, and they are lifeless, ludicrous, objects of wood and metal, fit only to be derided. The God Yahweh, by contrast, is the great creator and originator of everything that happens. This God does not dwell in the temple at Jerusalem but high upon the circle of the earth. The tent of this God is the heavens themselves. From this vast perspective, the inhabitants of the earth appear as mere specks. This is a God who reduces princes to nothing, and who makes the judges of the earth "as vanity". The God Yahweh is the God of all the nations, God of the universe, and God of every living thing. In the name of the great God Yahweh the heavens shout with joy, and so do the earth, the mountains, the forests and the trees.

As the God of history Yahweh anointed the Persian king Cyrus to perform the immediate task of liberating Babylon. It did not matter that Cyrus was not aware of who named and armed him (later, in the Book of Ezra, he acknowledges Yahweh), as it is Yahweh who is the active agent, who "hath wrought and done it." But Cyrus is only a channel for a much larger and continuing historical purpose, which is to bring true justice to all the nations. This role is assigned to Israel "my servant, Jacob, whom I have chosen, the seed of Abraham my friend." These are all metaphors for the people of the covenant; they point to Yahweh's closeness to the figures of Abraham and Jacob-Israel.

More specifically, the role is assigned to a chosen servant. "Behold my servant, whom I uphold; mine elect, in whom my soul delighteth; I have put my spirit upon him." This chosen one is called to serve the cause of righteousness. Yahweh gives this servant as "a covenant of the people" and "a light of the Gentiles" (nations of the known world), to open the eyes of the blind and bring out the prisoners from the prison.

We encounter here one of the most startling and original passages in the Hebrew scriptures. There are altogether four passages describing the servant of Yahweh. Like the God Yahweh, the servant is closely associated with Israel. But in the same way that Yahweh's writ extends throughout creation, so the chosen servant is to bring Yahweh's justice to all the nations and salvation to the ends of the earth.

But unlike the imperial Cyrus, this servant is no triumphal conqueror. He is one who is despised by the nations and the servant of rulers. Yet he is attuned to Yahweh as source of being and thus endures without resistance the abuse, the insults, the spittle, which come his way. "For the Lord God will help me, therefore shall I not be confounded." In an especially lyrical passage, the text proclaims, "how beautiful upon the mountains are the feet of him that bringeth good tidings, that publisheth peace." This passage became an inspiration to the apostle Paul, and in its Pauline form it has become more widely known through one of Handel's most elegant arias. It also inspired William Blake's celebrated poem "Jerusalem", in which the poet wonders if "those feet, in ancient times" might have walked "upon England's mountains green," and imagines the holy city rising amidst the "dark, satanic mills" of a modern, industrializing nation.

Unfortunately, the profoundly introspective prophet perceives that the servant is to be despised and rejected of humans, "a man of sorrows, and acquainted with grief … We hid, as it were, our faces from him; he was despised, and we esteemed him not … He was wounded for our transgressions, he was bruised for our iniquities," brought as a lamb to the slaughter and cut off out of the land of the living—just as was said of Abel, with whose imagined life and death this passage resonates. Christians, for their part, have seen in this mournful passage a description of the sufferings of Jesus. As the King James Bible editorializes, "Christ's sufferings foretold: the prophet, complaining of incredulity, excuseth the scandal of the cross, by the benefit of his passion, and the good success thereof." That may be. Certainly, Jesus and his followers knew the book of Isaiah well enough; and it is apparent from passages in the Synoptic Gospels that his life, and especially the passion event, came to be interpreted in part as an expression of the suffering and fulfillment of the chosen servant.

But it is possible to see this passage, and the passion of Jesus, as expressions of a broader, more universal meaning. For example, it is hardly possible to view the carnage of the Nazi concentration camps during World War II, the multitudes of abandoned corpses and charred bones found by the allied armies, and the gas chambers and crematoria which swallowed up six million people, without recalling, in sorrow and despair, this truly prophetic vision. "We hid, as it were, our faces from 'him'." Just so. And it was not just the Nazis, or the German people, who did that, but all those who knew about the destruction of the European Jews and other subject peoples and did not raise their voices against it. "He was despised, and we esteemed him not." True. "He was wounded for our transgressions." Only the blind and deaf could deny it. Prevarication and blindness helped then, and helps now, to condone persecution of others. "He was cut off out of the land of the living." It would be hard to imagine a more accurate, if terse, description of what happens when people are enslaved and robbed of their humanity. Isolated in prisons or camps or doomed cities, or in other ways rendered invisible (e.g. in ghettos, reservations, institutions of captivity, or jungle and desert encampments), they are left—as the prophet puts it—to be stricken, and to make their "grave with the wicked." The 20th century world has known about such ethnic and racial cleansing only too well, and in Dafur, Syria and Yemen it continues mercilessly to the present time. When we consider how this has happened across the world, we can hardly doubt that we are in the presence here of a universal trauma.

Another universal trauma, repeatedly addressed in the book of Isaiah, is that of oppression and abuse of the poor. This is a problem that remains largely invisible to the affluent, except on the occasions when famine consumes large areas, as in Ethiopia and Somalia, in such a way as to undermine political stability. By contrast, during 1958-1962 up to 40 million or more people died of starvation in a much greater human-induced famine in China, without the rest of the world becoming generally aware of it. Although the rate of childhood deaths has significantly declined since the year 2000, the World Health Organization reported that 5.9 million children under the age of five died in 2015 as a result of malnutrition and preventable diseases. Millions of others grow up starved of nutrition by parasites and intestinal infections. This is suffering on a global scale that goes on every day, every year, without cease—and yet remains a low-level priority in the policy framework of prosperous regions.

There is a tendency among some influential groups in the affluent world to regard this problem of individual and global poverty as beyond control—or even a necessary consequence of inner city or developing world mismanagement or wrongdoing. That is not the perspective of the book of Isaiah. When the poor are hungry and parched with thirst, the God of Isaiah will not forsake them. The God Yahweh is proclaimed to be a refuge for the poor and a strength to the needy in distress. The mission of the prophet is to bring good news to the poor. The responsibility of the favored is to share their bread and their homes with the dispossessed. For the poor, the captive, and the afflicted, are Yahweh's special concern. Yahweh's beloved servant, a "man of sorrows and acquainted with grief," takes on the suffering of the oppressed to enable their redemption. And woe betide those who oppress the poor! The just ruler will declare in favor of the poor and will in due course strike down and destroy their oppressors.

In short, the suffering servant is, in ways beyond our comprehension, working out the will of Yahweh. "By his knowledge," says the text, "shall my righteous servant justify (i.e. bring justice to) many; for he shall bear their iniquities." Through this kind of intentional surrender to divine will a great purging happens. Yahweh returns, to make an everlasting covenant. The servant people of deutero-Isaiah become a leader to the nations, a witness to the coming of the God Yahweh, "the God of the whole earth." A beautiful new Jerusalem will be created. The peoples "shall go out with joy and be led forth with peace: the mountains and the hills shall break forth before you into singing, and all the trees of the field shall clap their hands." It is a marvelous epiphany, made more profound by the image of nature modeling for humans the ways of joy and redemption. There are indeed new awakenings in human consciousness; and they are not cyclical, as with those of the fertility gods, or terminal, as with the flood myths, but historical, brought about through human suffering and redemption.

Other Exilic and Post-exilic Oracles

There remain sequences of highly charged passages throughout the book of Isaiah, including the last eleven chapters, which add to the profile of Yahweh as both an avenging and redeeming God. They include passages that savagely denounce Babylon and other oppressive regimes, as well as other passages that describe in apocalyptic terms the trauma brought upon the earth by human transgression. These latter passages depict an earth that is ravaged, defiled and consumed by a curse because its inhabitants have broken the everlasting covenant. The inhabitants themselves are burned, leaving few behind, but the poor earth also breaks apart, reeling to and fro like a drunkard. These are troubling passages; should the earth really have to suffer for the wrongdoing of its human inhabitants? But as we know from one human-induced disaster after another, that is what happens.

Yet the God who inflicts vengeance on the earth also strives to redress human corruption, to be a strength to the needy and a refuge from the storm. We are offered a picture of Yahweh, atop the mountain, preparing a banquet for all the peoples. On this mountain Yahweh swallows up death in victory, removes the veil of mourning covering all people, wipes the tears from every cheek, and lifts away the people's shame.

This imagery of Yahweh as God of salvation helped to sustain the captive Israelites through the long period of exile. At night, when the prophet's soul longed for Yahweh, there came visions of Yahweh's justice returning to earth. Humans had not wrought any deliverance on the earth, but with Yahweh it was different. When Yahweh returns, the eyes of the blind are opened, the lame leap like harts, and the desert is restored to life. A highway is provided, called the Way of Holiness. Along it passes the ransomed remnant of Yahweh's people, marching to Zion with songs and everlasting joy; and sorrow and sighing flee away. Let us note that this is an earth-based redemption. It is described by someone who understands deeply what it means, and how it feels, to be liberated from death and oppression and restored to a life of unity with the divine. In the words of a great nineteenth century Danish/English hymn,

> Through the night of doubt and sorrow
> Onward goes the pilgrim band,
> Singing songs of expectation,
> Marching to the Promised Land.

So, Jerusalem was rebuilt, and Zion was restored. The temple rose again, and the cultic sacrifices and liturgies were once again observed. But with the revival of contrite hearts came the revival of empty observance and the recrudescence of self-indulgence and idolatry. The text is compelled to address the subject of true atonement and fasting. True fasting: "Is it not to deal thy bread to the hungry, and that thou bring the poor that are afflicted to thy house?" Redemption is not achieved merely in order to renew cultic rites. The book of Isaiah is quite insistent that a fundamental ethic of serving needy people underlies the covenant. If you remove the yoke of oppression, draw out your soul to the hungry, and relieve the afflicted, then not only will your light arise but the God Yahweh will guide you continually. Sin is folly, because it drives Yahweh away. Darkness descends, and we stumble as if we had no eyes. "We look for judgment (justice), but there is none; for salvation, but it is far off." But Yahweh is a covenanting God and cannot indefinitely endure the oppression of God's people. Yahweh anoints the prophet and sends him to bring good news to the poor, to proclaim liberty to the captives, and to comfort all who mourn. From this concern for downtrodden human beings arises the image of Yahweh as a father-parent who cannot bear to see children suffering, and who must surely return to succor the people.

And with the return of this divine glory comes an ecstatic vision of Yahweh creating "new heavens and a new earth." The past is laid to rest and a vision beckons of a new Jerusalem, where there is joy and happiness and long life. But, as the text reminds us, the true temple of the Lord is the universe itself. Yahweh comes in fire, in chariots like a whirlwind, to gather the peoples of every language to see the glory of God. Others will go out and proclaim the glory of Yahweh to the nations. All humanity will come to worship Yahweh; and those who rebelled against Yahweh will become abhorrent to all who see them.

Commentary

There is much to reflect on in the book of Isaiah. Concern for the poor and a keen sense of justice pervade the text and give it much of its moral and spiritual force. This prophetic tradition is not just fired up by corruption and criminality. It embodies an ardent commitment to justice and a vivid expression of how justice, and a just society, is attained. Since the Isaian view is anchored in the Yahwist covenant, the prophetic explanation is based on that covenant. True justice comes from Yahweh and Yahweh's covenant, and from no one and nowhere else.

For a secular, rational consciousness, this conviction may sound jarringly otherworldly. In the secular world of modern democracy, justice is supposed to be secured by the law; and if democracies believe in anything, it is in the rule of law. Common law was developed and defended often in defiance of religiously sanctioned authority. It is built up on an accumulation of precedent and an understanding of what works in a social and political context. This seems a far cry from directly received revelation and puts the prophetic view at odds with the secular experience of law and justice. Can the two be reconciled, or is the prophetic view functioning on an ideal and impractical level?

A reading of the Isaiah discourse, as well as that of the other later prophets, would suggest that we approach this problem by recognizing that secular justice is itself an ethical and moral ideal. Full achievement of justice has not yet been attained in any secular context and is practically speaking beyond the grasp of human society. Does that mean that justice can only be achieved through divine intervention? The prophetic tradition is not arguing for intervention so much as for covenant: an agreement between humans and the Yahwist Deity as to the nature of the just society, and the means by which it can be achieved and maintained. Furthermore, the tradition argues that agreement about justice is the goal of divine-human discourse. The text of Isaiah is concerned first and foremost with social and moral order. Everything else is derivative, including international relations, physical defense, cultic observance, or accumulation of wealth. None of these activities, so ardently pursued by secular culture—and by some faith cultures as well—are considered viable where justice is missing. Only justice produces peace, and the only peace worth having is one produced through justice.

Another insistent theme in the book of Isaiah and the prophetic tradition is the problem of idolatry. What is it that so swiftly drives human society away from covenantal justice towards the more familiar terrain associated with the non-Yahwist cults? To be sure, such phenomena are tangible and recurrent, while justice and history are abstractions, dependent on memory and moral vision. Israel's Yahweh is invisible, and can only be observed in history, or through prophetic insight and revelation. Ordinary human beings need something more tangible, something which they can see and touch and feel, or which can satisfy the desire for material power or for economic security. This is the need that Aaron tried to satisfy, when he was said to have fashioned the golden calf.

But, as the Deuteronomic and prophetic traditions remind us, it is state power itself that is the principle source of idolatry. In the context of Israelite history, it is the rulers of the kingdoms of Israel and Judah (acting sometimes under the influence of spouses, who bring to the marriage their own cultic systems) who refurbish the totems, the gardens, and the high places, and who fashion the golden calves, through which idolatry can be cultivated. In the twentieth century it is easy enough to see how all this make-belief flourished in such bastions of state idolatry as Nazi Germany or Stalinist Russia, but harder—at least for inhabitants of the West—to see how it works in the so-called liberal democracies. It would not be a good idea, however, to assume that idolatry is not fostered by democracy. It is at its most graphic in media advertising, which lives and feeds on idolatry. But idolatry, in the prophetic meaning of dependence on non-Yahwist, materialist security systems, pervades democratic politics. Students of

John Watt

Biblical prophecy should hardly be surprised at this, as the prophetic tradition warns us that idolatry flourishes exactly where it might be least expected—in the heartland of the covenantal body politic.

And yet the text insists that all idolatry is fundamentally ludicrous and will get us nowhere. As the prophetic perspective evolves, it arrives at a point where idols are seen for what they are: mere bits of wood and metal, all image and no substance. There is only one divine reality in the universe. This divine reality is both transcendent and immanent. It is transcendent in that Yahweh combines the powers of creation and mercy with the powers of vengeance and destruction. Human consciousness returns to monotheism, but now it is a global monotheism, which demands that humans take account of their moral acts. It is immanent in that cultic observance gives way to introspection and surrender—and to what Jeremiah calls the covenant of the heart. This is the vision that still lies ready for us as we go about our daily business.

There is much more of interest that could be extracted from the book of Isaiah. It is one of the world's great literary masterpieces, full of powerful and lyrical poetic passages, and with an exceptional insight into human weakness. The Isaiah prophets have seen it all: greed, fear, hypocrisy, cowardly ambivalence, oppression, cruelty, alcoholism, self-destruction, and the heartache of captivity and isolation. They have also seen the earth suffering in torment, as human society drove itself towards destruction.

But they saw something else too: the possibility of redemption even amidst decay and disaster. The God of Israel is not merely a jealous overlord, threatening destruction to disobedient vassals, or an almighty power able to destroy what it has created. No: Yahweh is also a redeemer and savior, concerned to restore justice and peace to a broken world. In the text of Isaiah Yahweh is imagined as a shepherd, a bridegroom, a father, also as a woman in labor, as one who suckles her children, and as one who carries them since their birth. Amidst all the dramatic oracles condemning human depravity, it is possible to miss these nurturing images. But it is the image of Yahweh as nurturer, and as one who suffers along with humans, which sustains the prophets in times of crisis.

Above all, Yahweh is the God of history, who intervenes to restore justice and a world of peace and equity. This is the good news that the prophets tell us. Redemption from blindness or captivity is always possible and does in fact happen, once humans reconnect themselves to the divine power of justice and mercy. Redemption brings the Israelite pilgrim band out from the darkness of Babylon and the long night of doubt and sorrow, and back along the sacred way towards Jerusalem and the promised land. Redemption relieves the sorrow of oppression and puts in its place the joy of renewal. Redemption makes possible the reconstruction of Jerusalem on this earth and the possibility of extending Yahwist justice to other nations.

If, then, we shift our sights from the material to the spiritual plane, we too, might see a vision of a new Jerusalem, and a radiant power coming in chariots of fire to bring redemption to a suffering humanity. Thus inspired, we might even, like the visionary poet William Blake, see a way to building the new Jerusalem among the dark Satanic mills of our own times.

CHAPTER 8

The Individual and Covenant in the Psalms

I mean to sing to Yahweh all my life
I mean to play for my God as long as I live
Psalm 104, Jerusalem Bible

The world evoked in the Psalms

The psalms were originally the liturgical hymns of the people of Israel. Like all hymns they served a variety of human aspirations and needs, ranging from adoration of Yahweh to expressions of despair, anguish, shame and hope. Several of the psalms commemorate key moments in Israel's history, among them the Creation, the covenant with Abraham, the Exodus from Egypt and the covenant with the children of Israel, the Davidic covenant, and the exile in Babylon. Others are associated with liturgical festivals, or with Zion, the holy place that became the city and habitation on earth of Yahweh.

Important as the cultic features are, it is the theology and ethics of the psalms, and their ability to express the depths and heights of human experience, which should attract our attention. The great interest of the psalms today is in their understanding of what it means to be human. In them one can find expressed a wonder and awe for the beauty of creation and holiness, thanksgiving for relief from suffering, anguish over the success of oppressors, and a deeper anguish and contrition over one's own personal failings. The psalm writers are acutely aware of the fragility of human existence: its fleeting nature, its ambiguity, and above all the dependence of human beings on spiritual succor and friendship.

In the psalms Yahweh is the focal point of human utterance. It is to Yahweh that human beings confess their failings, their contrition, their pain, their hope for salvation, and their joy in being in the presence of the divine. It is to Yahweh that appeals for help and denunciations against enemies are addressed. And it is from Yahweh or Yahweh as creator God, who is slow to anger and full of mercy, that the protagonists or 'I-voices' anticipate forgiveness, relief, and the strength to overcome all difficulties. Some of this language draws on ceremonial formulas long used in appealing to divine authority for help against opponents. Some of it reflects the formal, liturgical expression of congregations in worship, in which individuals merge their personal concerns with the concerns of the group, which are presented to the Deity by an intercessor.

The association of many of the psalms with king David reminds us of the function of the psalms in expressing the establishment of the Davidic monarchy (in the course of which David triumphs over enemies and adversity), and the role of that monarchy in maintaining the Yahwist covenant. In certain respects, the psalms function as propaganda literature, proclaiming the virtue and empowerment of the Davidic monarchy and calling on Yahweh to honor the Divine commitment to uphold and safeguard it. As the Davidic kingdom of Judah was throughout almost all of its history very small in size and vulnerable to the aggressive policies of its larger neighbors, one can imagine the singing of these psalms as taking on a certain urgency, in much the same way that a national anthem, such as Britain's, which calls on God to "save our gracious king/queen", took on new corporate and personal meaning during the 20th century world wars.

Indeed, the world of the psalms is a harsh, dangerous world, swarming with enemies and awash with wicked, oppressive forces. In this respect it is surprisingly contemporaneous and familiar. Too often in this psalmic world the law of the jungle prevails over the law of the covenant. Yahweh's 'law' is ignored, and human greed and oppressiveness prevail. In such a world strong, aggressive people flourish, while the weaker ones sink to the bottom. This theme is also explored in the book of Job. Reading the psalms, one cannot help noticing that there is an almost obsessive preoccupation with wickedness and hostile forces, and an almost overwhelming desire to call in Yahweh/God to redress human wrongdoing. Yahweh is sometimes reproached for turning away the divine countenance and refusing to listen to the purgatory of existence on this earth. At times it seems as if there is no hope of salvation. Evil people will flourish, enemies will prevail, and the unfortunate victims of their oppression will die in vain. Sometimes the exasperated victim even cries out to Yahweh to "wake up!" But generally, there is the expectation that Yahweh's justice will prevail. Moved by this belief, the psalms appeal to Yahweh to overwhelm and destroy the opposition, so that justice and divine law can be reestablished on this earth.

To the modern Western reader some of this anathema against enemies and persecutors might seem a little tiresome. Since the Enlightenment era we have been used to a more nuanced and hopeful environment, in which enemies and friends are not always so clear-cut, and in which the object of life is to chart a course of progress and, where necessary, of compromise. Even today there is still an undercurrent of belief in the modern West that well-intended human agency can generally find a way around problems in human circumstances, thus resulting in progress for all and a general lifting of the body politic. But throughout the twentieth century this progressive bent has been battered by ideologies of greed and destruction, and it is once again under assault. Thus, we should not be surprised that it is not reflected in the psalms. Although the individual may accept responsibility for personal or corporate wrongdoing, and believe in hope of redemption for self, that hope is not extended to others who have fallen into iniquity. Unless they too plead to Yahweh for forgiveness and deliverance, they are doomed. There is no attempt in the psalms to negotiate on behalf of others, and there is no interceding for one's oppressor or out and out enemy.

No doubt this reflects the exigencies of covenantal history. People outside the covenant, who worshipped other gods, could not be reached through appeals to Yahweh. Not that the covenant is a closed system. The God of Israel, as depicted in the psalms, is creator of the universe and ruler of all nations. But those who worship idols—whether within or outside the land of the covenant—reject this premise and therefore reject the covenant that is the only guarantee of justice. Outside powers are liable to be hostile and predatory, and quite capable of overthrowing the Davidic monarchy and driving its people into captivity. History justified the revulsion towards enemies that is so conspicuous a theme in the psalms.

But of much greater concern for us as individuals is the corruption within the covenant, the interior decay that causes Yahweh to avert the divine countenance and ultimately to bring down destruction on Israel/Judah. This is the signal danger to which the psalms draw attention. The people of the covenant are themselves prone to corruption; and within the corruption of the people lies the corruption of individuals. This ethical focus on the I-voice is fundamental to the psalms. The individual, whether as corporate representative or as congregational member, is responsible not just for self but also for the collective security. Thus, every individual bears the responsibility to remember the history of Yahweh's mercy, to seek repentance, and to observe the law. Sung in the congregation, the psalms join individuals together in expression of this commitment to preserve self and people.

At heart the psalms recognize that the individual's existence is unique. One exists as a complete actor in oneself, and one stands or falls on one's own ethical and spiritual consciousness. This means that individuals are fundamentally free—if they so choose—to seek and find a personal relationship with Yahweh and to make this the anchor of their existence. The pathway to such a relationship is through observance of Torah, a message that is conveyed in the long acrostic psalm 119. But the psalms also express the conviction that the individual can appeal directly to Yahweh. To the individual who seeks a direct relationship Yahweh will listen. If one has failed in some way or fallen on hard times, all is not lost. The God Yahweh who made the universe is a caring Deity. Humans are broken, but recognition of one's brokenness brings the individual into a state of consciousness that is open to divine healing.

This awareness of human brokenness is a central theme of the psalms. It takes the individual beyond confession of wrongdoing to an understanding that human existence is damaged and yet is accessible to Yahweh's healing and salvation. It is through brokenness that individuals do wrong. Thus, confession functions less as an admission of wrongdoing and more as recognition of incapacitation. If I merely admit to wrongdoing I may be forgiven—or punished—for what I did wrong, without that process in any way transforming my consciousness. I remain a wrongdoer, viewed as such, and trapped in a cat and mouse game. There is no salvation in this route, and in fact it is one that merely functions to hold people down, not lift them up. It is one of the ironies of Western civilization that despite its supposed adherence to Biblical tradition, normative systems such as schools, courts of justice, and legislatures, have preferred to base themselves on establishment of guilt and infliction of punishment, rather than on a recognition of the human brokenness and incapacitation that is common to all. Partly that is because of a need to protect life, limb and property. But it also reflects the Augustinian Christian judgment, reinforced by centuries of theology and social practice, that human beings are born sinful. Those who contravene the law fracture the covenant that binds the people to God. They are therefore legitimate targets of condemnation and punishment, because they committed the sin of defying God's justice. But if I am broken to begin with, and you are too, what I and you basically need is not punishment but forgiveness and healing. I need that transformation of consciousness through which I can face the Divine with dignity, aware that I am an expression of God's intention in creating life.

We have here an expression of the theme of Yahweh as redeemer and recreator, transferred from the collective historical consciousness of the Exodus to the realm of individual consciousness within the collective identity. Individuation is the other side of the coin of collective consciousness. Just as collective consciousness preserves the experience of liberation achieved through the Exodus, and brings the collective into relationship with Yahweh, individual consciousness awakens memory of the God of Abraham, Isaac and Jacob who is also the God of Sarah, Rebecca, Leah and Rachel, and brings the individual into relationship with Yahweh. Redemption and restoration of the individual is one of the central concerns of the psalms. Development of spiritual consciousness enables the individual to survive pain and loss and enter a "secret" world of what the psalms call the "beauty of holiness." It is a world in which the poor are comforted and the meek inherit the earth. Yahweh's justice prevails, and the sounds of glory, praise, and salvation ring out.

In positing this alternative, salvational world order, the psalms do not suggest that it is in any way imminent. In that sense they are not eschatological texts in the way that the books of Daniel, Revelation, or even large sections of the Gospels and the apostle Paul's letters are. The alternative world of the psalms, from which the wicked are excluded, is achieved internally; its potential is always before and around us. However, the opposite possibility—of individual and collective disaster—is also always before us. That is because the psalms reflect the memory not only of the liberation from Egyptian captivity but also of subsequent defeat, destruction and exile in Babylon. Thus, the human condition, as experienced and reviewed in the psalms, combines the possibilities of both interior peace and joy and exterior chaos and loss.

Commentary on Individual Psalms

To illustrate these complex themes in a more tactile way, let us look at some of the better-known psalms in which they are explored. Psalm 1 sets out the basic idea that there are two ways: the way of Justice, which is "like a tree planted by the rivers of water" (an image used also by Jeremiah); and the way of the ungodly, which will perish. This idea of two totally contrasting ways runs throughout the collection. Psalm 2, made famous by Handel's Messiah, derides the way of the heathen and champions the king of Zion as Yahweh's ruler on earth. Its assumed messianic imagery was much drawn on by Christian writers. Psalm 6 is a simple appeal to Yahweh for mercy and help from someone experiencing oppression and clamoring for redress, such as Job, but without the theological sophistication expressed in Job. It is the first of a group of penitential psalms expressing the anguish of an abandoned soul at the mercy of enemies. Psalm 8 is a wonderful hymn about creation, praising Yahweh's way of righteousness, in which humans are "crowned with glory and honor" and given dominion over Yahweh's world. Psalm 18, encountered in the story of King David, is a song of deliverance from harm, witnessing to Yahweh's intervention in history and protection of those who give Yahweh their trust. Psalm 19, which praises Yahweh's law, ends with one of the most frequently cited Biblical prayers:

> Let the words of my lips and the meditations of our hearts
> Be now and always acceptable in thy sight
> O Lord, our Strength and our Redeemer.

(note: "O Lord" is the King James Bible's way of referring to Yahweh).

Psalm 22 strikes a darker note. The first lines are the words Jesus is reported to have cried out as he was breathing his last. "My God, my God, why hast thou forsaken me?" It comes in Matthew's version of the crucifixion. If one has heard Bach's setting of those despairing words in his Passion According to Saint Matthew it is hard to forget the haunting, almost heart-breaking cadences in the music. Another verse contributes to a memorable chorus in Handel's Messiah. The anguish of desertion in this psalm is acute. Christians have understandably assumed that in calling it out Jesus was giving voice to his own despair. But there is another equally important side to the psalm, indicating that when the afflicted one cried out, Yahweh hears. Because of this Divine hearing, the poor will be nourished and the whole world will return to Yahweh, "the ruler of nations." (Jerusalem Bible).

Psalm 23 needs little introduction, as it is one of the world's most famous and often cited texts. Numerous metrical versions exist, among them the lilting, seventeenth century Scottish hymn:

> The Lord's my shepherd, I'll not want,
> He makes me down to lie.
> In pastures green he feedeth me,
> The quiet waters by.

It is a song of personal deliverance and thanksgiving to Yahweh and is the inspiration for several modern hymns.

Psalm 24 is another eloquent and often cited hymn of praise. Psalm 25 traverses the problem of human transgression, and the dependence of the individual on divine mercy. "For thy name's sake, O Lord," cries out the I-voice, "pardon mine iniquity, for it is great." The text goes on, in wisdom fashion, to explore the change in consciousness that comes with fear of the Lord. Those who do so will dwell at ease. The "secret of the Lord," and Yahweh's covenant, will be with them. Psalm 30 introduces the very important theme of healing and makes the memorable observation that while crying may endure for a night, "joy cometh in the morning." Keeping watch through the dark night for the return of the light of day is an expression of faith, in psalmist theology, that dawn brings renewal of Yahwist grace.

Several psalms follow that recall the experience of David while he was living on the run. In psalm 31 Yahweh provides shelter to one surrounded by enemies. In psalm 32 Yahweh forgives the one who confesses a fault. Yahweh provides a hiding place and surrounds the penitent with songs of deliverance. In psalm 33 the virtuous ones "sing a new song" in Yahweh's honor and proclaim that Yahweh's love fills the earth. Psalm 34 is a great liturgical song of praise, in which the congregation cries out "I will praise Yahweh at all times … Proclaim with me the greatness of Yahweh … The angel of Yahweh pitches camp around those who fear (revere) him … How good Yahweh is—only taste and see!" (Jerusalem Bible) Enfolded in this aura of Yahweh consciousness, the people commit to practice good and seek peace. They learn that Yahweh is near to the brokenhearted and ransoms the souls of those who serve him.

Psalm 37 strikes a new note by encouraging downhearted people not to fret about evildoers. Trust in Yahweh, it advises, and do good. Cease from anger and forsake wrath. For evildoers shall be cut off, and "the meek shall inherit the earth." For those who let themselves become overly angered by wrongdoing, this is uncommonly valuable advice. It is also a thoroughly Biblical perspective. Leave judgment to God. It is pointless to obsess over the wrongdoing of others. The point is to be able to act oneself to bring compassion and healing into this world. The God Yahweh, the text assures, will not forsake those who show mercy and who are generous towards others.

Psalm 38 expresses sorrow and penitence in acute and graphic terms. The I-voice, vilely diseased and groaning with pain and fear, begs Yahweh not to be abandoned to those who would hurt and oppress for no reason. Psalm 39, which Brahms chose for his Requiem to express the anguish of facing death, addresses some of the same themes voiced by Job. "Do not make me the butt of idiots … Lay your scourge aside … Do not stay deaf to my crying." It introduces the metaphor of the individual human being as Yahweh's guest, a puff of wind, a shadow, a nomad. "Let me draw breath," pleads the I-voice, "before I go away and am no more." [Texts from Jerusalem Bible]. Psalm 40 expresses with great eloquence the hope and assurance of salvation. For those who have sunk into depression and despair, it is one of the great texts of deliverance and rejoicing. Right next to it comes another psalm about sickness and loneliness, reminding one that human existence can swing back and forth from abundance to misfortune. On this note of ambiguity, the first book of the psalms ends.

The second book introduces a famous psalm of exile (No. 42), which was used by the early Christian church as a baptismal chant ushering in the new life. It begins with one of the most striking images in the Bible. As a hart pants after streams of water, "so pants my soul after thee, O God!" My soul, says the I-voice, thirsts for God, for the living God. Just thinking about worshiping in the wonderful house of Yahweh, with the sounds of joy and praise on all sides, makes my soul melt within me. (Jerusalem Bible) The aching, crying soul turns to Yahweh, like deep calling to deep. "Why," it pleads, "hast thou forgotten me?" The enemy taunts, the soul is downcast. But hope is still in Yahweh, "for I shall yet praise him, who is the health of my countenance." The psalm became the subject of one of Felix Mendelssohn's characteristically melodious and spirited anthems.

By contrast, Psalm 44 introduces us—following the successes under Moses and Joshua—to a time of inexplicable crisis and defeat. Even though the people believe they are adhering to the covenant, the deity is simply not present to avert disaster. The people are being massacred all day long liked sheep led to slaughter. In despair they cry, "wake up Lord! Why are you asleep?" (From Jerusalem Bible)

In Psalm 46 hope turns to assurance. This psalm is another great text, full of rich metaphor and poetry, giving the people assurance of Yahweh's strength and help in trouble. It dwells on a frequent metaphor in the psalms, of Yahweh as our refuge, "a very present help in trouble." Therefore, we will not fear, though the earth be moved, and the mountains carried into the midst of the sea. Transported by this vision of Yahweh's power, the protagonist hears a voice proclaim, "Be still and know that I am God." This is a summons to live fully in the present, the dimension of the divine and the key to divine consciousness. It is consciousness of the divine as source of life that reverberates through the text. The psalm became the inspiration of one of Luther's most stirring anthems, "A Mighty Fortress is our God."

In Psalm 51 we enter deep into the experience of sin and brokenness, and the great desire of the individual to be released from this predicament. This is not a psalm to be passed over lightly. It expresses the anguish that comes with consciousness of our own shortcoming. The psalm reminds us that it is painful to be fully alive. We all carry such pain, and we need to acknowledge it in order to come to peace with ourselves and the world. To live is to confront this existential fault line. But the psalm makes the strong assertion that Yahweh desires inner truth and will enable the individual to find it. It is this process, rather than sacrifice and outward observance, which lightens and delivers heart and mind. This psalm is one of the greatest Biblical texts of healing and is a profound meditation on the human condition. It contains some beautiful liturgical passages.

Several psalms follow in which the I-voice again experiences great danger and a sense of almost intolerable abandonment. "Deliver me from mine enemies ... save me from bloody men," cries the I-voice in Psalm 59. In Psalm 61: "hear my cry, O God ... from the end of the earth will I cry unto thee ... for thou hast been a shelter for me." In Psalm 63 there is a moment of respite "when I remember thee upon my bed and meditate on thee in the night watches, because thou hast been my help ..." But in Psalm 64 the voice is once again calling on God "to protect me from this frightening enemy ... from this mob of evil men." (Jerusalem Bible) In such passages one again hears the voice of David, during the time when he was being hunted in the wilderness by the vengeful King Saul, who feared that David would usurp the throne from his descendants. In this predicament David learned to put his trust unequivocally in the God Yahweh, "my refuge ... strong tower ... shelter ... rock ... and fortress." But more: the fugitive learns to experience the deity not just as a military strongman but as an all-encompassing source of love, help, and joy. "Your love is better than life itself," says this protected soul. "All my life I will bless you." (Jerusalem Bible) It was in this spirit of profound assurance that Bach wrote his transcendent choral prelude "I call to Thee (Ich ruf zu Dir)."

On a lighter note Psalm 67 is a short but wonderful song of praise, written to celebrate the harvest. Psalm 69, however, is another extended exploration of the human predicament. "Save me, O God," it begins, "for the waters are come in unto my soul. I sink into a deep mire ..." (Modern translations substitute 'neck' for 'soul', presenting in some ways an even more despairing image). "I am weary of my crying," the text goes on. "My throat is dried, mine eyes fail ... Shame hath covered my face. I am become a stranger unto my brethren." Rejected by humans, and fasting and dressed in rags, the protagonist beseeches Yahweh "in the multitude of thy mercy hear me ... Draw nigh unto my soul and redeem it." The psalm goes on to curse oppressors roundly and explicitly. This clears the air and enables the speaker to end with the comfort of knowing that "the Lord heareth the poor and despiseth not his prisoners."

Following this cry for help, the next two psalms urge Yahweh to make haste to help the oppressed. Psalm 71, subtitled "an old man's prayer" by the Jerusalem Bible, describes how an old man, redeemed from the depths of the earth, gives thanks to Yahweh, saying "My lips shall greatly rejoice when I sing unto thee." The early 20th century Presbyterian minister, Henry Van Dyke, was inspired by these words to write his hymn "Joyful, Joyful we adore thee," to be sung to Beethoven's famous theme from the last movement of his ninth symphony. This hymn, in turn, became the inspiration for the wildly successful gospel version of Joyful, Joyful, once sung by a teenage choir led by Whoopy Goldberg and featuring Lauryn Hill in Sister, Act 2. How remarkable that the words of a tired old man, living 2,500 years ago, could be transformed into a paean of joy sung and danced by young people alive today.

Psalm 73, which begins the third book of the Psalter, is a useful text for those, such as the present writer, who have spent much too much time fretting over the prosperity of greedy and exploitative people and not enough on giving praise for being alive. After mulling obsessively over the sins of others, the protagonist finally enters the sanctuary of Yahweh, where all suddenly becomes clear. "Then understood I their end!" Probably those people familiar with the law of karma would have less trouble grappling with the problem explored in this psalm than those who worry that everything that happens must happen within one lifetime. From a karmic perspective, evil, greedy, bullying people may flourish today, but they are digging themselves a grave that could last for eons. The medieval European world, lacking the benefit of the doctrine of karma, depended on the universe of hell, into which all malevolent people would be dispatched when their turn came. The art of Hieronymus Bosch provides the most extended and imaginative visual treatment of this subject. His surrealist visions in The Garden of Earthly Delight depict both the absurdity of self-indulgence and its monstrous consequences. There are few visions of hell to match this in horror.

It is too bad that this imaginative perspective is so lacking in the modern mind, which has in fact created its own hells on this earth, in which people enjoying physical and/or political power have viciously persecuted and terrorized people without it. What we urgently need is for contemporary power-holders to develop a better understanding of the inferno to which they commit themselves in the act of raising their hands against other, more vulnerable human beings. Do we have to go back to Dante and Bosch, or to the great medieval poem Dies Irae (Day of Wrath) to get this vital message across? The psalms may not make this point quite as graphically as Bosch, but it is intrinsic to their outlook.

Meanwhile, the individual who becomes present to Yahweh enters a state of adoration as the Divine power reaches out and holds his or her hand. The experience is so intense that the I-voice exclaims "my flesh and my heart are pining with love." (Jerusalem Bible). This is one of the peak texts in the Psalms, inviting as it does the individual to let go of his or her obsessions and complaints and experience the rapture of undiluted love here on earth. A transformation of human consciousness occurs. The Divine power is experienced as "my heart's rock. My own, God forever." Such is the impact of the love of Yahweh when human beings open themselves to this power.

Yet in case one gets too carried away, the next Psalm is a lament on the destruction of the Temple and other shrines; the psalmist is fearful that this expresses Divine rage against the people. Several cultic psalms follow, of which two were introduced in chapter 5. Among them is a splendid pilgrimage song (psalm 84), which is the inspiration for a superbly eloquent, lyrical chorus in Brahms' German Requiem:

> How lovely is thy dwelling place, O Lord of Hosts.
> My soul longeth, yea, even fainteth, for the courts of the Lord.

The lyricism and intense feeling, so wonderfully evoked in Brahms' music, is in the words themselves and is the very essence of this psalm. Intoxicated with the beauty of this feeling, the protagonist exclaims "a day in thy courts is better than a thousand" (elsewhere). "O Lord of hosts", concludes the text, "blessed is the one that trusts in thee." One realizes, in reading such a stirring poem, what the psalms mean when they talk about the beauty of holiness. Just as there is an understanding of pain and anguish, so also there is a deeply felt expression of the blessedness and awe that arises from trust in Yahweh.

Psalm 89, the last in this third section, is an extended meditation on the majesty and faithfulness of Yahweh, now supreme ruler in the heavenly assembly. That faithfulness is manifested through Yahweh's covenant with David. Just as Yahweh is supreme heavenly ruler, David is the highest king on earth. He serves as Yahweh's viceroy, is armed with justice and righteousness, and can depend on Yahweh's will to crush his opponents. As if that was not enough, his dynasty will last forever. As a national or ethnic anthem, the psalm appears to be trumpeting the Yahweh Davidic covenant as the guarantee of Israel's future. But—and it is a very big 'but'—three quarters of the way through the psalm one discovers that Yahweh has repudiated the covenant, flung the king's crown to the ground and laid his forts in ruins. Worse, Yahweh has gone into hiding, and the victorious enemies are exultant.

Such a shocking denouement was to repeat itself again and again in the history of the children of Israel. It is a reminder of the folly of basing one's righteousness on assurance of military security. As one might conclude today, a strategy that relies on 'shock and awe' goes only so far. But why did everything fall apart? There is no direct answer in the psalm; the reader must ponder that question unaided.

Psalm 90, which begins the fourth book, lifts us out of the world of the here and now into a vision of Divine time in which human existence flashes by in an instant. The contrast between Divine and human time is profound; wisdom lies in understanding the difference. "Teach us to number our days," counsels the text, "that we may apply our hearts unto wisdom … And let the beauty of the Lord our God be upon us." This is one of several psalms that draw directly on wisdom theology. Isaac Watts, the great 18th century English hymn writer, based one of his most memorable and often sung hymns on this text ("O God, our help in ages past/ Our hope for years to come/our shelter from the stormy blast/and our eternal home"). Psalm 91 repeats the theme of God as "my refuge and fortress." In the dwelling place of God "shall no evil befall thee … for he shall give his angels charge over thee (and) they shall bear thee up in their hands." For reasons not hard to discern, this psalm is a deeply comforting text through which to wish Godspeed to someone whom one loves and may be grieving.

Psalms 95 and 100 are famous liturgical songs of praise, short, brilliant, and to the point. In Christian liturgical contexts they are often known by their Latin designations as the Venite (O Come) and the Jubilate Deo (O Be Joyful in the Lord). These are basically songs of joy, especially Psalm 100, which invites the individual to come before God's presence with a song. Singing is a way of entering fully into the present, and as we have seen, it is only by being fully and unequivocally in the present that one is able to access that which is beyond time.

We come next to two particularly powerful visions of the richness of life. Psalm 103 is a wonderful healing psalm that can stand being read many times over. The God Yahweh forgives, heals and redeems. "The Lord is merciful and gracious, slow to anger and plenteous in mercy." The days of a human being are as grass, or as a flower in the field. But Yahweh's mercy is everlasting, towards those that fear (revere) Yahweh. This psalm is about that secret consciousness of blessedness that enters the lives of those that fear Yahweh. Fear, in this context, does not mean that normal human reaction to imminent danger, but what the English poet Coleridge once called "holy dread"—a fear that sees though illusion and is natural to a consciousness of the august and radiant power of the Creator. It is the 'fear' experienced by individuals such as Abraham, Moses, and Job, who are conscious both of the overwhelming power of the divine and its creative and redeeming mercy. The psalm is a song of praise about that special quality of redemption. Like all those who experience redemption, the psalmist invites all creation, from angels and ministers down to armies and lesser beings, to bless Yahweh; but the psalm ends where it began, with an outpouring of individual thanksgiving.

Psalm 104 is another eloquent song of praise to the beauty and glory of Yahweh's creation. One cannot really do justice to this glorious poem by paraphrasing it. The text surveys the whole of known creation, from the astral bodies to the land and water and all the living things. Grass grows to nourish cattle and plants to nourish humans. There is wine that "maketh glad the heart", oil to make faces shine and bread to strengthen the body. There are trees for birds to nest in, mountains for wild goats, and rocks for the badgers. Everything has its place and purpose. Surveying all this the psalmist exclaims to Yahweh, "how manifold are thy works. In wisdom thou hast made them all: the earth is full of thy riches." All in all, the psalm is a profound meditation on the beauty and wisdom underlying the natural world in which we live.

The fifth and last book begins with a wisdom psalm, number 107, inviting the congregation to give thanks to Yahweh, whose love endures forever. The psalm surveys various examples of human folly, contrasting them with Yahweh's steadfast love and marvelous ways of rescuing those who ask for help. If you are wise, suggests the psalm, observe these things, and recognize Yahweh's loving-kindness. Psalm 110 is a messianic text that provided a locus classicus for the belief that the triumphant Messiah would sit at Yahweh's right hand. Psalm 115 is one of several cultic texts that extol the God of Israel while deriding the lifeless idols of silver and gold, on which other peoples have depended—and still do.

Psalm 116 is a song of thanksgiving to Yahweh for coming to the rescue of someone on the brink of death. This Yahweh, who listened to the entreaty of the anguished soul, is not only righteous and merciful but "tenderhearted" and a God to love with heart and soul. Here is the first great principle of Jewish salvation teaching addressed in the context of real human need. Filled with gratitude, the I-voice vows to walk in Yahweh's presence and give thanks in the presence of all Yahweh's people.

Psalm 117 voices that thanksgiving in one short verse.

> O praise the Lord, all ye nations
> Praise him all ye people,
> For his merciful kindness is great toward us,
> And the truth of the Lord endureth forever.
> Praise ye the Lord.

This short text sums up the essence of the human-divine relationship as laid out in the Psalms. It calls on all people and nations to begin and end by praising the divine, as the source of a great merciful kindness and an enduring, eternal truth. What this psalm is saying is that if one can grasp and truly enact with one's own life the act of praise, everything else begins to fall into place.

The text gave birth to one of the most inspired arias in sacred music. This is the Laudate Dominum (O praise the Lord) from Mozart's Vespers (Vesperae Solennes de Confessore). One might imagine that such a song of praise would generate triumphal, vigorous music in a declamatory key such as D major or G major. Instead, Mozart created an extraordinarily graceful meditation in F major for soprano voice with accompanying choir. It is one of his signature pieces and is from beginning to end slow, quiet, flowing, and exquisitely cadenced. Given the aria's atmosphere of thanksgiving and reverence, it is possible that Mozart had given careful thought to the message of Psalm 116 before choosing this text to voice his state of mind. Or he may just have reached a peak of spiritual awareness based on his treatment of the previous few psalms that form the body of the Vespers. In any case, what resulted is a compelling—and for this writer unforgettable—musical visualization of the Divine as embodiment of "merciful kindness", truth and blessedness. It is in recognition of these sustaining qualities that the human voice gives praise.

For Christian readers it is worth noting here that the Vespers liturgy concludes with a treatment of the Magnificat from the first chapter of Luke: "My soul doth magnify the Lord, and my spirit hath rejoiced in God my Savior," describing the feelings of adoration attributed to the young Mary, the mother-to-be of Jesus.

Let us move on to Psalm 121. This one ranks with Psalm 23 as one of the most deeply spiritual and affirming texts in the Bible. It is a very personal song of faith in the guardian of Israel. Yahweh is the divine power that does not slumber nor sleep. Yahweh preserves you from all evil; Yahweh preserves your going out and your coming in, from this time forth and for evermore. This psalm provides the inspiration for the powerful gospel anthem "Total Praise" by Richard Smallwood.

Psalm 130 is a Job-like cry for attention that is also an expression of tested and reaffirmed faith. Out of the depths have I cried for you, Yahweh; hear the voice of my supplications. If you never overlooked our sins, how could anyone survive? "But you do forgive us, and for that we revere you. (And so) I wait for Yahweh, my soul doth wait, and in Yahweh's word do I hope." (from Jerusalem and King James Bibles). What one notices so strongly in this psalm is the confident waiting of the soul that has passed through tribulation, as a watchman in the night waiting for a dawn that will come. This soul has passed from human to divine time, confident that when the time is right renewed strength will come.

Psalm 136 is another cultic text that reviews the redeeming history of the Exodus. It was made into a very fine hymn by the 17th century poet John Milton ("Let us with a gladsome mind/ praise the Lord for he is kind/ for his mercies aye endure/ ever faithful, ever sure"), of which a few brief verses are sometimes sung today. By contrast, Psalm 137 is one of the most wrenching poems in the entire collection. It is the classic lament of the exile, filled with anguished remembrance of the distant home and an understandable desire for revenge against captors.

Psalm 139 is another of those meditative texts that explores the conundrum of human existence. This psalm was very helpful to me at a time when I was almost completely adrift. The basic idea in this psalm is that God knows me through and through and is present to me wherever I go and am. No matter if I flee to the ends of the earth, "even there shall thy right hand lead me." Filled with this insight that Yahweh never rejects that which Yahweh has created, the I-voice declares, "I will praise thee, for I am fearfully and wonderfully made." What we see in this psalm is a discovery of the limits of the human ego and a recovery of God-perspective. Moved by this breakthrough in consciousness the protagonist exclaims "how precious … are thy thoughts unto me, O God! How great is the sum of them." Ah—how marvelous are the wonders of the human spirit and mind, when they are filled with God-vision! Was it just a dream? No, declares the voice. "When I am awake, I am still with thee."

The book ends with some resounding songs of praise and joy. Psalm 147 sums up much of what has passed before. The God Yahweh brings the exiles back home, heals their broken hearts and binds up their wounds. Yahweh raises up the weak and casts down the wicked. Sing praises, says the protagonist, to Yahweh, who has made the created world, and who takes pleasure in those who fear Yahweh and "rely on his love." (Jerusalem Bible) The final psalm, number 150, is a triumphal doxology of praise, drawing on all available instruments, and everything that has breath, to praise the Lord.

Commentary

As Psalm 150's trumpets and cymbals remind us, the psalms are songs that are meant to be sung. For centuries they were chanted in one way or another. In more recent times metrical versions were produced which were sung in Presbyterian churches to hymn tunes. Nowadays most protestant churches recite them antiphonally. I regret this way of reading the psalms, as it tends to reduce them to dry, disconnected texts, muttered in a shuffling undertone which skims over their poetic and liturgical power. Not that the metrical versions were necessarily an improvement. Many of them were badly done and better off forgotten. But singing or chanting the psalms, as is done in more liturgical services, reminds us that these are not mere improvised texts, put together one day to be set aside the next. They are deeply felt explorations of human experience and deserve to be treated as such, especially in liturgical settings, where the purpose is to try to access heart, soul and mind to awareness and praise of the divine.

The psalms also bring home the idea of covenant to the individual, corporate worshipper and its application of justice and mercy to the individual as well as to corporate life. One can of course study all about the covenant in the Torah; many religiously oriented Jewish people attend Torah classes year-round. Yet there is a cerebral aspect to Torah study, signaled by the extensive Rabbinic commentaries, which accompany traditional Torah texts. The psalms, through their combination of poetry and music, enable one to sense or visualize the presence of Yahweh and Yahweh's covenant in the spiritual life. That is why the Psalms should be sung with reverence, so that their intuitive power can be felt as well as understood. The psalms are particularly valuable texts for those not brought up on Torah study. As anyone knows who has listened to Psalm 23, you don't have to be Jewish to appreciate the psalms; you only need to be open to the presence of the divine.

Most of all, the psalms are written to help the individual embrace the meaning of justice and mercy and know what it is like to feel the sustaining power of Yahweh. The psalms ask each of us to function through the mediums of heart, soul and mind. Heart consciousness makes us privy to our fragility and need for divine succor, as well as to our ability to love and assist others. Soul consciousness, drawing on listening and visualization, gives us access to divine revelation and joy. Mind consciousness makes us privy to the fleeting nature of our lives, which go by, as the psalms reiterate, like a puff of wind or a summer flower, as well as to the presence of the divine that transcends the ephemeral. In order to deal with life's vicissitudes, we must first become aware of our fragility. Strength is available to us, but it is rooted in observance of the covenant and reliance on divine mercy. Externally such strength may be expressed through victory over national or personal enemies. Internally it is expressed as joy in the individual who 'fears' and trusts Yahweh as the source of deliverance.

Thus, we return to the conception of Yahweh as redeemer, whose power is accessed through empowerment of heart and soul. The hiddenness, deafness, and unconsciousness of Yahweh, so lamented in the psalms, are found to be reflections of our own lack of consciousness and fear of oblivion, which get in the way of accessing divine power. The psalms remind us that while we may go for years suffering misery or persecution, Yahweh exists as shield and refuge, with wings to protect us in our vulnerability. They also insist that we are a part of a great plan expressed in the formation and preservation of the world. Even though our physical lives are subject to calamity and brevity, the beauty and glory of life is always available to us whenever we seek it.

As for evil and wickedness, the psalms acknowledge their hold over human existence and protest fervently against those who abuse power over others. Wickedness is portrayed as a human choice, adopted by those who scorn or neglect the Yahwist world. The worst evil is the evil of those with access to the covenant of justice and mercy who turn their backs on it and spread corruption and apostasy. This hubris kindles Yahweh's wrath and abandonment of the covenant protecting the people. The way is then open to national destruction and exile and the heartache of individuals who survive such a catastrophe. As we can see from the experience of ancient Israel and Judah, the Yahwist world is not a haven against all comers. It is constantly being eaten away by interior rot. In that respect the Yahwist world of the psalms is no different from our own times, which reveal the same capacity for internal destructiveness.

But joy returns to those who put their trust in Yahweh. There remains an undercurrent of optimism running throughout the psalms that the world is at core a place of sacredness and beauty, expressed in the human context through Yahweh's power to reach out to those who cry for help. It is this core belief, and the confidence that it generates, that enable the individual to survive hardship and oppression and experience the joy of being alive.

CHAPTER 9

Covenant in the Wisdom Tradition

The Case of Job

Tell me, where does wisdom come from?
Where is understanding to be found?
Job, chapter 28

The Wisdom tradition is concerned with the consciousness and fate of the individual. It wants to know how individual trauma is to be experienced and interpreted, particularly when covenantal justice and mercy no longer suffice to ensure individual protection. One frequently expressed concern is why unscrupulous people so often seem to prosper, while others, who 'live by the rules,' may die abused and unrequited. If a person who appears to live by covenantal ethics falls on hard times, how is that to be interpreted? When justice and mercy fail to suffice as rules of conduct, are there other values accessible to human consciousness?

The author of Job refuses to accept that fate is a reflection on ethical conduct, and that what seems like bad fate equals bad conduct; therefore, a person should acknowledge whatever life deals out, because it is a consequence of his or her morality. This reductionist approach, as contemporary politics reminds us, tends to leave weak and disempowered people at the mercy of those who are strong and manipulative, so that worldly rewards end up gravitating to the latter, while the former get all the poverty and abuse. The Wisdom tradition rejects such a winner-takes-all (or takes-most) ethic as justification for what happens in human experience.

But unlike many psalms and prophetic utterances that deal with this problem, it does not assume that God will eventually 'wake up' (as in Psalms 44 or 73), see what injustice is being done, and then hammer the exploiters. Instead, it maintains that other levels of consciousness are available to guide human beings, and that these are accessible to individuals through what it calls 'wisdom' and 'understanding.' The question is how are these values gained, and in what do they consist? The author of Job explores this approach through a series of poetic dialogues that are laced with wit and satire. The book of Job is one of the great achievements of the literature of spiritual life. Its teachings are as relevant today as they were twenty-five hundred years ago.

The author approaches his theme (there is every indication from the content and form of the text that this is a male writer dealing with male problems) by making it clear that Job was a decent man, a leader in his society, one who upheld its values, worked for the common good, and enjoyed power and prosperity. Such men used to be called pillars of society, because like a pillar they upheld its structure and radiated the values of personal strength, good judgment, and worldly success.

Job was also a model citizen in worshipping Yahweh and acting to preserve Yahweh's creation. He even worshipped on behalf of his children, offering burnt offerings to protect them against any wrongdoing on their part. This information conveys the hint that Job, as a tribal leader, may have been too eager to manipulate the spiritual world—more specifically the Yahwist Court of Justice—on behalf of his family. The Satan (adversary or prosecutor in Yahweh's Court) evidently thought so. He claimed that Job's righteousness was too easily earned and untested, in fact even abetted, by Yahweh. This challenge took Yahweh by surprise. But once made, it could not be disregarded.

So, a plot was hatched to test Job's faith. In short order he was stripped of all his possessions and wealth, his servants and his children. So much for Job's dutiful sacrifices: the paragon of virtue now appeared to be sullied, impotent, and left to die without issue. When Job failed to lose faith because of these losses, the Satan obtained permission to strike him all over with boils (or malignant ulcers). Job's body became an agony to him and a source of uncleanliness and repulsion to others. He sat among the ashes mourning, while his traumatized wife yelled at him to curse God and die.

The story, however contrived, is lived often enough to call for explanation. The outward problem consists in Job's sudden, catastrophic loss of honor and power within the society to which he belongs. Externally he becomes unclean and therefore is required to live outside the security of the social structure. As a result, the man who was once an object of respect becomes a target of abuse. Internally he has lost his socially-defined power and with it his sense of honor and dignity. In addition, he has been cut off from contact—or so it seems—with what he had assumed to be the divine. His lifelines to empowerment are in danger of crumbling, and if they do, his life is doomed.

This experience of personal catastrophe sets up questions of great importance in the Wisdom tradition. From a Wisdom perspective, the world was formed out of primeval chaos through the mighty struggles of the Creator and is held together through the work of humans acting in accordance with God's covenants. What, then, happens when individuals get into trouble? Are they victims of their own making—or are they at the mercy of an eruption of disorder beyond their control? Or are they engaged in an interior journey uncharted in any existing covenant? Does the Sinai covenant truly control the acts of those who find themselves dumped outside the social order? How do individuals cast into 'outer darkness' make their way back into society? How do they survive while living in disgrace? Can they maintain their integrity without any hope of recognition? And how is such a crisis to be explained?

These are some of the objective questions. But subjectively speaking, we need to know as mortal human beings what the experience of darkness is all about, and where strength is to be found in this darkness. What is it like for an individual to live in a state of abandonment or chronic loss of integrity? Why does it happen? Why to me? What fosters our own interior darkness? What does the survivor learn from this experience, and what might we learn in that situation? Is the divine present in darkness, as well as in light, and if so how? How is one to deal with the destructive, shadow aspect not just of humans but of the divine—the aspect that can terrify and destroy what it has created? What lies beyond the human fear of the unknown and unknowable? What wisdom might accrue from the loss of normative reward and security structures?

We all know people who have fallen on hard times, and for many of us that is a personal experience. Some are expelled from their communities or countries. Others are abruptly driven from jobs and left without work, pension or health insurance. Many are evicted from their homes or thrown into prisons, labor camps, or isolation wards. Still others are victims of abandonment, violence, or self-degradation—such as millions of today's refugees—or of some indefinable yet incapacitating health problem. Beyond these instances of assumed victimization lie innumerable cases of personal turmoil and loss of vision occurring during periods of transition and disorientation.

If you have been in any of these situations, you probably found out what it is like to live outside normal society. You may have felt abandoned, deprived of power and self-respect, reviled and even in danger, and also insecure and self-blaming in your basic identity. The ordinary world of work and play goes on while you go into free fall. You become, or feel, an outsider and perhaps an outcast, an object of pity or contempt or indifference, a person who is no longer deemed necessary—or deems him or herself necessary—to keep the system going. What is worse, while you mess up, many who survive by going along with the tide, and even by exploiting and abusing others, appear to do just fine. Former friends become a burden and misery to you and may even, as in the Chinese Cultural Revolution, or the McCarthy era, become your worst persecutors.

When disaster happens to individuals who have led a wayward or antisocial existence, we don't normally express surprise. We could assume that the victims are in some way offenders and must have deserved their fate. If they got into trouble, why should we be concerned, except for their victims? The fact that millions of opportunists survive, prosper and die rich does not seem to matter so much, so long as those who fail in some way can be viewed as deficient, weak, or incompetent. The human capacity to blame those who fall on hard times is irresistible. And why not? No one is perfect, and everyone makes mistakes. If you get into trouble it shouldn't take me—or you—long to figure out reasons for your problems. People who seem to consider themselves, like Job, to be blameless are particularly prone to attack. They must be implicated in some wrongdoing or they wouldn't be in trouble; therefore, they had better stop whining and own up.

That is one reason why Job is depicted as a righteous man. The author wants to move beyond the ad hominem argument and the tendency to deal with adversity or dissent by blaming those in trouble. Blame may not always work. A person may be persecuted and oppressed for the wrong reasons. During the Chinese Cultural Revolution millions were branded as criminals and denounced as demons and ghosts, only to be rehabilitated (if they survived) ten or twenty years later when the political winds had changed. One may explain their trauma ideologically, but how is one to explain it in terms of individual conduct and hardship? At the same time the phenomena of catastrophe and blame need to be dissected from the subjective perspective. Since we all can find reasons enough for our own shortcomings and failures, what insights and options for growth in understanding do we have in times of personal crisis? Does crisis offer the option to reorient our awareness of who we are?

The argument of the Book of Job assumes that it is easier for the human conscience to find a linkage between trouble and failure in personal character than to search for explanation in what may be unfamiliar and unknown ground. When Job is battered by 'fate' and dumped out of his life of security, it is the tribally determined response that predominates. His friends and relatives desert him and parasites come and prey on him. Those friends who hang around become his greatest persecutors. But from the subjective experience of Job himself, his misery is incomprehensible. It is the challenge to find the meaning in disorder and chaos that lies at the heart of the book of Job. Wisdom seeks an explanation. What is it to be?

Three friends named Eliphaz, Bildad and Zophar, come and sit with Job, suffering with him in silence for a week. This act of mourning reflects their genuine friendship and concern. One can imagine that these good friends are wracking their brains as to what to say to their fallen friend. But no one dares to be the first to speak. Finally, the pressure to say something builds up. Job opens his mouth and, like the prophet Jeremiah, curses the day he was born. This leads to a full-scale debate about Job's crisis.

The account is divided into several parts. There is a first round of exchanges between Job and his friends. This is followed by two rounds of more heated exchanges. There is a short interlude, which explores some wisdom issues, and this is followed by Job's final peroration. But that is not the end of the matter. Job's crisis needs to be resolved before the account can come to an end.

Round One: The Moral Universe Defined

The argument, or rather the journey, begins with 'Job' wishing he had never been born and cursing the day and night that brought him forth. If only it could be swallowed up in darkness and oblivion. Would that he had died then and there. Then he would be resting in the peace of the tomb, along with rich and poor and slave and master. Why on earth give light and life to one so embittered? He feels obstructed and confused by God; his worst fears have come true.

As we see from this complaint, it is not the physical and social torment that bothers Job so much as the realization of his worst fears (Mitchell translation). His entire life is in vain; God is against him and has left him in turmoil.

Hearing this cry of anguish, his friend Eliphaz diffidently proffers advice. Innocent people are spared; it is only those who cause trouble who reap it. Despite these bland assurances Eliphaz has had a nerve-wracking vision that no human—and not even the angels—can be blameless before God. Humans are troublemakers: that is the problem. Job should appeal to God who wounds but also heals, who rescues the poor from their oppressors and the penitents from disaster and evil.

Obsessed with his own nightmares, Eliphaz does not stop to question Job about his. Of course: sin in some shape or form must lie at the core of Job's problems. Eliphaz's reply assumes that God is the source of Job's afflictions but draws on the mercifulness of the divine to show the pathway to redemption. How shocking, then, that Eliphaz's advice makes no sense to Job, because it assumes that the actor remains within a moral universe where repentance for social wrong-doing can elicit forgiveness. Job, however, has transitioned into a world of disorder, where God is experienced as enemy and a source of terror. His sense of righteousness is the only thing he still has left to protect his spirit from being crushed.

But how is Job to reach out to the divine? His friends are no use here because they are not in his predicament and see only a guilty man who needs to confess to some misconduct. Job curses his fate and echoing the language of Psalm 90 complains to God, what are mere human beings to you? Why have you made me into a target? Pardon me before I die and am gone!

Job's challenges disturb the friends. Bildad reiterates the point that God will neither cast off the upright nor embrace the godless person. But this again assumes a relationship with God that Job no longer feels. Job feels himself in a God-deprived state. He sees God as a force of overwhelming power that can crush and destroy as well as create and control the vast powers of the universe. Humans cannot compete in such a struggle. They will be crushed, whether innocent or guilty. When wicked people prevail, who lets that happen? If a decent, conscientious man like Job is accounted guilty and savagely punished, then there is no recourse. He longs for an arbiter to defend him, but there is none. He again challenges the divine: "Why do You judge me guilty when You know I am innocent? You are abetting the schemes of the wicked!" It is the cry of the oppressed for whom justice does not exist. "Let me alone", he exclaims; "I'll be gone soon enough to the land of darkness."

The author here focuses on a problem that had preoccupied the prophetic writers and the psalmists. How can the good fortune of wicked and unscrupulous people be squared with the existence of a righteous God? Evidently while Job himself flourished, he could have envisaged wealthy but unrighteous people as malefactors whom God would sooner or later deal with. But now that he himself has been cast down, the schemes of unscrupulous people no longer seem so tolerable. Their success casts the justice and mercy of the divine into doubt. The question becomes an obsession, which the protagonist must resolve before he can recover his integrity.

Meanwhile, to the friends Job's words are beginning to sound like blasphemy. Zophar turns on him. Stop your ranting, he warns, or God, who knows the worthlessness of men, will make you answer for it! How dare you vie with the Almighty? Cleanse yourself and renounce your sin, and you can still be saved.

This appeal also falls on deaf ears. From his perspective in the realm of disorder Job scornfully questions the morality of a world that sees his downfall as cause for disgrace. This is the same world in which robbers and parasites prosper. No: Job's downfall is the work of the Creator! Even animals and birds can figure that out. What is so myopic about humans? God is the author of crisis as well as order, the One who builds up nations and destroys them. Here is the prophetic image of Yahweh the Creator-destroyer, functioning not only in the cosmic context of world creation and upheaval but reaching out to touch a solitary individual.

Job now turns on his friends and rebukes them for misrepresenting God's power. The one in disgrace fires back. Feeling himself on to something Job now determines to challenge the Creator. "Hear me out", he shouts, "and don't frighten me! Why do You hide, as if I were your enemy? Why do You harass such a puny soul as me?" But soon his anguish and depression well up as he recalls the faults of his youth. The past comes back with a vengeance to haunt him. Is there anyone whose hands are clean? No, of course not. Trees survive, but man dies and that's it. Job begs for a reprieve, but there is none. God prevails and destroys the hopes of humans.

Round Two: A Vision of Horror

The story so far lets us know that Job feels abandoned by God and cannot reestablish communication. His old methods of contact with the divine are no longer working. The story also indicates that Job is mired in the past and unable to shake free from it enough to understand his situation in the present. But this is not how the friends see it. For them it is Job's behavior in the past that matters. And Job's past does not look good any longer.

Aghast at his truculence, the friends now turn up the heat on Job. Why are you so angry with God, demands the God-fearing Eliphaz? Your own words condemn you! Eliphaz paints a picture of the wicked man who defies God. He will suffer torment. A flame will wither him before his time. Vultures will eat his flesh. These scare tactics miss the mark because Job is sinking into a deeper anguish. Bereft of friends he is tormented by pain, exhausted and forsaken. God has given him over to the merciless hands of godless, mocking people and is raining blows on him. This is a development which goes far beyond the Satanic infliction of boils on Job, as recounted in the original legend, and it alerts us to the very real spiritual disorder that the author is addressing. Drawing on tribal custom,

Job pleads for his spilt blood to cry out to Heaven. But even as he does so, the relentless condemnation of well-meaning men wears him down. There is no way out except into the dead-end world of death and oblivion.

Job's friends are now beginning to feel rejected by Job! "Why attack us?" complains Bildad. He tries again to get Job to confront his 'wickedness'. Job lashes back. God has "covered my way with darkness", "stolen my honor away", and "taken the crown from my head." (Jerusalem Bible) My friends have abandoned me, my wife abhors me, even the children despise me. "Pity me, pity me", he cries out, "for the hand of God has struck me. Don't treat me as if you were God!"

These words include expression that would later be associated with the 'dark night of the soul'. Job is now experiencing the loneliness and terror which mystics report as occurring when the world of every-day illusion drops away. He is not only cut off from the security of human society but also deprived of communication with, and sustenance from, the divine. He is plunged into darkness and feels totally alone and even attacked by the very divine power on which he had once so dutifully relied.

Yet at this most disorienting of times Job continues to search for vindication. He falls back on the ancient notion of a tribal vindicator, who will avenge his loss of honor and see that justice is done. Somewhere there is such an advocate, who will come to his rescue in the divine court. Buoyed by this image of retribution, Job warns his friends not to forget their own day of reckoning; they should fear for themselves too.

And fear they do, and this drives them to intensify their attack. In greater detail than ever Zophar depicts the fate of the impious person. His crimes of greed and oppression are recounted. Such a one will disgorge everything he has consumed. He will sink into complete oblivion—just exactly what Job has feared—and heaven and earth will turn against him. This existential attack unnerves Job because it mimics so precisely his situation while completely misunderstanding what he now perceives. Job sees that truly corrupt people can flourish within the ordered, 'moral' world, particularly when that order weakens. They can even defy God and take power into their own hands. The ordered tribal world is itself a prey to disorder. Ask any traveler: monuments to evil potentates abound, and thousands mourn them when they die. This vision of evil triumphant makes a mockery of moral order and leaves Job in a state of horror.

Round Three: The Search for Wisdom

Two visions of order have been spelled out which appear to be in contradiction. In modern terms we might describe the first as a nineteenth century liberal vision of moral order, in which people believe the world to be guided and ruled by God's justice and mercy, with humans acting as divine surrogates. In such a world a social contract is established and maintained. Ethical standards are upheld, right prevails over wrong, and the integrity of the ordered, institutionalized world of human society is preserved. Wickedness and corruption are recognized as part of such a world, but such evil cannot prevail, essentially because God, aided by people of good will and devotion to right conduct and good causes, will not let it do so. God's justice is paramount, and human institutions, however imperfectly, strive towards the achievement of justice on earth. Education and law, backed by appropriate sanctions, instill this public vision of right and wrong into those inhabiting the social order. Religion acts as its ideologue and guardian. The upright person prevails over the scoundrel, and the righteous nation over the oppressor. Delinquents confess and then are punished and rehabilitated, while scoundrels are swept away into hellholes where they belong. In either case the values of the social order prevail over individual behavior. The inheritance of the past governs the present.

The alternative nightmare vision is one that re-emerged so strongly during the 20th century. In this nightmare world justice does not prevail. Nothing is stable. Even God's creation can be battered and destroyed. Human 'order' reflects the cosmic uncertainty. Evil can and does prevail over good. People corrupted by power in their thousands and millions can oppress their neighbors with immunity. More broadly, disorder can erupt without much warning. In this universe disorder mimics order and flourishes at its expense. This is the world which revealed itself to the full in the surrealist 'order' of Auschwitz, in the bombed out, terrorized cities of Europe, China and Japan, in the Stalinist purges and death camps, in the upheaval and bouleversement of the Chinese Cultural Revolution, in the annihilation inflicted by nuclear warfare, in the terrifying orderliness of the nuclear arms race, in the pitiless struggles for power in so-called 'third world' countries and territories. Under the influence of the drug culture such disordering order has taken over large areas of urban America. Ethnic cleansing in turn is 'reordering' the world in large parts of Africa, Central America, Europe, and Central Asia. Closer to home, domestic abuse seals up individuals in conditions of purgatory. These nightmare visions of entrapment, prophetically described by Franz Kafka, mock the ordered universe with their capacity to transfix human affairs.

In addition to these examples of publicly inspired disorder we have also had to acknowledge, however reluctantly, the human capacity for internalized pathology. Here we encounter nightmare visions of disease beyond the reach of modern medicine, or of internal mental disorder that defies explanation and treatment, such as the chronic depression or stress and violence commonly found among people living in modern society. In the face of radical change, the social meaning once supplied by schools, churches, cultural activities, patriotic agencies, political assemblies, and especially law courts, can no longer keep the world in focus for individuals experiencing acute personal uncertainty. Meaning dissipates; social pathology becomes individual pathology. As one set of illusions totters, others take their place. To tune into this subliminal disorder (today choreographed so cogently and brutally in rap music) is to risk the experience of radical disorientation, mental and physical exhaustion, and spiritual nihilism—of the sort that we see happening to Job.

Beyond these socially or materially-based paradigms of order and disorder is the paradigm of order associated with wisdom and understanding, that is of special consequence to the Book of Job. The author knows that such an order exists somewhere, and that it can only be accessed through abandonment of the tribally defined world of order, in which the values and institutions of the past govern life in the present. It is assumed that no one would willingly want to abandon this relatively safe and predictable environment, therefore a plot is concocted by the Divine order to eject a once valued individual out of it. We have observed the various ways in which the tribally defined order reacts to this ejection. The account has also explored what can happen when power falls into the hands of disintegrative forces capable of displacing or disregarding God and moral covenant, as well as the eventuality of God becoming deaf to entreaty or even engaged in the process of engendering disorder.

Are these latter alternatives aberrations which God, once "woken up" would clear up? Or are they rather built in to human existence, and therefore conditions with which humans must learn to contend? The author evidently realizes that humans cannot simply assume that God will come to their rescue whenever they get into trouble. From the author's perspective it is necessary to remove the structure of order from Job's situation if the search for wisdom is to go forward. To the friends' insistence that the covenantal God is no more than one phone call or confession away, the author responds that Job's personal circumstances make that proposition no longer certain, and even no longer viable. If the friends were right, God would surely heed the emergency call for help from a puny but decent human being. But God appears to be evading or directly oppressing Job—at least this is how Job experiences and reports his predicament. God may even be searching for a way to break Job from his attachment to a world governed by tradition.

But from the perspective of the three friends, who are locked into the socially determined logic of God as an all-powerful patriarchal ruler responsible for the protection of his subjects so long as they remain faithful, such a stance is blasphemous. Eliphaz, so muted at first, now rises against Job. God's judgment cannot be questioned. If Job is in a state of horror, it is a mark of his impiety and wrongdoing. Job's vision is perverse and impious, and its author is the epitome of wickedness. Eliphaz accuses him of one crime after another. "Repent!" he clamors, "and you can still be saved."

But Job is now bemused by his insights and doesn't really hear the friends any longer. What now concerns him is the disappearance of the God he thought he had always dutifully served. What has happened to that God, who had once served as Job's family insurance policy? Job searches for a response but in vain. A new fear seizes hold of him. The Creator cannot be influenced by the created and is beyond the latter's reach. Once more the specter of the world of evil rises before him. It is a Godless world of unmitigated social chaos, in which wicked and oppressive people accumulate power at the expense of those they oppress. While the poor (and disempowered) spend their days homeless and shivering from cold and hunger, thieves and rapists flourish. As we know, millions of inhabitants of slave labor camps, their abandoned relatives, and other millions of ghetto dwellers and refugees, could and do speak to this polarity.

The friends are tired out and reduced to silence. They fire off a few last whimpering blasts about God's power, but Job cuts in with a dramatic exposition of God as Master of the Universe. Another insight has come to him. If he, Job, is guilty of 'wickedness', it means that the world has been turned upside down and the truly wicked have prevailed over the innocent. Nevertheless, the innocent are innocent as long as they believe it. The body may be oppressed but the spirit can remain free. Seized with this thought, Job insists on his innocence. Let his enemies, he warns, fear for their own wickedness, for when those who wrong the divine run into trouble, why should God listen to them?

At this point in the text there is an interpolation on wisdom (chapter 28), which serves to reinforce Job's insight. Men can penetrate the uttermost depths of the world, and reach places unknown to bird or beast, yet the road to wisdom is still unknown. It is not in the land of the living, or in the abyss, or in the sea. It cannot be bought with gold or silver, or onyx or sapphire. One might add that it cannot be researched in a laboratory or found holding forth in a boardroom or other such human power centers.

"Then tell me", says the text, "where are wisdom and understanding to be found?" This is the critical question facing the individual for whom mercy and justice no longer suffice as assurance of God's presence in human affairs. Only God knows where wisdom and understanding lie. And why is that so? Because God discovered wisdom in the very act of creation, in measuring out the waters and making rules for rain and thunder. These are acts of wisdom, discovered in the act of confronting chaos, that in their grandeur brush aside the deeds of 'wicked' people and are the key to their ultimate irrelevance. The God of wisdom could say to man, what was never said to Adam:

> Wisdom is fear of the Lord;
> Understanding is avoidance of evil.

This is a simply stated proposition repeated over and over in wisdom literature. It ought to be easy enough to discern and follow; but if it had been regularly followed, there would be no need for covenants. Covenants are for the majority, for whom the journey to wisdom is too long and too frightening. But despite such difficulties the author insists that wisdom is accessible to humans. It enters the consciousness of the individual who has learned to embrace life in the act of struggling with disorder and terror. As we have seen, the germ of the idea is already in the Torah, where the holy is dangerous and to be respected at all costs. But in the Wisdom literature 'fear' of Yahweh has become a form of internally acquired consciousness, rather than a trained but uncomprehending response to life-threatening danger. It is no longer the fear that the holy will destroy that which profanes it. Rather, fear of the divine and terror in the face of the unknown is the gateway to wisdom and understanding.

Some commentators on Job regard this chapter as an editorial intrusion that does not belong to the basic text. Others see it as a point of demarcation, offsetting the traditionalist concept of God as patriarchal ruler and judge, imbued with male-oriented values of power and justice, which characterizes the perspective of the friends, and which had characterized the perspective of the Job of the introductory story. In contrast to that concept, the Wisdom chapter informs the reader that wisdom and understanding are beyond the reach of normal earthly expressions of human and specifically male power, such as wealth and material prowess, and beyond even the grasp of disorder or death. For the reader versed in the Hebrew wisdom tradition, the chapter serves to remind of wisdom's proximity to the divine, which "alone has traced its path." (Jerusalem Bible, Job 28).

The significance of exploring this insight into man's ambitions is because the protagonists in the Job story have all been male. Job's unnamed wife makes only a cameo appearance to rant about his initial failure. Then she exits from the scene, for this is a drama about patriarchal, tribal values and their limitations as a pathway to achievement of wisdom. Job must learn his lesson through the judgments of his well-intentioned male friends, and through the gap in explanatory power that their criticism reveals to him as he searches for understanding of his downfall. The wisdom chapter functions as a response to a request for wisdom amidst confusion and terror. It signals Job's readiness to reach further into the meaning of existence.

The Wisdom interpolation sets the stage not only for Job's final apologia but for an additional interpolation, which characterizes God as an all-powerful, all-knowing and all-judging ruler (values of patriarchy and judgmentalism raised to fever pitch). This is followed by the manifestation of the divine as creator and questioner, in which the gender attributions of the divine—and their accompanying values—are shrouded in ambiguity. If the mystery is to be unfolded, words alone will not suffice.

Reverting to the textual story line: Job now reviews his life and states his case. He recalls the past, when God was with him and he enjoyed honor and prestige. His strength then lay in his upright conduct, when he upheld the needy and opposed the wicked. In those days he felt his personal honor alive within him. Now he is abused by human inferiors who were once of no account. They revile him, threaten him with stones, and spit in his face. These remarks remind us that while the moral debate is going on between Job and his friends, objectively speaking Job is in the hands, and at the mercy, of unnamed but merciless people. "Oh God", he cries out from this state of impotence and dishonoring, "couldn't You help a wretched man, just as I once did? Don't leave me in this darkness!" Following this cri du coeur Job insists on his innocence. He enumerates and faces up to every crime he can think of. If he is guilty of any one of them then let him be punished. But at least let his case be heard. Let his accuser state the charge, and he will wear it like a crown.

This is Job's final plea. The man who is experiencing trauma is once again becoming sure of himself. Of the offense that matters most to him, namely a human proclivity to take divine mercy as accessible to people of stature and substance, he is innocent, and he knows it. He has now advanced beyond living unchallenged under divine protection. He has had to find his way, no longer as a social paragon but as one struggling to deal with rejection and abuse.

Job has in fact repented, but not in the sense that the friends assumed, as one who admits to wrongdoing and makes atonement. His repentance results from letting go of the identity and dependence on the past that had marked his former existence and his solitary struggle, through what is now often referred to as a paradigm shift, to transcend victimhood and search for meaning in the experience of total aloneness. The rich Job of old, living virtuously amongst the elect like a country-club businessman, and expressing justice and mercy every day of his life, has become an object of contempt, accused by humans of countless crimes, yet knowing that the real mastery of his fate lies within himself. This Job either abandons hope or struggles to find new meaning. Having first cursed his fate, Job goes on to reclaim it.

The Accuser

But this is not the end of the story. Job is ready in his own mind to be tested, so a human accuser is produced in the person of a brash and unpleasant young man named Elihu, son of Barahel the Buzite of the clan of Ram, in other words yet another tribal opponent. We could imagine him as one amongst the many who have been in the background persecuting Job. Elihu, it is claimed, has been listening in to the high-flown debate between Job and his friends. He is exasperated by the inability of the friends to pin a charge on Job. Since they have failed, the young prosecutor will now have his say.

Elihu begins with the ominous remark that God terrifies humans to preserve them from evil. Or a person is tortured with pain until brought to his senses. Such techniques have the benefit of saving the individual from perdition and bringing his soul back to the land of the 'living'. It is the classic rationale of the inquisitor and has been used throughout human history to terrorize dissidents. Elihu is advocating the doctrine of terror, which the Inquisition, the witch hunters, or such secular dictators as Lenin, Stalin, Hitler, Saddam Hussein, would enforce on millions as an instrument of church, state or party policy.

Following this intimidation Elihu charges that Job's innocence is a fiction. By criticizing God, he has revealed himself a blasphemer and a rebel. The friends had hinted at this, but their intention had been to befriend Job, not merely to accuse him. But as inquisitor Elihu's intention is exactly the reverse. He accuses Job of consorting with evildoers and reviling God. Elihu rushes to defend the Deity from such infamy. God cannot act wickedly. The One in charge cannot be an enemy of justice. To the contrary, God is constantly watching to detect and forestall criminal activity. There is nowhere for evildoers to hide. God turns at night and crushes them. Without a trial he breaks the mighty. Job has chosen to defy the Almighty and is adding rebelliousness to impiety. Let him be tried and judged.

To a student of twentieth century totalitarianism this approach is disturbingly familiar. Job is no more a rebel than millions of other victims of ideological extremism. But in an atmosphere of terror, the slightest hint of dissidence can be construed as treason. Every word of Job's has been overheard and analyzed. He is condemned out of his own mouth as a rebel and blasphemer. The wise, remarks Elihu ominously, will dismiss his words as senseless.

The accuser goes on to ridicule Job's crimes. What injury can they do to the Almighty? The wicked only harm themselves. But this does not mean that the All Powerful does not take notice. Job's case is already before Him. Let Job tremble! When the Almighty's ire is aroused, it will not bother Him in the slightest that a man should die. Elihu now proceeds to exalt the Almighty as the destroyer of the wicked and the vindicator of the oppressed. People who stray are punished, those who disobey perish. Those worth salvaging are instructed through distress. Take heed, warns the accuser. God is great. You should extol His work. Rising to a peroration, Elihu applauds the power of the Almighty. He challenges Job to ponder God's mighty works and awesome majesty. God is preeminent and owes no one an accounting. The people revere their invisible ruler.

The Elihu passage appears to be an interpolation in form, as well as in style and content. The logic of the argument, and of the rift between Job and the Creator, does not require an accuser at this point, since the reader (if not the friends) already knows that the original accuser was none other than the Satan, while Job has made it clear that in his mind it is God that is his accuser. Moreover, the subtlety of the argument in the main text lies in its test of the limits of covenantal ethics and its dissection of personal disorientation. The effort of the friends to heap accusations on Job fails, not because accusations are unwarranted but because Job is the only one who can fathom, and thus resolve, his predicament. To add further external accusations at this point serves to deflect the force of the original author's argument and its focus on the internal trauma shadowing the external crises experienced by Job. However, an editor of the text may have felt that since Job asked for an accuser, one should be forthcoming.

Nonetheless the Elihu interpolation adds some important dimensions to the case against Job. It shows considerable understanding of power and its capacity to terrorize and control human allegiance. If you can only learn through terror, it argues, then we will terrorize you until you learn. Elihu also attacks Job at his weakest points: his verbosity, his unorthodox views, his dangerous individualism. Job is a rebel—not against God but against human ideology. His critique attacks human values used to express property and power. The author of Job, like Kafka, advances new insight into the fragility of human order and the corruptibility of power. Such insights, Elihu and his kind insist, have no place in a strictly regulated social environment. They should be exposed, and their advocates coerced into submission. In presenting such a case the Elihu passage states the essence of the conflict between public order and individual conscience.

We might conclude that the force of this passage is to increase Job's fear of what awaits him. Is he on the edge of terror, or wisdom?

Yahweh Speaks

By presenting himself as God's defender Elihu has put the Creator's integrity on the line. Yahweh either supports the Elihu perspective, in which case Job is doomed, or has a different perspective. That problem must now be resolved. If the Elihu passage is omitted, the effect of Yahweh's intervention is to establish the fact of Job's shift in consciousness and consequent openness to a new vision of God's presence.

The author handles the appearance of Yahweh in a way that may at first seem quaintly archaic. The Creator appears out of a whirlwind and fires a volley of questions at Job. Was Job there when Yahweh was laying the earth's foundations and creating and giving life? The answer is no. Job is a mere mortal. He didn't 'create' anything in the way that Yahweh did. Then what is the point of the questions? One answer is that they serve immediately to differentiate Yahweh from the all-powerful doom-enforcer conjured up by Elihu. The Elihu argument is simply thrust aside, as also are the criticisms of the friends.

But the questions challenge Job (and the reader) to assess Yahweh's significance as the source of creation. Yahweh is depicted in the grand and arduous struggle to create a universe of order and beauty out of chaos. The Creator enters the abyss and brings the wild forces of chaos under control, containing them and setting limits around them. For example, Yahweh "pent up the sea behind closed doors … and marked the bounds it was not to cross." (Jerusalem Bible) A nurturing environment emerges, capable of sustaining life. Animals and birds come into being. The author describes them in some detail and in several cases with great eloquence. Yahweh, one realizes, hugely values life.

Yahweh has once again become present to Job, not as arbitrator of right and wrong but as creator and nurturer of life. This perception of Yahweh as life-nurturer is evidently a new vision, quite different from how Job had formerly perceived the divine, when he was in his palmy but fear-ridden days. Interestingly, the reader knows that that perception was always there. Yahweh is always the creative force nurturing life into existence; it's just that Job had gotten himself into a state of consciousness that was blind to the presence of Yahweh as creator and nurturer.

What has Job to say about all this? Does the critic still want to correct the Creator? Job's response is uncharacteristically muted. He mumbles a few words and falls silent.

From out of the whirlwind Yahweh then launches into another tirade of unanswerable questions. "Do I have no rights? Must your justification be at my expense?" Since Job's troubles were supposedly precipitated with Yahweh's concurrence, this question is left moot. Does Job have the capacity to control and cut down the proud and the wicked? "If so", says Yahweh, "put on your robes of authority and do it, and I will admit that you can save yourself." Evidently Yahweh has been listening in on all the argument between Job and his friends but waiting patiently while Job fought his way through the fog and gloom. Since the Book of Job is presented as an extended conversation, we are made aware that how one listens is as important as what one thinks and says. Yahweh has been listening to Job's questions; now it is Job's turn to listen to Yahweh's.

The passage continues with descriptions of the two fabled beasts Behemoth and Leviathan, symbols of Yahweh's mastery over the created world. One senses here an archaic reference to the puniness of the human creature as compared with many other much larger and terrifying inhabitants of planet earth, something missing from the Genesis creation accounts. Job, who has previously compared himself to Leviathan, realizes that he is out of his depth. At the same time, his need to exert control over the good will of the divine, so strong in his previous life of tribal virtue, has evaporated. Instead, he has become open to a life-transforming vision of the Creator's concern for the survival and wellbeing of the creation. Job withdraws everything he has said, and as a mere mortal formed from dust and ashes, who has achieved the wonder of a theophanic vision, he falls into an awed silence.

Commentary

Did Job give way to force majeure, or was he transformed by a renewed vision of a moral universe? There is certainly no surrender implied. Yahweh is not hostile, and Job is not intimidated. Instead, he experiences transformation through a vision of Yahweh as Creator-nurturer, who reminds him of the intense effort through which the universe was brought into being. Amidst struggle and pain the universe remains life-giving and beautiful. While destructive forces are not overthrown, limits are set around them. But it was not the Creator's intention to control everything. The creation must go through its own struggles to create and nurture life. To the extent that humans are surrogates of the Creator, that need to struggle applies to their lives also.

This necessity for creation to grasp its own creational and life-sustaining task is what motivates the search for wisdom and understanding. Ethical structures function within a societal framework to maintain social order. Wisdom and understanding, by contrast, are not limited by human convention. When people who disdain ethical norms come to power, ethical structures will not be accepted; rather, they will be turned upside down and anti-values enforced. The innocent will be declared guilty and the guilty innocent. The truly guilty, who are so because they defy God and scorn the covenant, will prosper and the innocent will fall into poverty and despair, or may even be imprisoned, enslaved or eradicated.

Such injustice will produce its own disorder and chaos, irrespective of who blames whom. The society will atomize, friends and relatives turn against each other, and victims will be demonized and destroyed. In the twentieth century one country after another has seen this happen, with Nazi Germany, Stalinist Russia, and the Chinese Cultural Revolution of the 1960s and 70s setting the standards by which all other such forms of ideological and racist hostility can be judged. But the solution, according to the author of Job, is not to curse God and die. Nor is it to cave in to the judgment of the times, whether it comes from well-intentioned friends or ill-intentioned enemies. A more life-sustaining answer is needed.

The course adopted by the Wisdom tradition was to focus on the act of creation and reflect on what that has to do with our capacity to live. As compared with the Priestly account in Genesis 1, which describes an orderly and all-powerful succession of creative intentions, the act of creation in the Wisdom tradition is much more arduous and unresolved. It is at heart a struggle to establish order over the chaotic forces that exist in the universe—and they include human society—and to bring a process of nurturing and caring into being. 'Yahweh' is the power by which that nurturing is achieved. 'Fear' or awe of Yahweh is acknowledgement of that power as the primal source of nurturing; and avoidance of evil, i.e. innocence, is avoidance of anything conducive to chaos.

The Wisdom tradition acknowledges the ambiguity of order, including the barely constrained chaotic forces that lurk in the background of the ordered world and are ready to erupt at any moment. But it also indicates that individual human beings can respond not just to the conditions of their own fate but to the broader fate and wellbeing of the world in which they live. Job becomes the paradigm of the wise and God-empowered human being, and the book of Job is the text in which that insight is worked out. Innocence in this context no longer means that I don't tell lies or suffer breakdowns, or that I don't have behavior in my past that I have good reason to regret. What it means is that I am not contributing by word or deed, or lack of consciousness, to fundamental cosmic disorder. More positively it means that I 'fear' the Source of creation, do not take Yahweh for granted as accessible at my beck and command, and respect with awe and wonder the will needed to make life possible. It took the author (and editors) of Job some 40 chapters to arrive at that conclusion. But can anyone doubt that the conclusion was worth the effort?

We might pursue this point at a more personal level by recalling the boils or ulcers with which Job was struck, when loss of human and material possessions failed to break his faith. From an external perspective, this kind of skin eruption would suffice to declare Job contaminated with disease and in some way polluted, and therefore to be excluded from society. Essentially Job is detribalized by his crisis; this is the sub-plot underlying the debate between the friends and accounts for the contumely with which he is treated by those who remain within the tribe, and for his own sense of dishonor and disempowerment.

But from an internal perspective it may be argued that Job's boils represent an eruption of toxicity from within his body and life system, comparable to the cancers and other systemic diseases which prevail in our times, and expressive of fears and nightmares that he harbored. Something happened to wear down Job's immune system and ravage his physical body. It is unlikely to have been the trauma of the random catastrophes that overtook Job, especially since we are informed that these occurred very suddenly and that they failed to break his faith. Some other crisis was attacking Job's faith, undermining his sense of strength and wholeness as a tribal leader, disorienting him, fulfilling his fears of impermanence and impotence, and causing him to wish he had never been born, yet at the same time sending him on an arduous search for renewed meaning. During the search Job's old world, represented by the tribal thinking of his friends, is cauterized and cut off. He is stripped of illusion, until he has only his own two feet on which to stand and find his way. Yet once the illusions of empowerment and disempowerment are cut away, that is when Job's internal recovery and epiphany can take place.

In the course of accompanying Job to his epiphany, the author makes some very important points about listening. The one who truly listens to Job, it turns out, is the one who also goes through profound struggle to bring into being a caring and nurturing world. Yahweh emerges as the compassionate non-judgmental listener, who takes no umbrage at Job's complaints and merely asks probing questions. By comparison Job's human interlocutors are unable to listen compassionately—even though the three friends attempted to do so—because they are too caught up in protecting their own standards and ideals to discern what Job is experiencing. Elihu, for his part, listens only with the ears of an inquisitor. The conversation that really matters is the one going on between Job and Yahweh. This is the all-important conversation through which wisdom is transmitted.

Just to make the point that even amidst trauma life is not without irony, the book of Job concludes with an account of what happened to the main protagonists. The three friends are chastised by Yahweh for misinterpreting Job's predicament and being blind to the struggles needed to attain wisdom-based consciousness. They are ordered to make sacrifices and to beg Job to intercede for them, which he does. Job is restored to wealth and property. His neighbors come rushing round to congratulate him. He has, once again, four sons and three beautiful daughters, and to the latter he gives special names denoting purification and consecration, as well as rights of inheritance. Women, or at least daughters, become a focus of gratitude and purification in Job's new wisdom-based world. He lives on to a ripe old age, enjoys his grandchildren and eventually passes on after years of domestic tranquility and happiness. An unresolved detail in the denouement is the fate of Elihu, which is left unmentioned. But it is enough to know that like a passing comet he fades from the scene, forgotten and unregretted.

More important than the fate of Elihu is the absence of the Satan in either the poetic discourse, the interpolations, or the end story. The Satan is not even around to guide Elihu in his frenzied accusations. It is evident that the wisdom tradition, as expounded in the Book of Job, found the concept of the Satan unsatisfying as an explanation for evil or chaos. Later wisdom texts, such as the Book of Wisdom, would attribute the Fall of Man to the Devil's envy that brought death into the world. But the Book of Job sought to penetrate the ambiguities and sufferings of existence by contrasting affliction and chaos to the work of the Creator-God, with a view to understanding how to survive and advance under such circumstances. It is not the search for Satan that preoccupies the author but the search for the Creator and for the elusive wisdom associated with the Creator. Where, and how, is the Creator to be found when chaos erupts?

That question, as Elie Wiesel reports, was asked at Auschwitz, at a time and place in which creation and human wellbeing—as understood in the Jewish Biblical tradition—seemed most at risk. It is a question that the hubris of the Cold War and the localized but savage breakdowns of order in the Post-Cold War era should continue to raise to our attention, particularly in the case of individuals whose consciousness remains grounded in the Biblical tradition. In such cases, when guilt no longer suffices to account for disaster or personal turmoil, and when justice no longer suffices to resolve it, we either search for a vision of the Creator in the maelstrom of chaos, or we assume the destructibility of creation, and its indifference to our own suffering and continuity. The occurrence in 2004 of the massive Southeast Asian Tsunami reminds us that the created order is itself part of the existential problem of life on this earth, a point that is explicitly recognized and addressed in the Book of Job.

The wisdom tradition, as expressed in the Book of Job, declines to account for disaster through either human guilt or divine judgment or indifference. Nor, as we have seen, does it look to the construction of an evil intervention who contends with God for the lives and loyalties of humans. There is no Satan to be found ruling the underworld or dragging the depraved into the fires of hell. Earthly affliction, like everything else, proceeds from the actuality of living in this world. Creative response to affliction depends on one's perspective.

According to the Book of Job, guilt is not a spiritually functional response to the problem of failure. Life is unpredictable and messy, and not always accountable in terms of right and wrong. An individual can go from riches to rags, success to failure, and freedom to oppression, without any guarantee of restitution. Observing this perspective, some commentators have concluded that the Job account reflects a collective experience of trauma, such as the Babylonian exile, or the persecutions occurring during the Greek Antiochite regime, in which the individual as such becomes helpless to control his or her wellbeing through right conduct.

Such an explanation could well be true, although it is not necessary as a condition for exploring the individual experience of chaos and darkness. What we could rather point to is the fragility of the line between order and disorder, and at the same time the capacity of one person to experience and work through the crisis of disorder while others, including close friends, remain within a socially determined construct of order.

In this respect, one very important and alarming lesson pursued by the author of Job is the incomprehensibility of the world of disorder not just to Job but to those remaining within a structure of apparent order. From such a perspective, the circumstances of an individual who has drifted or been shoved into disorder and away from the regular world are inexplicable except through categories applying to a world of mandated order. As a result, Job and his friends can no longer communicate with each other. This is agony for them all. Job's friends are his friends, and even though they may end up ranting and raving they don't desert him. Instead they appeal increasingly frantically for him to return to their world.

But Job goes on a lonely voyage of discovery, to see if God is still around and accessible in the context of darkness and disorder. Can a broken and humiliated human being find something that might elude people who are on the face of it in a situation of greater favor? According to the author of Job, the answers coming in from the perceptive travelers, as well as the animals and birds, are generally negative. The vast and probably overwhelming majority of those driven into oppression and chaos remain there unenlightened and die that way. They never get an answer to their questions. This is a great tragedy and yet an unrelenting fact of life. Here is where the Wisdom chapter provides a key to the problem and becomes such an essential clue to the Job problematic. Only those who learn to fear God and avoid evil have any hope of enlightenment.

But what does 'fear God' mean? Fear the God of Justice and mercy? Fear the God who could let the people of Israel be dispersed and their kingdom destroyed, and the people of Judah taken into captivity and their temple—Yahweh's temple—razed to the ground? Fear a God who doesn't answer when his faithful servants call? Fear a God who must be looking aside, or deaf to entreaty, or asleep, while decent people in their thousands and millions are trampled on, or have lost their moorings because of some catastrophe and are like so many refugees wandering around on the edge of chaos?

The book of Job doesn't try to answer such questions directly. But as a survival manual, its powers of insight are considerable. The oppressed individual, who discovers all kinds of reasons to fear humans, is led away from that focus and along the path towards what the Wisdom tradition calls fear of the Divine. But this kind of fear, it transpires, is quite different from fear of humans. The God Yahweh is not the terrifying judge-executioner represented by Elihu and caricatured with such brutality by 20th century dictators and their terror-obsessed followers, as well as by hosts of lesser tyrants. Yahweh is not even the hopefully merciful judge-punisher conjured up by the friends and the role model for so many orthodox rulers and administrators distributed amongst governments, schools, families, prisons and slave societies throughout history and throughout the world even today. In the discourse of the Book of Job, to fear Yahweh is to experience the crystalline beauty of the world beyond the terror of confronting disorder and hostility, to understand in that moment the essence of existence and to transform one's consciousness to engage with that vision. After Job had let go of his past and embraced the universality of the divine present, his turmoil dropped away. People not only left him alone but came under his sway, because they saw that he was graced.

The Book of Job, and other wisdom literature makes the case that wisdom is not to be found widely distributed among men in patriarchal cultures. Hebrew theology regards wisdom and understanding as essentially feminine qualities. This does not mean that they are beyond the reach of men brought up in patriarchal systems. But they do not come easily, and the implication of the Book of Job is that they are not achieved without substantial testing. Even so, wisdom advocates insist that nothing else is equal to them in capacity to understand and preserve life. It is this perception that makes wisdom so hard to access from within the reward structures of patriarchy. Thus, to be dragged outside those structures might even become an act of liberation, provided that the individual is lucky enough to survive the trauma and does not go astray or get killed while groping for new direction.

One final postscript about this remarkable story lies in what it teaches us about the consciousness of prayer and what I've called here the universality of the divine present. There is nothing new about this concept. The divine present is with us continually, but access to it is a very great challenge. We need to release ourselves from time-boundedness in order to achieve such access. This is something which most of us find very difficult to do. One should seek a setting in which it is possible for one's consciousness to become attuned to the now and to let go of both past and future. Disciplines allowing the possibility of complete release of ego, such as meditation, prayer, music and service to others, and exigencies such as complete deprivation of support from either the past or the future, are the key to any possibility of achieving this attunement.

But the seeker should beware. This is no simple journey on which to embark, for the tests for any of us while we are on it may be greater than we can bear. Part of the wisdom of the book of Job lies in making the dangers of this journey transparent. It is so much easier and less daunting if one can just slip back into the past, a behavioral preference urged by Job's friends, and one to whose seductive power I can personally testify. The magnet of the past, with its comforting parameters and familiarity, is hugely compelling. Nevertheless, if we truly want to seek wisdom, it is always there before us, awaiting the opening of our minds.

CHAPTER 10

Jesus and the Covenant of Redemption

Nothing—neither gold nor money
Costly stones nor pearls—
Can hide from me the eyes of the poor
Hildegard of Bingen

Then I saw a new heaven and a new earth ...
I saw the holy city and the new Jerusalem
Coming down from God out of heaven
As beautiful as a bride all dressed for her husband
Revelations 21, The Jerusalem Bible

Prophetic Conceptions of the Kingdom of God

This chapter explores ways in which the story of Jesus took on the covenant and mission of redemption proclaimed in the Hebrew scriptures. These scriptures were the source through which Jesus and his companions learned to think about the kingdom of God and to practice the two great commandments—to love God and love neighbors.

The idea of the God Yahweh as king over all has its origins in the prophetic texts. When the prophet Samuel anointed Saul as the first king over the Israelites, he did so with great reluctance. Yahweh was the true king; but Yahweh had been rejected by the people. This led, at Yahweh's insistence, to the institution of human kingship. When Saul failed as Yahweh's anointed one, Samuel anointed the unknown shepherd boy

David. Yahweh made a covenant with David to establish the monarchy in his family forever; but it was still a kingship derived from the power of Yahweh, who remained the supreme ruler. As David is said to have acknowledged—in words added to some versions of the Prayer of Jesus—"Thine, O Lord, is the greatness, and the power and the glory…., Thine is the kingdom…" (1 Chronicles 29, King James version).

After the Davidic monarchy began its downhill slide towards earthly power and idolatry, the kingship of Yahweh assumed greater significance, both as symbol of power and as promise of peace and justice. Entering the temple in the year of king Uzziah's death (around 742 BCE), the prophet Isaiah had seen a vision of Yahweh as king of kings, seated on a high throne. Seraphs stood around crying "Holy, holy, holy is Yahweh Sabaoth. The glory of Yahweh fills the whole earth." (Isaiah 6) This vision, as earlier discussed, had been followed by visions of a child of the Davidic line who would act as Yahweh's regent on earth; a "prince of peace", who would rule with justice and integrity. (Isaiah 9 and 11) Later the prophet Jeremiah, at a time of crisis for the beleaguered kingdom of Judah, warned that Yahweh, the true God and everlasting king, would leave Zion (Jerusalem).

The second part of the book of Zechariah, referring to a time of post-exilic restoration, envisions Yahweh's earthly king arriving back in Zion humble yet triumphant, riding on a donkey and proclaiming peace for the nations. The victory of the king is, nevertheless, military and total. The enemy forces wither with plague and rot, and all who survive go up to worship Yahweh as king over the entire world.[9] (Zechariah 9) The much later writer of the Book of Daniel saw one like a son of man, coming on the clouds of heaven. Appearing before one of great age seated on a throne of fire, this "one like a son of man" received dominion, power and glory over all people and nations. His would be an everlasting kingdom, given to the people of the saints of the Most High. (Daniel 7) These visions and others from the Book of Psalms, shaped the concept of an anointed redeemer, or messiah, who would deliver Israel from oppression. The hope of messianic deliverance became prevalent in late BCE Palestine as the Israelites fell under the yoke of first Greek and then Roman imperialism.

Since humans tend to associate kingship with the trappings of earthly

---

[9] This had happened to the army of the Assyrian king Sennacherib when it invaded the kingdom of Judah.

power, such as armies, military conquest, and accumulation of wealth and property, it should be noted that the prophetic kingdom of God was fundamentally a kingdom of justice and peace, which celebrated Yahweh's status as creator of, and lord over, all existence. Admittedly Yahweh was also viewed as strong and valiant in battle. The faithful David, as Yahweh's anointed one, had demonstrated Yahweh's military prowess. Centuries later the Persian ruler Cyrus, who 'liberated' Babylon, would be seen by deutero-Isaiah in the same light.

In fact the prophetic vision perceives Yahweh as having power over not only human dominion but also the universe itself. But despite the warlike imagery, it is the idea of Yahweh as eternal ruler of nations that is dominant in the prophetic texts and Psalms. As conceived in the Book of Isaiah, this Yahweh, with heaven as throne and earth as footstool, loves justice, proclaims liberty, and comforts those who mourn. Dismissing the corruption of earthly rule, the glory of Yahweh, coming in incandescent light, establishes the new heaven and earth—an early conception of what the Christian texts would call the kingdom of God.

Given the oppressive Roman occupation of Judea, the military aspects of messianic deliverance tended to prevail, leading to uprisings that the Roman occupiers invariably suppressed with great brutality. By contrast, the concept of kingdom advanced by Jesus and the early Christian communities rejected violence in favor of the Isaian concept of service to the poor and the guidance of wisdom and understanding, as spelled out in the Psalms and the wisdom books. This was not simply because of the appalling consequences of military rebellion against Rome. Rather, the Gospel kingdom proclaimed by Jesus recognized and drew on these alternative insights from the prophetic and wisdom traditions.

Jesus and the Kingdom of God

When Jesus begins his mission in Galilee he is pictured as proclaiming the good news of the kingdom of God and issuing a call to repentance. In the words of the Mark gospel (reiterated in Matthew) he declares that, "the time is fulfilled and the kingdom of God is at hand. Repent and believe the good news."

Several prophetic themes are sounded here. The advent of the kingdom of God is always good news, since it proclaims the end of oppression and the dawning of a new age, in which Yahweh Sabaoth, the Lord of Hosts and the everlasting King, will return to Zion and reclaim the people of the covenant. Chastened by suffering, the people are ready to turn back to Yahweh, and Yahweh is ready to turn back to them. Thus prophetic calls to repentance always come with implications of political as well as moral restoration.

Repentance means turning away from idolatry and returning to the values of justice and mercy spelled out in the Torah and prophetic texts, high among which are the protection of weak and indigent people. As the book of Ezekiel put it, the upright person oppresses no one, returns pledges, gives food to the hungry and clothes to the naked, never charges interest, is fair to all, and adheres to Yahweh's laws (18: 5-9). In particular repentance involves a conversion of the heart. We see this stated most strongly in the Books of Deuteronomy and Jeremiah. Those who repent cry out in anguish. In a characteristic Deuteronomic phrase, they circumcise their hearts, so that they can once again love Yahweh with all their heart and soul. As a Psalmist puts it (Psalm 51), "the sacrifices of God are a broken spirit; a broken and a contrite heart, O God, thou wilt not despise."

The prophetic mission of kingdom proclamation is to bring good news to the poor, bind up the broken hearted, proclaim liberty to captives and comfort all those who mourn. There is no theme more prominent in prophetic proclamation than this theme of identification of the kingdom with the poor and oppressed and wounded. No theme has meant more to Christian mystics and saints, whether it be Hildegard of Bingen, Saint Francis, Bishop William How, Mother Theresa, or Dorothy Day, to name only a few. The kingdom liberates those who are enslaved politically, ideologically, economically, socially, or spiritually. The most commonly mentioned victims of oppression and intended beneficiaries of justice and mercy are widows, orphans and aliens. This reminds us that the kingdom of God, as envisaged by the prophets, applies most fundamentally to the individual in the context of social structure and human relations. It applies especially to disadvantaged women and children, and to people without legal rights. This is why prophetic kingdom consciousness, as an expression of human relations, is located in heart and soul. When there is love of God and love of neighbor, kingdom consciousness is never far away.

Building the Kingdom Community

As recorded by the gospel writers, Jesus took his mission of kingdom deliverance to people who were sick, defiled and oppressed. Much of his early work is said to have focused on healing the sick, particularly people coping with defiling illnesses and those possessed with evil spirits. People with polluting diseases or bodily discharges were among the most oppressed, since they were cut off from contact with society or access to purification. Healing in this context became an act of liberation, restoring to the healed person a sense of wholeness, identity and access to community life.

As well as restoring individuals to wholeness, Jesus proclaimed the kingdom in addresses delivered in synagogues and more informally to crowds who followed him wherever he went. Many of his remarks were brought together in the gospels of Matthew and Luke, notably in the famous Sermon on the Mount. Many of its themes strike a familiar note. Blessed are the poor and destitute, for theirs is the kingdom of heaven. Blessed are those who mourn, such as children and widows, for they shall be comforted. Blessed are the humble; blessed are those who hunger for righteousness. Blessed are the merciful and the pure in heart. Blessed are the peacemakers, such as Isaiah's herald of peace proclaiming salvation. Blessed are those—such as the prophets, for example—persecuted for the sake of righteousness. Theirs is the kingdom of heaven. Such people are the salt of the earth and the light of the world. "Let your light so shine before others", says the text, "that they may see your good works and glorify your Father which is in heaven."

In a dramatic revisioning of this text, the Franco-Jewish scholar and interfaith activist André Chouraqui redefines the concept "blessed" as an active invitation to "arise and walk forth"—exactly the message given by Jesus to those whom he healed. Thus, the arrival of the kingdom enables the poor and destitute to "arise and walk forth," because their time of deliverance has come.[10] It enables those who are mourning to "arise and walk forth," because their time of consolation has come. It enables the humble, the merciful, the peacemakers, to "arise and walk forth," and to be

---

[10] The words "arise and walk forth," translated from the French "en marche," are taken from a work by Jean-Yves Leloup.

recognized as guardian angels. It enables the prophets to "arise, walk forth," and proclaim the arrival of the kingdom. All this arising and walking forth is a reminder of those feet, once beautiful upon the mountains, of the Isaian servant-son of Yahweh, whose very appearance brings good tidings of peace and deliverance, and the advent of the heavenly kingdom.

In case anyone should misread the Gospel kingdom as novel and unbiblical, the sermon text has Jesus insist that he has come not to abolish but to fulfill the law and the prophets. Torah teaching is integral to the kingdom of God. The sermon addresses various Torah commandments and teachings, particularly on male adultery and divorce, and reaffirms them. In the spirit of Deutero-Isaiah it addresses the problem of aggression by urging people not to resist violently. If someone hits you on one cheek, offer the other one. This is meant not as passive non-violence but as active non-violent engagement with an opponent. Similarly, if someone in need asks you for something, give it.

The most controversial passage in the sermon urges hearers to "love your enemies, bless them that curse you, do good to them that hate you, and pray for them which despitefully use you." This early Q passage points out that God causes the sun to shine on the evil as well as the good, and the rain to fall on the just and unjust alike. In other words, the wicked have a place in the sun. Those construed in one context as 'wicked' may in fact be functioning to fulfill some divine intention. Your enemy may be your teacher. Furthermore, Yahweh takes no pleasure in the death of wicked people and would rather see them renounce their sins. (Ezekiel 18 and 33) What, in words recorded of Jesus, is so special about loving your own? It is learning to love neighbors, strangers and enemies that is the test of your integrity, and the mark of your internal access to kingdom power. This is the supreme challenge of life on this earth, towards which all of us are invited to "rise and walk forth".

Another aspect of this teaching consists in its capacity to transcend normal patterns of forgiveness, by which we intend to relieve someone whose actions may have harmed us from the guilt they presumably feel or should feel. Important as this act may be for the other, it does not necessarily cleanse ourselves. For that to happen, the teaching asks us to transform our sense of having been 'harmed' into a moment of enlightenment. From that perspective we could choose to engage actively in seeking the wellbeing of those whose actions resulted in harming or, alternatively, enlightening us. A whole different perception of self and other is involved here from that which we normally carry around. The 'other' is transformed from oppressor into teacher and becomes someone worthy of our active engagement and intercession.

The sermon goes on to address the subject of prayer, one of the most important elements of spiritual practice. It introduces the prayer of Jesus. "Our Father, who art in heaven, hallowed (holy) be thy name. Thy kingdom come, thy will be done..."[11] In its Greco-Latin and European versions, the prayer is the prayer of the poor, of people for whom the kingdom of God alone promises a life of wholeness. "Give us today our daily bread," it requests, "and forgive us our wrongdoing, as we forgive those who wrong us." The prayer of Jesus is the prayer of the spiritually fragile, and that includes all of us, for the wrongdoing often happens when we are enjoying an access of power and are most liable to abuse it.

"Lead us not into temptation," the prayer continues, "but deliver us from evil." Some modern translations have tried to soften the first of these appeals, as if God could not possibly lead us into temptation. But if we have read the book of Job and other wisdom and prophetic writings, we know that this is within the capability of the wisdom God and essential for our spiritual development. The journey of the soul is predicated on encountering danger or misfortune. While some have evil thrust upon them, others may never come to grips with it unless they are led into temptation, or tested to the limit of their endurance.

Indeed, testing body and soul is one of the characteristics of Yahweh— so much so that Paul was obliged to reassure his Corinthian followers that God "will not let you be put to the test beyond your strength." (1 Corinthians 10, from Jerusalem Bible). Still, the prayer of Jesus recognizes our fragility and need for deliverance. It also puts the onus for our integrity on us. Forgive others, it concludes, and God will forgive you. If you don't forgive others, why should God forgive you?

The sermon calls on people who are in need of food and clothing to set their hearts instead on God's kingdom and righteousness. This is the unequivocal call of faith, to surrender to the greater and unfathomable

---

[11] In Aramaic the text is "oh Birther, father-mother of the cosmos...focus your light within us." Douglas-Klotz, Prayers of the Cosmos, 12-18.

wisdom of the divine. Surrender of self-identity is central to this teaching. To take up the larger agenda of redemption it is necessary to let go of personal agendas. Then ask, and it will be given. Search, and you will find. Knock, and the door will be opened. To those who have knocked in vain, these words might sound naively unrealistic, except that Jesus is recorded as having demonstrated their power in his own life. In your dealings with humans, he affirms, treat others as you would like them to treat you. In other words, there is a way, and state of mind, to do with asking and knocking.

The sermon warns that the road to the kingdom is a hard road, which only a few will find. Drawing on wisdom thinking, it compares a wise with a foolish person. The former builds a house on rock, the latter on sand. When the floods rise and the winds blow, the house built on rock survives, but the house built on sand collapses. "And great was the fall of it." (Matthew 7)

Kingdom Consciousness

It is apparent from such passages in the gospels that kingdom consciousness is not easily acquired. If one's consciousness is formed by structures of control and oppression, such as colonialism, slavery, or the patriarchal system controlling first century Palestinian family life and still active to this day, one learns, often at considerable cost, how to survive within such systems by becoming obedient to their dictates. One can also rebel, or find small areas of psychic freedom. But kingdom consciousness involves not rebellion but transformation and renewal of the soul. Kingdom citizens pay taxes to the government and thus are loyal in terms of their material goods, while spiritually they commit to the values of kingdom ethics and wisdom. As we have seen, the term used in the synoptic gospels to describe this process of spiritual conversion and turning to kingdom consciousness is 'repentance'. John's gospel describes it as being 'born again' or 'born anew'. Familiar as we are with systems of oppression, it is hard to comprehend the reality of spiritual freedom. Ethics alone, even miracles, are not enough to convince us. We need to be persuaded by example what the kingdom is like.

Recognizing this need, Jesus is recorded as employing several metaphors to describe the kingdom. It is, he says, like a farmer throwing seed on the ground. Day after day, of its own accord, the seed sprouts and grows: first the blade, then the ear, then the full corn in the ear. When the corn is ripe the farmer reaps, because the harvest is come. This homely agricultural metaphor recalls passages in Deuteronomy and Isaiah, in which the fertility of the seed represents Yahweh's care for the land and presence among its people. It is a reflection of Yahweh's fulfillment of the covenant. By the same token, a failure on the part of the people to abide by the covenant, leading to rejection of Yahweh, will result in a blighting of seed and crop. But as a metaphor, seed refers also to the health of the people themselves. Indeed, in one of his most famous stories Jesus uses the metaphor of a farmer sowing seed to distinguish journeys towards, and away from, the kingdom. Fertile seed, in short, is a metaphor for the word of Yahweh going out into the world through human agency and accomplishing Yahweh's will. As for the harvest, it provides one of the three great annual occasions for bringing the people into ceremonial communion with Yahweh. As such the harvest becomes a prophetic metaphor for the day of salvation or judgment.

Another more famous metaphor is of the kingdom being like a mustard seed. It is a diminutive seed when sown, yet it grows into a large shrub, with big branches on which birds can shelter. The kingdom, in other words, can grow out of the smallest of small expressions of life. One small gift may turn a corner in someone's life. Or it is like a farmer, who sows good seed in the field. But while he sleeps, an enemy comes and sows weeds. When the good seed ripens, so do the weeds. The farmer and his laborers see that an enemy has been at work. The farmer decides to let the wheat and the weeds ripen together. At harvest time the reapers collect the weeds and burn them; but the wheat they gather into the farmer's barn.

Normally Jesus did not explain his parables, except to his disciples, and when they were alone. But recognizing messianic symbolism in the parable of the wheat and the weeds, the disciples pressed for an explanation. They were told that the farmer is the son of man. The field is the world. The good seed are the children of the kingdom. The weeds are the children of the wicked one. The enemy that sowed the weeds is the devil. The harvest is the end of the world. The reapers are the angels. As the weeds are gathered and burned, so shall it be at the end of the world. The son of man will send out his angels. They will gather up out of his kingdom everything and everyone that is evil and throw them into a furnace of fire. There will be weeping and gnashing of teeth. Then the righteous will shine like the sun in the kingdom of God. Whoever has ears to hear, comments the text, let them hear.

This passage, for all its symbolic language, sends out a fiercely confrontational message. We are introduced to a struggle, expressed in messianic and apocalyptic language, yet reflective of polarization experienced in the day to day world. There are different strategies for accessing the kingdom, and they are bitterly contested. According to gospel accounts, the 'Pharisees' went about it through very strict observation of Torah regulations. John the Baptist and his followers fasted strictly and prayed. Jesus and his followers, by contrast, wined and dined, consorted with tax collectors (Roman agents) and people defiled in various ways, ate without properly cleansing themselves, and bent the sabbath observance to their own agendas. Evidently taken aback by this conduct John was moved, while in prison, to send representatives to Jesus querying whether he was "the one" for whom they were waiting. Pharisees and scribes are recorded as following Jesus around, taking notes of his breaches of sabbath observance and assumption of messianic powers, and planning how to get rid of him. The gospel accounts are very unspecific (at least on the surface) about the personalities and power issues underlying these conflicts, but they do make it clear that Jesus was a marked man, and that his claims on the kingdom were vigorously opposed by other groups seeking Yahweh's favor.

Of particular interest in the explanation of the wheat and weeds parable is Jesus' reference to the farmer as the 'son of man'. This term is used frequently throughout the synoptic gospels to apply to Jesus himself. Its use in early Q texts is associated with the efforts of early Jesus communities to create a community of equals, as opposed to the hierarchical, patriarchal system that governed the social relations of the time. The apocalyptic meaning takes over as the pressures for non-conformity are brought to bear on the early Jesus communities.

That the Jesus of the Q texts defined his mission in opposition to patriarchalism is not disputed, although the circumstances of his family relations leave many questions unanswered. The legitimacy of his physical conception was first said to have been questioned, then covered over, by his 'father' Joseph. His relationship with his siblings/cousins is never clear. Once Jesus is launched on his mission to proclaim the kingdom, his relatives try to rein him in. Jesus forthwith repudiates his natal family and names his followers—those who do the will of God—as brother, sister and mother. 'Sonship' is redefined to accord with the leadership of the new house communities of Jesus-followers. Later, as the kingdom passages are knitted together with the Christ-as-Savior traditions, the 'sonship' of Jesus would be aligned with the chosen servant of deutero-Isaiah and the virtuous man of the wisdom tradition.

Kingdom People

Liberated from family, and surrounded by a community of people disadvantaged in various ways, the Jesus of the early textual sources begins to articulate his vision of the human kingdom community. If few can enter this domain, and if it is not to be accomplished simply through strict Torah observance, who gets in, and in what order? These questions are hotly debated by Jesus' close followers. Their teacher comes down hard on such speculation. Whoever wants to be first must make themselves last and servant of all. Children are the true citizens. Whoever does not receive the kingdom as a child will not enter into it. Jesus takes children and embraces them to drive the point home.

In such ways Jesus begins to model himself as a servant. He tells his followers that the 'son of man' comes not to be served but to serve, and to act as a ransom for many. According to Torah, ransom was the money paid by males and set aside as a poll tax for Yahweh, in return for the gift of life. Each male paid the same amount, regardless of their wealth. For the poor of Roman Palestine the ransom was an oppressive burden and a symbol of their servitude to the occupying power and the hierarchy in charge of the temple. But in prophetic declaration ransom was also the price paid by Yahweh to deliver the captive people. The ransom paid by Yahweh redeems the people so that they can return to Zion, the heartland of Yahweh's kingdom, "with songs and everlasting joy upon their heads." (Isaiah 35) Thus ransom is a gift to those languishing in servitude. Payment of ransom is a mark of kingdom service, through which many in bondage are redeemed. In Paul's teaching, Jesus as Christ becomes the ransom whereby humans may be delivered from sin. The purchase price is the sacrificial blood of the lamb, paid via the crucifixion. That is the essence of the Jesus covenant.

We can observe this thinking about service in the examples Jesus gives of those whose behavior identifies them as close to the kingdom. An impoverished widow comes to the temple and donates two small coins. Compared to the gifts of the wealthy, this looks like a token. But no. They gave from their surplus. She gave what she had to live on. As in a comparable story from the Buddhist tradition, her motivation surpasses that of other givers and indicates the difference in her spiritual capacity. Here is a farmer with a hundred sheep. One strays from the flock and gets lost. Is the farmer going to cut his losses and go home? Not this one: he goes looking for the lost sheep, and on finding it returns home rejoicing. Or take a scribe, who becomes a disciple of the kingdom. This is like a householder who brings "forth out of his treasure things new and old." (Matthew 13)

The kingdom is also discriminatory. Here are fishermen hauling in a catch. They collect the good ones and throw away the rest. So it will be at the end of time, when angels separate the wicked from the just. Here is a king with a servant owing a huge debt, which he cannot pay. The servant is to be sold with his family and all that he has, to meet the debt. He pleads for respite. Moved with compassion, the lord remits the debt. The servant turns around and grabs another servant who owes him a small pittance. The victim also pleads for respite but is thrown into prison. Distressed by this cruelty, other servants report it to the Lord, who seizes the unjust servant and delivers him "to the tormentors" until he pays up every last penny. "And that", Jesus is reported as saying, "is how my heavenly Father will deal with you, unless you too forgive your debtors." (Matthew 18)

One of the most poignant stories is about a wealthy, powerful person interested in saving his soul. He comes to Jesus asking, "Good Master, what shall I do to inherit eternal life?" (Mark 10, Matthew 19, Luke 18) Jesus stiffly tells him to follow the Torah. "I have done so", he proudly rejoins, "from my youth up". This sounds more promising. "There is one thing you lack", says Jesus. "Sell everything, give the proceeds to the poor, and you will have treasure in heaven. Then come and follow me!" When the man heard this, he was sad, as he was very wealthy. Jesus draws from this exchange an unforgettable wisdom image. It is easier for a camel to squeeze through the eye of a needle than for a rich person to enter the kingdom. In that case, ask his listeners, who on earth can be saved? Jesus responds, "what is impossible for human beings is not impossible for God." The disciple Peter exclaims, "we have left all to follow you!" 'There is no one," Jesus insists, "who has left home and family for the sake of the kingdom, who will not be repaid many times over."

There were also times when the idea of the kingdom seemed to strike home, or when it was tangibly felt. Here is a scribe, who has just witnessed a battle of wits between Jesus and some of his opponents. "Which is the first commandment?", he asks. Jesus responds by reciting not the first of the ten commandments but it's much more emphatic iteration in the Shema, his favorite heart centered passage from Deuteronomy about loving Yahweh. The second commandment, he adds for good measure, is the commandment from Leviticus to love your neighbor as yourself. These are the core values of the covenantal community of equals, on which Jesus has staked everything. "Well said!", responds the scribe enthusiastically. "To love God with all your heart and soul, and to love your neighbor as yourself, is worth much more than any sacrifice." It was a meeting of minds liberated from temple worship, tradition, narrow patriarchalism, ethnic exclusiveness, anything which confines and subjugates the human spirit. Jesus looks at him with admiration and exclaims, "you are not far from the kingdom of God."

Walking the Walk, Talking the Talk

In due course there came a critical occasion when Jesus, preparing to submit to his enemies, was anointed by a woman, claimed in John's gospel to be Mary, sister of Martha and Jesus' friend Lazarus. In performing this service, the woman used nard—a very expensive ointment that graced the bride in the Song of Songs.

This shocked some of his disciples. "Why such a waste?" they complained. "It could have been sold and the money given to the poor." This was not the first nor the last time that male disciples failed to understand the significance of what was happening in front of their eyes. So, Jesus intervened. "Leave her alone," he responded. "The poor are always present, and you can help them at any time. But I will be gone soon enough. She has done what she could. She has anointed my body for its burial. Wherever the good news (of the kingdom) is proclaimed, what she has done will be spoken of, in memory of her." (Mark 14, Matthew 26).

"She has anointed my body for its burial:" these words let us know that Mary performed an essential act to proclaim the sacredness of Jesus' sacrificial death. This would be no normal crucifixion. His body and his death had been hallowed by a woman friend in an act of pure love, sufficiently to carry him through the fearful ordeal that lay ahead. It was a critical intervention by a woman who had grasped the significance of the situation and performed a vital priestly rite, while the male disciples remained blind and deaf to what the situation needed. The huge irony is that while Mary's gift supported Jesus, it had little if any impact on the evolution of Christianity as a religion. The good news of the kingdom still needs to focus on this event.

The story reminds us that the Jesus covenant is a proclamation about love and reconciliation between friends and equals, men and women, who give everything they have as a gift to the other. This is the expression of loving with heart and soul, by investing one's fullest means into the life of the other. The equality of human beings before God is expressed through the mission to the poor and the sick, since before God they are held to be no less human than the rich—or even, for that matter, than the wicked. Jesus himself by this time had nothing to his name beyond the clothes he wore. But that did not matter. What he did was to proclaim the kingdom, heal the sick, comfort those in mourning, and bring good news to the poor.

Thus, the anointing by Mary validates Jesus and proclaims his enlarged mission as redeemer and divine ransom. It gives him the confidence to move forward and face the crisis that lay ahead. No wonder he wanted Mary and her deed remembered. For in any kingdom worth its salt, this act of anointing is the culminating act of human recognition, bracketing, as it were, the descent of the Spirit that initiated Jesus' mission. Could Jesus have endured the trial of crucifixion without it?

John Watt

Sacrifice and Redemption in the Covenant of Jesus

As portrayed in the gospels the Jesus mission had to embody, in the passion experienced by its leader, the meaning of the covenant ascribed to the prophetic kingdom of God. Several motifs from the Hebrew scriptures are drawn together to convey the essence of the "new" covenant, of which Jesus was proclaimed as both harbinger and fulfillment. Approaching the holy city of Zion Jesus is depicted as riding a donkey, triumphant and yet humble. This symbolism is supposed to usher in the Messianic restoration of Israel. Yahweh will sound the trumpet and his arrows will flash like lightning. Yahweh's armies will devour the sling stones of the enemy like bread and drink their blood like wine. What joy and beauty will be theirs! (from Zechariah 9, paraphrased from the Jerusalem Bible)

But although this kingdom covenant of Jesus is to involve the offering of bread and wine, the imagery is to be of sacrifice, not conquest. The battleground is both terrestrial and super-terrestrial; and the chief protagonist, in battle with the forces of evil, is to assume the sacrificial and redemptive role of lamb of God and servant-son. The bread to be eaten is not the sling stones of the enemy but the body of the sacrificial lamb, given as an act of atonement and ransom for the transgression of the people. Similarly, the blood to be drunk is not that of the enemy but that of the servant-son, wounded and pierced through for the sins of the people and led like a helpless lamb to the slaughterhouse.

To convey the significance of this imagery of defeat Jesus is recorded as developing a simple ceremony of bread and wine, now commemorated as the Eucharist (giving or returning thanks). In it the bread represents the body and the wine represents the blood of the Lamb and the new covenant, poured out as an act of atonement for the forgiveness of sins. Following this ceremony, psalms of thanksgiving and sacrifice were sung, and then Yahweh proceeds, again in words from Zechariah 13, to strike the shepherd and scatter the sheep. A terrible testing awaits the servant-son and the people-sheep of Yahweh before the day of redemption can arrive.

This new covenant imagery of sacrifice and redemption achieves its full expression in the crucifixion of the servant-son, followed by the martyrdom and scattering, first of the people of Jerusalem and then of the early followers of the sacrificial victim. Crucifixion is the brutal means by which the occupying power of Rome got rid of thieves and rebels. In the year 70 Roman soldiers suppressed a Jewish uprising with great brutality. In later times Rome would hand over its victims, including thousands of confessing Christians, to be massacred by conquering armies, or torn alive and devoured in public arenas by wild animals. The Jesus covenant, now anchored in the servant imagery of Isaiah and the virtuous man and suffering son of the Book of Wisdom, was intended to take on this violence towards underdogs and embrace it as the means to spiritual redemption and healing.

But there is another element to the imagery of the Jesus covenant, which draws on the "new covenant" described in Jeremiah. That is the covenant written on the hearts of the redeemed people of Israel. To comprehend the significance of this heart-centered covenant we need to enter the sorrow of defeat and exile, hear Rachel weeping and crying for her children, and go on to beat our own breasts with shame and repentance. Yahweh needs to hear the deep grieving and moaning of Ephraim, crying out in exile, "bring me back, let me come back, for you are Yahweh my God." (from Jeremiah 31, in Jerusalem Bible).

This act of repentance is central to the new heart-centered covenant of Jeremiah. Hearing it, Yahweh responds by giving the people a different heart and an everlasting covenant of goodness and restoration. Likewise, the Jesus covenant, as described in the letter to the Hebrews, anchors itself in this act of repentance. Christ as symbolic high priest performs the act of redemption with his own blood, thus inaugurating the new heart-centered covenant spelled out in Jeremiah. The followers of Jesus, bodies washed in baptism and hearts cleansed, are ready to enter the heavenly Jerusalem and the kingdom of Yahweh.

Modern commentators see in this mixed symbolism some of the heartache experienced by the small band of followers who inherited the Jesus mission. Could the scandal and trauma of a rebel's death truly inaugurate any kind of new covenant worthy of the name? And which of the mixed messages of Zechariah was to be believed: the Yahwist victory in battle or the scattering and martyrdom of the sheep?

Looking forward a few hundred years from the events of the crucifixion, we can see that Christians did in the end come together and achieve a victory in the legitimization of Christianity by the Emperor Constantine. But that event threatened to discount the Isaian suffering servant imagery on which Jesus had based his mission. The kingdom covenant of the Jesus mission is not achieved through co-opting the power of Caesar. Instead it is the Jesus mission itself, which ever since the time of Constantine has been repeatedly co-opted into supporting worldly power. In the established, state-approved or state-tolerated church, eating the bread and drinking the wine too easily becomes an act of righteousness, rather than contrition and realignment of heart and soul. The imagery of sacrifice and ransom is lost in the splendor of earthly ceremonial. Beneath the grand edifices, the soaring arches, vaulted ceilings, and stained-glass windows of the established church the sounds of Rachel weeping for her children risk turning into faint echoes. Ephraim, secure in national or corporate identity, has little, or not nearly enough, sense of what to grieve and repent about.

The urgent message of the Jesus covenant is to focus on redemption and renewal. Human beings have much to repent, and none more so than those of us who have lived through much of the twentieth century. That century saw altogether too much oppression, racism, bloodshed and murder, of which far too much was committed or condoned by warring nationalisms. Anyone confronted with the history of world war and genocide and taking the Jesus covenant seriously would have to adopt the will to repent deeply and with aching heart acknowledge the terrible abuse and destruction of human and terrestrial life that has taken place in our time, much of it carried out by people supposedly espousing Biblical teaching. In the United States, much life goes on in the political, economic and domestic arenas without much evidence of commitment to the covenantal spiritual and moral values proclaimed by Jesus and his prophetic predecessors. There is, in short, no end to the grieving and repenting which serious followers of Jesus and kingdom adherents need to do. But perhaps it is asking too much to expect ordinary people to assume this kind of responsibility. We all have enough trouble facing our own personal difficulties and inadequacies, without having to take on the collective responsibility for the racism, war and murder, with which our nation among many others, has been so scarred.

But don't followers of Jesus need to bring some solace to all the Jews, Africans, native Americans and African-Americans, and other oppressed peoples who have been on the receiving end of modern Western militarism? Without such solace the Jesus covenant remains dormant, unable to redeem and pay ransom for all the suffering that it confronts. Then there is the constituency of poor, alien and underclass people—including widows, aliens, orphans, prisoners of conscience, refugees by the millions, people suffering from psychosomatic trauma, and women and children generally—to which the Jesus mission was directed. What about them? Are we to witness a turning away from such constituents? And what about the intentions of all those millions of secularized people, many of them spiritually adrift, for whom the Christian tradition has become a shadowy memory of things past and presumed to be better forgotten?

Redemption as an ethic for transforming and renewing public life is not at the present time much in vogue. But it is at the heart of the Jesus covenant and the prophetic teaching on which that covenant is based. In the early 14th century, when redemption enjoyed higher public recognition, the population of Siena, in Italy, gathered in the streets to witness the ceremonial procession of one of the greatest artistic creations of the medieval world, the Maesta, by the now not very well-known painter Duccio di Buoninsegna. This elaborate work proclaimed the majesty of the Madonna, to whom the Cathedral of Siena was dedicated, and at the same time recreated in stirring imagery the life, personal struggles, prophetic teaching, and redemptive death and resurrection of her son Jesus. The Maesta was ceremoniously deposited in the Cathedral, where it remained through the age of faith, until later generations cut it up into small pieces. Yet the mysterious power of Duccio's masterpiece has managed to survive its dismemberment. Although parts of it are now widely scattered and some pieces are lost, the message that it conveys remains unforgettable.

Further north, in early 15th century Flanders, the populace around Ghent was treated to a magnificent visualization of the Lamb of Redemption buying back the followers of Yahweh with the blood of the new covenant. This painting, by the brothers Hubert and Jan Van Eyck, and now in Ghent Cathedral, likewise remains to this day one of the truly great expressions of medieval and universal faith. One cannot help but admire such imaginative and deeply felt representations of a life devoted to the rescue and salvation of others.

But these works were not just made to elicit admiration. They are a reminder to Christians, as the apostle Paul put it, that it is within their power to share both the suffering and the glory of the covenantal tradition, and its expression in the life and mission of Jesus.

CHAPTER 11

Paul and the Covenant of Redemption

> When I survey the wondrous Cross,
> Where the young Prince of Glory died,
> My richest gain I count but loss,
> And pour contempt on all my pride.
> Isaac Watts (original text)

The Making of an Apostle

Most people on the edges of Christianity would probably know that Paul was the driving force behind the organization of the early Greek-speaking Christian communities. His travels and persecutions are recalled in Acts of the Apostles; and his views are preserved in his letters or epistles. Consequently, his words or deeds appear quite frequently in formal readings of Christian scripture. The 13th chapter of his first letter to the Corinthians, extolling love, has become such a staple of the modern wedding ceremony that it is hard to think of that event without recalling Paul's words.

But Paul was not primarily a commentator on marital love. He was first and foremost a Jewish rabbi and Pharisee, who radically modified his approach to Torah Judaism under the influence of a growing attraction to the Christ story among the Hellenistic communities of mixed Jews and non-Jews (gentiles or pagans), among whom he lived and worked. That conversion, which happened (according to the much later accounts in Acts) while he was en route from Jerusalem to Damascus, transformed Paul from a zealous persecutor of the followers of Jesus into the most ardent exponent of their new covenant of redemption. How could this radical switch have happened?

The first thing to note about this transformation is that it embraces Paul's interior and private as well as his exterior and public life. In terms of his public life, the Hellenistic Jew, narrowly but ardently obedient to the Torah covenants of Abraham and Moses, becomes committed to the new covenant associated with Jesus, because that covenant claimed to make the blessing and grace of the Yahwist God accessible to people outside the legal recognition of the Torah covenants. The transformation, through which Paul accepted that claim, gave him the justification necessary to advocate the cause of the Yahwist Divinity envisioned in the Isaiah and other prophetic texts, whose salvation would reach to the ends of the earth. Accepting the idea of Jesus as obedient to that mission in his life and death, and as such the instrument and expression of Yahweh's grace to the non-Jewish nations and peoples, Paul became its most fervent protagonist.

At the same time an interior transformation occurs in the man who sought to live blamelessly but could not. For individuals such as Paul, who felt themselves living in a messianic era, the Jesus story struck a resonant chord with both the story of the Isaian suffering servant, who took the faults of many on himself, and that of the virtuous man of the Book of Wisdom obedient to the mystery of Divine justice, whose soul is pleasing to, and loved by, God. Suddenly it became possible, through the mystery of the crucifixion and its resonance with these themes of redemption and grace, for the individual human being to be liberated from the sins and the anguish of failure in what Paul calls "this present wicked world." (Galatians, 1, 4.) A new world led by the Spirit appeared to emerge, through which ego-centered and self-mortifying life can give way to a liberating and life-expanding love of the Divine and of the human as other-than-self. "Self", in Paul's vocabulary, is "crucified"; in place of the identity of "self" the individual heart receives the Spirit of the Redeemer, calling the divine to the newborn child-person as "Abba" (father, parent, nurturer, source of love and spiritual freedom). These personal mysteries of the life of the redeemed spirit are as vital to the life and teaching of Paul as are the doctrines by which he interpreted the Christ event as a mandate to bring the Yahwist covenant to people outside the scope of Torah covenantal law. The Yahweh covenant of redemption is nothing if not good news to all people as individuals, including the messenger.

As contemporary scholars have pointed out, we must presume a long internal struggle between Paul's adherence to the Torah covenants and practice of the Law on the one hand, and on the other his reflection, recorded in his early letters, on the Isaian and other texts proclaiming the universality of the God Yahweh and the liberation of the redeemed spirit. Paul's adherence to Torah was unquestioned and was the basis of his reputation as both a strict Pharisee and a scourge of Jesus followers. Yet, as a Hellenistic Jew and Roman citizen, Paul evidently realized that the universalism of Roman imperialism, the Jewish-gentile admixture of Hellenistic society, and the interest of gentiles in the Yahwist faith and its practice in Hellenistic Jewish communities, created circumstances favorable to the development of a Yahwist mission along inclusive, Isaian lines.

But it was the Christ event, and its explication by early (pre-Pauline) followers of Jesus as the Christ Messiah making Yahwism accessible to gentiles, that persuaded Paul to change course and proclaim a Christ-centered, Isaian Yahwism to the nations. This proclamation, in the forms adopted by Paul, did not go unchallenged by other Christic adherents. Indeed, Paul reports in his letters that he constantly had to defend and justify his mission to Hellenistic gentiles. It says much for the powerful consequences of Paul's conversion that decades after it had taken place the author of Acts found it necessary to recall or create a specific event (and repeat its telling several times) that made that transformation theologically explicable, as well as convincing to those followers of Jesus as Christ who were not yet persuaded about Paul's apostolic credentials. What Paul records in his letters is that he did go through a fundamental change in consciousness, though not specifically while en route anywhere, nor at any one moment in time. Having done so, reportedly over a period of years, he went about applying the same drive and determination that had characterized his former life as a Pharisee to his new understanding of Jesus as personification of a new universal covenant.

Whatever the circumstances of Paul's conversion, the events described in Acts as happening on the road to Damascus have had the most profound consequence for human history. Indeed, in terms of its historical significance, the encounter is comparable with that of Moses and the burning bush. Paul brought the authority of a Pharisee, a mind steeped in scriptural learning, and a passionate desire to understand and explain life's meaning, to the mission of proclaiming Jesus as the Christ. He applied that passion with soul force to the dissemination of the story of Jesus in the multifaceted roles of Christ, Redeemer, and Lord of all. He became a missionary, in fact the paradigm of missionaries who fearlessly devote their lives to a cause. In the name of the Christ Jesus, Paul traveled up and down Asia Minor and into southeastern Europe, proclaiming the "good news" about Jesus and the new Jesus covenant, and undergoing harrowing experiences, without ever losing heart or sense of direction about what he was doing.

But Paul was not just an eager missioner for Jesus as Christ-redeemer. Before there were any gospels, he developed a sophisticated theology focused on the crucifixion and resurrection of Jesus and the significance of this event for gentile salvation. Paul's theology was based on an intimate knowledge of the Hebrew scriptures, particularly on doctrines of redemption and salvation found in the prophets and the psalms. He embraced the experience of the Christ Jesus as a fulfillment of those doctrines, a way of reconciling humanity to God through an act of grace on God's part.

It was this insight, elaborated into his doctrine of justification by faith, which made Paul such a tireless advocate of Jesus as Christ/Messiah, Redeemer and Lord. The Christ Jesus had literally saved him from what he came to regard as a life of sin and had commissioned him to go out into the world and preach the good news. For Paul this good news was overwhelming, since it involved not merely his own personal salvation but the much larger reconciliation of the human and natural order to the Creator. The world had gone wrong, but Paul, in a blinding flash—or after long and intense reflection—had grasped how it could be put right. This vision propelled the new faith into the Hellenistic world, where it took root and eventually spread all over Europe. In the long era of the European Reformation that ushered in the modern world, Paul's vision became a world-wide force. The famous and hymn by Isaac Watts, cited at the beginning of this chapter, is an example of Paul's transformative vision at work.

Over the last two centuries secularization has done much to weaken the hold of Christianity, and Pauline theology, over modern consciousness. The secular world has been governed by economic and political, rather than religious, ideology. For many people in the contemporary West, the secularism of the European Enlightenment brought about an era of modern progressive liberalism, which would address itself to social concerns to which the dogmas of traditional religion seemed confining or irrelevant. In addition, throughout much of the 20th century an ill-defined anti-clerical humanism filled in the gap for millions of educated people who had turned their backs on the organized church and Christian practice. Other tens of millions were won over to more aggressive and nihilistic substitutes for religious doctrine.

But the 20th century has not been kind to secular ideologies. Those that seized control of state power in order to overrun their opposition succeeded only in causing untold destruction and misery. Can we ever account adequately for the crimes and mass genocides committed in this century in the name of secular ideologies? In much of the world the secular ideologies of Imperialism, Fascism, Nazism and Communism, have been tried and found emphatically wanting. Thus, in this era of trouble and uncertainty, a redemptive and generally inclusive vision such as Paul's is something worth examining. Our contemporary world has also gone—and is going—wrong. The abuse of the created order—whether we are talking about ethnic cleansing, or racism, or the drug trade, or arms trafficking, or human or natural pollution, or terrorism—is staggering. We too need a vision of how these terrible troubles could be put right. We need a vision that focuses not on conflict and conquest but on reconciliation, one that is sufficiently powerful to transform the way we view ourselves and our place in the world in relation to other living beings. We particularly need a vision that provides an alternative to the hatred and fear that affect so much of contemporary life. Could it be that Paul's vision has something to teach us? The turmoil of our times is so great, that even for the most skeptical it must at least be worth considering the matter. Indeed, it was to skeptics that Paul directed his greatest efforts.

Paul's Letters

The substance of Paul's experience and teaching is contained in his letters to newly established communities of Christ followers. Modern scholarship generally divides these letters into three groups. The main group, consisting of the first letter to the Thessalonians, the surviving letters to the Corinthians, the letters to the Galatians and the Romans, and the letter to the Philippians, contain the essence of Paul's teaching on the crucified and resurrected Christ Jesus and the doctrine of justification by faith. The letter to the Romans gives the most systematic exposition of his views on these matters. The second letter to the Thessalonians, and the letters to the Colossians and the Ephesians, convey a much more eschatological perspective. The latter two letters project a revelation of the hidden 'mystery' of Jesus as the eternal Lord, battling and overcoming the cosmic powers of darkness and thereby retrieving souls from a life of sin and falsehood. To be sure, the theme of Jesus as cosmic Lord is present in credal passages reported in Paul's early letters but not substantially developed. For this and other reasons having to do with developments in liturgical and social practice, these other Deutero-Pauline letters are widely viewed by contemporary scholars as belonging to a later date than those that concentrate on the Jesus crucified in this world. Similarly, the 'pastoral' letters to Timothy and Titus belong to a later period, when the early communities of Jesus followers had begun to develop an organizational structure. It is the first group of letters that give the most direct indication of Paul's vision about how to make Yahwism accessible to gentiles, and to gentiles as individual human beings accessible to Yahwist grace and mercy.

The first letter to the Thessalonians introduces prophetic themes that preoccupied Paul throughout his mission. The most urgent was the fear that the Yahwist God would one day tire of human wrongdoing and strike back. That Day of the Lord was coming sooner than people realized. Paul was very moved by the concept of Divine retribution and the critical need to find a way to salvation. The good news for the Thessalonians was that Jesus, who had died and risen from death, would come to save both the living and the dead when that terrible day arrived. Those who would be saved were those who believed in the good news of Jesus and the living power of the Spirit to transform human existence. That transformation was manifested through living in holiness. What Paul meant by living in holiness was that people would treat themselves with reverence and treat each other with love and compassion. Those transformed by faith in Jesus had now become children of light who would win salvation through his intervention.

This letter is one of the shortest expositions of Paul's teachings. The problems that he would encounter in preaching to 'Gentiles' are barely touched on. The new converts are reminded that they would have persecutions to bear, just as Paul did. They are advised to "live quietly" in order to appear respectable to those outside the faith, and to arm themselves with faith, love and hope.

The letter to the Philippians, although written from prison, is the most optimistic and warmly eloquent of Paul's writings. It is also one of the most personal. One can feel Paul's frustration at being chained in prison. He admits how much he misses his friends and how much he agonizes over those who misinterpret the good news. But what makes him happy is that the Christ is proclaimed. His friends in Christ are together with him in the struggle to spread the good news. He prays that their love for each other will increase and so prepare them for the Day of the Christ.

Warming to this theme, Paul invites them to liken themselves to the Christ Jesus. He quotes from an early hymn about how the divine Jesus humbled himself, taking on the form of a servant, as in deutero-Isaiah, and becoming "obedient unto death". Then the God Yahweh raised him on high, above all powers and principalities, so that at his name every knee should bow and every tongue confess him as Lord. Paul urges his friends to work for their salvation with fear and trembling, so that they become perfect children of God, shining like bright stars.

Then the issue of circumcision comes up. As missionary to the Gentiles Paul had concluded that circumcision denoted obedience to the Judaic Torah rather than faith in the glory of the risen Christ. Seizing on the Deuteronomic idea that true circumcision was of the heart, Paul claimed that converts to the Christ were the real people of the circumcision, because they "worshipped in accordance with the Spirit of God." If circumcision, as traditionally defined, was the issue, Paul as a Jew was surely qualified for salvation. But penile circumcision now symbolized for Paul righteousness through his own efforts to follow the Judaic Law. That is what had characterized his early, dysfunctional life. Now it obfuscated the brilliant clarity of faith in the Christ-redeemer. Paul had argued this issue out with the Christian community in Jerusalem and obtained their reluctant consent to convert Gentiles without circumcision. But his mission was harried by exponents of "cutting", who were no better than "enemies of the cross of Christ." Paul countered that such people were caught up in earthly things. But our home, he affirmed, is in heaven, where our Savior, the Lord Jesus Christ, will transform our "vile" bodies "like unto his glorious body."

As we see from this striking passage, the physical body constituted a serious problem for Paul. A celibate himself, he railed against what he regarded as abuse of the body by others, whether in the form of fornication, homosexuality, or other activities outside of monogamous and heterosexual marriage. Yet he was an ardent lover, and one can hardly doubt that he felt pangs of attraction for others, especially the young men, such as Timothy and Titus, who were his most devoted companions. In the case of Timothy, whose father was Greek, Paul had even carried out the intimate and highly painful operation of adult penile circumcision. Some scholars have hypothesized that Paul felt in himself the pangs of homo-erotic love, and that this could have constituted the guilt which underlay his pre-Christian existence. Whether or not that is the case, there is no doubt that Paul suffered greatly through his body. At one point he recounts that he was five times given 39 lashes, and at other times beaten, stoned, or thrown into prison, as well as enduring all kinds of hardship on road and sea. Paul tried to sublimate this physical and mental anguish by striving ardently for the perfection of Jesus as Christ. Circumcision was a challenge not only to his theology but to his spiritual wellbeing, by giving physical expression to values that challenged Paul at the core of his mental and spiritual life.

In the letter to the Galatians, his conflict with the circumcisers comes to a head. This letter is virtually a single-issue document. It says nothing about the coming day of retribution, or about how to prepare for that time. It is focused on Paul's authority to put aside circumcision and proclaim faith in Jesus as the Christ. Evidently circumcisers had been challenging Paul and pushing circumcision behind his back. Paul comes right back and warns that anyone promoting such a line—even if an angel from heaven—is to be condemned. Drawing on Deutero Isaiah, he likens himself to the servant of Yahweh, called from his mother's womb to become a light to the nations. He recounts his meeting with the elders of Jerusalem and confirms that he was commissioned to preach the good news to the uncircumcised.

Paul casts the issue starkly in terms of slavery versus freedom. What justifies a person is not accordance to the Law but faith in Jesus as the Christ. Jews no less than Gentiles had to become believers in the Christ Jesus. No one will be justified by adhering to the Law. To conform to the Law after turning to the Christ is to make us sinners like the rest. If justification is through the Law, then Christ's death was pointless. Paul draws on various biblical themes to advance the case of justification by faith. He seizes on the fact that Abraham put his faith in God before he was circumcised. As an avid reader of Isaiah, Paul insists that scripture foresaw that the God Yahweh would justify the Gentiles by faith. More, those who live by the Law are under a curse (that is, the curse of Adam and the broken Deuteronomic covenant). The righteous person finds life through faith. The Christ redeemed us from the Law by taking its curse on himself. The Law merely specifies crimes. We are all in the grip of sin, enslaved to idols and godless gods. Freedom comes only through faith in the Christ Jesus.

Paul exhorts the Galatians to stand firm and not to submit to the 'yoke of slavery'. What matters, he insists, is faith experienced through love. The Law can be summarized in the command to love one's neighbor as oneself. This is the critical issue for Paul: the life of the Spirit versus the life of the body. Living by the body leads to a whole catalog of corrupting sins. Those who live by that way will not inherit the kingdom. Living by the Spirit brings love, joy, kindness, and self-control. Those who sow through the life of the Spirit will become new beings, who will harvest eternal life.

The issue of circumcision had become the pivotal point for the missionary seeking to unfold the life of the Spirit. But there were other issues that Paul had to address before he could put his theological defense together. Some of these problems are reviewed in his two letters to the Corinthians. One of the problems in Corinth was that factionalism had broken out among the followers of Jesus. Paul addresses this problem in terms accessible to a Hellenistic audience, by arguing that the only meaningful difference is between spiritual faith and intellectual reason. Belief in the cross of Jesus is a matter of faith, not reason. It is a manifestation of God's power to save. This, said Paul, may seem "foolish", but that simply reveals the limits of the human intellect. It may seem "weak", but that is a sign of God's hidden wisdom at work. This wisdom, ordained before the world began, is unknown to the powers that had crucified Jesus. It is revealed through the spirit. That is why Paul teaches not by philosophy but by the spirit. A follower of the Christ must learn to become 'foolish' before being able to become 'wise'. Paul reminds his readers that the Day of Judgment is coming. It is the gifts of the spirit that will prepare them for that Day.

Paul then turns to problems concerning human sexual conduct. He reiterates the point that those who abused their bodies would not inherit the kingdom. The body, he proclaims, is the temple of the Holy Spirit. This argument provided a telling application of a central theme in Jewish salvation history to the anguish and drama of individual wellbeing. Followers of the Christ whose bodies had been "purchased with a price", should use them to glorify God. In an extended passage Paul offers his views on marriage and celibacy. Then he addresses the question of idolatry. Could food sacrificed to idols be eaten by believers? This might seem today an arcane problem. But the point Paul makes is that food itself has no spiritual value. The point is not to use food to abuse others. Paul, it turns out, has become a vegetarian, in order to avoid eating sacrificial meat that might become a cause of trouble to others.

The broader problem is that abuse of food is a sign of abandonment of the life of the spirit and a turning towards idolatry of the body. This sounds alarm bells for Paul. It reminds him of the misconduct of the children of Israel while they were wandering through the desert away from Egypt, and of the appalling punishments that befell the wrongdoers. For people who are living at the end of time, this must strike a warning bell. Paul reminds his readers of the eucharistic meal (a sacrament of thanksgiving), through which believers become united with the Christ and with each other. One can commune with the Lord or with idols, but not with both.

Mention of the eucharist leads Paul into a discussion of liturgical practice, particularly as applied to the agape love feast and the eucharist itself. Christian worship no longer requires the agape feast, but the eucharist remains the central ceremony, intended to bond Christians now as then. What Paul said about it has in turn become the central text of the eucharistic liturgy, heard by millions every weekend. Those who participate in the eucharist, says Paul, proclaim the death of the Lord on their behalf. They should conduct themselves accordingly.

Having dealt with the eucharist, Paul goes on to discuss the vital question of the nature of spiritual gifts. These include preaching, prophesying, healing, the gift of tongues, interpretation, etc. Paul uses the analogy of the body to make the point that these gifts all have their place when used properly. But it is the higher gifts that count. The gift of tongues, without love, is mere noise. The gift of prophecy, even of faith, without love, is nothing. Even the gift of my body, without love, is nothing.

What then is this love, on which all other gifts depend? Rather than directly answering this question Paul responds by describing how love manifests itself in relation to others. Love, he says, is patient and kind. Love does not insist on its own way. It rejoices in the right, not in the wrong. Love believes, hopes, and endures. Love, says the great evangelist of love, never ends. All the other gifts of tongues, prophecy, one's body, etc., pass away. For when perfection comes the imperfect disappears—leaving only the expression of what is perfect. It is like leaving childhood to become an adult, or like peering through a mirror and then seeing face to face. What I know now is imperfect; but in the fullness of time, I shall know as I am known. It is faith, hope and love that endure; but above all, love.

If Paul had written or recorded nothing else, these words would have sufficed to preserve his memory. They express for him the essence of human consciousness transformed by the power—in other words, the love—of the Christ-redeemer. These famous words came out of that power and were not written in abstraction. More than any other passage in Paul's writings they encapsulate his deepest beliefs about the life of humans inspired by the personal sacrifice of the Christ Jesus. It was love that enabled Paul to endure all the hardships that he experienced, love that kept him going on the road and in prison, love that kept him hopeful and focused on the life of the Spirit. Love was like a compass for Paul, always pointing forward, never back, always towards others and away from self, always towards the heart and spirit. Without love he would have been an angry zealot pursued by guilt; he would have doubtless remained just another itinerant rabbi or preacher who has disappeared from the pages of history. Love transformed him; he applied it to transform others.

Paul ends his letter with a recapitulation of his teaching about the Christ raised from the dead. He turns to the analogy of Adam, through whom death came, and the Christ Jesus, through whom came the 'resurrection'. At the end of time the Christ will return in triumph, having defeated all his enemies. The last defeated enemy is death, for then the dead will be raised. Some people wondered how this could happen. Paul replies, in a unique passage in chapter 15 of this letter and commemorated in a powerful, dramatic aria in Handel's Messiah, that we would then all be changed, in the twinkling of an eye. "For the trumpet shall sound, and the dead shall be raised incorruptible." And death will be swallowed up in victory. And for those who know Brahms' Requiem, this is the climactic text of that powerful composition written to comfort those in mourning.

Between this letter and what we now have as the second letter, Paul was obliged to visit Corinth and sort out some of the problems referred to above. Evidently Paul was under attack and in anguish, for this subsequent letter is much more defensive in tone. Indeed, a previous letter, of which a portion is believed by contemporary scholars to have been tacked on here as chapters 10-13 (verse 10), was written "in tears". According to this passage, people had accused Paul of hiding behind his letters, because his bodily presence was weak and his speech "contemptible."

Behind this abuse was the more substantive charge that he had encroached on other people's turf. Others in the area were competing with Paul for converts. They accused him of muscling in, pretending to preach for nothing, but in fact living off other people. These charges, coming from other Jewish missioners, were especially painful. Paul accused his critics of being false apostles and deceitful workers. He recounted all his hardships and degradations. He had nothing to boast of but his weakness and his visions. But his weakness was viable, for in that lay his strength. Exhibiting this strength, he warned his readers to prepare for a third visit and meanwhile to examine their own lives. He would wish to build them up; let them not fail the tests of faith!

In the main body of the letter Paul reverts to the question about his authority. The problem here was that he was not one of the designated twelve apostles (men certified by the risen Jesus to proclaim the faith, who had known Jesus in the flesh.) Paul knew him only through a vision. Since he had been once such an ardent enemy of followers of Jesus, the elders in Jerusalem never quite trusted him. Perhaps they were afraid of his rabbinical skills, his understanding of the Hellenistic world, his empathy with uncircumcised males in that world. In any case, he possessed no letters of recommendation. His mandate, he had to argue, came from God, who had appointed Paul and his associates as ministers of a new Covenant, one which was made not of written letters but of the Spirit.

Here too Paul distinguished himself from those who still adhered to the covenant of the written law. The one, in his view, administered condemnation, the other justification. Paul, who seems to have felt condemned by the covenants of the law and of circumcision, refused to apologize for adhering to what he proclaimed as the new covenant of the spirit. "We preach not ourselves," he said, "but Christ Jesus, the Lord, and ourselves your servants." We, admitted Paul, are only earthenware jars. The power comes from God. Life on earth is like a "tent", soon folded up. But the truth would be brought out before the judgment seat of Christ. It was in the fear of the Lord that they tried to persuade others. If they sometimes got "carried away", it was because of the love of the Christ, who died for humans so that humans could live for him. It was through that critical and dramatic event that the God Yahweh had become reconciled to the world, and that the time of salvation had arrived.

Paul and the Covenant of Redemption

The defensive tone of this letter (or letters) suggests that Paul and his companions were getting dissatisfied with the problem of having to respond to attacks on one issue after another. They needed a statement of faith, an apologia, which would spell out their position on the key issue of justification by faith, on which Paul based his mandate as an apostle and evangelist. The letter to the Romans was written as an answer to that need. Paul had not yet visited Rome therefore Rome was not yet within his mission territory. He planned to go there on his way to Spain. He wrote to tell the Roman believers about himself, perhaps also to set out his views for the benefit of his existing constituency.

The letter that emerged is less a letter than a proclamation of faith. It is one of the most minutely studied texts in theological history. It has exercised enormous influence on the unfolding of Christianity. Reformers, such as Luther and Calvin, anchored their doctrines on this letter. As a theological text it does not make easy reading. The non-specialist reader can do no more than settle for the gist. But because of the profound influence that this letter has exerted on Christian practice, it is essential to know something about what it is saying.

After the usual introductory courtesies, the letter wastes no time in getting down to the gist of Paul's beliefs. The good news he was called to proclaim is that God has the power to save all who have faith, and that faith is what leads to life. This proposition seems so deceptively simple as to require little further explanation. But it gets right to the heart of the challenge facing Paul: how to translate a revelation founded on Jewish historical experience into terms that can include people living outside of that experience; and for himself personally, how to justify by faith what could not be justified by formal appointment. In short: how to include outsiders within the covenant of redemption.

The standard assumption among Jewish missionaries of the time was that anyone seeking to become a participant in God's salvation would have to be circumcised (if male) and become fully compliant with Judaic covenantal law. Paul had become convinced that this approach would not work. It confined the universality of God's power, and it undervalued the power of redemption. Paul based these conclusions on a minute reading of the psalms and the prophets, particularly Isaiah. But it was the experience on the road to Damascus (or some similar defining awakening) that catalyzed his belief. The zeal of the man determined to stay afloat through his own efforts ran into a revelation about God's power to save the individual person who is unable to help him or herself. It dawned on Paul that God's power cannot be circumscribed by human behavior. The essence of God's grace and mercy towards humans is that the power of redemption is freely given. The proof was in the freely given death and resurrection of Jesus. As a Pharisee Paul believed in resurrection; he just had not regarded the death and reported resurrection of Jesus as a manifestation of God's grace. On the "road to Damascus", that insight came to him with overwhelming impact.

It may help in understanding the force of this revelation to recall the apocalyptic times in which Paul lived. Within the Jewish orbit it was widely felt that the day of God's judgment against the wicked world was fast approaching. The spread of Roman power and idolatry, coming on the heels of an epoch of Greek Hellenistic oppression, had hastened the day of reckoning. Apocalyptic texts, such as the book of Daniel, and others outside the Biblical canon, warned of unparalleled distress to come. Whole communities, such as the Essenes, had retreated into the desert to prepare themselves for the end times. Paul shared this apocalyptic perspective, even if not in the extreme forms adopted by the desert communities. He looked around at the scale of human sin and felt the burgeoning of God's wrath. No humans anywhere were exempt from it. All who sinned would perish.

But the prophetic vision, which warned of God's anger, also spoke of God's anguish and mercy, and the power of the God Yahweh to intervene in history to save humans. In Paul's view the Christ event, proclaiming the long-awaited Messiah as spiritual redeemer, constituted such an intervention. It reached beyond Judaic Law and tradition to reach both Jews and Gentiles through faith. To illustrate the power of faith Paul turned to the example of Abraham. Yahweh's promises to Abraham were freely given and secured through Abraham's faith. Abraham's strength consisted not in obedience to the Law (which did not yet exist), or in circumcision (which came 'later' in his life, after he had made his commitment to Yahweh), but in faith, through which he became father of many nations. Paul's argument here draws on intricacies in Jewish salvation history, but the main point, that faith is the key to salvation, is clear enough.[12]

In short, wrote Paul, it is by faith in the Christ event that humans today can access God's grace. The Christ's death was freely given so that we who are sinners and enemies to God (or to God's covenant) could be reconciled to the Almighty. Or, as the King James Bible text puts it, picking up on Paul's end-time fears, "being now justified by his blood, we shall be saved from wrath through him." (Romans 5.9) As sin and death had entered the world through Adam, so grace and life had entered through the Christ Jesus. The Christ's death and resurrection set the believer free from sin—but not, Paul quickly added, free to sin. "For the wages of sin is death". The gift of God, by contrast, is eternal life, through the Christ Jesus.

Having established this argument, Paul turned to the relationship of the Law to sin. As a believing Jew, he made it clear that he was not against

---

[12]

the Law. "We know that the law is spiritual", he wrote. The problem is that humans are carnal and sold on sin. They just can't help themselves. Reason tells them to serve the Law of God, but the flesh compels them to sin. "O wretched man that I am!" he cried out. "Who shall deliver me from the body of this death?" As we see from this passage, Paul did not preach anything that he had not struggled with in the intensity of his own body and soul. It was the grace of the Christ Jesus's example that had enabled him to feel redeemed and "delivered from the body of this death." Living in the likeness of sinful flesh Jesus had overcome sin in the flesh, manifesting the glory and transcendence of a life lived by the power of the spirit.

That glory awaited all those who turned to live by the fruits of the spirit. But beyond human redemption the whole of creation was awaiting the time of liberation and the hope of salvation. That time of total salvation had not yet arrived; yet those who were called into reconciliation would not be refused, for nothing could come between them and the "love of God, which is in Christ Jesus our Lord."

Paul followed this passage on individual salvation with a long statement arguing that the intervention of the Christ event was not to be viewed as a denial of, or terminal point in, Jewish salvation history. On the contrary, the Jewish people, or at least a remnant, remained firmly within God's plan of salvation. It is a great pity that this long passage has so frequently escaped the attention of Christian theology and professing Christians. The idea that God had somehow "cast away" the chosen people and replaced them with gentiles (a notion with which I grew up, and one that as a child I assumed without question) was not what Paul intended. The Jewish people were, as he pointed out, his own blood relatives, and they were still the chosen people. We need not go into the details of how Paul explained God's salvation plan for Jewish people. It is enough that he had an explanation, and that it was central to his conception of God's mercy.[13]

Paul ended his letter with a miniature Sermon on the Mount, urging his readers to love each other, bless those who persecuted them, prefer good to evil, and make their bodies a "living sacrifice", holy and acceptable to God. In a passage that would resonate with Luther, he adjured them to submit to civil authority. They should love their neighbors as themselves,

---

[13] The debates as to whether the Christian covenant replaced the covenant of Moses in terms of its access to salvation lie beyond the argument of this book.

and live and let live. As the time of reckoning was drawing near, they should wake up and "put on the armor of light." Various greetings and postscripts followed, and then a final word of praise to the everlasting God, who alone is wise.

The Challenge of Faith in Action

The letter to the Romans, as I hope this brief account may indicate, is a virtuoso exercise in theology. It displays an incredible grasp of Biblical text and a remarkable ability to apply Jewish theology to the universal problem of human sin. It is also moved by an urgent desire to save human beings from the consequences of wrongdoing. As such it is an intensely personal statement. The anguish of human existence is never far below the surface of Paul's argument. He longs for individual people to be able to throw off sin and experience the renewing power of love and Divine glory in their lives. As a follower of the Isaian teachings, he even longs for all creation to experience this renewal.

We can imagine this man, who had found renewal in his own life, setting out to bring that vision to communities of people living up and down Asia Minor and on into southern Europe. Apart from small numbers of Jewish people, these communities knew nothing of salvation history. The idea of a redeemer God, who could transform a life of anguish and guilt into one of hope, did not exist for them. The challenge of proclaiming this good news took hold of Paul and gripped him. From then on, his whole life was devoted to that end. He could have become a great Rabbinic scholar or an admired exegete. But he was happy living out his life on the road, creating little communities of faith and nurturing them through his letters.

The Pauline mission, conceived in faith, represents that element in the Christian tradition that is intent on communicating the hope of self-renewal, embodied in the redeeming covenant of the crucified and risen Jesus as Christ. As compared with the tradition, associated with Peter and the Jerusalem community, which is founded on apostolic appointment, the Pauline mission is rooted in the experience of personal redemption and vocation. That is still its greatest strength and appeal. Paul's vision of covenant concentrates on its attribute of Divine reconciliation freely given. Children of the covenant are those, such as Isaac and Jacob, who receive that promise given to their mothers and embrace it. Gentiles, once excluded from the Yahwist covenants, are brought within their scope through the freely given sacrifice of Jesus as the Christ.

The fact that Christianity has found room for both these apostolic traditions has been a source of both strength and weakness. The weakness consists in the polarity and tension that exists between the two traditions and the internecine violence, often brutal and disastrous, which this has spawned. Such religious violence built up during the Reformation and reached its peak in the Thirty Years War between Catholic and Protestant forces, which devastated central Europe during the mid-17th century. Bloody ripples of that religion-inspired violence lingered on in Northern Ireland until recent times. The strength consists in understanding that there is a place for both traditions in the overall conception of a life of faith. Because of the strength of Paul's convictions and the life of faith that he created as a missionary, Christianity is still to this day shaped by his unique part-Jewish, part-Hellenistic vision.

Not only that, his message of hope to people torn between competing secular and religion-inspired visions is relevant to polarities central to our own times. Paul was one of the very few missionaries who was determined, to bridge the chasm between the urban, mundane, and substantially secular world of Greco-Roman culture and the spiritually demarcated and exclusive communities of those people preparing for the end times. Paul, too, was preparing for the end times when God's judgment would prevail, but not—like the Dead Sea communities—in isolation from the rest of humanity. He absorbed the Isaian idea that the kingdom of God reaches out to people of all nations and made it his business to put that idea into action. He addressed the doubts of people teetering between the demands of material and spiritual existence, confronted their problems, and insisted that the values of Jewish salvation history applied to their circumstances.

This belief in the universalism of Yahwist grace was more of a stretch than many followers of Jesus could countenance. How could the idolatrous, uncircumcised, unclean, and hostile world of Roman Hellenism be accessible to a divine power notorious for forbidding idolatry and uncleanliness and demanding circumcision? But Paul, as a Greek-speaking Roman citizen, took up that challenge. Why leave people out of consideration, when they were also part of God's creation? It is a question that continues to demand attention, whether on the southern borders of the United States or among the many thousands of refugees occupying barebones camps on the edges of Europe, Asia and Oceana.

III

Covenants and Contemporary Problems

CHAPTER 12

Covenant and Management of Androcentric Power

> When I consider thy heavens,
> The work of thy fingers,
> The moon and the stars
> Which thou hast ordained,
> What is man, that thou art mindful of him?
> Psalm 8

We move now from discussion of covenantal relationships in the Hebrew and Christian scriptures to the question of their capacity to provide us with spiritual and moral direction today. We are certainly in need of spiritual and moral guidance. Our civil society, as manifested in the United States and other developed Western countries, is in theory admirable but in practice leaves all kinds of spiritual, emotional and material problems unresolved. Can the wisdom of the Covenants help us deal with today's material and spiritual problems, and if so, how?

In approaching this question, I emphasize two related aspects of the Biblical covenant. One involves the so-called 'kingdom' or realm that is of and alive to Divine and spiritual power; the other the prophetic mission to bring good news to people living on the edge, or as the King James Bible puts it, the "poor and broken-hearted." In this chapter I concentrate on the realm of the spiritual kingdom in relationship to the secular kingdom of man. I am using the terms 'man' and 'kingdom of man' intentionally, in order to emphasize the dominance of patriarchal, male values in human, worldly power systems. The question for this chapter is what is man, and how do these two different kingdoms define the nature of manhood?

Recognition of male dominance and phallocentric management of power in human organization, language and culture—and therefore the need to set boundaries to it—is at the heart of the Yahwist covenant. This is a matter which recent feminist scholarship has attempted to bring to the attention of the religious world, so far with limited results. This is due partly to the dominance of religious and other power systems by men, and partly to reluctance by both men and women to question whether this male dominance, as currently manifested, fully reflects the intentions ascribed to the covenanting God—or, for that matter, is in accord with the values of spiritual life as such.

Religious androcentrism itself reflects the broader fact that men have taken possession of worldly power and have used it to advance male agendas. Contrary to what one might have expected, given the last 200 years of European enlightenment and liberal progressivism, the world of the 20th century saw the intensification of male, phallocentric power. With the access of the age of terrorism, the imbalance between male and female power—what the Chinese call yang and yin—and the dominance of manifestations of male power, such as the essentially male-developed nuclear bomb, ICBM delivery systems, and male terrorist regimes, brotherhoods, and systems of religious domination, has reached a crisis point.

The Biblical perspective is that the fundamental problem of imbalance in male-female relations arises from the supremacy of phallic power. In the realm of God phallic power is subsumed within a broader, spiritually inclusive power relationship between humankind and the divine. But in the realm of man phallic power is its own justification as a source of male preference and domination. We can see this comparison in divine versus human power in the accounts of Abraham and King David, but in view of the immediacy of the problem for our times we need to pursue the matter further.

Subsuming of Phallic Power in the Abraham Covenant

The Exodus covenant has its Priestly counterpart in the covenant supposedly made hundreds of years previously by Yahweh with Abraham. According to this patriarchal covenant, found in Genesis chapters 15 and 17, Yahweh promised to make the faithful Abraham heir to the land of Canaan and progenitor of a great nation. This is the origin of the selection of Israel as the sacramental nation and the Israelites as the 'chosen people'. As with the Exodus covenant, the agreement came with a condition. In return for Yahweh making Abraham most fruitful, a progenitor of nations and kings, and possessor in perpetuity of the land of Canaan, Abraham, his sons, and the males in his household should be circumcised. From henceforth, all Abraham's male descendants must have their foreskins cut off from their penises, in acknowledgement of this sacramental phallic covenant. According to the account, Abraham that same day took his son Ishmael and the males in his household and cut off their foreskins. Abraham was 'ninety-nine' years old when he cut off his own foreskin, and Ishmael thirteen. In this way the phallic covenant was ratified. Circumcision has remained since then a central rite of Jewish life.

It is interesting to note that Yahweh's original promise to Abraham of land and descendants was unconditional and was ratified through an ancient sacrificial ritual recorded in the J tradition that has nothing to do with circumcision. When Moses travels from Midian to assume the burden of leading the Israelites out of Egypt, he is, in a very strange episode, also from J, attacked by Yahweh. To ward off the danger his Midianite wife Zipporah takes a piece of flint, cuts off her son's foreskin—which evidently to that point had not been circumcised—and touches it between Moses' legs, in his own phallic region, murmuring "truly you are my bridegroom of blood." This phallic offering appears to satisfy Yahweh, who withdraws. One gathers from this episode that circumcision was not fully acculturated at the time of Moses or even quite possibly much later; it is considered mandatory, however, to demonstrate adherence to Yahweh.

The covenant of circumcision in the Abraham cycle was evidently a later addition, introduced from the Priestly tradition into the text at a point after Abraham and Sarah had finally succeeded in giving birth to a son. Priestly power here asserts its importance for the management of the Yahwist covenant, and as guardian of that covenant's tribal and sacramental purity. From the perspective of the myth, the old man and his wife had at long last achieved mutual fertility and now could hope to establish descendants. But Abraham's dynastic fertility was to be won at the cost of a painful operation, inscribing on the penis the immutable evidence of man's covenant with, and recognition of, the authority of Yahweh over the energy expressed through the phallus. Management of phallic power should henceforth be recognized as a central aspect of Yahweh's covenant, inasmuch as it is recognized as an expression of Yahweh's power and plan for the ongoing creation and support of human life. The priestly act of circumcision (the bris) became the ritual repeatedly affirming the adherence of Israelite patriarchy to its covenant with Yahweh as Creator and Progenitor. The physical energy of the phallus produces genealogy, new life, and a fruitful tribal existence. All the "begettings" enumerated in the Torah are thus intended as witness to the continuity and fulfillment of the Priestly covenant. Phallic power is subsumed within the divine creation plan, whereby humankind should multiply and fill the earth; the children of Israel, as the expression of Israelite covenantal phallic power, are elected as the prime actors within that plan.

But as with all power systems, phallic energy can be abused. Thus. the Exodus covenant stipulates substantial boundaries that are placed around the use of the penis. Adultery, that most blatant abuse of phallic power, was forbidden. Men who committed it must be put to death. Men were also forbidden on pain of death to lie with other men, to have intercourse with animals, to commit incest or to have intercourse with other close female relatives. After having a seminal discharge, a man must wash his whole body with water and remain unclean until the evening. After sexual intercourse both parties must wash all over and remain unclean until the evening. The practice of handing over young offspring to be burned before the god Molech was proscribed and offenders sentenced to death. When Israelite men on the trek to Canaan went whoring with Moabite women and worshipped their gods, their leaders were sentenced to be impaled and the rest to be killed. The Israelite man who brought a Midianite woman into the camp was speared in his groin and killed.

These proscriptions are nowadays seen by many people as old-fashioned, if not sanctimonious and destructive to life. As with all human proscriptions they can be abused and violated in the very process of attempting to prevent abuses. We should therefore attempt to understand these ancient phallic proscriptions as a way of intending to honor the generative properties of phallic energy and the relationships by which generation and human creativity are accomplished. In the Kabbalistic tradition the sefirah (emanation) of Yesod, the phallus, embodies our "energy need to form sacred unions with other human beings, unions from which the continuation of life comes … the sefirah of Yesod naturally draws us to those with whom a sacred union is possible."[14] From this perspective, covenantal circumcision of the penis, and the accompanying proscriptions, can be described as intended to recognize the sacredness of sexuality and sexual union, and not just to legislate against its pervasive abuse.

But, as can be seen from the story of King David, the covenantal horror towards misuse of phallic energy did not stop the Israelites from developing systems of authority based on phallic rather than divine power. David himself was one of the worst offenders. He cut off the foreskins of two hundred dead Philistines as a bridal trophy for his jealous king and father-in-law to be, used his own penis to commit adultery with Bathsheba (for which neither were put to death), and condoned the rape of his daughter Tamar by his son Ammon. David compounded his own crime by arranging for the husband of Bathsheba to be slain on the battlefield so that he could then take her as his wife. David's son and successor Solomon, after constructing the temple for Yahweh, indulged in an orgy of phallic power by accumulating a vast harem of wives and concubines (allegedly 700 of the former and 300 of the latter; one can reasonably interpret these figures as meaning a very large number). Under their influence he reintroduced worship of the cultic gods of the Sidonians, the Moabites and the Ammonites, including Molech, the infernal child-consumer and epitome of the burning and destroying aspect of phallic power.

After the Davidic kingdom split into two parts (Israel and Judah), a succession of claimants seized power in the northern kingdom of Israel, each time massacring the entire extended family of the previous ruler, thus obliterating his primary evidence of phallic power. Jereboam, the first king of the northern kingdom, set up two golden calves as objects of

---

[14] Myss, Carolyn, Anatomy of the Spirit. New York: Harmony Books, 1996, 82.

worship. After this act of apostasy, worship of cultic gods took over and the covenant of Yahweh was replaced by the rule of human dictators. The impact of the covenant remained stronger in the southern kingdom of Judah, partly because of the influence of the temple at Jerusalem. But even in Judah cultic idolatry and prostitution flourished, especially during the 45-year reign of the tyrant king Manasseh.

It was Manasseh's reign of bloodshed and child burning that had precipitated the original Deuteronomic reform. As we have seen, that reform demanded not merely a restoration of the covenant but an intensification of human commitment to Yahweh. The revised, exilic Deuteronomic text raised the power and scope of Yahweh to new heights, in order to establish that the power of Yahweh sufficed to protect the people of Judah and to prevail under all circumstances short of apostasy. It demanded that the people commit themselves to Yahweh heart and soul and called on them to 'circumcise' their hearts. Whereas the phallus is the symbolic source of male procreative energy and negatively of male gender dominance, the heart is a gender-inclusive symbol of love and constancy in its positive aspect and of obstinacy and brokenness in its negative. Circumcising the heart would therefore mean covenanting with the seat and source of human emotional power.

This application of phallic imagery to the heart meant covenanting heart energy to the service of Yahweh. In sacramental manner the heart is symbolically cut and bled; in this way the people would become a people holy and sacred to Yahweh and under Yahweh's special providence. Phallic consciousness had assured procreativity and bred tribally defined bodies, but it had not bred covenantal loyalty and emotional constancy, much less the sacramental quality of phallic energy. Phallic man had proved obstinate, rebellious and 'hard-hearted'. Yahweh had consequently 'punished' those phallic Israelite men (and their families) circumcised only in a physical sense in the flesh of the penis, by allowing the tribal groups inhabiting the kingdom of Israel to be driven into oblivion and tribally eradicated by the Assyrians, and the leadership of those living in the kingdom of Judah to be captured and exiled by the Babylonians. The covenant's chosen people were on the verge of physical extinction. So much for the power of the circumcised phallus. For the few who survived these catastrophes a new, Deuteronomic covenant had to be called into existence, inscribed, this time, on a cleansed and 'broken' heart.

It is worth noting that the heart covenant advocated in the texts of Jeremiah and the Deuteronomic tradition represents a considerable raising of the stakes in the conceptualization of the divine-human relationship. The heart covenant does not replace the phallic covenant; rather it indicates that the human condition cannot any longer progress without a heart covenant. It develops recognition of the divine human relationship from progenitiveness to compassion as essential to sustain life. The male-dominated tribalism and human warrior bonding achieved through the phallic covenant is now seen as necessary but insufficient to survival. The compassion and love of Yahweh, so powerfully advocated in the prophetic writings, is now the focus of attention. Human existence, to the extent that it models itself on the Hebrew covenantal tradition, must henceforth take that into account.

In short, apostasy and phallocentrism had undone the human kingdoms set up by the successors of David. The idea of covenant as a commitment to recognize and deploy in God-attuned ways the power of heart energy took its place alongside the phallic covenant, to be incorporated into the Torah text after the end of the Babylonian exile and the restoration of the exiles to Jerusalem. Henceforth the concept of 'hardening of the heart', which in the Bible is applied particularly to males out of touch with the divine, would signify not just an emotional but a covenantal state of discord.

The Kingdom of Man from a Covenant Perspective

When one looks at the kingdom of man from a covenantal perspective, it becomes apparent that human authority comes in many different guises, ranging from some much more repressive than the covenant to some considerably more libertarian. Nevertheless, dominance of male and specifically male-phallic power is found in virtually all major cultures. The occasional appearance of a great queen such as England's Elizabeth I or Russia's Catherine the Great, or a powerful woman prime minister such as Mrs. Thatcher, Golda Meir or Indira Gandhi, does not impair the patriarchal and phallic-oriented structure of the societies over which they ruled. Even the fledgling Christian church, founded on the communal kingdom teaching of Jesus, soon adjusted to the patriarchal values of Greco-Roman society.

This resulted in the rapid evolution of a structure of all-male bishops and priests, by which the church was guided into the modern era. Protestantism reinforced male dominance, inveighing—in the voice of John Knox—against the "monstrous regiment (i.e. rule) of women" leading the royal houses of late 16th century Scotland, England and France. Protestant males, with a zeal equal to, or worse than, that of Catholics, sent multitudes of empowered women to be destroyed as witches. Eve resumed her role as the great corrupter of masculine virtue, and in Christian society women were relegated to Pauline roles of silent subservience. The professions excluded women from their ranks, and it was only with the greatest difficulty that in the late nineteenth century a few medical schools were persuaded to admit women as students. Even today, influential fundamentalist Christian texts place a high priority on supremacy of males within the basic building block of family life.

But phallocentric power tends to repress men as well as women. For example, in the British subculture in which I grew up, education of middle-class boys and girls was separated at a very early age, sex education was virtually non-existent, and any male sexual narcissism, such as masturbation, was regarded with abhorrence and punished appropriately. Approved physical contact between males was limited to handshaking, contact sports, and that hallmark of repressive phallocentric cultures: corporal punishment. Legitimization of paddling and caning, by both older boys and men, on the prostrated and often naked buttocks of subordinate boys provided a culture of fear and male dominance necessary to the development of heart-hardened and tear-repressed male values as well as submission to male hierarchy. Contact sports, such as football, rugby football and boxing, reinforced the values of obedience and team spirit, as well as deployment of trained aggression and intimidation, by which patriarchal power is greased and oiled.

Out of this heart-hardened and buttock-tested (in Germany also face-slashed) male culture emerged in modern times the millions of armed and uniformed men, who would march obediently to their killing fields in the trenches and slaughterhouses of World War I, as well as the millions more who would be swallowed up in the Second World War. Male obedience to the culture of phallocentric violence is deeply instilled, and breaches of that culture are very risky. Whereas the uniformed schoolboy who evaded school could be paddled or caned as a truant, the uniformed man who evaded the battlefield could be (and in World War I was) shot as a deserter. Thousands of German and Russian military deserters were shot by their own military forces during World War II. Even today draft-evasion, although widespread in the United States during the Vietnam war, is regarded by most people with distaste, as an evasion of public duty and an act of cowardice rather than courage and moral virtue.

In seeking to point out the negative impact of patriarchal culture on male behavior we should not overlook its positive aspects. Modern patriarchal culture at its best has produced brilliant administrators, empire builders, industrialists, scientists and military leaders. From it there emerged in the West a powerful missionary and Christianizing movement which has spread its influence throughout the world. The glories of modern Western patriarchal faith are recorded in such triumphalist Victorian hymns as Onward Christian Soldiers (once a favorite of English congregations) and The Church's One Foundation. Out of modern English patriarchalism came the radar which confused Hitler's Nazi air force, and the 'Hurricanes' and 'Spitfires' whose pilots shot it down and saved Britain from invasion in 1940. Out of modern patriarchalism came also the much more ambiguous Manhattan project and the atomic bombs that ended the Pacific war.

But such rigorous, phallocentric masculinity is achieved at a cost, which spreads out across less overtly masculinized males, as well as across women, children, servants, and subordinate peoples. Religion itself becomes the mirror of the culture, serving the interests of nationalism, empire building and conquest. Man exists to serve God, king, flag and country, but God too has nationalist obligations, as the famous German curse of World War I, "Gott strafe England (God punish England)," so vividly demonstrates. Churches even are nationalized into institutions promoting patriotism, loyalty to the flag and state service. On the upside, they celebrate national days, sing patriotic anthems as thanksgiving for military victory, and when necessary justify war and lead soldiers into battle. On the downside, they bury and memorialize those who fall in the line of patriotic duty. Some national religious shrines harbor the tattered flags recovered from the battlefields of male conflict, as if these are somehow icons of service to the divine rather than to the power conflicts of mortal rulers.

In such a dominantly patriarchal culture the Deuteronomic idea of the male (and heart-covenanted) ruler subordinating himself entirely to Yahweh's will is unthinkable. In truly patriarchal and phallocentric cultures it is unthinkable for men to cry, to show pity to each other, or to respect 'unmanliness'. Male-male relationships operate within severe restraints: no kissing (as in 'decadent' France), no hugging either. The intimacy characterizing the love between David and Jonathan, or between Jesus and the beloved disciple, could hardly be dreamed of, much less practiced. It is hard even to imagine the kind of inter-generational male bonding that the Bible records as occurring between Moses and Joshua or Elijah and Elishah. From the perspective of covenant sexuality and heart-centeredness, male emotional life is crippled by the need to appear strong, silent, and in control. Where the covenant calls for return to a merciful God, and to the singing of psalms of reconciliation and forgiveness, man in the modern kingdom of man is expected to be disciplined, self-reliant, hard-nosed, assertive, and silent about failure and hurt. And any self-respecting boy in the kingdom of man had better avoid sniveling while being bullied, punished, or sexually abused.

But this depiction of androcentrism in microcosm hardly begins to explore the excesses that have been carried out in modern times by excessively phallocentric regimes. It is easy enough to point to the atrocities inflicted on subject peoples and social groups by the Nazi and fascist regimes of central and southern Europe, and their miserable duplicates in Latin America and elsewhere. These regimes which idolize the male leader, male uniform, male leg-strutting, male organization, male bonding, male athleticism, and male violence, torture, and terrorism, are clearly out of balance with human society. They are paradigms of what the Bible means by idolatry and are a fearful reminder to us that idolatry is not a thing of the past but lives and flourishes in our own time. Such regimes reject covenantal values serving the interests of creation, justice and mercy, and they are particularly vicious towards the 'alien' in their midst, such as Jews, Gypsies, indigenous ethnic peoples, illegal immigrants, or 'abnormal' males. Men in these cultures are not merely trained but culturally authorized to oppress, beat, degrade, torture, and if need be destroy, people weaker than—or in some way different from—themselves, including, if necessary, their own women and children. No covenantal justice is deemed necessary for a culture that is organized to survive and dominate.

A more complicated ideological perversion permitted Soviet Communism and its counterparts in other nations to enslave subject classes and peoples, consign millions of men and women (but predominantly men) to slave labor camps from which the majority never returned, channel natural resources into heavy industry, militarism and strategic weaponry, and drag opponents in tens of thousands (again principally males) before male firing squads. The ideological perversion of ethnicity is now committing similar crimes. Indeed, as this passage was being drafted, UN teams were setting out in Bosnia to search for the bodies of 7,000 Bosnian Muslim males missing as a result of the Serbian capture of Srebrenica in 1995. In short, for most people living outside a few favored Western countries, the materialist advances of the twentieth century have been paid for very dearly.

But favored Westerners should not dwell on the failings of other cultures of mammon without examining those of our own. Countries such as the United States, Canada, or Britain, so advanced in many respects, remain primitive in terms of the excessive respect paid to male power. Since 1776 there have been no women presidents of the U.S., very few governors or senators, and hardly any mayors of major cities. Men still head up almost all major corporations. There are no women priests in the Catholic Church and still very few women priests or ministers in other denominations. A handful of women have become presidents of major universities, but men still predominate in the upper echelons of the academic world.

In such an unbalanced environment one cannot expect social resources to be distributed in any way approximating the terms of the covenant. We could hardly expect the interests of widows, orphans, and the "alien in your midst" to take precedence over those of such male-dominated sectors as national security and the corporate economy. It does not matter that Biblical prophetic witness explicitly condemns state policy that prefers to rely on human rather than divine power. In the cultures of realism and neo-realism, which govern contemporary Western state policy, the idea that Yahweh could have neutralized Soviet or other country ICBMs would seem absurdly ludicrous—the stuff of Old Testament fable, perhaps, and the sort of thing one might occasionally hear about on Sunday mornings, but hardly relevant during business hours. More significantly, the collapse of the Soviet Union was widely acclaimed by American political leaders and their choruses of admirers as the result of 'standing firm' against the menace of Communism, as if inner resistance within the Soviet populations, or the judgment of a farseeing Providence, had nothing to do with it. This implies on our part a not very veiled form of hubris, precisely the attitude of mind that led the United States in the 1980s and 90s to neglect its own internal problems, such as inner-city decay, health insurance, or the national debt, until they reached crisis proportions. A comparable hubris preceded the crises that erupted in 2008.

Dangers of Androcentrism

Behind the obstinacy of male hubris there lies a much more significant defiance of creation as an expression of sacred power. I am referring here not so much to the increasingly troublesome environmental degradation, although that is catastrophic enough, but specifically to the degradation of human society. The two problems are linked and are products of the same mind-set; but we will not be able to appreciate the harm that is being done to the environment until we take responsibility for the harm that our social structures are doing to our own kind.

Let us assume, for the purposes of this argument, that the damage occurring to people living in famine-stricken lands belongs in the same category as the environment, i.e. something happening to creatures other than 'ourselves' and therefore not 'our' responsibility. For most Americans, who still feel identified with the power structures constituting their government, damage to people living in inner cities—although publicized daily in the media—also belongs in the category of 'other' and therefore outside 'our' responsibility. For those who continue to benefit in one way or another from androcentric power, the troublesome problems of domestic violence—most of which is committed by men—are insufficient to raise questions about the values which either license men to be abusive or are unable to prevent them from being so. Female encroachment on the professions and on public power continues to be widely contested, for reasons as powerful and irrational as those fueling racial prejudice. Power, as has often been noted, is seldom voluntarily surrendered.

We must therefore begin by looking into the problems that the values of androcentrism inflict on men themselves. One can observe, for a start, the damage to the male body that results from the stresses of competing in the androcentric world. Stroke, heart attack, emphysema, lung cancer, alcoholism, and cirrhosis, all lie in waiting for the ambitious, workaholic male, along with such other peculiarly male afflictions as prostate and testicular cancer and sexual diseases resulting from careless use of the penis. The great scourge of AIDS, that ultimate pathology of phallocentrism, has not yet struck at the core of the advanced androcentric world, although it is ravaging populations elsewhere. AIDS has spread rapidly into central and southern Africa, the Indian subcontinent, Southeast Asia and China; and businessmen from advanced capitalist countries, along with countless other traveling males, are helping to transmit it. We are long past the time when AIDS was dismissed as a problem of androcentric 'misfits' such as gays, 'queers', and drug users. AIDS, along with drug abuse, has long since entered the androcentric bloodstream.

But recitation of the physical diseases resulting from the abuses of androcentrism hardly begins to get at the problem. The terrible emotional problems lying under the surface of the androcentric world would have to be faced if we are ever to move beyond the crippling hardness of the male heart that has so characterized the cold war world and all the worlds dominated by androcentric values. I personally do not think that most men are ready yet to admit to the emotional pain and destructiveness with which so many of them live. Work, alcohol, sports, sex, money, divorce—almost anything seems to be preferable to the hard work necessary if a man is to deal with his own inner pain and fear. In the androcentric, competitive world, mastery of pain and fear are necessary ingredients to survival and success. Admission of pain or fear is admission of weakness and therefore unthinkable. It is unacceptable for men to cry in public, admit to emotional fragility, or display a weak inner core. Men who shed tears, or whose voices crack, do not normally get elected President. The statement "I do not cry", inconceivable among women, remains common among men. The fact that Jesus wept (or is reported as having done so) is beside the point. Jesus was Jesus—a person who comes off in terms of modern androcentric imagery as frankly long-haired and effeminate and unlikely to have made it in the national football world, much less as a marine commando. Can one imagine Jesus training in bayonet practice or the use of high explosives? That, too, is unthinkable, but it is what millions of real and even not so real men have to do.

In my experience in workshops and men's groups, the pain of men is both tragic and at times terrifying to witness. It is often expressed in violent outbursts of yelling, screaming and frantic pounding on floors, walls, or any available surface. Along with this violence comes a stream of profanity uttered at an earsplitting pitch. Once the dam breaks, a tidal wave of anguish and rage spills out.

It is the rage that captures one's attention. Altogether far too many men are sitting on a suppressed volcano of anger. The men to whom I am referring here, and whose pain I have personally witnessed and shared, are for the most part white middle class males holding responsible jobs in the corporate and professional worlds. They include engineers, bankers, architects, professors, teachers, lawyers and entrepreneurs. What are these mostly well paid, affluent and materially rewarded men so angry about? Quite often it is hard for them to identify what makes them so angry. On the surface it may be some setback in work, some loss in career opportunity, or trouble in relating to women and children. But by the time men get themselves to workshops, some are ready to look beyond the surface. Dare they then admit that they are angry at their very own fathers and mothers, angry at their teachers, priests, and peers, angry at themselves, angry at everything that has suppressed their ability to be affectionate, loving and fully human? Such admissions are easier fantasized than made in real life.

Unfortunately, the chances are that their own fathers and peers were also angry and living in a state of suppressed pain and fear. Anger and pain here come up against the very values that enable men to succeed in the mundane world. The father may have swallowed his anger or pride, allowing it only to leak out in the privacy of his family, so that he could have a career, pay the bills, and enable the children to grow up and compete for their own share of the good life. The father, in other words, lived a selfless life, concealing his own emotional pain and fear behind a screen of affability or silence and getting himself to work day in and out. How could one rage at such a model of rectitude? How can one rage even at a damaged human being who cannot confront his own inner life? Surely compassion, or at least pity, would be more appropriate responses.

To point out the ambiguities facing males who strive to improve their emotional lives is not to condone the forces giving rise to such ambiguities. Male emotional pain is one of the most serious problems afflicting our culture. I have merely drawn brief attention to the pain of white middle class males. The pain of black males is much better documented and much more socially visible. One can more readily see the social consequences of the pain of black males, particularly if they are young men living in urban ghettoes. What we all need to understand better, however, is the social and systemic consequences of the pain of mainstream males, males who are on the surface 'making it' in this world and who have the most power over how we live our lives.

As a rule, such consequences are more likely to have been sought for, or admitted, at the personal and domestic level, in abuse of self and abuse of family. Angry men, such as I was for years, not infrequently turn their anger against themselves, rather than admit to working it off at the expense of others. This, after all, is the safest way to channel rage. If I abuse myself, most likely I will be the one to suffer the brunt of the consequences—unless I die, for example, of a sudden heart attack or a driving accident. However, we do live in a narcissistic culture, and striking at others, physically or emotionally, is still socially if not legally permissible. Middle class family life, with its all too frequent script of domestic violence, infidelity, and divorce, provides a rich and tragic terrain for the study of androcentric pathology.

But we must look to the male dominated world of work and public policy if we are to comprehend the full dimensions of a world of unbalanced androcentrism and male hardness of heart. Here it becomes necessary to look critically at the things that men do particularly well, e.g. their ability to define power and mobilize it to achieve social and political ends. The governments, the military systems, the corporations, the research establishments, the underground gangs, are all products of male ingenuity. Until quite recently, science and technology have been almost exclusively the product of the male 'rational' mind. Women scientists stood out by their rarity. Men design the strategies and build the military hardware and armed services through means of which nations compete.

Most notably, men have developed the military applications of the atom, constructed and used the atomic bomb, and created the vast strategic arsenals of nuclear, chemical and biological weapons that dominate our world. So great has been the investment of human and natural resources in nuclear stockpiling that it is almost sacrilegious to suggest that the expense may have been contrary to the best interests of those responsible, not to mention the rest of the world including its other, non-human inhabitants. Where so much cumulative male ego has been invested, it must be foolish for anyone to suggest that the whole effort has been not merely wasteful and dangerous but even idolatrous and nihilistic. The idea that public policy today could be idolatrous seems absurdly antiquarian, particularly when applied to a society that pays so much lip service to the honoring of God. How could anyone seriously suggest that American strategic policy has been and still is idolatrous and destructive, and why should anyone in the policy world take such a criticism seriously? To be sure, Soviet policy was idolatrous, but this was because it worshiped the false god of communist utopianism. The vast Soviet ICBMs that once paraded through Moscow each May day could be easily seen in the non-Communist world as monstrous evocations of destructive, phallocentric power. American ICBMs, almost as vast and monstrous, and with considerably more warheads, were discreetly kept in their underground chambers, away from the public eye, as mere statistical quantities without substance or image. We did not supposedly idolize these dogs; we merely built them as a regrettable necessity, to keep Communism at bay.

Now, as a result of this policy, we live in a nightmare world of activated plutonium. How is this material to be neutralized? How are the missiles to be defanged? How are the weapons of mass destruction to be contained? What happens to all those missiles and nuclear stockpiles outside of adequate Russian government control? What happens to the technology and scientists on sale to countries seeking the strategic power that comes with nuclear weapons? What, in short, happens when—not if—the governments of India, Pakistan, Iran, Iraq, North Korea, Saudi Arabia, etc., acquire nuclear and missile capability? What if they develop chemical and biological stockpiles? Will they suddenly become models of compromise and decorum, ready to sit down and do business with the 'rational' countries already in the nuclear club? What happens when—not if—male terrorist organizations acquire the capacity to construct medium or short-range nuclear armaments? How long will it be before a nuclear weapon is set off in New York or Washington or London?

One can assume that there are people in the policy world contemplating these nightmare scenarios and trying to figure out ways of containing them. One doubts, however, that prayer is among the resources being applied to these problems, unless as an act of desperation. It has been a long time since Yahweh's views have been included in the counsels of nation-states, and it is hard for an ordinary person to have any sense of what Yahweh's views on such contemporary problems might be. Does anyone imagine that Yahweh's views are also being consulted over the disposition of the U.S. national debt, or the proportion of debt payments to be balanced against tax reductions versus reductions in social services, or over any of the other manifold problems affecting public policy? "Frankly", one can hear the politicians and the interest groups muttering, "such matters are none of Yahweh's business. Let Yahweh, or God—whatever—deal with the saving of souls; let us deal with the management of governments and public finances. We're in charge here. Leave this absurd religiosity out of it."

In such a division of labor let it never be admitted that the same attitudes controlling the solutions are the ones that have created the problems. It is not all the debt, the plutonium, the social and environmental degradation, that is the basic problem. It is the kingdom of man itself.

Rethinking the Human Kingdom

As a man I am deeply worried by the belligerence so often employed by males to sort out their problems. Take the conflicts in Bosnia or Chechnya, for example. Here, barely a few years beyond the Cold War and into the so-called New World Order, male behavior is looking nastier and more brutish than ever. In Bosnia a civil war featuring relentless ethnic cleansing was accompanied by widespread reports of rape and murder by combatant soldiers. The world was shocked back in 1936 when Japanese armies seized the Chinese capital of Nanking and indulged in an orgy of killing and rape. Armies were then naively supposed to conform to certain standards of behavior reflecting a dim echo of medieval chivalry. Civilized men, it was supposed, simply do not rape women. To the contrary, they revere and seek to protect them.

What rubbish! A casual glance at any commercial advertising lets us know that civilized men are only too ready to convert women into dehumanized sex objects. Whole industries of female and child prostitution have mushroomed in contemporary megacities, feeding the voracious penises of men. Such prostitution is nothing else than commercialized rape. But rape in contemporary society extends far beyond the arenas of prostitution and civil war. It is working its way into 'normal' society like a systemic cancer, concealed from public view and doing its dirty work behind closed doors. Increasingly states are having to recognize marital rape as a crime, not an expression of male entitlement. According to data compiled by the U.S. National Council on Crime and Delinquency, women have a one in five chance of being raped during their lifetimes and a one in three chance of being molested as children. If rape and child molestation were infectious diseases, we would call this rate of incidence a pandemic and demand that the U.S. Centers for Disease Control and Prevention do something about it. In short, the crime that 'we' Americans abhorred in belligerent Serbs, etc., is going on to a shocking extent in the cities and suburbs of America. At least military rapists might claim in self-defense that they chose to rape their victims rather than be shot for disobeying an order.

Rape is the ultimate expression of phallocentric power out of balance with the rest of creation. We rightly apply the word 'rape' to systemic abuse of natural environments such as the tropical rain forests or the southwestern deserts of the United States. Those environments, and their human and animal inhabitants, have been violated, generally in the interests of commercial development controlled by outsider organizations. 'Rape' is not too strong a word to apply to this kind of social and environmental degradation. But rape here is used symbolically rather than literally. We cannot talk of businessmen, engineers and oil-riggers thrusting their penises into the rain forests or their inhabitants. That, one presumes, does not happen. Thus, the image of rape is diminished by the fact that it applies principally on a symbolic level. Can we not, however, bring ourselves to visualize hostile Serbian soldiers shoving their penises into the vaginas and rectums of helpless Bosnian and Croatian women? That kind of savage violence took place. If it is not a war crime, what is? Why shouldn't the perpetrators of such crimes be arrested and locked up for years? Could 'we' also, perhaps, bring ourselves to visualize angry and degraded American men raping and abusing helpless American women and children? These crimes are not symbolic. They are real, and they occur on an everyday basis, to people all around us.

Contemporary society, and especially women, should not be so surprised that men have difficulty visualizing other men committing rape and accepting this as a violent crime. The values of medieval chivalry died long ago. In any case, they never applied to more than a small proportion of people. The values that apply today are those proclaimed by Madison Avenue, where use of female images to stimulate male phallic appetites is a fact of life. I do not want to make Madison Avenue the scapegoat for the degradation of our sexual ethics. This is a systemic problem that extends far beyond the advertising world. Madison Avenue—and Hollywood, for that matter—are merely a reflection of the problem. The problem is the decontrol of phallic power itself, the concentration of power in the hands of males, and the abandonment of any ethical structure comparable to the covenants to restrain and channel human behavior towards moral ends.

The covenants of Abraham and Moses, as noted earlier, set out to control and channel phallic energy to constructive service of Yahweh's creation. This is not a subject generally discussed in Sunday school, and I have yet to hear it discussed in a Sunday sermon. Christianity is curiously silent about the phallic ethics of the Yahwist covenant. This is not altogether surprising. As we have seen, the apostle Paul fought tooth and nail to convert Greco-Romans to the fledgling Christian faith without having to circumcise the men. And men had to be enrolled; otherwise Christianity would have remained largely a woman's faith and outside the male power structure.

Instead, baptism took the place of circumcision. Spirits and bodies were to be symbolically cleansed, while penises were spared from the knife. The conservative Christian community in Jerusalem objected strongly to this compromise; but Paul and his supporters prevailed. The patriarchal Hellenistic world, which in its Athenian phase had long adored and celebrated the male phallus, was uncircumcised. How could its adult males be expected to submit themselves to a painful sacramental operation in order to be of service to an unknown and invisible God? Thus, Christianity took the fateful decision to sever itself from its Jewish origins. It became an uncircumcised religion, dependent on the rite of baptism and the 'new' covenant of the crucified Jesus to establish a commitment to Yahweh, now transformed into a Greco-Roman Theos or Deus, and later into a Germanic Gott or God. Yahweh and the covenants of the patriarchs disappeared from Christian discourse, relegated to the irrelevant Old Testament world of Rabbinic Jewry. In the Nazi era the circumcised penis became the mark of Cain, condemning every European Jewish male to fear of extinction. Not until recent times has the concept of Yahweh as Yahweh been reintroduced into Christian biblical discourse, and then only at a theological or sectarian level.

Interestingly, Christianity's abandonment of sacramental circumcision did not lead to the disappearance of phallic consciousness. Far from it. Early Christian spokesmen such as Augustine regarded the phallic properties of men as evidence of their superiority over women and even speculated as to whether women would regain penises—as if they had ever lost them—in the life after death.

Nowadays it is difficult to regard such sententious theologizing with any degree of respect. But consider it we must, if we are ever to understand the extent to which phallocentrism and religious consciousness are intertwined. On the one hand we have the Yahwist covenant, which takes phallic energy seriously as essential to the business of life and insists on a sacramental commitment of the phallus, and subsequently the heart, to the covenantal bond. On the other hand, we have a 'new' Christian covenant, which ends up permitting patriarchal, phallic power to take full command of the physical body while the covenant supposedly manages the life of the spirit, as if that life had not already been contaminated. The longstanding spirit-body dualism that has characterized Christianity has its genesis in this abandonment of the sacramental phallic covenant. No wonder the subject is off limits in Sunday school, as well as in the Sunday discourse of Christian adults. The idea of a minister or priest devoting a Sunday sermon to an account of the sacramental functions of the phallus is inconceivable. Consequently, there is no phallic education in Christianity, no phallic sacrament, and no control of phallic power. We have shut our eyes from the consequences of that which we dare not discuss.

Does this imply that the 'kingdom of God' is incomplete and irretrievable without sacramental circumcision? On this troublesome question I must join the apostle Paul in answering no. It is inconceivable that upwards of two billion males would readily submit themselves to adult sacramental circumcision, and equally inconceivable that this reluctance to be circumcised would place them beyond the compassion and mercy of a divine power truly concerned about living beings. Prophetic proclamation was certain that Yahweh's kingdom reached, or would reach, to all nations. From a Biblical perspective the uncircumcised millions (now billions) of males living outside the covenants of Abraham and Moses are also Yahweh's creatures. From this perspective, uncircumcised Christian males, baptized into the new covenant of the crucified Jesus, have entered into commitments with divine power. Under what circumstances does that enable them to function effectively as citizens of Yahweh's 'kingdom'?

The Jesus Mission in Relation to Men

The gospel accounts of the views of Jesus are quite explicit about male roles in the kingdom of God. In the Greco-Roman patriarchal world, said Jesus (I am editorializing here only slightly, otherwise following the translation of the Jerusalem Bible), the so-called 'rulers' lord it over their subordinates, and "their great men make their authority felt." Indeed, it is not hard to find out about the many ways in which these great men did make their authority felt. The owner of the stronger phallus always tends to dominate the owners of the smaller, weaker phalluses. "But", Jesus is reported as telling his male disciples, "anyone who wants to become great among you must be your servant; anyone who wants to be first among you must be slave to all. For the Son of Man (new male human being) did not come to be served but to serve." (Mark 10, Matthew 20).

We have here a typical example of the contrarian thinking consistently ascribed to Jesus when dealing with the affairs of the world. We are also offered another twist on the phrase "Son of Man". The 'Son of Man' modeled by Jesus is also male and as such an offspring of the androcentric, patriarchal world. But as 'son' this male becomes something else: last, not first; a servant, not a master; like a child, not an adult; and slave to all, not free. Among these various male role reversals, that of servant and service, drawn from Isaiah, provides the central motif. "Behold my servant, whom I uphold", proclaimed Deutero Isaiah on behalf of Yahweh, "mine elect in whom my soul delighteth. I have put my spirit upon him. He shall bring forth judgment (justice) to the Gentiles." (Isaiah 42) This is the model for male kingdom citizenship: a servant in whom Yahweh's soul delights, and who receives Yahweh's spirit and commission to bring the values of covenantal justice to people living outside the covenant.

A transformation of consciousness is intended here, from the patriarchal world of phallocentric domination to the covenantal world of justice, mercy and service to others. This is not a world populated by bonded males who kowtow to their superiors while disregarding the traumas of oppressed people. The male servant envisaged in Isaiah is expected to be peculiarly strong, consistent in advocating justice, and willing to accept injury and violence in the process. He must even be able to bear the sorrows of other people and face death without flinching. This is strength that very few 'real' men have. This kind of quiet strength exposes godless phallocentric power as a facade that has nothing to do with justice and salvation, and that crumbles in the face of real confrontation.

One is reminded of the young David facing Goliath, the epitome of Philistine phallocentric violence. This male giant had made strong but lesser 'men' tremble. Yet one well aimed stone from a mere youth was enough to bring down the miracle of phallic power, who had defied an army of supposedly real men for forty days. Of course, it is not always that easy. Count von Stauffenberg's bomb failed to bring down Hitler in 1944. Hundreds of honorable German men, including the Count himself and the revered theologian Dietrich Bonhoeffer, not to mention additional hundreds of thousands of honorable Jews and other oppressed ethnic peoples, suffered horribly for that misfortune. Phallocentric power has its strength too, and it is insanely cruel when challenged.

But the strength of deutero-Isaiah's vision, which inspired Jesus, and which has inspired covenantal males everywhere, lies in its trust in Yahweh's power, particularly as that power is revealed in the prophetic covenant of the heart. If we merely counterpoise one phallocentric power with another, we end up with the Cold War stockpiling of strategic missiles and the likelihood of Mutually Assured Destruction. This is an example of patriarchal phallic power uncontrolled by any covenantal ethic or sense of justice and compassion. There is no salvation whatever in that path, and no trust in the Divine; only a faltering equilibrium and ceaseless competition for mastery. The alternative image of male strength, visualized in deutero-Isaiah, is hardly what is taught in the mundane world. We have a long way to go before most men and boys could be persuaded to model themselves even minimally on the Isaiah vision. But that is the direction—and the only one—in which lies the kingdom of God.

It is interesting to note that Jesus found it unnecessary to lecture his women associates on kingdom behavior. With not much to gain from the kingdom of man, the women were less blinded by its allurements and more open to the message of the kingdom of God. As feminist scholars point out, there is no record in the gospels of women betraying Jesus, denying him, or failing to be on hand in his time of crisis. It is the male disciples who try to keep women and children at bay, who debate about their own superiority, and who misunderstand what the good news is all about. It is men who sleep when Jesus is praying in Gethsemane, while it is women who enter the tomb in search of his body. The kingdom consciousness of Yahweh has always required more self-transformation from men than from women, because men have always received the greater rewards and power from the kingdom of man. But covenantal kingdom consciousness is not gender, race, or age-specific. It applies, as the Isaiah text pointed out, to all peoples everywhere.

CHAPTER 13

The Strange Fate of Women in the Covenantal World

*If the Teacher held her worthy,
Who are you to reject her?
The Gospel of Mary*

Subordination of Women

If androcentrism and male dominance have been characteristic of mainstream Christian culture, what is the nature and what are the reasons for the subordinate status of women? To what extent is the subordination of women intrinsic to Christianity, in its aspect as a patriarchal religion, and how is that subordination engendered and maintained?

Male readers should recognize that subordination of women has been required and practiced by Christianity well into the 20th century and to a large extent still is, particularly in fundamentalist denominations.[15] Until recently women, 'defiled' by menstruation, as well as hampered by lack of professional education and by alleged lack of rationality, were not admitted to the priesthood. They are still not admitted to the Catholic priesthood, on the grounds that Jesus—being a man—chose only men as his certified twelve disciples; and their admission to other priestly and

---

[15] This observation is based on the work of Philip Greven. See his book Spare the Child: The Religious Roots of Punishment and the Psychological Impact of Physical Abuse. New York: Vintage Books, 1992.

ministerial offices has been a matter of fierce controversy. The staunchly male Trinity of God the Father, Son, and Holy Spirit (the latter male in the Latin language and Roman tradition), has militated against admission of women to priestly roles. So long as Christian and Judaic deity is taken by mainstream culture to be gender-restricted to masculinity, we should expect women as priests or as rabbis to seem intrusive to those, including both men and women, for whom the religious sanctuary remains the ultimate male preserve.

In addition, there is for Christians all that commentary in the Pauline letters about the subordination of women to men in the management of both religious and secular life. Although acknowledging the leadership of women in the fledgling Christian community, Paul followed the Eden myth in regarding woman as emergent from, created for, and subordinate to, man. When in church, he admonished, a woman should cover her head, as a symbol of the authority over her. (I Corinthians, 11) A possible interpolation in the first letter to the Corinthians adds that women are to remain quiet while at meetings, as they have no permission to speak. If they have questions, they can ask their husbands at home. Otherwise they should defer to their men, as stipulated by Yahweh in the fate assigned to the fallen Eve.

The Pauline position, reinforcing perspectives on women in the wisdom literature of Ecclesiasticus, is laid out more emphatically in the later deutero-Pauline letters. Wives should submit to their husbands, as the Church submits to Christ, because the husband is the head of his wife, just as Christ is the head of the Church. (Ephesians, 5) Women should be dressed modestly "with shamefacedness and sobriety." They should learn in silence, with all subjection; and they are not permitted to usurp authority over the man. The reason, according to the writer, is simple: Adam was first formed, then Eve. (I Timothy, 2) Chronology of birthing, when archetypal and mythic, counts.

Furthermore, claimed the writer of the first letter to Timothy, Adam was not the one who was deceived; it was the woman who was deceived and in transgression. Her salvation, consequently, lay in not vying with male authority but in childbearing and in living a faithful and sober life. Men alone, according to the Letter to Titus, are identified as church elders and leaders. Women, for their part, should avoid gossiping; old women must not spread false accusations or indulge in alcohol. They should teach young women to be sober and obedient to their husbands, so that the word of God is not blasphemed.

It would be a mistake to regard these sentiments from the Pauline tradition as quaintly old-fashioned or of "historical interest only" (as in The Interpreter's Commentary on the Bible, 1971 edition). To the contrary: this vision of woman as subordinate and secondary to man continues to dominate Christian theology and humanism, even if its expression has been toned down in more liberal church circles since the days of Augustine and Thomas Aquinas. Moreover, these views are part of a much larger pattern of societal expectations regarding the roles of women and men. We do not have to go back to the Pauline letters to note the subordination of women to men. The evidence is still all around us. But the Pauline letters lay the groundwork not merely for the relationship of women to men in the Christian context, but more broadly for the Christian view of the character of women that developed within the Roman world. Thanks to the Pauline letters and volumes of later patristic theology, men could be permitted to regard and treat women as they were depicted in these letters; and a view of woman, arising from the subordinate birthing and primal 'transgression' of Eve, would develop, which still greatly influences the way in which women are perceived in modern Western culture.

Recent studies by theologians and historians have shed considerable light on the elaboration of female inferiority by early Church fathers, indeed even by gospel texts. Augustine and Thomas Aquinas were particularly influential in linking women with commission of the 'original' and fundamental sin by which humanity was condemned to death. The sexual act constituted the moment at which that sin took place. Androcentric moral theology labored to devise ways of protecting men from sexual entrapment and of punishing women who lured men into sin. More broadly, the early fathers laid out a general theology of the inferiority of women in relation to men, based on such criteria as the subordinate status of Eve to Adam, women's defilement through menstruation, the subordinate and lower status of their souls compared with those of men, and their danger to the preservation of male virginity and purity. As we shall see, the doctrine which identified Eve as a handmaid of the devil played a particularly fearsome role in equating the activity of women with sin, death and corruption. In the anti-feminist traditions of Western Christianity, a woman could affirm her Christian obedience only through perpetual chastity and virginity or through marriage, child-bearing, and subordination to men as lords and masters.

The Christian male-determined conception of femininity as virulent, prone to temptation, and therefore to be subordinated to male authority, owes much of its tenacity to the influence of three basic archetypes of womanhood, which emerged over the centuries: Eve, the presumed original transgressor and seducer of man; Mary, the Virgin, Mother of God and unsullied by male sexuality, but at the same time less than God; and Mary Magdalene, the alleged transgressor-whore who loved greatly, and who atoned for transgression through extreme privation. The characterization of these archetypes has shifted over time, nevertheless the fundamental characteristics of seducer, virgin, and repentant whore have clung to their exemplars, and these exemplars have exerted a powerful influence over the imaginations of men and women and the positioning of women in a male-dominated Christian world.

Eve, the Seducer

Eve is the primal woman in the Christian tradition. To say this is to point out the inherent distrust of that tradition towards women and womanness. Eve it was, according to the J tradition as modified by the Deuteronomists, who, after being formed out of Adam's rib, succumbed to—or ganged up with—the serpent, seduced Adam into wrongdoing and destroyed his innocence. Specifically, she destroyed his sexual innocence, since after they had eaten the forbidden fruit, they 'discovered' their sexuality and tried frantically to cover their 'private', sexual parts. According to Augustine, who pondered on these matters, Eve's duplicity robbed Adam of control of his sexuality and initiated the demon lust by which men have been obsessed ever since.

Eve's punishment for committing what became the original sin, by which all humans were brought to shame, sexuality and death, was great. According to the standard (Deuteronomic) interpretation of the text, Yahweh decreed that "I will greatly multiply thy sorrow and thy conception; in sorrow thou shalt bring forth children; and thy desire shall be to thy husband, and he shall rule over thee." Or, as so superbly paraphrased by Milton:

> Thy sorrow I will greatly multiply
> By thy conception; children shalt thou bring
> In sorrow forth, and to thy husband's will
> Thine shall submit; he over thee shall rule

But long before Milton's time Eve's sin had entered European folklore through the graphic arts and the mystery plays. To quote from a play, Adam takes one bite of the forbidden fruit and cries out in horror:

> Out! Alas! What eales (ails) me?
> I am naked, well I see;
> Woman, cursed must thou be
> For both now we be shente (destroyed).
> I wotte (know) not for shame whether to flee,
> For this fruit was forbydden me;
> Now have I broken, through rede of the (advice of thee),
> My Lordes commaundement.

Eve tries to blame the serpent, but Adam goes on muttering, "Yea, soothe said I in prophesie / when thou wast taken of my body / man's woe thou woldest be witlie (knowingly)." Eve urges that they cover themselves; Adam does so, knowing that it will do no good. Sure enough, God arrives, sees through their chicanery, and pronounces the doom. To Eve:

> And, woman, I warne thee wytterlie
> Thy mischiefe I shall multeply;
> With pennaunce, sorrow and great anoye
> Thy children shalt thou beare.
> And for thou hast done so to-daye,
> The man shall mayster thee alwaye,
> And under his power thou shalt be aye, (ever)
> Thee for to drive and deere (suffer).

Eve receives her doom in silence, but Adam, after getting his, continues to complain. "Now all my kinde," he advises his fellow men, "Is by me kent (warned) / to flee womans intisement. / That trusts them in anye intent / Truly he is decayved." Moreover—and here we enter more dangerous ground—

> My licorous wife hath bene my foe
> The devilles envye shent (destroyed) me also,
> They twayne together well may goe,
> The sister and the brother.
> His wrath hath done me much woe,
> Her glottony greved me alsoe;
> God let never man trust them twoo
> The one more than the other![16]

These lines were written in the late 15th century. Around that time, in 1487, there appeared a work, entitled Malleus Maleficarum (Hammer of Evil-doers), which along with the Papal Bull of 1484 ushered in three centuries of brutal persecution against alleged witches and sorceresses. The Malleus rooted the problem of witchery in the unholy alliance between women and the devil, which had first borne fruit in the Garden of Eden and had subsequently been exposed in anti-Christian heresy. The devil tempted Eve to sin, and Eve seduced Adam. "And as the sin of Eve would not have brought death to our soul and body unless the sin had afterwards passed on to Adam, to which he was tempted by Eve, not by the devil, therefore she is more bitter than death. More bitter than death again, because that is natural and destroys only the body; but the sin that arose from woman destroys the soul by depriving it of grace and delivers the body up to the punishment of sin."[17] Under the aegis of the authors, the sin of Eve now spread its shadow over women of all ages. Armed with the Papal Bull, the Church was now able to go after witches and sorcery, and it did so with a vengeance. Protestants raged with equal fury against witches, with the result that tens of thousands of women were burned at the stake or hanged because of the alleged sin of Eve.

This persecution, which lies like a dark and barely admitted shadow

---

[16] From Happé, Peter, English Mystery Plays, Penguin Books, 1975, 62-78.
[17] From Delumeau, Jean. Sin and Fear. New York: St. Martin's Press, 1989, 265-266.

over the history of modern Europe, virtually eliminated women from public and professional life. The survivors of this oppression and murder were brought to heel and domesticated. Not until after the mid-nineteenth century would Western women dare to venture forth to knock at the doors of public institutions such as colleges and universities and begin to seek admission. Another fifty to a hundred years would pass before women were permitted to vote or felt strong enough to bid for ministerial positions in mainstream churches—or in democratic governments. Meanwhile the image of the witch as nocturnal terrorist remains embedded in popular folklore and children's stories. It was the subject of Tam o' Shanter, Robert Burns' most famous and satirical poem; and the Wicked Witch of the West still reigns over the Kansas sky.

Thanks to all the witch-burning and denouncing, Eve as seducer continues to forge on, alive and well, into the 21st century. The temptresses who lure eager men into buying expensive automobiles or who seduced young people into becoming lifelong smokers come straight from the pages of Genesis. Smoking leads down a one-way street to disease, disability and death. There could be no better image than that of Eve—or her ludicrous Marlboro country boy—to entice people into doing something that they sense could have life-destroying consequences. The fact that these images are almost always created and manipulated by men should come as no surprise to those who take the Bible seriously. Biblical imagery continues to dominate not just our thinking but our imagination. Men fear Eve, but they continue to find her irresistible. Eve draws men and their companions into restaurants, movies, night-clubs and strip tease joints. Eve smiles from the pages of glamor magazines and magazines for men, teasing them with notions of male virility, dominance, and self-gratification. Eve models the clothes that men sell to women or want their women to wear. Eve lies waiting on sun-drenched beaches and beckons with breath-taking nudity from vacation advertisements or skin flicks. Wherever a hint of seduction is needed to overcome male resistance, the face or body of Eve is ever ready to draw men on.

But the primal role of Eve, from a male perspective, remains to lure men into doing something that they know to be wrong. We should see the myth of Eve underlying the misconduct of men such as Macbeth, or even Hamlet's uncle, who killed out of lust for his brother's wife and possessions. Eve is the ancestor of Biblical women such as Jezebel, Bathsheba, and Salome, who 'provoke' rulers into committing crimes. Eve's naked, lissome body beckons from the walls and windows and even seats of churches, as well as from the paintings of some of Europe's greatest masters, tempting man to commit the ultimate offence of disobeying divine authority, and then dumping him into a world of incessant labor, hardship, anxiety, and death. Underlying this powerful archetype is the subliminal acknowledgement that the life that comes forth from woman is fated to be lived under the burden of sin and to end with decay and death. In the Pauline Christian tradition, only the redemptive power of God and the resurrected, sinless Christ stand between man as Adam and a life of sin and mortality begotten of Eve.

On the other hand, from the theologically neglected female perspective Eve is the original victim, deracinated from earth religion by the triumph of an intrusive sky God, and reduced to becoming man's possession, the object of his carnal desire, and breeding sow for his offspring and begetting. She is demeaned as the creature of impulse, unable to resist temptation or see the consequences of her actions. Worse, she is made the handmaid of the evil one, and the target of a patriarchal theology that saw in her the procreator of sin and death. She is the manifestation of earthly flesh, a secondary incarnation who grew out of Adam's rib, while Adam bore within him the spirit of the Deity. The equation of Adam with the Creator Deity and Eve with the sins of the flesh and the destroyer devil is not intrinsic to the original story; but Christian theology came up with this formula, and once it was in place Eve's reputation, and the lives of women, would be in continuous jeopardy. It would be at best her duty to obey her husband and bear children; and woe betide her if, like Joan of Arc, or innumerable women who came before and after Joan, she should arise and challenge established patriarchies.

The archetype of Eve strikes deep into the biological and cultural ambiguities dividing men and women. As temptress she appears as a projection of male patriarchal fears, a being in tune with the hidden powers of the earth, which are themselves in conflict with the power of the male-oriented and increasingly sky-inhabiting Yahwist God. To defeat these powers and to establish male primacy, this God reverses the biological order of creation, more accurately reflected in Genesis chapter

1. In the Yahwist world order described in Genesis chapter 2, the man was created first, before even a plant or a seed grain had sprouted. After the man has been created, Yahweh plants the garden of trees (no crops yet, because this is a pastoral myth) and puts man into it. Eden becomes a male domain. Yahweh populates it with animals and birds, creatures of a pastoral economy, so that man can find a partner among them. Considering the extent to which pastoral men use animals as companions, this is not such a bizarre idea as it may at first seem to modern, science-trained city dwellers.

Nevertheless, something, or someone, is still missing. As if through an afterthought, Yahweh puts the man to sleep, extracts a rib from his body (thus mythically establishing the male origin of woman), shapes it into woman and brings the new creature to man's side. Finally, after all other life of any human-centered importance has been made, we have a woman. "This, at last," says the man, "is bone of my bone and flesh of my flesh." A true partner to pastoral man, in the form of a projection out of his own male body, has come into being.

As a creation myth, this one places the male order in the center and reduces the female order to a secondary projection out of masculinity. As satire it is astounding. Everyone has always known—and that includes all Christian male saints and theologians—that in the natural, biological order by which existence lives and dies, males emerge from females and not vice versa. But the myth is describing not a biological but a cultural and political order, in which patriarchy is intentionally defined as a reversal of the natural order. Patriarchal religion, aligned with pastoral culture, serves notice of a rejection of the power of cultic worship of the earth and of female deity and life force. Mythically speaking, patriarchal man now comes first and is the progenitor and namer of all human existence. Woman comes last, after all the animals and birds necessary to support the pastoral economy have taken their place. Woman not only comes last, she is created out of man, and is a projection of his power and world orientation. Her birthings are a function of his seeding of her; they come under his ownership, just as she does.

Nevertheless, in a backhanded way the myth affirms with surreptitious irony the continuance in the Yahwist world of female cultic power. Man is seduced by that power and abandons his covenant with the Yahwist God not to eat of the tree of the knowledge of good and evil. Female cultic power rather than Yahwism introduces man to the knowledge of good and evil, and specifically to a consciousness of sexuality and nakedness.

After they are driven out of the Yahwist pastoral Eden and into the densely cultic world of Caananite agrarian culture, Adam and Eve copulate (figuratively 'know' each other) and she gives birth to Cain. Irony of ironies! Woman re-emerges as birther of man. This problem is resolved by turning her first born, a non-Yahwist tiller of soil, into a monster who slays his newer, 'younger', and pastorally minded Yahwist brother. The strife and bloodshed between different cultic systems are given mythic explanation. Cain the agriculturalist is branded and expelled from Yahweh's presence in a second and definitive act of banishment. He goes off to till and populate the land of Nod, and back home, at Adam's place, the Yahwist pastoral order begins to take hold.

The new world order of Adam and Eve, redefined by this powerful and ironic myth about the beginnings of patriarchy, takes shape in a context of seduction, betrayal, copulation, and fratricide. Eve's body is needed to produce offspring for the new Yahwist order. But in all other respects she is the earthly cultic shadow infiltrating and spreading doom within the male pastoral order. As the author of Ecclesiasticus put it, "sin began with a woman / and thanks to her we all must die." (Ecclesiasticus/Sirach 25). Sin and death are connected, and the blame is pinned on the female order. In the hands of the early church fathers the burden of woman's prideful sin would be greatly enlarged; she is chastised as the "devil's gateway" and the destroyer of God's image, man. The way is now clear to link Eve with the Augustinian doctrine of original sin.

So powerful has been the Augustinian myth, that efforts by creationist thinkers, such as Hildegard of Bingen, to redefine the role of Eve in the overall business of creation could not shake the dominant Augustinian view. But given the life-negating definition of womankind that has dominated the Christian patriarchal view of Eve, another male-defined model of femininity would be badly needed to redress the force of evil and male undoing unleashed for Christians by the imagery of Eve. It was found in the life and character of the Virgin Mary.

John Watt

Mary, the Immaculate Madonna

The cult of the Virgin Mary is one of the most powerful and compelling aspects of Catholic Christianity. Mary is the great intercessor with the heavenly powers. Revered as mother of all, her manifestation at such holy shrines as Lourdes and Fatima has brought healing and relief to innumerable followers. In her capacity as black Madonna, her image has inspired millions more and has become a source of solace and inspiration for entire peoples. As Madonna and mother of the infant Jesus, particularly in the guise perfected by the Italian Renaissance painter Raphael, her image of tender and loving maternity adorns thousands of churches, schools and homes, and hundreds of art museums. At the cross she is the lonely parent who mourns the body of her dying child. A powerful medieval poem (Stabat Mater/The Mother Stood) reified this perception of Mary as anguished and devoted mother. Yet as queen of heaven, reunited with her son, she is the human being exalted to a state of radiant bliss. Apart from the Crucifixion scene itself, Mary's depictions as handmaid and Madonna are certainly the most preponderant images to be found in Christian iconography.

The power of the Marian myth begins right at the start of the gospel narratives, through the event described in Luke's gospel as the Annunciation. In this repeatedly imagined and illustrated episode, the angel Gabriel appears to the young virgin. Although the text only says that Gabriel "came unto her" (in Latin ingressus), in the images the angel drops down from above and kneels, as is appropriate in the presence of one since recognized as mother of God. "Ave … Maria," says the angel, words now massively popularized through the music of Schubert and Gounod/Bach. "Hail, full of grace, blessed art thou among women." The drama of this moment is compellingly visualized in a painting by the great 14th century Sienese painter Simone Martini, now in the Uffizi Gallery in Florence. Gabriel announces the forthcoming birth of Jesus and explains to the startled young woman how it will happen to one still virginal. "For," concludes the angel, "with God nothing is impossible." This remark was lifted from Yahweh's retort to Abraham when the latter was informed that his barren and cynical eighty-year old wife Sarah would give birth. Mary replies, "Behold the handmaid of the Lord. Let it be done to me (fiat mihi) according to thy word."

With that ultra-important 'fiat mihi' Mary is revealed as reversing in two words the sin of Eve. She expresses not merely obedience but faith, and it is that faith that is to usher in the Christian covenant. What we find depicted here is the representation of a power whereby women (Mary and her 'cousin' Elizabeth—the one a virgin, the other an elderly Sarah) once again become central to the divine-human relationship. Yahweh's procreativity is once more about to break into history. The central point of this new inbreaking, as pointed out on an earlier occasion in the Isaiah texts, is a young unmarried woman of modest expectations. But the spirit of the innocent young Mary is equal to the charge. And this time the new man, although theologically conceived via the Holy Spirit, will not be created out of clay, bones or dust but born of a woman's body.

To celebrate this moment the gospel writer created (or inserted) a magnificent canticle, generally known by its Latin name The Magnificat. As recorded in the King James Bible, "and Mary said, 'My soul doth magnify the Lord, and my spirit hath rejoiced in God my Savior, for he hath regarded the low estate of his handmaiden.'" The canticle is generally sung in evening services. It has been set to music many times, of which there is none better than Bach's inspiring D Major version in enabling the listener to appreciate the extraordinary event that this canticle proclaims.

Thus, a woman was restored to a central role in the creation of the new covenant. Patriarchalists might well ask themselves why Yahweh should have chosen to make use of a sin-and-death-delivering woman's body to create the new, sin-free Adam, instead of starting ab initio with clay and vital breath uncontaminated by woman's flesh. No woman, after all, had been considered necessary to the creation of Adam. Perhaps the new Adam was not intended to become another stock-in-trade of triumphal patriarchalism.

But prophetic precedent plus centuries of tortuous theological reasoning could not accommodate such a possibility. Instead the problem of Mary as contaminating birth-source was resolved by the early Christian myth-makers and theologians through her gradual elevation to a position of unassailable freedom from sin. Against a theological background contrasting Mary's retention with Eve's loss of virginity, she was declared

John Watt

theotokos (God-birthing) in 431, and virginal in perpetuity in 553. Her own immaculate conception by her parents was debated over many further centuries, vigorously affirmed by the medieval theologian Duns Scotus, celebrated as a feast day from 1476 on, and affirmed as Catholic dogma in 1854. Her bodily assumption and heavenly coronation likewise became widely accepted and a standard image of medieval and renaissance culture, long before being officially decreed by the Papacy in 1954.

This apotheosis of a young and unknown woman into a universal model of immortal feminine purity has served a very crucial need in the establishment and maintenance of patriarchal Christianity. A universal religion could not have sustained itself indefinitely without developing some channel for the expression of female power, particularly in its aspect of mother-protector. The acknowledgement of female divinity, widespread throughout the world, would not simply disappear with the advent of Christian patriarchalism. The history of Judaism itself, as recorded in the Hebrew scriptures, provides gripping evidence of the struggles between male and female divinity and their human advocates, which continued long after the establishment of the Mosaic Covenant. Human society showed itself most reluctant to let go of female deity.

What is fascinating to contemplate is that the generally celibate men who committed themselves to the spread of Christianity throughout the Roman empire could not themselves operate without the elevation to heavenly status of a virginal, God-birthing and immaculate woman. Needing Mary for themselves as a model of all-protective motherhood and sexual abstinence, they also needed Mary for the people as a bridge and intercessor between the travail and pain of human existence on earth and the justice and mercy promised in heaven. The model of Mary as virgin also served young women proselytes who dedicated themselves to virginity, and often to martyrdom, as a way of preserving their bodies and souls from the downfall of Eve. Patriarchal theology vigorously advocated this defeminization, seeing it as a necessary step in the quest for spiritual salvation, through the reversion of Eve to the aboriginal male form from which she had originally 'sprung'.

But the myth of Mary could not have spread so deeply into human consciousness if it had been only the product of religious minds. The radiant virginal queen and intercessor finds her way into the final pages of the Divine Comedy, where Dante, guided by the great Cistercian Mariologist and meditator on spiritual feminism, Bernard of Clairvaux, prays to her as "she who did man's substance glorify."

> Within thy womb the love was kindled new
> By generation of whose warmth supreme
> This flower to bloom in peace eternal grew
> ....
> In thee is pity, in thee is tenderness
> In thee magnificence, in thee the sum
> Of all that in creation most can bless

With Mary as intercessor, the poet then of her grace so much power "doth beseech / that he be enabled to uplift even higher / his eyes, and to the Final Goodness reach." The request is sustained, and the great poem ends with this final vision.[18]

Beside this depiction in words, we could imagine the kind of vision of Mary vouchsafed to the poet by examining a painting done by the incomparable 17th century Spanish artist Velazquez while he was still relatively young. It is of Mary as youthful and immaculate virgin, standing on a crescent moon under a halo of pearly stars, and offset by a golden aureole and banked clouds in a deep nocturnal sky. The radiant young woman, dressed in a pink robe and black cloak, her hands together in prayer and her face suffused with light, looks down tenderly on the earth below that is shrouded in darkness and yet still accessible to her power. The symbolic forms are borrowed from other sources, but they are expressed with a tastefulness and concentration of vision that are the hallmark of the Spanish artist, and that make this picture such a powerful image of Mary as universal intercessor to all people living under the grip of darkness.

In the aftermath of World War Two, Mary as sacred mother became the subject of an extraordinary symphony (#3) by the Polish Composer Henryk Gorecki. In slow, sacramental cadences the grieving mother invites her crucified son to share his wounds with her, and she becomes the object of an anguished invocation by Helena Wanda Blazusiakowna, an eighteen-year old young woman imprisoned by the Gestapo in their headquarters

---

[18] Milano, Paolo. The Portable Dante, New York: Viking, 1953. Paradiso, Canto 33.

in Poland. The symphony ends with the voice of an unknown mother mourning the death of her son - perhaps at the hands of a cruel enemy – and imagining birds and flowers protecting his body, somewhere.

To see the power of Mary at a less sacramental level, we can turn again to the mystery plays, for which the assumption and coronation of the Virgin are a part of the cycle. Jesus in heaven looks down on his dying mother and recalls, "my flesh of her in erthe was tone (taken), / unkindly thing it were i-wis (for sure) / that scho (she) shulde bide be hire (by her) allone / and I beilde (live) here so high in blis." He sends angels to accompany Mary "meke and mylde" to Heaven. Mary, as always, accepts the summons as God's will. After she has arrived in Heaven, her son tells her:

> Be-fore all othere creatours
> I schall the (thee) giffe both grace and might
> In hevene and erthe to sende socoure
> To all that servis the (thee) day and nyght.
> I graunte thame grace with all my myght
> Thurgh askying of thi praier
> That to the (thee) call be day or nyght
> In what disease so that thei are.

As to some of the 'diseases' for which intercession was made to the Virgin, we learn from poems of the Hebridean islanders that problems of women's health were very much in mind. Consider this Mothering-nut charm:

> See the woman, O Mary mild
> Thy smile of grace above her head
> Freedom give thou unto the child
> And keep the woman from the dead

Mary eases swollen breasts and wards off the evil eye. She weaves spells of purest white:

> The spell of purest white was sent
> From Mary Virgin forth it went
> To Dorail's daughter lovely bride

> Of golden-yellow tresses tied
> . . . .
> To thwart the eye, to thwart the snare
> Malice to thwart and hatred's stare
> To repel debility bred
> And to repel the measles red
> To repel running from the nose
> And to repel the deadly rose (smallpox)

Beyond the physical and social ailments, Mary eases the soul in anguish and near physical death. She is "dark mother of woes", "maid of the poor", and "well-spring of grace." She is also the "Queen of sweetness of heart", and the "fountain of mercy mild." Beyond that, her grace encompasses the earth and sky:

> Thou the Queen of the sea so bright
> Queen of all the heavens on high
> Queen of the angels of the sky
> in light
> . . . .
> Since thou art the full ocean wave
> By sea be my pilot at hand
> Since thou art the dry shore, by land
> o save[19]

But it is the image of Mary as the "Mother so sad and kind" that particularly impressed itself upon people for whom distress was never far away. The ubiquitous iconography of the Madonna and Child served to remind ordinary people that Mary in her infinite grace had given birth to the Savior and thus was the assurance of redemption and forgiveness to all. To a world living under the yoke of original sin, the image of Mary was the reminder that humans could still crawl out from under the burdens to which they had been born. Her maternal love, encompassing the Child-Savior, was her gift to humanity. And having delivered and nurtured, as

---

[19] From McLean, G.D.R., Poems of the Western Highlanders. London: SPCK, 1961.

well as grieved, the Savior, she would remain eternally watching over his children and interceding for them throughout the centuries.

Despite the maternal and intercessory powers attributed to Mary, there were certain aspects of life to which the Marian myth could not apply. Her well-established meekness, obedience, and abstention from sexuality, put her beyond the reach of people for whom sexuality was a major preoccupation. To be sure, the Marian myth was not completely disembodied from carnal matters. As Queen of Heaven she became the bride of Christ the King, and the latter would address her in the mystery plays as "my mayden schene (bright)" and "my dere darlyng." But this was a heavenly union, beyond the scope of earthly existence. On earth an image of sinful woman redeemable by Christianity was needed. It was provided through the myth of Mary Magdalene.

Mary Magdalene, the 'Repentant Whore'

In her fascinating study of Mary Magdalen: Myth and Metaphor, Susan Haskins relates that as a child at a convent school she once asked, who was the red-cloaked, golden-haired, and weeping figure at the foot of the cross. It was of course Mary Magdalene, weeping for her own sins and those of mankind. What sins? Those of the flesh, "that I would understand ... when I was older."

In this terse exchange we have the essence of the Magdalene myth: a woman branded for unmentionable sin (signaled, however, through the redness of her robe and the wild, unkempt, golden, hair), yet who was acknowledged to have loved greatly and documented to have been at the foot of the cross. She was also documented by John's gospel as the first human being to have greeted the risen Savior, and to have received from him the first apostolic commission.

How this could have happened to a woman was one of the great mysteries awaiting patriarchal mythic solution. The eventual resolution was developed through analogy with the Prodigal Son of Luke's gospel. Mary Magdalene was indeed a wayward prostitute who had returned to Jesus seeking remission for her sin. Her contrition and humbleness had brought her forgiveness and earned her the special attention and protection of the Savior. But that she should be made primus inter pares, the first apostle of the Christ with the first apostolic commission, was going a bit too far, particularly since heterodox texts had accentuated this aspect of the Magdalene story. The orthodox myth-makers finessed these details (as does the post-Crucifixion account in Luke's gospel) and then banished Mary to serve 30 years of post-Crucifixion penury, asceticism, and solitary repentance. By the time she returned from all this remorse, she was suitably elderly, haggard and emaciated: a perfect picture of repentant and de-sexed womanhood.

The biblical episode permitting the construction of the myth comes from a passage in Luke's gospel which is not directly associated with the Magdalene. Instead, an unknown woman around town who was a 'sinner', approaches Jesus while he was dining with a Pharisee named Simon, and begins to anoint his feet, crying and kissing them and drying them with her hair. Astonished by this bold behavior, the Pharisee wonders to himself how Jesus, if he were a true prophet, could be letting such a person defile his body. Jesus divines his thoughts and tricks Simon with a story about a creditor who releases two debtors, one of whom owed a substantial amount. "Which one would love him the more?" "I guess the one whom he forgave the more," replies the unsuspecting host. "Exactly!" comes the swift response. Jesus then compares Simon's empty formality with the woman's heartfelt gifts. "I tell you, Simon," he concludes, "her many sins are remitted, because she loved much. He to whom less is forgiven, loves less." (Luke 7)

This story is characteristic of Jesus' contrarian thinking and his openness to women. It is not characteristic of what is directly known from the gospels about the Magdalene. The latter appears in Luke's gospel in the very next passage, as a companion of Jesus who had been cured of possession by seven demons, themselves evidence of defilement. The myth results from a conflation of the above story with all the passages directly naming the Magdalene, as well as those naming Mary of Bethany, the sister of Martha and Lazarus, who also anointed Jesus' feet, and an unnamed woman who anointed his head.

These conflations, developed over several centuries and approved by the great Pope Gregory VII, took the steam out of the text identifying the Magdalene as first post-resurrection apostle and anchored her for good in the role of repentant whore. In that capacity, she could be permitted to attend the crucifixion and deposition of the dead Savior. Even better, she could be depicted in the dramatic post-resurrection scene, in which Jesus would have obviously said to her in her capacity as a former prostitute, following the Vulgate text, "don't touch me!" (in Latin noli me tangere). (John 20) It was this apparently rejective post-resurrection scene that would engage the attention of the image-makers, rather than that in which Jesus as the risen Christ commissions her as apostle to the apostles. Then with Mary safely tagged as rejected sinner, she could be sent off into the wilds for decades to ponder, and atone for, her sexual misconduct. Later magdalens, e.g. in Ireland, would be confined to Church-ruled institutions no different from prisons to do their atoning.

The power of this myth has waxed and waned according to the agendas of succeeding ages. But until recent times, little theological effort had been made to deconstruct the myth and separate out the biblically recounted episodes attributed to the Magdalene from those that were not, as well as from all the non-Biblical elaborations. Mary Magdalene as repentant whore is embedded in the tradition of patriarchal Christian culture. Such a role could counteract any notion of her as special companion to Jesus, which could otherwise be inferred from her presence at the Cross and her unique meeting with the resurrected Christ and commission as apostle to the apostles—a commission which was in any case, according to various surviving early Christian texts, vigorously rebutted by the apostle Peter and other male disciples. In addition, accounts in the Mark and Luke gospels report that the male apostles (still at that time just disciples) would not believe the Magdalene and her companions when they reported having met with the risen Christ, and according to Luke, Peter had to run to the tomb and see for himself.

From this Petran tradition we get a sense of the controversies surrounding the Magdalene's role as the special intimate of the Savior and the one who most passionately and persistently mourned him. We do not need the Lucan story of the repentant and assumed whore to understand that the woman who is clearly the Magdalene passionately loved Jesus and, according to the original Greek text of John's gospel, embraced or clung to him after discovering him outside the tomb. This privileged Magdalene, later rejected as expression of an anti-male-apostolic heresy, also constituted a serious obstacle to a patriarchal religion committed to abstinence, for which an untouched and sexually uncompromised Savior was a sine qua non. The myth of the Magdalene as whore reduced her to the level of other fallen women and permitted her to be viewed as an object of pity and forgiveness, consistent with the well-established empathy of Jesus for female sinners.

Moreover, the Magdalene of myth, as repentant whore, could perform a vital role in advancing the theology of repentance. A sinner and copulater, just like Eve, and thus a source of contamination and death to men, her case could be used to demonstrate the power of the new covenant of Jesus to excite repentance and atonement, in short to redeem carnal and defiling womankind. Whereas the Virgin Mary, as the complete obverse of Eve, had to be elevated to a status of purity beyond the reach of ordinary male mortals, the Magdalene could be displayed as a fallen woman, who in the presence of Jesus repented mightily of her sins of the flesh, who could acknowledge her guilt by crying and weeping, and who could spend all her later years in solitary remorse. This archetype presented a real flesh and blood woman, moreover an Eve tainted with sexual sin and pride and in crying need of remorse and renewal—exactly the type of woman whom the Savior could and would redeem and set back on her feet—or at least on her knees.

The myth could also be used to articulate the Church's policy towards women and prostitution. As prostitute par excellence, the example of the Magdalene could be called upon to reveal the way forward for women needing to seek repentance from accusations of sexual misconduct (the theme so trenchantly explored in recent movies about the Irish magdalens). Beyond that, the 'example' of the Magdalene as solitary recluse, who abjured the pleasures of body and flesh, could be used as a model for fallen women seeking to purify themselves by means of Christian mortification and abstention.

In short, the mythic Magdalene could be utilized in all kinds of ways to advance patriarchal agendas. In addition to those mentioned above, we should appreciate the special frisson created by the juxtaposition of male Savior and female slut. Celibate men seeking, not always successfully, to model the assured abstinence of the Savior could find in the myth of Jesus and the Magdalene a paradigm for the management of their own sexuality. The Jesus who dined with Simon, and the resurrected Christ of 'don't touch me', illustrated how it should be done. The fact that Jesus also sat with the mythic Magdalene, in her capacity as Mary of Bethany, demonstrated the fruits of his influence in the conversion of the former 'whore' to a self-possessed woman who was content to sit in humble admiration at his feet. Later, according to John's gospel, the Magdalene, in her guise as Mary of Bethany, would go further and once again anoint those same feet before Jesus faced his own sacrifice.

The power of this myth has been able to stimulate some very striking, and in certain respects discordant, artistic images. Many such images are discussed in studies by Haskin and Margaret R. Miles. We will limit ourselves here to examples illustrating key episodes or attributes in the establishment of the myth, which at the same time introduce other perspectives on the Magdalene.

To begin with the episode of the Magdalene as repentant whore, a dramatic and highly articulated study was created by the 16th century Venetian artist Veronese. This depicts the feast in the house of Simon as occurring under a huge Venetian loggia opening out to an urban scene of palatial buildings and arcades, symbols of patriarchal achievement and power. The Magdalene kneels in the exact center of the picture drying the feet of the Savior with her telltale long orange hair. Simon looks on disapprovingly, as do several other diners. But it is the moment when Jesus has just told the story about the debtors and is challenging Simon to perceive her love. Above the diners two cupids hold aloft a pennant proclaiming Jesus' well-known statement that there will be joy in heaven over one sinner that repents, more than over ninety-nine just persons. (Luke 15) The painting is a statement about repentance and true joy, proclaimed in full view of the urban aristocracy, and challenging establishment males to check out their own receptibility in the afterworld that awaits them.

Another very powerful image of the Magdalene was created by the brilliant Venetian artist Titian, an older contemporary of Veronese and one of the seminal influences in the creation of Renaissance and Baroque esthetics. This is an intensely dramatic depiction of the 'noli me tangere' scene, done while the artist was still in his early to mid-twenties. In this picture the Magdalene in her hallmark red robe and long, unkempt orange hair kneels before the risen Christ, one hand on her jar of unguent, the other reaching out to touch the Christ. A large tree rises behind her, beneath which the body of the Christ as gardener sways away, eluding her outstretched hand. As befits Easter, it is a beautiful, sunlit day; it is also a day in which not only the Christ and the Magdalene, but the divine and human orders, are physically drawing apart.

Some twenty years later Titian produced another vision of the Magdalene, in which there is no hint of rejection of her proffered love. This exists in several versions and has become one of the most famous images of the Magdalene. It shows a young woman of powerful, sensual beauty, with her head uplifted in a state of adoration towards the unseen yet clearly envisioned Savior. Her famously provocative orange hair is entwined around her breasts and body and in the original version constitutes her only covering. The shocking fact conveyed by this picture is that a basically naked woman clothed only with the unkempt hair of a seductress could be depicted as in the rapture of unconditional love with the Christ, without requiring any mediation on the part of religious authority.

In his final painting, done when he was around 90, Titian produced an austere and glowering version of the Pieta scene. In front of a tomblike architectural shroud the dead Christ lies in the arms of his mother, while the Magdalene, standing to the left, flings out her arm in anguish. To the right the friend and follower Nicodemus, shown as a self-portrait of the aged artist, kneels in suffering before the Christ. On either side two harshly fanged lion heads enclose the drama of the human event. If Nicodemus and the Christ project the suffering of death, the Magdalene projects a defiance that refuses to accept death as finality. Her urgent, standing figure reaches out, as if to summon life back into a scene of dread mortality. No repentant whore here, she personifies with dramatic intensity the urge to life crying out amidst the pall of death.

Another artist who pondered the story of the Magdalene was the exquisitely sensitive 15th century Flemish artist Rogier van der Weyden. One of his most poignant pictures shows the Magdalene, in her guise as Mary of Bethany, preparing to anoint Jesus before he goes to his death. The Magdalene is shown in half portrait in front of a serene Flemish landscape. She has the long orange hair, but it is pinned together, and she wears over it a beautifully tailored Flemish hat and veil. She is dressed in an austere blue tunic and robe, but with richly brocaded arms. In her right hand she holds the jar of ointment. She has an expression of sadness and pensiveness, which is heightened by the teardrops on her cheeks. But she also projects a character of spiritual strength and beauty, and an air of readiness to carry out her sorrowful task. Her image is that of a woman of true compassion and steadiness.

Van der Weyden also depicted the Magdalene as Mary of Bethany in her contemplative mode, seated and reading a book, but with her jar of unguent not far away. But then, in one of his most famous paintings, he presented a very intense and dramatic representation of the deposition of Jesus. In this picture, now in the Prado Museum in Madrid, the Magdalene's neatly braided hair is covered, but her body writhes in pain as she sees what has been done to the body of the man she loved. She is portrayed as a woman recoiling in agony from an unjust and terrible death. In all these images of the Magdalene, the artist sees far beyond the stereotypical myth into the heart of a woman who loved deeply and passionately. It is the Magdalene as Magdalene (or Magdalene and Bethany), undiminished by any trace of theological error.

Another stunning image of this scene by Botticelli, the Florentine artist who loved above all to depict women, shows the Magdalene kneeling and cradling with her hands and cheek those injured feet, once "beautiful upon the mountains", of the anointed and beloved Isaian servant-son. Discreetly this act is depicted in the lower left-hand corner of the painting. But as an expression of deep and loving reverence, its meaning could hardly be clearer.

Finally, we should note the statue, done by the 15th century Florentine sculptor Donatello in the last years of his long life, showing the Magdalene returning from her mythic thirtyyear period of fasting and remorse. What we see here is a gaunt, haggard and toothless old woman. We are presented with the image of a saint who has devoted herself to a life of extreme austerity. If there was ever any error in her past, it has long since been eliminated by years of penance. But the face is that of a woman who seems to have lived with an unbearable memory. This is not the Magdalene who might have embraced the risen Christ and received his mandate as first apostle. It is instead an old woman consumed by suffering and remorse, who has lived too long with bitter memories. She reminds us of the ongoing agony symbolized and experienced in the crucifixion.

In all these depictions the imaginations of the artists take us far beyond the agenda of the myth towards an interpretation of the Magdalene as a flesh and blood human being who lived in intimate relationship with the Savior. The gospel words that linger in the mind of the artists are those declared by Jesus of the unknown 'prostitute', that "she loved much" (dilexit multum). Esthetically the Magdalene emerges as the woman who truly loved Jesus: with intensity, as in Titian, with gratitude, as in Veronese, with heartfelt devotion, as in van der Weyden and Botticelli, or with painful anguish, as in Donatello. These of course are all male projections into the meaning of the story of the Magdalene. But they are projections that work around the myth of the Magdalene as repentant whore to uncover a more emotionally satisfying representation of love between woman and man, as revealed in situations of crisis. For example, the abject pain of the Magdalene at the foot of van der Weyden's cross is contrasted with the swooning mother. One drops into a lifeless faint, the other stands and writhes. Although the Magdalene stands to the side of the picture, it is her lively agony, as contrasted with the Madonna's immobilizing faint, which catches the viewer's attention. The Magdalene lives her agony, and in Titian's Pieta she is the one who alone stands and cries out to the world. Indeed, at the very time that theologians and opportunists were rabidly pursuing the destruction of women as witches, the great Titian chose to project the Magdalene as a solitary life force, defiant amidst a world of death.

The Status of Women in the Kingdom of Heaven

A subject of critical importance to the future of Christianity consists in how its founder related to women, and women related to him. Was Jesus an equalizer in terms of gender roles, or did his attitudes towards women fit in with modes of patriarchalism prevailing in both secular and religious life in his time? Depending on that answer, can the present-day world of Christianity reform itself sufficiently to adopt a positive stance towards Divine and human power in female or gender-neutral manifestation? More broadly, can men and women find the means through the religious life to create an equal playing field, in which both expressions and functions of humanity on earth can be fully empowered and realized?

To take the matter of the Jesus mission first: one of the sticking points in the way of defining the mission as gender-equal has been the Biblically reported focus of Jesus' training on male discipleship. The twelve disciples (apostles once they were commissioned to preach) were male, and when one (Judas) dropped out, the others found another male to replace him. In addition, Jesus prayed to God as Father, at least so far as we have it in the received text. However, our English text is translated from the original Greek and the Latin Vulgate versions, which have already patriarchalized Jesus' reported diction. Translations from Aramaic—the language that he spoke—put it differently. "Our Father, which art in Heaven" is in various versions translated from the Aramaic as "O Birther! Father-Mother of the Cosmos."

This suggests, so it would seem, that Jesus' thought and diction in Aramaic lacked the patriarchal emphasis that emerges in our translations from Greek and Latin. What if the God of Aramaic thought and speech is regarded as beyond the divisions of gender and sexuality, or combining both? What, at least, if Jesus' God is Oneness? If Jesus considered God, not only as Father, but as Father-Mother, or Creator-Birther, or Breather of Life, Christians could be invited to do the same: to reconsider two thousand years of sitting, kneeling or bowing to an all-powerful Father figure and expand their minds beyond gender-limitation of the Divine— as Jewish and Christian esoteric traditions, and as Christian Scientists through the words of Mary Baker Eddy, already have.

But this, it may be objected, is mere semantics. What about the twelve apostles? What about the commission to Peter: the rock upon which Jesus would build his congregation, and the guardian of the keys to the kingdom of Heaven? One might interpret the Peter commission by noting that the text reporting it is immediately followed by a lacerating criticism of Peter ("Get thee behind me, Satan"); moreover, the commission is more prominently asserted in the late first century non-Pauline text of Matthew than it is in the earlier, mid-century letters of Paul, which are in places quite critical of Peter. Paul applies the foundation stone metaphor only to Jesus. The Peter depicted in Paul's early letters to the communities in Asia Minor is a rock made of sand rather than granite.

But to return to the twelve apostles: we have noted that the first post-resurrection apostolic commission was, as reported in the John and Mark gospels, given not to a male disciple but to the Magdalene, to whom also was reportedly accorded the first sighting, touching, and discourse with the resurrected Christ. Women, in fact, are reported as playing a critical role in the Crucifixion and post-Crucifixion events. Women are also reported as accompanying Jesus on his mission and supporting him out of their resources. All four gospels recount that it is a woman or women who at one stage or another anoint Jesus with precious ointment. In three instances, that anointing is the act that identifies Jesus ceremonially as the Christ (Anointed One) and prepares him to undertake his entry as Messiah-king into Jerusalem and his arrest and execution at the hands of the Roman imperium.

So important did Jesus (and his chroniclers) consider this ceremony of anointing that he insisted that wherever the gospel should be preached throughout the world, this deed that the woman anointer had done would be told about, "in memory of her." To have a woman perform such an act is itself of enormous significance in defining Jesus' assertion of the sacramental role of women. The sacramental priesthood for Jesus, it would appear, is a female priesthood. Last, but not least, is the role accorded to Mary the mother, not simply in the infancy narratives, but as participant in his adult mission, mourner during his crucifixion, and commissioned by the dying son as apostolic matriarch.

To sum up: Jesus was birthed and reared by a woman, supported materially by women during his mission, sacramentally anointed by a woman in preparation for his entry as Messiah into Jerusalem, surrounded by women in his suffering on the cross, and as resurrected Christ greeted by a woman who had come to attend to his burial and who passionately loved him. The evidence is clear: women were critical to the conduct and the denouement of the Jesus mission. Many of them were also its direct beneficiaries; and as reported in the Acts and the early letters of Paul, many women became missionaries of the new covenant. Many women also became martyrs for the cause of proclaiming Christianity.

All this suggests strongly that Jesus treated women as intrinsic to his mission and not only accepted their participation but actively depended on it. The authorized gospels also intimate that he had very close personal relations with one or more women, valued what they did for him, and wanted the memory of one woman's sacramental deed remembered in perpetuity. No doubt if women had been co-directing the Christian church over all the subsequent centuries, that deed would be better remembered, and its significance better understood and ritually incorporated into modern liturgies than is currently the case. Our modern-day liturgies and creeds are still for the most part those inherited from the early patristic church. If Christianity is to be rebirthed in our time, these liturgies will have to be changed and the priesthood of women acknowledged.

There is a great need in contemporary Christianity to rethink and reformulate from the ground up the role of women as bearers of religious and spiritual tradition. In terms of progress in this matter among the general public, we are still too close to zero. The appointment of a few women to ministerial positions does little more than tinker with a closed system and does not get at the question of women as bearers and channelers of divinity. The language, culture and traditions of modern Christianity are still fundamentally patriarchal. This was evidently not the intention of its founder. The renewal of Christianity will occur when the energy, language, spirituality, and recognition of women as carriers and channelers of divinity are fully engaged, as Jesus had intended.

For this to happen, men and women will have to find the means, and the myths, to create an equal playing field in which the religious resources of both can be fully developed. In this time, women are no longer going to be deprived of the opportunity to give full expression to their religious power, in ways that do not simply advance patriarchal agendas. That will occur either inside of organized Christianity or outside of it. A few Christian churches have already fully empowered women as religious leaders and activists. But mainline Christianity is still too timid and cluttered with tradition to make this kind of unconditional commitment. Until that happens, men and women living in Christian cultures are both the losers.

At a more personal level, men reared in Judeo-Christian traditions need to search out the spiritual and religious power represented by the female element in existence, and women as human bearers of that life force on this earth need to reactivate it in a way that is definable and sustaining to men. Our non-Christian myths about women, such as those inherited from Classical Rome and Greece or from pre-Christian European Goddess cults, are themselves sufficiently powerful as to present aspects of female power that are extremely appealing and attractive to men. One need only study Botticelli's great mythic paintings of women goddesses to see how appealing these myths are. But within a dominantly Christian cultural tradition, the mythic power of such figures as Venus and Diana or Morgan La Faye, potent as it is, cannot been seen outside the primal mythic context of Eve as seducer and betrayer. In any case, part of the potency of the Venus myth in Christianized culture derives from the problems associated with the myths about the Virgin Mary and the Magdalene; while attitudes towards the pre-Christian Goddess cults and their heroines are still infected by the centuries-long persecution of women as witches.

At present, men and women are still trapped by these myths, as is reflected daily by the institutional forces and gender assumptions, both religious and secular, under which we labor. The myth of woman as seducer lying at the heart of patriarchal religion still lives on and flourishes, even though it has long since lost its utility as a means of preserving cultural power. The Eve myth is in fact now seriously damaging our culture, as is indicated by the far too pervasive male degradation of, and violence towards, women which infects our culture, as well as the violence towards, and damage of, the earth, which has long been mythically identified with female power. At least Adam, so far as the Bible is concerned, never beat or raped his wife and children or polluted the earth. But today, in America and elsewhere, too many contemporary Adams are doing just that.

Yet the Adam and Eve myth, as I implied in the previous chapter, is also damaging males. As a male I feel compelled to point this out to other males; at the same time, I am compelled to ask women to acknowledge their own complicity in perpetuating these female-distorting myths. If I am angry with people of my own gender for shaping me into another Adam and my wife into another Eve, I also recognize that the latter has the power to undo the myths binding her and me. The female, just as much as the male, is the manifestation and image of the "Birther-Mother-Father of the Cosmos." To put this more formally, existence is both unitary and dyadic: unitary in respect to the oneness of the source and emanation of life; dyadic in respect to its manifestation in reproductive and gender-related form. If a renewed cosmos or kingdom of heaven is to be birthed, it will be done through the linked power of both genders.

The Christian myths about women have gone most astray not with Eve or the Virgin Mary but with the Magdalene. The Eve myth long predates

Christianity; and although it is less guilt-ridden in Rabbinic Judaism, the association of Eve with death is a Jewish myth inherited through Paul by Christianity. The Virgin Mary myth, although in its full expression unique to Christianity, is constructed on elements, such as virgin birth, that were common throughout the middle east well before Christianity made its appearance. The concept of Mary as intercessor and protector has brought healing to innumerable people and is by any measure an active and valuable expression of spiritual life for millions of men and women.

On the other hand, the myth of the Magdalene as repentant whore is an artifact that reflects far more about its makers than it does about the Magdalene herself as an avatar. It exploits the 'prostitute' archetype in the priesthood of women (a subject reflected in Biblical texts) and distorts that into a depiction of woman as purveyor of death-dealing sin rather than as sacramental channeler of divine energy and blessing—a service that women in antiquity performed. The Biblical records, coupled with artistic insight, tell us something about the Magdalene that is quite different from the standard myth constructed by orthodox Christian theology. Instead of the deathly and repentant whore, what we see is a woman who deeply loved and may well have consecrated Jesus, and who was deeply loved by him.

Indeed, according to early Christian records outside of what became the orthodox canon of the "New Testament", she was his most intimate companion. Recent scholarly translations of, and commentaries on, the Gospel of Mary [Magdalene], and other related writings from what is generally labeled the 'Gnostic' tradition, draw attention to the inner teaching that Jesus reportedly imparted to Mary, little hints of which can be found in the standard gospels and some of the writings of the Apostle Paul. Through the partially recovered discourse of this gospel, we can see that Mary (or an archetype representing Mary) gains access to a way of envisioning resurrected being, as well as to the pathway of the soul to the attainment of spiritual grace. She becomes a living witness to this gospel teaching imparted by Jesus. This powerful and complex way of nurturing the soul was not apparently conveyed to the male disciples and is a major—if not the major—reason for the privileged status of Mary (or Miriam, to use her Hebrew name) and the reported frustration of the apostles Peter and Andrew as depicted in the gospel text. According to that text, the men simply could not believe that Jesus could have accepted a woman as primary companion in any discourse about the mission of the beloved teacher or the good news to be propagated, when it was them whom he had selected as his companions and disciples.

It is this aspect of intimacy, rather than the apparent choice of Mary as apostle to the apostles, that seems to have caused most trouble to orthodox Christianity. The possibility that the Magdalene and Jesus might have had a relationship of loving, even sacred and spiritual intimacy was simply too much of a challenge to a religion whose priesthood (and monkhood) was for centuries anchored on a foundation of male celibacy and to a considerable extent still is. In addition, the notion of the Magdalene as primus inter pares ran up against powerful belief systems that regarded male expression as the ultimate image of divine spirituality and female expression as a secondary and corrupted manifestation of human existence. These beliefs, rooted in arcane patristic theology, underlie continuing Western notions about the superiority of male in relation to female life. More specifically, they ensured the suppression of a text that countered the dominant patriarchal ideas on what Christianity was all about.

Several recent studies, both scholarly and unscholarly, have explored the notion that Jesus might in fact have been married and, if so, was very likely married to the Magdalene. The arguments, as sociology, are certainly plausible, but they run up against two thousand years of patriarchal certitude that Jesus, as depicted in the four authorized gospels, was a single person whose life was dedicated solely to the propagation of the kingdom of heaven and the assumption of suffering on behalf of a sinful humanity. Christianity is still a long way from considering, much less accepting, the notion that Jesus might have been married, that the Magdalene might have been his spouse, and that together they might have borne children.

In this respect, Christianity differentiates fundamentally from religions in which union between divine avatars, or between gods and humans, is a given. Outside of the Church of Jesus Christ of Latter-Day Saints there has been no accepted Christian theology that could permit us to construe Jesus and the Magdalene as spiritual lovers or partners in any physical, earth-bound way. Indeed, until contemporary scholars began to focus on the recovered but damaged text of the Gospel of Mary Magdalene, there had been no biblically based theology even legitimizing a spiritual union, anchored in cultivation of the soul's pathway to divine enlightenment.

John Watt

This denial of a fully worked out spousal theology within Christianity means that the latter comes up short on the single most important human relationship within human existence. In that respect there is a great need to root out the corrupt and pernicious Magdalene myth and replace it with one that can be broadly sustaining to men and women alike.

CHAPTER 14

Marriage as Sacramental Covenant

> From the beginning of creation
> God made them male and female
> For this cause shall a man leave his father and mother
> And cleave to his wife
> And they twain shall be one flesh
> Mark, chapter 10

Problems with Contemporary Marriage

In this age of global materialism hard problems are grinding away at the contemporary family. Divorce, domestic abuse, abandoned children, and abortion, represent the most serious damage to individual lives searching for love and stability through marriage and family. But underlying these abuses are all the doubts about personal identity in a constantly shifting culture. The public institutions that have served in the past to define identity, such as church, school, community, and job, are no longer as strong and reliable as they once were. Even rural communities, once oases of stability, are having to grapple with transience and pressures from sources beyond their control, while in the urban world anonymity has become a fact of life, confronting us whenever we encounter a stranger. Individuals searching for identity in such an atomistic environment must increasingly depend on the strength of their own inner resources to carry them forward.

The problems of the individual are seen most clearly through the stresses of making a living in a culture more driven by market share and profit margins and less concerned about the security of individual lives and atomized, nuclear families. For most people living in the United States, vocational and job stability can no longer be expected—and for many it never could. The economic and social forces bearing down on the family lives of underclass people, especially ethnic/racial minorities, are now seen to be at work in the larger society. As a result of this spreading instability, the survival and wellbeing of the family have metamorphosed into a public, political concern, because when the values of mainstream culture begin to unravel, there is nothing for anyone to look forward to but further drift and anxiety.

Americans hear a great deal about abortion, and that is because abortion is the ultimate expression of marital and family values in disarray. Family values are designed to bring stability to adult relationships and to secure the protection of children. Abortion negates the latter objective. Consequently, concern about abortion reflects a deeper anxiety that marital and family values are becoming less functional in protecting and nurturing human life. To abandon a fetus before it is born implies that the fetus was carelessly or wrongly conceived, with all that that entails, and that there is an inadequate basis of material, emotional and spiritual support to convert the fetus into a child whose legitimate needs can be sustained. Each abandoned fetus is a sorry reminder that family values, in our culture, are in trouble.

This anxiety about the problems and wellbeing of the family matters greatly. Marriage and family are the basic structures holding human social systems together, and marriage is the basic bond supporting the family. It is impossible to imagine human history and human survival without the existence of marriage. Marriage is not necessarily part of the perceived content of history, because as a basic social institution it tends to function below the level of consciously recorded events. But take away marriage, as would be the case in certain utopian or libertarian communities at one extreme, or in slave labor camps at another, and one is immediately confronted with the presence of unstable and transient conditions. The surprisingly shallow or conditional commitment of contemporary society towards marriage is not a sign that we are moving towards a liberation from social convention—as if libertarianism and utopia resulted from the withering away of social institutions. It is rather a sign of malaise in the social fabric that allows us to function as social beings. It may be true, as Jesus was once provoked to remark, that in 'heaven' there is no marriage. But as far as life on earth is concerned, there is no evidence that human society can survive and flourish without the existence of marriage as a formal social relationship.

As a social institution marriage is an expression of trust achieved between negotiating parties. Here we are primarily concerned with marriage as an ethical and covenantal institution, and with the way in which these aspects of marriage are reflected in cultures such as those within the U.S., that are based on Biblical tradition.

The glue that cements this kind of sacramental marriage consists of pledges made in a formal, public manner. Those pledges are the expression of a covenant of trust between two individuals, undertaken most often in a sacred setting. "Undertaken in a sacred setting" means—or should mean—that the covenanting parties seek to make their pledges in the presence of the divine and agree to unite as an expression of divine intention for human existence. Gifts expressing those pledges are exchanged in the form of rings, and society is invited to witness and celebrate the enactment of a covenant bringing two people together into a sacramental union. The witnesses contribute gifts, blessings and expressions of goodwill as part of the covenantal ceremony. All that is lacking in the modern Biblically-derived marriage ceremony is an expression of the curses and maledictions (such as "may your offspring all be abused, aborted or die young, and may you die penniless") that should accompany a breach of a marriage covenant made in a sacramental setting. But as we know, such maledictions can in fact come true whenever a marriage is irreparably breached. Indeed, many thousands of women and children with dead-beat fathers can attest to the impoverishing consequences of divorce.

But what happens when the institution of marriage itself is discounted? In our culture today, we have innumerable instances of sacramental marriage ceremonies being carried on by and for people who have little or no conception of what a sacramental ceremony is all about. For such people churches function as little more than ceremonial drop-in centers. The parties seeking ceremonial endorsement 'drop in' whenever there is need for a wedding or a funeral, and then, having obtained that endorsement, they drop out. When it comes to discussing such matters as what is a vow, why do we want to conduct the wedding in a sacramental setting, what do the concepts of 'sacred' and 'spiritual' mean to us, what commitment do we bring to the marriage, and what promises do we want to make in the presence of the divine and our fellow humans, many soon find themselves in beyond their depth. The wedding ceremony goes ahead, but it seems to be more about costumes, photography, lavish flower arrangements, limousines, big receptions and expenditures, in other words everything to do with material abundance, than about the enactment of a sacred covenant. When the ceremonial gloss wears off, which it does soon enough, and when the guests are gone, the champagne emptied, and the honeymoon over and done with, the marriage then survives or falls on the basis of an individual human relationship, which society as a whole has little interest in preserving.

Beyond such disregard of marriage as a covenantal enterprise lies a broader lack of trust within the society as a whole, and the consequent effect of this lack of trust on personal relationships. Contemporary society has come to have little trust in politicians, employers, celebrities, journalists, or other such symbols of material empowerment. Now, as we see in our social legislation, it has become similarly distrustful of the poor, the immigrants, the homeless, and other such disempowered people. Gunfire crackles in inner cities, and gun-ownership among suburbanites and those living in rural areas proliferates as a response to fear of violence on the part of hostile-looking—e.g. ethnically or racially different—individuals. In certain areas of the U.S. the home is shifting from a place of tranquility and hospitality to an armed camp to be protected with guns; and individuals 'courageous' or unlucky enough to have to venture into the public arena feel they must do so with legally concealed weapons capable of killing assailants.

This kind of environment is not conducive to the kind of social cohesion intended by covenant, marital or otherwise. It breeds a culture that instead favors casual or restricted relationship above long-term social commitment. Marriage depends on trust; and trust, as we can see all around us, is a perishable commodity. By contrast, casual personal intimacy is convenient, sexually functional, and free of the risks associated with making long term commitments. Less casual relationships can involve both commitment and love, but stop short of the level of trust implied, if not fulfilled, by marriage.

Why is this? When it comes to trust and other emotionally defined values, no amount of material abundance or institutional security can act as a substitute. Trust grows out of inner strength; and inner strength cannot be assumed in a culture as shifting and impermanent as ours. Those who stop short of marriage are letting us know that marriage by itself cannot act as a substitute for the emotional strength that we bring to the relationship.

Furthermore, marriage and parenthood play a key role in inculcating trust and emotional bonding in human beings; while absence, indifference, lovelessness, abuse, dishonesty, and divorce, play a similarly important part in engendering mistrust. Children learn trust primarily from their parents or guardians. Consequently, the widespread occurrence of abuse, dishonesty, absence, and divorce characterizing contemporary families should make us very worried about the lack of trust being passed on to children, and the effect of that lack of trust on the future of marriage and family. Can it be wondered that many younger people today hesitate before committing themselves to institutions that have become so damaged by the decline of trust in our culture?

The discounting of marriage, the ease of separation and divorce, indeed the conversion of a sacramental covenant into a legal and finite contract, is to all intents and purposes a fact of contemporary life. Nobody but the most romantically blinded believe any longer all the well-intentioned and sacred promises evoked in wedding ceremonies to hang on through sickness and health "till death do us part." How many people have uttered those words, only to go back on them within months or years? The typical wedding ceremony has become a well-intentioned charade that traps people into making promises they cannot sustain. It may be unkind to call such an expensive event a sham, but that is exactly what it has so frequently become. Perhaps we should instead say that society today lacks adequate belief in marriage to commit to it as an enterprise through bad times as well as good. What does it really matter now if a contractual marriage, like a start-up business venture, doesn't survive some unexpected misfortunes? Apparently, one should simply pick oneself up and look around for other opportunities and people.

But the breakdown of marriage as covenant does matter. Without the certitude of marriage and the commitment to human relationship embodied in marriage as covenant, problems connected with breach of trust are inevitable. Among those listed so far, the one most reflecting the malaise in our social fabric is abortion—the abandonment and destruction of human life because there is not enough personal and social commitment to sustain it. Since covenantal marriage functions to conceive and support human life, and abortion functions to get rid of conceived life, covenantal marriage and abortion lie at opposite poles of the continuum supporting human birth and human welfare. The urgency and grief in contemporary America about abortion is thus a reflection of the underlying social trauma that it expresses. One single, solitary abortion may be a "reproductive decision" or an expression of choice; but over half a million a year is an epidemic and a national disaster. In case anyone thinks this is the conclusion of a hard-line right-to-lifer, let me clarify that I strongly oppose epidemic abortion, not choice per se. Abortion in the amount carried on in the US is as radically destructive as female infanticide was in Imperial China, which Americans rightly abhor. It puts Americans in roughly the same unflattering and vulnerable status as the inhabitants of any so-called developing country, which cannot or will not find the means to sustain its human offspring.

Unfortunately, the abortion debate in this country is vitiated by the way in which the onus for abortion—as for so much else relating to marriage, family, and human welfare, especially emotional health—has been placed predominantly on women. When unwanted pregnancy occurs, it is the woman's body that is implicated and the woman who is forced to decide what to do (except in countries where abortion may be state-mandated). Women must bear the burden for the fault-lines in human relations that make an unwanted pregnancy possible in the first place. Women's lives, already stressed by the nuclearization of families and the changing relationships of women to family and workplace, must now take on the additional stress of determining the fate of the unborn. Clinics providing family planning and obstetrical services become the battlefield where these decisions are played out.

But where are the males in this national trauma, whose sexual activity fathers over half a million annually abandoned fetuses? Without male sexuality and intercourse there can be no abortion, because there will be no fetus to cause any trouble. Ah: if only sexual intercourse could be guaranteed without risk of pregnancy! Then it would hardly matter that the average age of first sexual intercourse for American males is 17 years, way before the average age of marriage, or that over 60% of high school seniors have had sexual intercourse. We could simply entrust sex education to high schools and mandate that boys practice copulation under formal supervision before being turned loose on girls. Informally this is what is already happening now, except that society is reluctant to assume any formal responsibility for it. Boys will be boys, meaning they must have their sexual fun; and if girls don't watch out, it is their own responsibility.

The patriarchal double standard, much reviled by feminists, is at work here. But to be fair to formative patriarchy, in the times of the ancient Greeks and Romans boys got their sexual initiations with other boys, not with girls, thus diminishing and even obviating the problem of teenage pregnancy. The modern British, and those who emulated them, attempted to continue this arrangement by insulating precocious boys in boarding schools, where their erotic drives could be kept in check by discipline and athletics or carried out in secret.

But the leveling of class lines and the invasion of male preserves by women, have broken down efforts to keep boys and girls apart. Patriarchalism, ironically, has now been let loose across the board. With or without the easy availability of condoms, boys can now engage in sex—if necessary, on the spur of the moment—without more than one in four having received any sexual, much less moral, education. Hollywood movies now routinely advertise and display teenage sex.

Ironically—for people living in Christianized countries—we have come a long way from the early days of Christianity, when it was believed that male semen alone produced life and that women's bodies functioned merely as fetal incubators. Human life was governed then, too, by patriarchy, but this androcentrism could be rationalized by the claim that life was solely the product of male fertility. But the way the abortion debate is conducted today, there would appear to be little connection left between male ejaculate and the unwanted fetus within the female body. A new and disturbing female parthenogenesis is upon us. Where abortion is concerned, it is a problem pre-eminently for women, both financially and morally. The 'choice' is theirs. If they take it and spend the money, then they are pro-choice but anti-life, while if they conform to the patriarchally managed ideology of the 'family' they are pro-life but devoid of choice. Meanwhile an apparent majority of male ejaculators (many well beyond high school age) remain in the background, eluding fatherhood and the responsibilities that the public imposes on women. Could one imagine a killer of abortionists, such as John Salvi, ever taking his gun to the heads of sexually active but irresponsible males?

How did Americans ever get to the sorry situation of engaging in a national shouting match on abortion, without having the honesty to face the underlying problems of which abortion is an expression? Why, indeed, do we have so much trouble acknowledging the very great material and emotional problems confronting modern marriage, and admitting to the emotional impoverishment and decay of trust within—as well as outside of—marriage that affects so many people today? How can we expect not to have problems like domestic abuse, divorce, dead-beat fathers and abortion, when our most basic social institution, the basic glue on which social cohesion depends, is so much at risk?

To approach these questions from a Biblical perspective, we need to know whether the Biblical covenant tradition, on which our social institutions are founded, can have any guidance for us in this non- or post-Biblical age. What does the Bible have to say about marriage? What does it mean by marriage, and how has that meaning been interpreted? And can the wisdom of minds at work two or three thousand years ago still guide people of our generation, who live with such personal and social uncertainty?

Marriage in the Biblical Tradition

One cannot read beyond Genesis chapter 2 without coming upon a text about marriage. In the passage describing the creation of Eve, we are told that Adam exclaimed, "this at last is bone from my bones and flesh from my flesh" (Jerusalem Bible). Then follows an ironic interpolation. "She shall be called woman", Adam remarks in punning fashion, "because she was taken out of man." But then the textual redactor adds, as if somehow in logical continuity, "therefore shall a man leave his father and his mother and shall cleave unto his wife; and they shall be one flesh." There is in fact little ground in the literal ingredients of the story for this "therefore." Adam had no father and mother to leave, nor had he and Eve gone through a wedding ceremony. Yet Adam's much later and probably post-exilic 'descendants', for whom this "therefore" passage was intended, did have parents and did marry. It was through marriage that the early patriarchs and their descendants were able to fulfil the God-given injunction to "be fruitful, multiply, and replenish the earth." Indeed, the very fact that the earliest patriarchal figures, Abraham and Sarah, are described as having had for decades a barren marriage, is intended to reiterate the Divine agenda intended by marriage.

Thus, marriage emerges as the mythical founding institution of Biblical society, defining the function of human beings on earth and, according to the text, countenanced by God in the very act of creation. Rabbis, who assiduously taught the primacy of marriage in the Torah, would cite a well-known passage from Proverbs stating that "house and riches are the inheritance of fathers, but a prudent wife is from the Lord." A man's marriage partner, they insisted, was not a matter of human dispensation but came directly from the Holy One.

Early Christian teaching followed the Genesis line on marriage. Paul himself recommended marriage primarily as an antidote to lust. He personally preferred celibacy, with the proviso that those who were already married should stay married. Paul's emphasis on celibacy, and concern about the worries of marriage, resulted from his apocalyptic belief that time was growing short and the material world would soon pass away. Consequently, he wanted his followers in Corinth to concentrate on preparing for the end of the world, not its continuity.

But Deutero-Pauline letters to Paul's followers and successors in Ephesus and Colossus are very much concerned with family morality, precisely because the family is regarded as the body and substance of the life of community and thus as the body of Christ. These early Christian communities are in a sense also 'exilic', in that they post-date the destruction of Jerusalem in CE 70 and represent the implanting of Christian fellowship outside the land of its origin. Thus, there are interesting parallels between their attempts to arrive at self-definition and the efforts of the earlier

Israelite exilic communities to insert their thoughts about marriage and family into the Biblical tradition.

The letters to the early Christian communities search for ways to promote security and survival. They argue that men must love their wives as they love themselves—because their wives are indeed an expression of their bodies. For this reason, notes the letter to the Ephesian Christians—harking back to Adam and Eve—a man must leave his father and mother and be joined to his wife, and the two become one body. Wives, in addition, must respect and submit to their husbands, because the husband is the head of his wife, just as Christ is the head of the community of faith. Children, as proclaimed in the Decalogue, are to honor their fathers and mothers; those that did would prosper and live long. Parents, in turn, should not provoke their children to wrath but bring them up in the nurture and admonition of the Lord.

This kind of advice, with its reflection on wives as the 'weaker vessel', took hold and indeed sat well enough with patriarchal Christian cultures even until current times. The Gospel teachings, however, add a sterner note. In answer to the question is it lawful for a man to divorce his wife, Jesus is led to respond with his own question: what does Moses command? The answer, in Deuteronomy 24, was that in case of certain improprieties a man could divorce his wife. Jesus comments, however, that this was permitted because of the hardness and lack of feeling in men's hearts. (Mark 10) We should note well this pointed comment on the hardened state of men's hearts in patriarchal culture. So much of the Jesus mission could be defined as an attempt to repair the patriarchally hardened male heart. But from the beginning of creation, Jesus continues, referring to the gender-egalitarian Priestly creation account in Genesis chapter 1, God made them male and female. Because of this creational dualism a man shall leave his father and mother and cleave to his wife, and they shall be two in one flesh. So, they are then, he adds, not two but one flesh. In other words, marriage functions to counteract the division brought about by the creation of dual genders and individualized lives, by recreating one body out of two. Marriage, in short, comes to symbolize the principle of sacred union. That is the principle underlying the use of the word "therefore" in the Adam and Eve text; and that is why the Jesus text is placed at the head of this chapter.

Furthermore, the woman does not so much come to the man as the man leaves his parents and comes to the woman. So much for the assumed dominance of patriarchy. In marriage a new life is born. What therefore God has joined together, concludes the text, let not man put asunder. Back in the house the disciples question Jesus about this. Indeed, the Jesus of this text is articulating a radical theory of marriage, one which serves to set his followers apart from those living under rabbinic, not to mention pagan, guidance. So, he is shown as repeating the point more strongly. Any man who divorces his wife and takes on another woman commits adultery against the wife. If the wife divorces her husband and marries another man, she also commits adultery. (Mark 10, Matthew 19)

Adultery in those days was no light matter. According to Torah, if a man committed adultery with a married woman, both must be put to death. Various other breaches of marital relations were also punishable by death. Incest was punishable by burning. The Hebrew scriptures were, in short, tough on breaches of marriage. Such actions were regarded as defiling and hateful. Casual sex was also frowned on. When Shechem got together with Jacob's daughter Dinah, had intercourse with her and then wanted to marry her, her brothers Simeon and Levi tricked and then slaughtered him and his compatriots. But to equate divorce with adultery is a way of shocking the listeners not just with the threat of the law but at the core of their being, because it argues that divorce is defiant of God's 'creational plan' of producing gender duality, so as to create life through its bonding.

But Jesus, while condemning divorce and adultery as anti-creational, could not stand hypocrisy. When a woman accused of adultery was brought to him by men who were lusting to kill her, he invited anyone who had not sinned to be the first to throw a stone. The he bent over and scratched on the ground. The accusers slunk off; who, even today, has not sinned? Jesus, who condemned the offence, would not condemn the offender or even, one might note, those who sought her death. To her he is recorded as saying, "go and don't sin any further."

The letter to the Hebrews took a similar line to that reported in the Gospels, saying that marriage was honorable to all and the marriage bed immaculate (and therefore an appropriate place for sexual intercourse); nevertheless, God would judge fornicators and adulterers. The Book of

Revelations put fornicators into the same category as dogs, sorcerers, murderers, idolaters and liars. When the day of judgment came, all such vile creatures would be cast beyond the pale. The first of the letters named for Peter urged wives to be obedient to their husbands, partly as a means of attracting pagan males and husbands into the life of the Christic community.

Some of these sentiments today might seem more a source of bemusement than of serious guidance or self-questioning. It might be jarring, but more likely bizarre, for the contemporary reader to find a Bible text that lumps fornicators together with dogs and murderers. It might also be jarring, yet less absurd, to see how adultery is treated. Adultery (meaning sexual intercourse between a man and a woman, both of whom already had marital partners) attacked the institution that lay at the very foundation of Biblical society. The most exemplary case of adultery in the Bible involved King David, the king most loved by Yahweh and the recipient of a unique covenant that underlay the myth of the Messiah. David's adultery with Bathsheba, the wife of Uriah, did not result in his or her death but did result in the death of their first born, as well as the slaughter of the hapless Uriah. It also marked the turning point in David's career and was the act which more than any other precipitated his decline and fall as a monarch, as well as the rape and slaughter that broke out among his children. Nor is ancient Judea alone among pre-modern cultures in abhorring adultery. An act of kingly adultery underlies the rift between the Catholic and Anglican communions, which has continued for nearly 500 years. (Perhaps it is not so surprising that Henry VIII, the English king who precipitated that rift, would die of syphilis.)

Even in modern times misgivings about adultery die hard. There are still denominations, church communities and ministers who cannot countenance the idea of celebrating the marriage of someone who has committed adultery. But does this mean that we should all be gathering rocks to hurl at well-known practitioners of sexual intercourse with other people's spouses? If death were today the consequence of adultery, Hollywood would be decimated, and the silver screen deprived of one of its most enduring themes. Dear Abby and Anne Landers and other such social counselors would lose much of their business. Not a few of our own political leaders would find themselves in serious trouble.

Obviously Biblical injunctions regarding adultery and fornication are as out of place in the contemporary world as animal sacrifice or the slaughter of idolaters. Indeed, much of Biblical ethics simply no longer applies. With already seven billion people on this earth and eight billion anticipated within a few decades, how can any serious person imagine that it is the function of marriage, as implied in the first chapter of Genesis, to enable humankind to be fruitful and multiply? Even the Chinese, still the most fruitful of human societies, understand that the world does not need and cannot sustain many more people. The globe is finite. Such a marital ethic has run up against that finiteness. That kind of ethic, surely once necessary to the survival of a primitive society, no longer works to assure our present survival. It now has the potential to bring about a world of increasing starvation and misery for humans and non-humans alike. Consequently, those who still take the trouble to read the Bible cannot afford to accept its ethics uncritically. If Biblical ethics are to survive in our time and be of use to contemporary and future society, we are going to have to do some critical sifting of ethical wheat from chaff.

At the same time if we ask, what is marriage for today, inhabitants of Western societies cannot altogether ignore the Bible. Anyone who has read this far will appreciate how much of Biblical imagery still influences thinking in Western cultures about marriage. When it comes to getting married, we are still descendants of Adam and Eve, taking our most important step away from our natal families and struggling to "cleave" together as "one flesh." If we have been through a Christian marriage ceremony, we may still recall the words attributed to Jesus, "What therefore God hath joined together let not man put asunder." We will probably also have heard a reading of Paul's famous paean to love, if not his exhortation to his Corinthian followers that "you must want love more than anything else" (Jerusalem Bible). We will have sought the blessing of a sacramental experience, as if acknowledging that marriage is, or should be, something more than a legal contract or a business deal.

Similarly, if we want to find ways of strengthening family life, we may not be able to make do by putting our trust solely in secular and materialistic solutions. Human consciousness strives for deeper meaning than can be satisfied by the materialism of the secular world. In addition to a new sofa or stereo system, we also want beauty, joy and happiness.

We want to be able to trust that life will not always betray us. We want to experience love. We may even want to do the great deed of conceiving life itself. These are fundamentally emotional desires that can only be fulfilled through human relationships. We may also want to go deeper still and search for spiritual consciousness. We may want to seek the experience of loving God. We may want to know what it means to love others—those who are our neighbors, as Judaism puts it. We may want to experience the capacity to be compassionate, to comprehend and ease the pain of others. Some may even, as Christianity and Buddhism advocate, want to develop that rare quality of being able to love our enemies, or as Judaism also advocates, to experience their pain.

It is in the context of such desires that the institutions of marriage and family begin to take on freight. So long as life is directed to the rational, secular world, and to the accumulation of material power and influence, we cannot expect much of institutions that now offer little in the way of material rewards. An institution whereby two people make the decision to cleave together as one is not designed or equipped to advance specifically material goals. According to the Bible, it asks us to leave father and mother, in other words take ourselves out from under the protection of parents, where we can function as dependent children and receivers of the material bounty accumulated by our forebears. Men are asked to go out from under the family 'roof', find a partner, and "cleave" together as if they were one. According to the rabbis, and according to Torah, finding that partner is not a matter of simple inheritance. It is likely to involve a journey, and the discovery of the partner cannot be attributed solely to human agency. As the writer to the Ephesian Christians was forced to put it, "this is a great mystery", beyond the explanation of words or rational phenomena. Or as the rabbis concluded, it is the work of the Holy One.

Such views, with their acknowledgement of Divine intervention, remind us that the world in which early Christian thinking and writing about marriage developed was not like ours. As scholars such as Elaine Pagels have pointed out, much of early Christian writing follows Paul in strongly advocating celibacy for both men and women. Those authorities that favored marriage did so because of its importance to conceiving and raising children, rather than as an archetype of the creative will. Some of this ambivalence towards marriage is reflected in the Gospel accounts, especially that of Matthew, which on the one hand is less adamant than the Mark account about divorce, and on the other hand esteems extreme celibacy.

Thus, in attempting to interpret the meaning of marriage teaching as recorded in the Christian scriptures, we need to bear in mind the apocalyptic beliefs prevailing in first century Jewish communities, which as we can see in the letters written directly by Paul had the effect of dampening interest in marriage. Early gentile Christian communities were much more interested in marriage. But at the same time there existed within them an ardent sentiment favoring celibacy and radical self-denial. This ardent advocacy of 'celibacy for Christ' underlay the development of monasticism as well as the celibate priesthood and profession of teaching. The influence of celibacy is not nearly as strong today as it once was, so far as the clerical and teaching professions are concerned. Yet opposition to sexuality continues to affect contemporary Western attitudes towards family planning, as well as to push people into marriage as a means of sanctioning the sexuality of those for whom celibacy is not an option. More basically it nurtures seeds of doubt about the function of sexuality as phallic energy in the overall scheme of things.

But marriage, in both Judaic and Christian doctrine, was never intended to be nothing more than a means to sanction sexual intercourse. Nor is it merely a means to sanction procreation. Beyond these factors lies the idea of marriage as a symbolic expression of the basic plan and design of creation. It is significant, in this regard, that both the gospel and Pauline traditions draw directly on the redactional commentary implanted in the Adam and Eve story to show that marriage is intrinsic to the Divine plan. In the Pauline and early Christian tradition we see marriage set forth as the basic building block in the creation of the Christic community of faith. Women draw their men into the Christic community, where their hearts may be exposed to the saving grace of personal redemption. Hierarchically speaking man is still regarded as head of the union of woman with man, as Christ is head of the union of Church with Christ. But within this hierarchical mindset, what matters is union. Marriage is the glue by which the community of faith is constructed, and the means by which pagan men might be brought into that community. That glue is not merely an institutional concoction; it the expression of an emotional bonding based on love and trust between individual human beings.

In the gospel traditions we see emphasized another idea in the Adam and Eve myth, namely the separation of man from the patriarchal inheritance and the cleaving together of man and woman as one. Marriage, in other words, functions to unite what is separate and to transform duality into unity. Existentially marriage brings about the unification of gender duality and all that inheres to gender duality, from biology to personhood to expression of human life in myth and reality. Through marriage male consciousness and female consciousness are to be drawn together into a consciousness that is created from that union. Monism is to be the fundamental mode of existence, not duality, yet it is a monism that has the capacity to be expressed, and in fact can only be expressed, through the duality defined by gender. Without gender duality and sacramental unity, in other words, there is no creational achievement.

Thus, we should not be surprised to find the gospel tradition insisting that what God has joined together let not man put asunder. This is the conclusion to be drawn from the marital doctrine built into the Adam and Eve myth. The Bible insists that marriage is not just a human arrangement put together for reproductive or sociological purposes, or even as the formalization of an emotional bonding. It is, at its fullest, an expression of the divine power at work in the human order. One could even claim, in line with this reasoning, that marriage is the essential expression of the divine at work in the human order, preceding church, temple, monastery, and all the other ecclesiastical superstructures reflecting clerical assumptions about how divinity likes to operate and be housed and represented on earth. Putting this in simple theological terms, God makes marriage happen because God wants marriage to happen. Putting it in more existential terms, definitions of human bonding that are reproductive, contractual, sociological, even emotional, fall short unless they bring marriage into some overall structure of consciousness functioning in relation to the process of creation itself. Marriage as an expression of the creational process makes sense and is humanly speaking satisfying. Any lesser definition is in the long run unsatisfying and insufficient to keep marriage going.

Making Sense of Modern Marriage

If marriage is really intended to function at such a substantively creational level, how then are we to make sense of the messy state of contemporary marriage and human relations generally? Here again it is worth noting that Biblical myth is not without relevance. Following on from the definition in Genesis, chapter 2, of marriage as intrinsic to the creational plan, we find Eve apparently seducing Adam, Adam letting himself be seduced, Adam blaming Eve, Eve blaming a snake, and the two of them getting into such trouble that they are driven out of Eden and dumped in what is to them an inhospitable and lonely terra incognita. They procreate and manage to raise two sons. Hardly have these sons achieved adulthood than they have a falling out and one murders the other. Even today family life is not often that bad.

What are we to deduce from such a bleak characterization of the 'first family'? To begin with, the text informs us that the Biblical first family is not so unlike other families, which began with the blessing of God and then proceeded to sin by transgressing the commandments and in one way or another defiling the sacred land. Fratricide, so shocking in the myth of Adam and Eve, had its more shocking historical counterpart in the family of king David, the king especially beloved of Yahweh.

But why should we be so surprised to discover that David's children raped and murdered each other? Sin and violence, from the perspective of the myth-defining Torah, is the way of human kind. It is human to transgress, and that transgression begins, and is found within, the basic building blocks of marriage and family. What better way to make this point than to show it as functioning at the mythic origin of human consciousness itself? The veracity of the point can then be confirmed only too readily by everything we know about history and the conditions of our own times. Or, better, the unconscionable data of our own times acquire mythic and symbolic explanation.

Yet the Adam and Eve story does not come to a grinding halt with Cain's murder of Abel. Adam and Eve start another family. They give birth to Seth, and after him they have other sons and daughters. Seth in turn has a son named Enos, and then other sons and daughters. And so it went on, down to Noah and then on to the time of Abraham and Sarah and later generations. Although wives/mothers are generally not mentioned in the earliest genealogical accounts, the function of marriage as enabling humankind to be fruitful and multiply is genealogically 'established'.

More important, in terms of marriage as a moral enterprise, the birth of Seth restored the primal family to God's good graces. Seth replaced Abel and provided a line of descent that would "invoke the name of Yahweh." (Genesis 4) So too, in the more historical story of the Davidic family, for which the mythic story supplies a deep echo, the birth of Solomon could be characterized as a new start. This much younger son was to be the recipient of Yahweh's grace and approval and the inheritor of David's kingdom; and through his progeny the Davidic covenant would be passed down to later ages.

In early Christian doctrine, as we have seen, the institution of marriage is given meaning as the genesis of the human society forming the Christian community of faith. Here too we need not assume that marriage and family, albeit sanctioned by God, functioned in a truly loving and spiritually wholesome manner. Paul, for example, was shocked to discover that one of his followers in Corinth was living with his father's wife. It confirmed his fears about the dangers of sexual urges and the need for marriage as an antidote to sexual misconduct. Bothered by the proximity of his followers to the sexual life and myths of ancient Greece, he exhorted the males to stay away from prostitutes, since even in that kind of liaison the two "become one flesh", corrupting the whole purpose of human intimacy. But for Paul the primary purpose of the human body was to do what he himself did, and that was to proclaim the glory and grace of God. The body, in Paul's theology, is the temple of the Holy Spirit, redeemed by the Christ as the new Divinely graced Adam. Consequently, the redeemed body belongs to its redeemer and to the purposes for which that act of redemption took place. As he put it bluntly to the Corinthians: "you are not your own property; you have been bought and paid for." (I Corinthians 6, Jerusalem Bible)

As the letters of Paul and his successors indicate, early Christians had no easier a time grappling with the problems of marriage than we do today. Marriage is not a solution to life's problems but a stage on which those problems are acted out. Marriage, in Pauline theology, does not convert us from frail human beings into new, spiritually reformed Adams and Eves.

If anything, it serves to accentuate our fragility as the price of developing consciousness of the meaning inherent in our own lives. On the other hand, marriage does have the function of making two humans responsible to and for each other. It provides an objective basis to satisfy the human yearning for attachment, or as Paul and others sometimes thought of it, to legitimize sexual ardor.

More broadly, marriage has the larger purpose of functioning in some measure to guarantee not only the present but also the future. In contrast to all the forces leading humans to look backwards within their own personal lives or into the history and origins of their culture as explanation for transgression and failure, marriage, more than any other social institution, turns our attention forward and into the future. It functions this way not only in terms of creating children and grandchildren but more basically in terms of creating human and social bonding. Whereas the destruction of Israel by Assyria and the ravaging of Judah by Babylon forced the exilic Jewish community of the 6th century BCE to look backwards for explanations of the disasters which had come upon them, the institution of marriage, which was believed to express God's will in the very act of creating human society, helped them to look forward beyond the troubles of the present into the potential of the future. That, in other words, is the symbolic meaning of leaving father and mother and cleaving to new life and thus to the present and future.

So too the early Christian communities, functioning as little more than tiny nodules within a vast sea of hostile or indifferent paganism, leaned on marriage as the institution that could provide an oasis of personal stability and assurance through the "immaculateness" of the marriage bed. But beyond that personal reinforcement, marriage provided the human building block for the development of the body of Christ's church on earth, and thus as the physical and earthly guarantor of its future.

Marriage as Resource for our Present and Future

Given the powerful associations in our Biblical heritage of marriage as a force in building present and future, we can now look at contemporary marriage as a reflection of how we ourselves view the future. What emerges from this discussion about contemporary and Biblical marriage is how conditional our trust in the future appears to be. If marriage is a guarantor of the future, then domestic abuse, absentee fatherhood, divorce, and abortion, function as massive assaults on the future. Thus, to read in 1996 that the number of abused or neglected children in the US more than doubled in the previous 10 years to nearly 3 million, is a way of letting us know the extent to which our future is being compromised. To continue along these lines: every day in the US three children reportedly die from abuse or neglect. Between 1985 and 1996 the proportion of homeless population consisting of families with children increased from 27 to 36 percent. This kind of data must trouble anyone who is interested in preserving the present and building for the future. Current initiatives to reform welfare that do not take these trends into account are likely only to intensify them. (Data from Boston Globe, 3/22/1996)

Has marriage today lost its capacity to restrain these chaotic trends and provide our society with emotional and existential strength? Or perhaps the question should be rephrased. Do we care sufficiently little about marriage today that we no longer regard it as a necessary means to secure our personal and collective future? To ask the question in this way may require some rethinking about how that future is supposedly secured. Politically we have tended for decades and even centuries to regard the nation-state as the guarantor of public safety and thus of our ability as individuals to get from today to tomorrow and to the next year and the next.

But today in the US as elsewhere the nation-state is pulling back from this role. The economy, in a much more insidious way, is also pulling back from this role. Global forces, far from guaranteeing the future, appear to be raising further questions about its security. The global economy may be a source of growing wealth, but as we all know, that wealth is not well distributed and has little bearing on our communal, much less personal, prospects. The forces of industrialization and material development now seem to threaten global warming and environmental degradation as much as to assure global development and diversification.

With such systemic destabilization all around us, marriage would seem to be a puny means by which to restore some sense of order to our atomized lives. How could one marriage make any difference in a culture permeated with evidence of personal and communal anxiety? Without a broad grasp of how marriage fits in to the larger scheme of things, our individual marriages remain dependent for survival on our own capacities to make sense and meaning out of life. When that capacity eludes us, marriage loses its vitality, because there is no broader flow of meaning to carry our own frail vessels.

Here is where the Bible can still teach us a lesson about how life survives. As an institution ordering two lives, marriage cannot get us very far. Conceived in human terms, marriage contains within it the same potential as any other human enterprise to go astray and cause harm. To understand this, we need still look no further than to the myth of Adam and Eve, a myth that remains very functional in explaining the human predicament. But as a microcosm of the way of ordering human existence, marriage is another matter. It remains the basic building block of human order. Even with all its faults, nothing else has been found to serve us better. And as the exiled Israelites could remind us, it is in times of collective stress and disorder that the significance of marriage as a human bond appears most clearly.

But to understand fully the force of marriage as a social bond, we must make the effort to peer into our own personal and collective futures. What are we collectively endeavoring to create and construct? What, apart from the accumulation of material resources, or responsibility to those with claims on us, energizes each of us to live for the next day and the next? Are we attempting, as were the Israelites of the Torah, to create a covenantal society? Are we trying, as were those Israelites living in the anguish of Babylonian exile, to hold together, or restore, a sense of sacred community that had been brutally ripped apart? Are we even, like the early Christians, looking for ways to build a community of faith in a social environment of considerable indifference or hostility to faith-community? In our time, defined since the late 1940s by the possibility of nuclear destruction, and much more recently by such troubling clouds on the horizon as terrorism and climate change, are there ways in which these earlier models of future-building can help us to proceed?

It may be useful to recall here that when the exilic Israelites confronted their own bleak prospects, they were able to find new meaning in reinterpreting the ancient, archaic creation myths. Although sitting down in Babylon and lamenting over the memory of Zion, they also put together a revised Deuteronomic explanation of history and myth that would enable them to achieve a renewed sense of divine purpose and the fulfillment of that purpose in human history. A future arose which was constructed on the one hand from acknowledgement of failure, and on the other through the possibility of redemption. As inheritors of their reflection, we are reminded of our own capacity for transgression when we review the creation myths and the Deuteronomic histories of the kingdoms of Israel and Judah. Similarly, we are reminded of that ardent encounter with redemption when we read the wonderful passages of hope in the later Isaiah prophesies, or the passages in Jeremiah, Hosea, and other prophets, that deal with the restoration of covenant and the creation of new bonds between Yahweh and the chosen people.

But the possibility of redemption is implicit within the Deuteronomic interpretation of the creation myth itself; and at the center of that possibility is the institution of marriage and family. It is as if the exilic Israelites found in the myth of Adam and Eve a microcosm of their own history: of creation itself, of covenant enacted and betrayed, and of a renewing of life after the betrayal, exile from Eden/Jerusalem and fratricide. Even though humans fail, the divine purpose continues, and the agency for that continuation remains human. In the myth of Cain and Abel we are asked to look at fratricide as being at the core of our history and consciousness, but at the same time to recognize that each of us can engage in the task of post-fratricidal renewal. History itself is changed. After the destruction of Judah there are no longer kings, tribes, or landownership; the temple is in ruins, as is Zion itself. Consciousness must be rebuilt from the ground up.

It is as if Washington and New York were to be bombed out of existence, the US seized by invaders, and a few residual Americans left to survive and rebuild in Chiapas or Guatemala. If this is too unlikely a scenario, we could take note of the Tibetan exilic community of today, forced to abandon its homes and communities to invading armies, which led in turn to the destroying of its holy places as utterly as the Babylonians destroyed Jerusalem and the Temple, so that the surviving Tibetans must try to restore a sense of community and faith while subordinated to force majeure or scattered in foreign lands. This apocalypse has already happened, and is continuing to happen, in our own time.

Other such apocalypses are happening all around us, Rwanda, Bosnia, Kosovo, Chechnya, the Congo, Darfur, Afghanistan, Yemen and Syria being the most currently newsworthy examples. Despite such destruction of life and consciousness, the Deuteronomic perspective maintains that from the Israelite exilic 'remnant' a renewal of the divine plan, based on redemption, can be constructed. At the most basic level of human functioning, Adam and Eve, having lost both of their sons, start a new family. Life, though badly chastened, is to continue, albeit along a humbler and more circumspect path.

It is not surprising that the deutero-Pauline letters and the gospels should draw heavily on this interpretation in attempting to create their own structure of reality. They too sought to forge a new consciousness in which a man would leave his own (quite possibly pagan and Hellenistic) parents and seek to cleave to his spouse and partner, and in so doing create a new community of faith. 'Leaving one's parents', as we know, is easier said than done. One may choose to put a gap of two or two thousand miles and more between us and them; but physical distance has little to do with it.

It is the development of consciousness that is at issue. Do we draw ourselves clear from our inherited consciousness and attempt to direct our efforts to the present and future? Can we take charge of our destinies and seek to deal with the world as it is, and not as we might have wished it to be? Such an obvious question hides a multitude of problems. The past is baggage that we all carry with us. We worry about it at night; and many of us, like the exiled Israelites, have reason to worry about it during the day. The waters of Babylon flow through our lives too.

But Christianity, and for that matter Rabbinic Judaism, insist that life continues to be given meaning through divine purpose. The meaning has once again been given a new interpretation. Early Christian communities found it in the faith-story about the crucifixion and resurrection of Jesus. They built community around that story, anchoring their structure of community in the institution of marriage. The resurrected Christ became the new Adam, the faith community the new Eve. Within that symbolic marital community each married man and woman, by bonding together as one, became a metaphor for the bonding of the larger community. Even if marriage had an ulterior purpose as a recruiting mechanism, its primary purpose lay in its capacity to be the human expression of the divine plan. God was the power that drew man and woman together, and man and woman together formed the power that embodied the faith community.

The question for a fundamentally secular and materialist age is whether it can still find meaning in this conception of marriage as the energy driving the survival and re-creation of human and global community. The whole concept of a divine plan seems archaic today. Are the Holocaust and the Nuclear Bomb also part of the divine plan? Does divinity any longer have any control over what humans do to each other? Is divine plan to be seen in all the torture and repression going in the world today? Is divine plan to be found in all the corporate downsizing and lay-offs, in cigarette smoking, drugs, AIDS, and other contemporary traumas? Is divine plan to be found in domestic abuse, or in the catastrophes that now confront millions of refugees? And what, in any case, can marriage do to forge a better future?

As we enter the new millennium and the dangers lying not so far away, it is an appropriate time to consider anew what are to be our basic strategies which to engage the future. Over the past half-century Americans have placed increasing reliance on armaments as the guarantor of the future. Star Wars has been the preeminent example of a collectivist approach to future-management. As individuals we pay taxes to the State, and the State assembles a vast enterprise to guard our collective future. On the domestic front, millions of Americans trust guns and ammunition as the guarantor that when confronted with violence they may live to see another day.

But as a strategy for securing our collective future Star Wars did not get us very far. It could not protect us from our mythic enemies in the now former Soviet Union; and it certainly was no solution to all the domestic abuse, infidelity, divorce, abortion, abandonment of children, or all the self-inflicted abuse that comes from doing drugs, alcohol, tobacco, or careless sex, or all the community abuse that results from tolerating or engaging in racism and sexism, or participating in new wars on the poor, on illegal immigrants, gays, lesbians and transgendered people, African-American males, and all others categorized by the dominant culture as social misfits. These are problems within our society from which all the armaments, prisons and exclusionary legislation cannot ultimately protect us. Efforts to legislate against violence and social strife do not add up to a coherent human plan for securing a future worth living for.

Amidst all this incoherence and evasion of responsibility, marriage still beckons as an enterprise that points the way ahead. In a biological sense marriage creates future generations. But this can be done without marriage. That is why the Deuteronomists were right to insist on the moral and symbolic contexts of life and on marriage as the fundamental union by which morality is defined and made possible. Where else is morality to be anchored, if not in the union of two individuals?

In this respect, it must be clear that the Deuteronomic approach, and its reiteration in the Pauline and gospel texts, gives primacy to marriage—rather than to family—in defining the human structure of morality. Before there can be family values there must be marital values. Marriage comes first. That is the fundamental teaching of the Adam and Eve myth. The reason is that marriage addresses the level of the individual human being in relationship one to another. Marriage is thus the basic building block for creating moral order. Ethically speaking, family is the result of marriage, not the cause of it. Humans leave their birth families in order to become married. They cleave together and with luck become a unity; and as the gospels would put it, this is the divine plan at work, so humans should beware of messing around with it. To put family values ahead of marital values, as seems to be so often the case today, is to put the cart before the horse. It is to misunderstand the process of union through which raising new life is achieved, and through which an individual attains moral significance as a participant in the process of creating the future.

A great rethinking of marriage by our culture is needed. A culture of marriage in which divorce is rampant is too leaky a vessel by which to convey ourselves into the future. We need a more comprehensive understanding of what is meant by marriage and what it can do for us. We need to understand that marriage is the basis of emotional bonding and creative community, and that if our culture is plagued by domestic abuse and dishonored pledges, we need to look for the cause within the disorder of marriage itself.

By the same token, troubles with marriage reflect troubles in our symbolic understanding of the past and the future. As individuals we have for too long abandoned the future to the collective enterprise and neglected its dependence on our own individual lives. We have forgotten, also, that marriage is a covenant between two people to address the promise of the future. For marriage to work, one must release the past and 'cleave to' the future. It is especially hard to release the past, containing as it often does much personal and collective trauma. But as the Bible rightly insists, personal and community renewal depends on our doing so.

CHAPTER 15

The Covenant and Economic Justice

> Let not mercy and truth forsake you
> Bind them about your neck
> Write them on the tablet of your heart
> Proverbs, chapter 3

One of the hardest problems for inhabitants of advanced capitalist countries to comprehend is the problem of economic injustice. Our economic thinking is based on a hierarchical model of social organization. Reduced to its crudest elements, the idea is that those at the top of the hierarchy should enjoy the greatest benefits of human existence, in such forms as power, wealth, service and leisure, while those at the bottom should enjoy the least. Within that lowest common denominator called the nuclear family, the traditional hierarchy consists of husband at the top, followed by wife and then children in order of birth. In more traditional societies male children take precedence over female, as the latter are expected to marry into other families and therefore are unable to function as fully-fledged members of their natal families. More extended traditional families provide for further hierarchical orderings, such as mother-in-law over daughter-in-law, first wife over concubines, and family members over servants and slaves. In all such arrangements, those at the top get to control the power and wealth, and those at the bottom are subject to the authority of those above them.

Critical social observers, such as Marx and Engels, noted the division of societies into what they called classes. Power devolved over time from one class to another, without changing the essentially hierarchical structure of society. Feudalism was extremely hierarchical, but capitalism replicated feudal hierarchy in its economic structures. In today's capitalist world corporate chairmen sit at the top of the hierarchy, with the largest salaries and benefits, the biggest offices, and the broadest decision-making power. Under them come presidents, and then in various organizations executive vice presidents, senior vice presidents, vice presidents, assistant vice presidents, and on down the corporate line to the lowest levels of management. Those higher up the hierarchy control the economic prospects of those lower down. Few imagine that such layers could be done away with, or that individuals in different layers should receive the same access to power and wealth. Below management comes staff and labor, also arranged in hierarchies. Similar hierarchies are to be found in the military and all such command structures, including the Catholic and Episcopal churches, political party organizations, and school systems.

A discovery that in retrospect should not have surprised anyone is that socialist systems are also pervasively hierarchical. Revolution may change the ordering of classes, so that landlords and entrepreneurs fall from the top to the bottom, while landless peasants and workers take their places. But egalitarian communism remains a distant ideal, beyond the reach or desire of the 'real world', where socialist party hierarchies determine what happens. In socialist societies as in all others, those at the top of the power structure receive the greatest benefits, while those at the bottom receive the least. Any shifting in the hierarchical reward system, as happened in China since Deng Xiaoping unleashed the market economy, was received with tremendous alarm by those who had been its primary beneficiaries. No one likes to be shoved downhill.

Countries, too, are organized hierarchically. During the Cold War era the United States and the Soviet Union stood at the top of two vast pyramids of interlocking multinational systems. For a considerable period of that era the U.S. enjoyed a commanding lead in standard of living, overall wealth and enjoyment of power. On the capitalist, or 'free world' side, the next level was occupied by an assortment of Western powers, and a rising group of East Asian powers. Below them came various countries in Asia, the Middle East and Latin America, which enjoyed various advantages in natural assets. Below them came an increasingly impoverished number of countries in Central America, Africa, Asia, and Oceania. Political scientists might discover that the pecking order of the countries was not naturally ordained. Human exploitation, in such forms as imperialism, colonialism, or internal dictatorship, as well as vulnerability to natural catastrophes, might well be factors in determining a country's relative positioning. There could, in short, be extraneous reasons underlying the organization and maintenance of such hierarchies of wealth and power. But few would conclude from such analysis that the countries at the top should make serious efforts to organize a level playing field with the countries at the bottom. For any number of reasons, such a policy would make no sense and would not be politically feasible. Consequently, countries such as Bangladesh and El Salvador have no choice but to pull themselves up by their bootstraps or go on existing at the bottom of the pile, along with Somalia, Afghanistan, Haiti, Zimbabwe, Southern Sudan, Syria, and other such marginal 'nations'; and their unprivileged citizens will have somehow to get by living on next to nothing, while those living in the U.S., Japan and Germany add to their investments in good times, or tighten their belts in bad.

Most people lucky enough to live in the advanced capitalist countries know that this situation is unfair. But what can be done about it? There are simply far too many destitute and abandoned people in this world to be taken care of by well-intentioned citizens living in capitalist suburbia. In addition, deep down we cannot help wondering if such an arrangement isn't somehow ordained. Perhaps it was karma or predestination that caused us to be born to affluence and security and them to destitution. If that is the case, to be soft hearted about it is pointless. What good can be accomplished by wringing one's hands? In addition, one will from time to time hear about the ingenuity and hard work characterizing those who made it to the top and the sloth and incompetence of those who remain at, or sink to, the bottom. But this is moral window-dressing. Hierarchy constitutes the human condition. To live ethically within one's limits would seem to be the most that can be reasonably expected.

"Not so!" said Jesus. To make the point he is reported as having told a very odd story. There was once a landowner who got up early to hire laborers for his vineyard. Having agreed with them on a penny a day, he sent them into the vineyard. Returning to the market place several times he found other workers looking for employment. "Go to my vineyard", he told them, "and I'll give you a fair wage." When the day was nearly done, he found still more workers standing around. "Why are you standing there idle?", he asked them. "Because no one has hired us", they replied. "Go to my vineyard", he told them, "and whatever is right I will pay you."

When the day was over, the owner called his steward and told him to pay all the workers, beginning with the last. Each of those who had arrived at the eleventh hour received a penny; so too did those who had been hired during the day. When it came to those who had been hired first, they now expected to be paid more, but instead they each received a penny. "Why do you pay them the same as us", they complained, "when we have borne the burden and heat of the day?" "My friend", replied the owner, "I am hardly being unjust. Did we not agree on a penny? Take what is yours and go your way. I will give to the last just as I give to the first. Why be envious because I am generous?."

This story is quite often heard during church services. What is one to make of it? Does Jesus really mean that those who have worked for just one hour are to be rewarded with the same benefits as those who worked for a whole day? "Those lazy bums? Give me a break!" Naturally the full day workers yelled and screamed. Why shouldn't they? Wouldn't you? This landlord is saying that my ten hours work is worth no more than their one hour. I am worth no more than them. I have just donated nine hours of work for nothing. That's not fair!

But Jesus can't be wrong or unfair, so perhaps he is saying something else. Perhaps the story is about morality and repentance. Those who repent late in life will still be recognized and compensated, and—what is even more important—admitted into the vineyard. This story is, after all, about a landowner who goes out looking for people without work or prospects, who are dependent for their 'living' on the goodwill of people with money. Perhaps the story is even saying that the rich should support the poor. Perhaps it is about binding mercy and truth to your heart. If you've got money, you should spread it around, so that those without it can manage to subsist.

But such explanations have unpalatable inferences. The first implies that people can spend decades squandering their lives and still be admitted to the vineyard in their last hours, along with those who have worked for a living all their days. There is something inherently offensive about this notion. If I have lived honorably, working my way through life, while you have lived like a parasite, why should you be treated the same as me? Where were you at the beginning of the day, when the landowner first came out looking for workers? What is there to induce me to work, if my reward is no different from yours? As to the notion that the landowner should distribute his largesse to all those in need of work, this flies in the face of reality. Economic man pays for services rendered. One does not hire people merely for the sake of paying them money. Businesspeople who spread their money around in this way would not remain competitive for long.

The most difficult notion to swallow is the idea of paying people who are barely distinguishable from freeloaders. Nobody should get something for nothing. Nobody should shake their cup in my face. Even though I may be making a six or seven figure income, I am working for mine, and you aren't. If you can't compete, that is your tough luck. Get out of my face and go back to your hole where you belong.

I may be stating this point a little harshly, but I think it is a fair guess that most Sunday congregations do not identify with this story; or if they do, it is only in a Sunday context, i.e. in terms of the story's salvational meaning. Even that context is a little hard to swallow. As a good Christian, I may be happy to see you admitted into the vineyard. But do I really want you getting in on the same reward basis as me, when I have paid my dues all life long, and you haven't? Certainly, I might be willing to organize a soup kitchen to provide for the unemployed, or even to make sandwiches once a month. Grudgingly I might accept a slightly higher tax burden (questionable, these days), or contribute a few dollars to some charity, so that down-and-out people could be kept from starvation.

But how could their work be valued similarly to mine? Work is just about the most discriminatory aspect of human existence. Some of us are corporate or institutional executives, some of us are house cleaners. Some of us have job tenure, most of us are temporary labor, while others are on the bread lines. During the Chinese Cultural Revolution party executives were dispatched in droves to clean pigsties and human latrines. Former capitalists went to prison for years. Intellectuals were hounded into stockades and then sent off to labor in frontier areas. For some ten to fifteen years the human social structure was turned upside down. But it could not stay that way. The party executives, the capitalists, and the intellectuals are back in their offices. The lower order workers are back cleaning the latrines and shoveling the pigsties. As the Chinese economy advances, disparities in wealth, earnings and access to work are increasing year by year. That is the human condition.

Or rather, it is the condition in the kingdom of man. The Jesus story describes conditions in the kingdom of God. "Now the kingdom of heaven is like …" is the way the story begins. We are confronted here with two starkly different realities. We all know what the kingdom of man is like. It is a place where people looking for work at the end of the day do not normally get hired. Or if they are lucky enough to find a job, it is likely to be as temporary or contract labor, at a lower skill level and at a wage thirty or more percent less than what they were earning before. It is a place where economic predators abound, and where ordinary people had better watch out. It is a place where changes in economic trends can move thousands, even millions, of jobs across the globe, leaving large numbers of people stranded and suddenly unemployed. In recent years the kingdom of man has been becoming a place where income disparities are increasing rapidly. We see these disparities ballooning every day on the streets of cities across the world, but we can see them more clearly in the contrast between the lives of those who live in the affluent suburbia of the West and those living in such places as Somalia, Afghanistan and Haiti, or in the streets and shanties of third world megacities. This is how things are happening in the kingdom of man.

But in the kingdom of God, according to one of its prime exponents, things happen otherwise. The 'king' has assets and uses them to go out looking for people who need 'work'. As Isaiah put it, the righteous person shares bread with the hungry, shelters the homeless poor, and clothes people who are naked. (Isaiah 58) The God Yahweh anoints the prophet to bring this good news to the poor. For Yahweh loves justice and hates robbery and all that is wrong. (Isaiah 61) As the prophet Micah put it, Yahweh hates rulers who devour the flesh of the people, loathe justice and pervert all that is right, build Zion with blood, and demand bribes for favorable verdicts. (from Micah 3) The prophets are clear about it: Yahweh loves justice and hates economic injustice, particularly when committed by people supposedly in a covenant relationship with their God.

A terrible fate awaits such people, because this is no laughing matter. The covenant is very specific about economic justice and injustice. According to the Deuteronomic version, people with property must tithe their harvests every three years and deposit the proceeds at their doors, so that dispossessed people, such as aliens, orphans and widows, could come and eat all they want. Every seven years debts are to be remitted. If there are poor people among you, notes the text, do not harden your heart or close your hand. Give generously, and Yahweh will bless you. The text acknowledges that there will never cease to be poor people, so it exhorts the reader always to be openhanded to anyone who is in need or poor. The poor are accorded certain rights, such as to eat their fill of grapes in the neighbor's vineyard (though not to carry them away), and to pick the ears of his corn (though not to cut them with a sickle). Property owners are forbidden to lend on interest to fellow citizens. If they take pledges, they are not to enter the debtor's house to seize them, and they are not to keep them overnight. They must not exploit hired servants, whether fellow citizen or alien, who are poor and needy but must pay them their wages before the end of the day. They should not beat their olive trees, or pick over their harvests, a second time, but leave what remains for the dispossessed. (from Deuteronomy 14, 15, 23, 24).

Of course, this kind of legislation, designed for an archaic, agricultural society, doesn't appear too relevant to the present day. Nowadays most people live off salaries or wages. They don't have harvests or vineyards to tithe. They pay taxes and expect the government to provide for widows, orphans and aliens and their contemporary counterparts living on the margin. Interest is loaned by institutions, not individuals. If a bank loans at high interest to poor people and forecloses on those who cannot pay, how can I as a solitary individual do much about it? It is impossible to police every company that exploits ignorant, disadvantaged people, especially when so much of this exploitation goes on overseas or out of sight and unreported. If corporate executives and raiders skim off pension funds, or savings banks invest their deposits in junk bonds, or downsizing and outsourcing corporate executives lay off tens of thousands of trusting employees, it is hard to see how the private citizen can be held responsible. We live in a society in which individual responsibility has been diminished by the rise of huge corporations and public institutions, with powers far beyond the means of control of any single human being. Economic justice is fine in theory, but in practice it must compete for public support with huge, well-organized interest groups that are not bound by commitment to any archaic covenant. The only thing these contemporary institutions have in common with the past is that they too are expressions of human social organization.

Yet in following this line of reasoning, we should be careful not to oversimplify the past or to assume that its simplicity permitted the sanctioning of individual responsibility, while the complexity of our social organization does not. Behind the details of the Deuteronomic covenant and its precursors lies the principle that Yahweh loves economic fairness and abhors exploitation. As the prophet Micah put it, "He hath showed thee, O man, what is good; and what doth the Lord require of thee, but to do justly, and to love mercy, and to walk humbly with thy God." (Micah 6) The just man, as we have seen in Ezekiel, returns pledges to debtors, does not oppress others, never steals, gives his bread to the hungry and clothes to the naked, never charges usurious rates, takes no interest, and avoids iniquity. (Ezekiel 18) The Book of Proverbs even holds that someone who has pity on the poor "lends to Yahweh." (Proverbs 19)

Indeed, the just person 'loves mercy' (or 'loves tenderly') and 'walks humbly' with Yahweh. Here we get a feel for the moral basis underlying economic fairness. 'Just people' identify with others because they are conscious of their own vulnerability. Perhaps they too had been debtors, or servants, or slaves in Egypt. Or perhaps they had once been guilty of oppression and fraud and had learned through repentance about the mercy of Yahweh. In the words of Hosea, the prophet of repentance, they have learned to turn again to God, to hold fast to love and justice, and to put their trust in God. (Hosea 12) Or as the Psalmist puts it, they have learned to wait patiently for Yahweh, not worrying about those who made their fortunes at the expense of the poor and needy. (Psalm 37) They are free from the bondage of greed and covetousness, see nothing virtuous in amassing wealth through junk bonds, derivatives, and corporate takeovers, and see other people not as objects to be exploited but as candidates for Yahweh's justice and mercy, just like themselves.

As for oppressive people, there are two views about them. Wisdom literature points out that such people have a habit of flourishing at the expense of others. They may even go to their graves unrepentant and apparently unpunished, leaving their swindled millions to other oppressors. Wisdom literature, which takes the long view about such matters, dismisses such perversion of social order with the question, what is that to you? The psalms also take the view that the wicked will eventually perish from their own wrongdoing and disappear. The psalmist would rather encourage honest people to be generous and openhanded, and to do what is right and avoid doing what is wrong. Yahweh loves what is right and will take care of people who lead decent, honest lives.

The prophets, however, are more skeptical about oppression. They fulminate against corrupt, oppressive people precisely because the latter violate the covenant and in so doing violate Yahweh's justice. They predict a terrible fate for those who exploit and oppress others. The fundamental fact here is that economic injustice is a violation of the will of Yahweh, through which the world came into being and attained the order that enables it to function. A natural law operates to maintain the natural world. Yahweh set the boundaries on natural forces, enabling them to function in balance with each other. Human society is the wild card in the created order, rebelling against the divine will, not once—as in Eden—but repeatedly, and therefore necessitating additional action to restore harmony to the divine kingdom. We have seen this additional action expressed in a series of covenants, through which Yahweh mediated with human society to lay out a just social order. With the establishment of the covenants everything is now clear. Humans know what they need to do to keep things in balance.

But covenants and the threat of dire punishment do not suffice to control greed and oppression, and do not suffice even to control rationality. Human authority seems compelled to defy the covenanting God. On the one hand comes idolatry, on the other economic injustice. Both represent defiance of the covenants, precipitating the curses with which the covenants are provided. For the covenant texts are well armed with invective against economic injustice. A curse on him, says Deuteronomy, who displaces his neighbor's boundary mark. A curse on him who perverts the rights of the stranger, fatherless and widow. A curse on him who takes a bribe to slay an innocent person. The most terrible curses, including destitution, plague, cannibalism and enslavement, are called down on those who disobey the covenant.

Taking their cue from these imprecations (or perhaps creating the morality that gave rise to them), the prophets point the finger at those guilty of economic injustice and oppression and curse them vehemently. Woe to those, says Isaiah, who amass property, turn values upside down and consume indiscriminately. Should a nation of indiscriminate consumers, such as the people of the United States, take note of this curse? Woe to those who issue unrighteous decrees, who refuse justice to the unfortunate and cheat the poor of their rights. Woe to those, such as some of our perverters of justice, who make widows and orphans their prey. What will you do on the day of punishment? To whom will you flee for help? Where will you leave your riches? The prophet Habakkuk included a special section of curses on oppressors, defined as people who amassed goods not theirs, exploited the labor of others, built cities with blood, drugged people with alcohol, and beguiled them with idols.

As a result of all this perversion the idea developed not just that wickedness would be punished with invasion and conquest but that a great day of Yahweh would arise, when purveyors of wickedness and oppression would meet their doom. The classic statement, in Zephaniah, predicted the coming of a "dies irae," a day of wrath, ruin and devastation, when Yahweh would bring such distress on men that their blood would be poured out as dust and their flesh as dung. On that day, said the Messenger (Malachi), Yahweh would personally stand as witness against the sorcerer, adulterer and perjurer, against those who oppress the wage earner, the widow and the orphan, and those who rob aliens of their rights. "How", respond these insolent criminals, "are we cheating you? Can a man cheat God?" "In the matter of tithes and offerings," comes the terse reply. "You are cursed with a curse, for you have robbed me, even this whole nation." Let us take note: according to this perspective, to cheat the wage earner, the widow, the orphan, the alien, is to cheat Yahweh; and that kind of behavior has consequences. For the day is coming, continues the Messenger, that shall burn as an oven. All the arrogant and wicked people will be reduced to stubble and burned up, leaving neither root nor branch. The righteous will trample on the wicked, who will be like ashes under their feet.

Is this kind of prospect believable, or is it more prophetic mumbo-jumbo? Does the world really work that way? Jeremiah, the greatest curser of them all, agonized over the prosperity of the wicked. "Why do wicked people live so prosperously," he demanded of Yahweh? "How long will the land mourn and the grass wither? Animals and birds are dying because of their wickedness! Come Yahweh", he begged, "drag them off like sheep to the slaughterhouse." (Jeremiah 12) We see here a distinction between the prophetic view that violation of economic justice would bring its own retribution, and rage against its moral repulsiveness. The prophets are not determinists. They are people who feel passionately about justice and are enraged by oppression. There is nothing determinist, or antiquarian, about this.

In medieval times these views did not go unnoticed. The justly famous poem on the Dies Irae (Day of Wrath), written in Latin and traditionally attributed to Thomas of Celano, became the central subject matter of requiem masses for the dead performed in Catholic churches. It was through observance of these requiem masses, and through meditation on this intensely vivid and shocking poem, that living Christians gained an opportunity to ponder their own personal conduct and destiny. Even today anyone who hears requiem masses built around that poem, such as those written by Mozart and Verdi, can still engage in that kind of introspection, or at least realize that this was the motivation driving the creation of these extraordinary compositions.

But unfortunately for us, we live in a secular world, in which the modern, rationalist view of economic justice is considerably more determinist than that of the prophets or the medieval poets. This is partly a reflection of the breakdown of the covenantal commitment to the poor and its replacement by doctrines promoting individual and national self-interest. The condition of the downsized and destitute in our time may be seen—in fact it is quite often shown on television—but it is for the most part not felt in any personal way by those in charge of worldly affairs. Nor should this be surprising. Few of those who manage corporations or who establish and administer social and economic policy are, or have ever been, truly poor. Even commentators, such as myself, who have spent time visiting third world ghettos, have really no idea what it is like to live in them day in and out, year after year. Cushioned by affluence, we are out of touch with the feel and the smell of poverty and with the fragility of life and hope that is lived on the margin. We may have experienced hell on a personal level, but we have not experienced it as a pervasive and inescapable social phenomenon.

Consequently, we do not, unlike the prophets, reject the idea that the destitution of others is tolerable, or that policies, such as those of the International Monetary Fund, which have had the effect of imposing harsh economic discipline on people already living on the margin, are morally questionable. The 1980s and 1990s have seen the application of such policies in both the international and local contexts. Debt management of developing country debt has been administered considerably more harshly by international lending institutions than debt management of the United States. But even within the United States, social budgets at all levels of government have been substantially cut in the interests of tax reduction and stricter debt management. People who are not vigilant or lucky enough to secure stable salaries, health insurance and pension funds, are the ones who are having to pay for these cut backs.

Looking into the near future, it does not appear that these conditions will change any time soon. The pressure of national and international debt on poor and marginal people will continue to grow, even though their responsibility for the debt, and their ability to manage it, is miniscule when compared with that of the people who have held the power and set the policies. The rising flood of corporate downsizing in the 1990s is now bringing these dog-eat-dog conditions closer to the heartlands of the market economy. As the 2008 economic melt-down made only too clear, the global economy emerging in our time has little in common with the covenants.

Economic Justice and Kingdom Consciousness

As solitary individuals we cannot alter the circumstances of our birth and upbringing, but we can alter our adult consciousness. A person who has striven for years to become a successful taker can become a successful giver. A person who has for years disparaged the meek and lowly can learn to walk humbly with them. A person who has been scared to death by poverty, or who has regarded it with contempt and disapproval, can learn to see it in a different light.

The key to all these transformations, as has so often been pointed out, lies in moving beyond an ego-centered view of the world. So long as we conclude that we alone can secure our wellbeing and that nothing else matters, we are unlikely to be able to revise our views about economic justice. Economic justice will mean justice for us and for those like us. The 'alien', the stranger, the dispossessed, will be likely to fall outside this rubric. So too will downsized, impoverished and destitute people, as the story of Job so vividly illustrates. According to ego perspective, what those people need is not to receive economic justice but to confess their incompetence and get out of the way. But with a shift in consciousness, this fear for ourselves, and disdain towards others, can still be replaced by an attitude of awe for the magnificence of Yahweh's world that transcends our personal materialism.

An approach to this shift in consciousness is described in Psalm 49, which is itself a wisdom text. "Why should I be afraid in evil times", says the psalmist, "when malice dogs my steps and hems me in, of men who trust in their wealth and boast of their riches? Man could never redeem himself; it costs so much … it is beyond him." This is a text appropriate to our times, when people who thought themselves economically secure are being laid off in droves and are facing the prospect of impoverishment and even penury. In the kingdom of man there is no economic justice for these people, any more than there is for the inhabitants of Haiti or Somalia or Zimbabwe or Syria. The psalmist, however, grasps the idea that only Yahweh can redeem human life. There is never enough material wealth, because in the last analysis, material wealth is evanescent. It has never bought spiritual redemption and it never will. In addition, one cannot take it with one, and we all die sooner or later. That is why it is, claims the psalm, that "man, when he prospers, forfeits intelligence; he is one with the cattle doomed to slaughter." Death will herd him and his kind to pasture, and the upright will have the better of them.

Agreement with this last sentiment depends on one's perspective, but the point that the psalm makes is clear enough. If it is not, we can look to another psalm, such as number 15, which clearly delineates the upright person. Such people do what is right towards others. They stand by their pledges, they do not ask interest on loans, and they cannot be bribed to victimize the innocent. What if such morality had prevailed in the United States during the 1980s? What if it were to prevail now? The nation might still be deep in debt, but there would be a good deal less scar tissue on its unemployed. The psalmist, too, affirms that Yahweh loves virtue and hates wickedness. Therefore "for the plundered poor, for the needy who groan, now I will act", says Yahweh. (psalm 12) And for the virtuous, as we hear so repeatedly in psalm 23, "the Lord (Yahweh) is my shepherd, therefore I shall not want." Yahweh, assures the psalm, revives my soul and even prepares a table before me under the eyes of my enemies. "Ah", exclaims the psalmist in lyrical rapture, "ah—how goodness and kindness pursue me every day of my life; my home, the house of Yahweh, as long as I live."

Turning back now to the kingdom of God as defined in the Jesus mission, we can see that this idea of home as the house of Yahweh is central to the approach of Jesus to economic justice. Indeed, psalm 23 might be taken as the text for the kingdom of God in its economic guise. We may recall that Jesus always asked his followers to abandon their material goods and place their trust in Yahweh. Even when going out as missioners he asked them to take nothing with them except a staff: no bread, no backpack, no money, no spare clothes. Stripped down and unencumbered by materialism, they are to become a channel for Yahweh's power. Hosts take them in, as happened to Jesus repeatedly, and when crowds gather around, supplies materialize. "Don't worry about your life", he said to them, "about what you are to eat or wear. It is unbelievers who worry about these things. Set your heart on the kingdom, and these other things will be given you." (Matthew 6)

To those who worried about getting their fair share, Jesus advised them to guard against possessiveness. People's lives were not made secure by what they owned. A story: there was once a rich man who had a big harvest. He thought to himself, "what am I to do? My barns are too small. I need bigger ones. I will build bigger ones and store my goods. Then I can rest secure and eat, drink and be merry." Then God said to him, "you fool! This very night will your soul be demanded of you. What good will all your wealth be then?" (Luke 12)

Another story: there was a rich man who wined and dined every day, and a poor man, named Lazarus, who lay at his door eating garbage. Dogs came and licked his sores. When Lazarus died, he was taken up by Abraham, while the rich man died and went to hell. "Father Abraham", implores the latter, "I'm burning and in agony here. Please send Lazarus to moisten my tongue." "I'm sorry", replies the patriarch, "it's just not possible. You've had your good times. In any case, there's a gulf between you and us, and no way of crossing it." "Then send him to warn my brothers!", pleads the unhappy miser. "Why?", asks Abraham, ever the skeptic. "Let them listen to Moses and the prophets." "Oh no", cries the miser, who knows his greedy brothers only too well. What do they care about Moses and the prophets? "But," says he, "they will repent if they hear from a dead man!" "What bull", one can imagine the patriarch thinking. Aloud he tells the doomed plutocrat, "if they won't listen to Moses and the prophets, why should they listen to an apparition?" (Luke 16)

It is a fair question, and a question for our times. This story is not a Sunday school story but a deadly serious parable about economic justice. It is a story about rich people and poor people, rich countries and poor countries, glorious wealth and wretched poverty, and the consequences of abandoning economic fairness. On the one hand we have a picture, all too common in our day, of a wealthy corporate executive who has climbed to the top of the pile and is enjoying the fruits of his wealth. One can safely say, in the context of this story, 'his' wealth, since 'he' clearly regards it as his own and is not about to share any of it with destitute beggars. One could even imagine him saying, after downsizing thousands, "if you're doing what you think is right … then you're fine. So, I'm fine." (From an article by Charles Derber, Boston Globe, 4/2/1996)

This is a man, in other words, who is operating way outside of the covenant. He has forgotten—assuming he ever knew it—all about the three-year tithe, the sabbatical year, the rights of the poor, everything designed to maintain a relationship of justice and mercy between the rich and the poor. He has forgotten what Mr. Derber called the sense of common good. He has forgotten what the Torah calls his duty to participate in Yahweh's covenant and contribute to the great work of maintaining justice and order in our world.

We do not have to look far to remind ourselves of such miserable people, who degraded themselves and their countries, particularly during the 1980s and early 90s, and who are doing so again in the new millennium. Their names were and are constantly in the newspapers as their thieving and swindling came to light and some of them were dragged before the courts of justice. The worst of these people preyed on the fears of old age pensioners, raided their trust funds and savings accounts, raided corporate pension funds and sent tens of thousands of workers into unemployment, or bribed their way into insider trading deals and kickbacks. They lived high off the hog and enjoyed the adulation of the times, while their victims skidded towards disaster.

Why, one wonders, should such parasites not be sent to burn in hell, or at least to spend decades behind bars? Look what happens to the people they trash! It is not a pretty picture that Jesus describes. We have a destitute person groveling at the rich man's gate, pleading for a few scraps from the rich man's table, while dogs come to lick his sores. One can see hundreds and thousands of such people in third world megacities. Some of them have the amputated limbs of lepers and can barely drag themselves around, but if they are to live from one day to the next, they must still get to somewhere where they can beg. Such people are also showing up in increasing numbers on the streets of first world cities or clamoring at the borders or in the refugee camps of first world countries, because their own countries are too poor or too violent to sustain their lives. Today's world is full of millions of refugees, fleeing from economic and/or political oppression and living wherever they can on the margin, while people in first world countries tighten their immigration laws and barricade their frontiers.

Meanwhile, time runs out on rich and poor alike. In death Yahweh's mercy elevates the beggar and Yahweh's justice bears down on the corporate magnate. The soul of the latter is sent where it belongs, to hell. We now are treated to a supremely ironic dialogue. The rich man still disregards the poor man, whom he refuses to address and continues to regard as an errand boy; but he has just enough morality left in his soul to remember his worthless brothers. He expresses no remorse for his own life, but he does fear for theirs, because he now knows in what direction they are headed. These people obviously regard the covenant with derision, or at the very least imagine that it is irrelevant to the real world. Nobody can persuade them to dip into the Torah or waste their time reading the prophets. The very thought is ludicrous. These people are hell bent on amassing profits and getting rich. How is Torah going to help them? One might as well ask, how is the Torah going to help arbitragers, bond bundlers, and specialists in greenmail. No, these people are not about to consult the Torah or ask themselves if economic ethics counts for a damn. But perhaps they might just listen to an apparition. Perhaps after a particularly drunken evening they have come home and had a nightmare and wondered for a moment what life is all about. Perhaps, like King Saul, they already have seen an apparition or two.

But the covenantal answer to this is "no deal." No helpful apparitions for the rich. No word of warning from the other side. That is not how the kingdom of Yahweh works. The kingdom is rooted in the work of creation and historical consciousness. It is experienced, and struggled for, here on earth, not in some limbo for departed souls. It is formulated in and through the lives of living human beings. The values of kingdom ethics are spelled out fair and square in the Torah and repeated ad nauseam in the prophets and the psalms and the books of wisdom. And for Christians they are laid out in the gospels. One must be morally blind not to be able to figure them out. Why should wealthy people be treated to some heaven-sent angel, who should come in and save them without any struggle on their part? No! Let them look around for themselves and figure out how Yahweh's world really works. If they need any guidance, they know where they can get it.

As I said, this is not a Sunday school story. It is one aimed at the politicians and corporate executives responsible for how the world is managed. Corporations are supposed to be judged by profitability and therefore unable to be deflected by commiseration for the poor. Their business is to maximize wealth. Functions that detract from that goal merely decrease their competitive status. How can their managers be expected to think about economic justice? In any case, economic 'ethics', from their perspective, is for sanctimonious liberals, the clergy, and old women. As we have seen, it hardly belongs in the hard-hearted male, androcentric world governed by phallic power. How can one scramble for money and power and at the same time pause to assist those over whom one scrambles? In the androcentric world the race is to the swift, not the ethical.

I realize that there are ethical people who are struggling to square their consciences with the demands of the rational world. U.S. policy has struggled for several years with the problems of the Haitian refugees, or with the conflict in the Northwest between environmental groups and the logging industry, or more recently with oppressed people in the Middle

East and Central Asia. The Chinese government is struggling to trade off political reform, which is feared as destabilizing, against economic growth, which threatens to increase income disparity and strengthen the eastern provinces at the expense of those further west. The UN has been struggling to salvage human rights in such places as Guatemala and Bosnia while brokering settlements that reflect the power realities. In such situations it is considered reasonable to look for the center, where hopefully one can work out a compromise. In the absence of covenants the center, it may be argued, is the only reasonable alternative rallying point.

But the covenants, and the kingdom of Yahweh that it represents, are not concerned with brokering compromise but with establishing a just order. There can be no compromise about justice, unless one takes the position that the lives of the poor are inherently less valuable than those of the rich. In a world governed by profitability, one could argue that that is indeed the case. The rich create the wealth that is necessary for all to survive. This is the underlying ethos of the trickle-down theory, which continues to this day to be the basic theory driving economic behavior in the kingdom of man. No wonder increased taxation is regarded with such suspicion, for it is not just a liberal panacea to mitigate poverty but a threat to the basic system on which competitive economics depends. Thus, if competitive economics is your game, you are bound to oppose anything which gets in its way.

But you do so at a price. Biblical ethics is quite adamant about this. The world was not created as a resource base to satisfy the needs of power-hungry, competitive executives. It can function only through a process of balance, in which all created forces recognize their limits. Biblical order means recognition of limits. The Sinai covenant established limits binding on human society, and the prophets sought to uphold and reestablish those limits. This is the basic meaning behind the principle of covenantal justice. Every living organism has its place in Yahweh's world, and Yahweh takes delight in each one. The covenant is not an instrument to enable humans to exploit each other and the natural world as well, but a way of reining in human excess and reminding humans—even those as special as the chosen people—that they did not create the world in which they live. That achievement belongs exclusively to Yahweh. Wisdom and long life begin with the acknowledgement of Yahweh's transcendent power.

The prophets also insist that Yahweh's kingdom is merciful as well as just. That means not that there is some lowly and contemptible place in it for the poor who lack economic power, but that the kingdom does not materialize unless it is built around the poor. In Yahweh's kingdom the poor receive preferential attention. Jesus knew this, so did the gospel writer Luke. That is why he had Jesus begin his mission in Nazareth with the text from Isaiah announcing his prophetic mission "to bring good news to the poor." The mission of Jesus focuses on the needs of underprivileged people such as lepers, widows, servants, children, and people crippled in body or soul. "Blessed are the poor", he tells his followers, "for theirs is the kingdom of heaven." The rich are informed in every conceivable way that wealth will only bar them from entry to the kingdom. Wealth cannot buy access to Jesus' kingdom; nor can it to the psalmist's.

The kingdom of God, however, recognizes that wealth wreaks its damage also on the wealthy person. Yahweh's mercy is available to all, even to rich people, and is precipitated through the process of repentance. The evangelist Luke illustrates this process in the story of Zaccheus. Zaccheus was a wealthy person who made his money collecting taxes. In Roman Judea this was a lucrative but ignoble profession. Zaccheus had money alright, but he knew it was not well earned. When Jesus came into Jericho, Zaccheus came looking for him. He was too short to see over the crowds, so he climbed up a tree and peered down. Jesus looked up and saw a potential host. "Come down Zaccheus," he calls to the tree-bound tax collector, "I must stay at your house today." Zaccheus rushes home and welcomes him joyfully, while all the people who think they know better criticize Jesus for visiting with a fat-bellied collaborator of Rome (the occupying and taxing power). But surprise, surprise! Zaccheus has not forgotten the covenant, and this visit has turned him around. "I'm going to give half my property to the poor," he exclaims, "and if I stole from anyone, I will repay them fourfold." "Today", comments Jesus, "salvation has come to this house." The evangelist concludes the account with a version of one of the more memorable sayings attributed to Jesus, that the Son of Man has come to seek out and save what was lost.

Thus, we see that in the kingdom of God economic justice works both ways: to save the rich from their own spiritual hell as well as the poor from the physical hell of starvation and misery. Kingdom justice is not merely redistributive but salvational. This is what distinguishes it so profoundly from the redistributive secular ideologies that sprang up over the last 150 years. In post 1949 China, for example, Maoist justice shot or stripped-down millions of landlords and rich peasants, redistributed their property to the poor peasants, then soon converted it all into public ownership. Bureaucratic mismanagement of agriculture in the late 1950s resulted in one of the most crippling famines in human history, during which up to 40 million or more people starved to death. It took Chinese agriculture years to recover from this horrible and man-made redistributive catastrophe. Since Mao's death in 1976 agriculture in China has been substantially privatized, and a new cycle of competitive redistribution is under way. This latest development may be good for business and the economy, but it has little or nothing to do with salvation.

Kingdom economics, however, is both transformative and salvational. It is a means for bringing the kingdom of God into the lives of human beings whilst replenishing their material existence. Hundreds of thousands of people, who have taken seriously the mission to bring good news to the poor, have felt its transformation in their own lives. Kingdom economics invites people of means to lighten up, and to bring their energies and resources to the aid of people without means, or to people who have lost everything through some calamity, such as children and families living off third world garbage dumps. Much to their credit, many people of means have taken on this challenge.

As to how this is done, there are famous passages in both Isaiah and Matthew 25 that tell one all one needs to know. To cite the latter: "I was hungry and you gave me food, thirsty and you gave me drink, a stranger and you made me welcome (a thought that goes back to the story of Abraham), naked and you clothed me, sick and you visited me, in prison and you came to see me." Christians should understand that every phrase in that famous passage from Matthew's gospel is drawn from the Hebrew Scriptures. "And when did we do this?" ask the bemused but virtuous ones. And the king replies, "just as you did it to the least of my brothers and sisters, so you did it to me."

A different and less pleasant message is addressed to the takers of this world. As I have tried to indicate in this chapter, kingdom justice applies to the greedy as well as to the merciful. But it flourishes through mercy, not revenge.

CHAPTER 16

The Relevance of Covenant to the Natural World

The land belongs to me
And to me you are only strangers and guests
Leviticus, chapter 25

To Yahweh your God belong indeed heaven
and the heaven of heavens, the earth and all it contains
Deuteronomy, chapter 10
From Jerusalem Bible

The Torah texts that introduce this chapter make the blunt and non-negotiable statement that the earth and all it contains, as well as the universe beyond it, belong to the Power that formed the entire environment, through means of which we live. It is not there simply to benefit humans. The idea that humans are merely strangers and guests is a consistent view throughout the Hebrew scriptures.

This thinking runs contrary to actual human experience of governance, as found in every leading civilization. In virtually all recorded history androcentric power has held sway over the destiny of the world. The only difference between our age and previous times lies in the degree of power accessible to the androcentric world. In our time science and technology, by unlocking powers inherent in the natural world, have greatly increased the resources of material power, while centralizing them in the hands of androcentric power elites. The old Cold War model in which power lay in the hands of androcentric elites in Washington and Moscow—and ultimately in the hands of two men with their fingers on the 'button'—has now given way to a more complex model of elites and sub-elites competing for access to the rapidly increasing powers being uncovered and exploited in the material world. The competition can be very cruel, as we have seen in Croatia, Bosnia, Cambodia, Iraq, Syria, and any number of other places. Cruelty goes with the pursuit of material power and is the epitome of that power in action, whether it is occurring within the American home or corporation, or on Balkan, Iraqi, or other battlefields.

An additional aspect of material power is its indifference to the wellbeing of the material order itself. One reason for this is that in a hierarchical power system all power is subordinate to power at the top of the hierarchy and must yield to it. There is no inherent difference between subordination of human power to power at the top and subordination of natural power emanating from the non-human natural world. All power must maintain the hierarchy, otherwise the hierarchy may crumble, and then the power system that the hierarchy had maintained is left at the mercy of competing power systems (as in Iraq, Afghanistan and Syria today). As power is constantly increasing with the increases in human population and in technical-scientific access to natural power, hierarchies must constantly increase their control and management of power in order to stay competitive. That means they must strive to increase control over any and all power, natural as well as human.

It has been customary in liberal circles to denounce power systems for their exploitation of natural environments and their feverish efforts to extract every particle of power from the natural and human worlds. One may be sympathetic with this critique of power, but I believe it misses the point. Secular hierarchies operating outside of any covenant have no other power than that which is accessible to them from the material world. We should expect secular hierarchies to maximize the extraction of power from the natural universe (including its human elements); and from a secular perspective we should criticize such hierarchies whenever they fail to do so. Maximization of power, as history has demonstrated time and again, is the only way to maintain competitive edge. It is counterproductive to assume that imperialism and other such secular power systems prevailed because of their superior ethics or religions. This is not what secular power is

John Watt

about. Whether it is the hegemonism of ancient China or the imperialism of the modern Western world, secular power seeks to maximize itself by expanding and consolidating control over power. The Cold War proved to be yet another episode in the human quest to consolidate secular power. It is just that science and technology have greatly broadened that quest by making the universe of non-human material power much more accessible to secular human power systems.

Thus, human history is beginning to expand its attention to include the history of consolidation not only of human power but also of natural power. As the exploitation of atomic power revealed, natural power has vastly greater potential than human power, particularly when brought under control of human hierarchical power systems. We humans are therefore beginning very slowly and reluctantly to focus our attention on the ethics of maximizing control over natural power, particularly in its form as weapons of mass destruction. People are increasingly drawing attention to the abuse of the natural world, as if justice and mercy should somehow prevail in our management of the latter, just as they have in theory in our management of the human order. But we would have to be selective about our use of history to conclude that justice and mercy have prevailed in the management of human affairs. I may be a cynic for arguing that justice and mercy are used as window dressing by secular power, which is interested preponderantly in maximization of material power. Nevertheless, development of a covenantal perspective shows us that within the 'Judeo-Christian' traditions justice and mercy apply only within the context of covenant and never outside it. (The ancient Chinese struggled over the development of a comparable but different system of ethics, which they called the Mandate of Heaven, to contain and manage secular power). Thus, we should expect secular power to maximize control over the natural universe, just as it has over the human order.

Part of the problem in understanding the struggle for control over power lies in the widespread Western captivation with the Enlightenment theory of progress—according to a simplified version of which the human condition is gradually getting better and more enlightened—and with the Western and especially American notion that people living in the Western countries (and a few select Asian countries) are much freer in relation to power systems than those living elsewhere. What this freedom usually means is that they enjoy much more access to economic and material power, as do their governments. They are also free to speak their minds, because what they say has very limited impact on the control and management of power by governments and corporations.

Freedom, however, is not the same thing as the exercise of justice and mercy. Nothing, for example, said or done by the anti-nuclear power movements as an expression of free speech had any serious impact over the obsessive development by the US and Soviet governments of gigantic nuclear stockpiles and strategic systems. History will almost certainly show that what caused both governments to switch direction away from additional stockpiling was 1) cost factors, making further stockpiling of enhanced weaponry counterproductive in terms of power accumulation, and 2) the development of new risks, such as the breakdown of the Soviet Union itself, requiring the development of new strategies to control and manage power. In countries such as Egypt, Iran, Pakistan, or North Korea, where the institutionalization of power is much less stable, we should not be surprised to find a much greater effort exerted to maximize power and control public opinion.

But whether we are looking at competition between East and West or North and South, we cannot fail to notice the continuing scramble by governments and corporations to increase control over power systems, whether economic, military, nuclear, molecular, chemical, or electronic. The rapid consolidation in the early and mid 1990s of corporations catering to the U.S. Defense industry is a recent example of this ineluctable pressure to control access to material power. Since the material power of the natural world is now being 'accessed' with greater urgency and speed than ever before, governments and corporations that want to compete have no option but to move in this direction.

In the face of such rising pressures and uncertainties it may seem unrealistic and even unwise to suggest that boundaries be placed on the exploitation of the material order. That order, as we now know from astrophysicists, electrical engineers and microbiologists, is virtually limitless, as well as containing within itself enormous power systems. All we need is the human ingenuity to 'access' the power residing out there in space, or down in the oceans, or deep in other materialistic structures. Space missions are already moving us slowly in the direction of extra-terrestrial exploitation. So far as space exploration is concerned, we are still in the 'Stone Age', Yet we are moving slowly along. If there are no limits to space, why should we talk of imposing boundaries? Similarly, we are still in the Stone Age in terms of our explorations of the worlds of molecular biology, genetics, gene transplantation, cybernetics, etc. There may be powers lurking in these worlds that would make the discovery of steam power or the internal combustion engine seem of trivial consequence. Why impose boundaries when we don't know yet what we are bounding? In any case it is the nature of humankind, as the myth of Adam and Eve tellingly depicts, to challenge boundaries and defy authority. Whenever the gods try to beat us back, we human beings recoil and challenge them more defiantly.

On the other hand, there is a growing worry, with which the contemporary world must wrestle, that while the universe may be infinite, planet earth has its limits. News reports about the greenhouse effect, the decline of ozone, the melting of polar ice, the gradual warming and freezing of the planet, the increasing loss of species, and other potential disasters, have some people worrying that the planetary environment is being degraded and may soon no longer be able to renew itself. Stories about the shocking levels of environmental pollution uncovered in parts of East Europe and the former Soviet Union, coupled with such environmental and human catastrophes as Chernobyl, Love Canal, the Alaska oil spill, the drying up of the Aral Sea, or Bhopal, remind us of the environmental dangers posed by worldwide industrialization.

In short, scarcely have we learnt to accommodate our thinking to one such problem when another one erupts. Certainly, we have only to look at the huge increase in human global population over the last hundred years to perceive the growing human pressure on the earth's resources. In large parts of the developing world population numbers continue to increase as relentlessly as the growth of the U.S. national debt. Between 1980 and 2007 the world population grew by 50 per cent from 4.4 to around 6.6 billion people. According to the World Population Clock it is now already up to 7.6 billion in 2018 and increasing at around 200,000 people every day. This expansion in billions of humans may not be visible other than as an abstract statistic, nevertheless it is happening. It is changing the structure of the international economy, but more importantly, in terms of the argument here, it is changing the relationship of humankind to the rest of the earth's life systems. Long ago it used to be thought, as in the beginning of Ecclesiastes, that "a generation goes, a generation comes, yet the earth stands firm forever." Not so long ago—and within many people's lifetimes—that assumption would have been taken for granted. But today even the most optimistic or foolish among us must doubt that the earth can truly remain 'firm for ever'. As Ecclesiastes also states, "the more knowledge, the more sorrow." This sounds more like a contemporary mindset.

The message of the covenants, and of the kingdom of God, is that boundaries are necessary if justice is to be established. Justice involves boundaries—between what is mine and yours, ours and theirs, or the scope of one life form versus another. There must be boundaries between humans and the divine order, boundaries between one person and another or one society and another, and boundaries between the human and natural environments. Maintenance of boundaries is necessary if suprahuman power is to support human existence. It is of course possible for humans to exist without the divine, but history is not very encouraging about the terms of human existence in which the divine (in one or another manifestation) is missing. As the Job story reminds us, and as Ecclesiastes insists, human systems can flourish in the absence of the divine. Cruelty and oppression can go unpunished, and exploiters go to their graves unrepentant. Similarly, it is possible for human powers to pay lip service to Yahweh, or Deus, or Dieu, or God, or Gott, or Allah, or Shang-di or Tian, etc., while exploiting and punishing subordinates mercilessly. Yet most people seem to feel that such behaviors are unsatisfactory and do not deserve our approval. We would prefer the divine to approve what we are doing, even if that means setting limits on our desires—provided, of course, that everybody else agrees, or is required, to do the same. But then, if we want the approval of Yahweh/God/Allah, we need to take account of the covenants.

Creation, the Sinai Covenant, and the Natural Order

The Bible contains not two but several versions of how creation came into being. Those who have attended Sunday School or sat in church pews, and many who have done neither, are more or less familiar with the creation stories in Genesis chapters 1,2 and 3. As we have seen, in the Priestly account of the creation, with which the Bible begins, God proceeded from the division of light and darkness to the parting of the waters, the formation of dry land and sea, vegetation, astral bodies, sea monsters, fish and birds, animals and reptiles, and man and woman to have dominion over all other creatures. Seeds and fruits were to be the food of humans and leaves the food of the animals. All that took six days, then God, the great architect of heaven and earth, rested on the seventh day, blessed it and made it holy, thus instituting the sabbath.

People such as myself, who were brought up on the view that the Bible was basically about the origin and development of the natural and human world, took it as given that the account in Genesis chapter 1 established the theological basis for the creation of the world. In Genesis chapter 2 we got a rather more detailed look at the creation of the human order. In other words, creation started as described in chapter 1 and proceeded on as described in chapter 2. This narrative approach to the story of creation seemed to be indicated by the arrangement of the Genesis accounts. One proceeded from the general to the particular, in due course arriving at the story of Adam and Eve. In addition, we learned that everything up to the arrival of the humans had moved along in a nice, orderly manner. Only with the creation of man and woman did things begin to go awry.

We are, of course, operating here with two differing traditions about creation, which Bible redactors organized into one relatively seamless account. The Priestly writers set the stage with their vision of an orderly birthing of the universe presided over by a Supreme Being in complete control of the process. Everything in this account happens as planned. Finally, humans are created in the image of God and given dominion over all moving creatures. That is the picture of how things began that they would wish us to assimilate. Once that stage was set, the redactors turned to the powerfully ironic creation story recounted by J. Readers and auditors, who were not told otherwise, could assume from this that the J version exists within the context of the P version, and that the same stately God who fashioned the world out of apparently nothing was the Yahweh God who made man out of dust and breathed life into his nostrils. This Yahweh God, moreover, plants a garden with rivers and trees and sets man in it as cultivator. Man may eat of all the trees in the garden except of the tree of the knowledge of good and evil. There is nothing here about stars, waters and firmaments, but it is still a creation story, and one with a moral edge.

So far so good, but not good enough. So, Yahweh God fashions all the wild beasts and birds, as if they had not already been fashioned in Genesis chapter 1, and brings them to man to name them. Still there was something lacking. As Harold Bloom points out, we are in the hands of a great satirist and comedian. Man is given a soporific, his rib and lung (source of breath) excised, enclosed in flesh (life form) and fashioned into a woman. This improvised gynecology is far from the stately creationism of chapter 1, nevertheless it seems to work. Yahweh God brings the newly fashioned woman to man, and they become husband and wife, naked and without shame! From body creation we go to instant marriage and shame-free sex, without any inconvenient babyhood or adolescence. This looks too good to be true. Indeed, both parties, as most people know, have been set up for a fall.

The downfall of Adam and Eve, as Bloom points out, is one of the great ironic masterpieces of human mythmaking. Although Adam as man is Biblical Creation's First Person (of which male Christian theologians from Paul on have made so much), under pressure he turns out to be a craven sneak. Adam is not the ideal character from which to build ideologies of androcentrism. As retribution for eating from the tree of knowledge of good and evil, he is to labor to get his food from the soil and from wild herbs (but not from the flesh of servile chickens, cows and pigs). The woman who got him into trouble must give birth in pain and suffer her husband, with his feet of clay, to put her in the family way.

Here is the real human punishment of the 'fall', as seen from a gynocentric perspective. How ironic that androcentrism is made mythically possible by the masochism inflicted on childbearing women. The serpent fares even worse, condemned to eat dirt and to live in enmity with the woman's offspring. So much for the old gynocentric cosmic powers. Yahweh then makes clothes out of animal skins and expels the humans from the garden, before they can eat from the tree of life and live forever. Cherubim, reminiscent of the exclusive temple cult, are posted at the doorway to keep the humans from the forbidden tree.

Before long expulsion has led to fratricide, and to promiscuous sex with the 'sons of heaven' and the 'race of giants'. (The Deuteronomic editor may well have been alluding here to contemporary 'goings-on'). Yahweh God suddenly is sickened by the earthlings and decides to get rid of them, except for a few lucky ones who are bundled into an ark along with the upright Noah and his family. The rest are all drowned like unwanted cats and dogs, or like the ancient kingdom of Israel overwhelmed by the onrush of Assyria. When the floods recede, Noah builds an altar to Yahweh and sacrifices some birds. Yahweh repents and promises never again to judge the earth and its creatures. Noah cultivates a vineyard and gets drunk. That story completes what might be called the creation cycle in the J source.

We also encounter the richly dramatic account of the creation in the book of Job. This begins with architectural metaphors. But soon the Creator is struggling to impose boundaries on vast, inchoate forces. The author's imagination leads us from the depths of the ocean to the patterns and movements of the stars far above. We are taken to gates of death and darkness, storerooms of snow and hail ready to be unloaded in a day of terror, and thunderclouds that will pour down (like the 2017 hurricanes Harvey and Maria), turning dust into mud. In this created order chaos is never far away. This Creator hunts prey for the lioness and exults in the wild animals. The wild ass scorns the driver's whip, and even the cruel ostrich 'makes sport' of horse and rider. Most compelling is the image of the battle-charger, a magnificent horse that is fearless under stress and charges joyfully into the din of battle. Where is 'man' in all this noise and confusion? Not only is man not master of the universe, he is not even lord of ox and ass, much less of hawk and vulture. Certainly, he is a paltry creature when compared with the mighty Behemoth and Leviathan described in Job chapters 40 and 41. If we regard these latter images as metaphors of power rather than mythic land and sea monsters, they will remind us of the vast powers latent in the universe created by Job's God.

The Job vision of creation as mighty struggle is not unique to the Bible. Psalm 74, after describing in graphic terms the obliteration of the temple, recalls God's vast power in splitting the sea and smashing sea monsters and calls on Yahweh to avenge the destruction of the temple. A God who split the sea and smashed sea monsters can surely punish those who smashed a mere temple. Psalm 89 contrasts the human onslaughts against the Davidic covenant with Yahweh's mighty power over all other natural and terrestrial forces. Psalm 90 compares the agelessness of Yahweh—God before the world came to birth—with man whose life is dust and ashes. "You brush men away like waking dreams … our lives are over in a breath." Psalm 104 depicts Yahweh as reproving the waters and creating a vibrant and complex world. During the night savage lions roar for their prey; during the day humans go out and labor until dusk. Yahweh is the force that gives breath and renews the world, and at whose glance earth trembles and mountains smoke.

It is necessary to recall these vibrant but destabilizing images of creation because so much is made by the theologically orthodox of the Priestly version in Genesis 1, as if that was the only account that mattered. It is the Priestly version which is so often cited as the text authorizing mankind to "be fruitful and multiply, and replenish the earth, and subdue it: and have dominion over the fish of the sea, the fowl of the air, and every living thing that moveth upon the earth." There is not a whisper here of the power of Behemoth or Leviathan (the great sea monster), not to mention the power reserved to Yahweh, which alone holds creation in balance, but which can also equally well destroy what has been created. According to Genesis 1 and its latter-day apologists, God has delegated power to man to populate and subdue the earth. The entire globe, not just the oasis of Eden, is to be 'man's' terrain. There is no J vision here of man with his feet of clay, expelled from Eden and sent off to cultivate the dust, or of Job as the puny earthling, who was not around when the earth was formed, or of the psalmist's humankind who enjoy a mere few fleeting hours on the earth before time whisks them away. But it is these visions, not Genesis 1, which define the dependency of humans, who cannot even survive politically without covenantal support. The entire thrust of the Hebrew scriptures is to emphasize man's feet of clay, not man as global imperialist. It is the breakup of the Davidic kingdom, the destruction of the kingdom of Israel, and the Babylonian exile of the people of Judah, which shape the Biblical imagination. Even in the Priestly account of creation, God is transcendent while humans are the renters, brought in after everything else has been set up.

When we turn from accounts of creation to the place of the natural order in the Sinai covenant, we find again the imposition of boundaries on the exercise of human power. In the first place, humans are to do no work on the seventh day. This immutable law is now honored largely in the breach. Such are the exigencies of international affairs that we could hardly imagine the President taking his finger off the nuclear button on Sundays, much less stop worrying for 24 hours about whether Saddam Hussein, Slobodan Milosevic, Fidel Castro, Osama Bin Laden, Mullah Omar, Kim Chung Un, or other demonized individuals such as ISIS operatives might be up to no good. No: in the secularized world of flux and inconstancy, eternal vigilance is the price of democracy. Yahweh is not there to do our worrying for us.

Economic institutions also rest at their peril. The Chinese work six days a week, at a minimum, and their economy has been booming. We also, in the West, are working longer and longer hours as the incomes of most of us shrink relative to costs and former incomes. Yet the covenant derides this compulsive industry and even forbids it. If God can rest one day a week—so the thinking goes—so can and must humankind.

The decalogue (ten commandments) also forbids such common economic practices as stealing and coveting what others have. It could hardly approve of the modern economy, which we are reminded so often is fueled by greed and covetousness. Without greed and covetousness how could junk bonds have flourished, how could savings banks have gone off on a wild spending spree, how could Keating, Milken, Ken Lay etc. have become in their time avatars of contemporary economic man? Where would we be without such people? I do not mean to scorn greed in the United States at the expense of greed in Japan, or Italy, or China, or Russia. Greed and corruption are as ancient as human history and are endemic in contemporary society. Despite constant corruption, the world so far has survived. But must we assume that when practiced within certain limits greed and corruption are an inevitable and even desirable fact of economic life? Can we afford to put up with greed and corruption without paying a price?

The book of the covenant found in Exodus 20-23 goes on to proclaim that every seven years humans must allow the land to lie fallow and "forgo all produce from it." The poor and the wild animals are to be permitted to collect what they can find. This idea is an extension of the weekly sabbath, which is intended to allow beasts of burden, slaves, and aliens, to enjoy a breathing space. The notion of allowing the land to rest for one whole year already assumes the dominance of humans over nature but attempts to set limits and boundaries around that dominance. For one day out of seven and one year out of seven humans must stop exploiting their economic assets. This text does not see the land as having independent integrity any more than the donkey, the slave and the alien. All can be exploited six days and years out of seven, but they are finite assets and they need rest. The poor also need a break, which it appears they would not otherwise receive.

Leviticus 25 amplified the idea of sabbatical rest by formulating a jubilee year (taking place after each forty-nine-year period), which would be a year of special rest. People would return to their ancestral homes and do no cultivating, gathering or planting throughout the year. Yahweh would make sure that there was enough food to tide the people over until the next planting and harvesting seasons. Leviticus also insists that land could not be sold in perpetuity as it belonged to Yahweh; and to Yahweh humans "are only strangers and guests." Patrimony sold because of need must be redeemed on the jubilee year. Only dwellings within a walled town were exempt from this rule, except in the case of property of town-dwelling Levites, which came under the protection of the law of redemption. The text justifies this legislation by stating that when the people lived according to Yahweh's laws the earth would yield its produce and Yahweh would dwell amongst them. When they broke the laws, the reverse would happen. The people would be punished sevenfold, and the land would lie fallow and desolate.

Another idea we get from Leviticus is that the land is itself subject to the laws of cleanliness. It is not a mere inert mass on which humanity acts out its fate. When people pollute, the land becomes unclean and must "vomit out" its inhabitants. According to this thinking, the land of Canaan was given over to the children of Israel because the previous inhabitants had polluted it with idolatry, incest, and child burning, and the land had to vomit them out. This powerful image, equating human pollution with terrestrial rejection has come true again in our time as we witness the pollution or desertification of huge tracts of land, which now refuse to support human life. "Ye shall therefore", says the King James Bible, "keep all my statutes and all my judgements, and do them: that the land, whither I bring you to dwell therein, spue you not out." (Leviticus

18). The Biblical redactors could not have envisaged the kind or degree of defilement which modern civilization brings to the exploitation of land; but they did understand that the land was part of God's creation, and therefore "good" and not to be polluted.

The Deuteronomic code, for its part, emphasizes that the land flowing with milk and honey is a gift from Yahweh. In return for that gift those who enjoy the land must set aside first fruits and tithes, lay them before Yahweh, and bow down in the sight of Yahweh. Every third year they should assure Yahweh that they have given the tithe to all those in need, so that Yahweh could bless the people and the land that supported them. The land, in other words, was part of the covenantal exchange. It was needed to support the poor as well as the rich. Provided the landowners guaranteed before Yahweh that they had truly given their tithes to the poor, Yahweh could be expected to bless the land that supported them all. (Deuteronomy 11, 26) Furthermore, not just the land but the entire universe belongs to Yahweh alone.

Behind this concept of the land as blessed of Yahweh lies the idea of Yahweh as the great liberator and savior of the children of Israel. Yahweh adopted them in the wilderness, fed them on the yield of the mountains, and brought them out of the narrow and desert-surrounded land of Mitzrayim (Egyptian Nile valley) into a land flowing with milk and honey. The people, however, grew fat and restive, forgot the Rock that birthed them, and sacrificed to demons. It is a familiar enough picture, for our age as well as that of the Deuteronomists. All that is lacking in the modern world is the notion that Yahweh might retaliate without simply taking such contempt on the chin. The ancient Jewish mind was quite capable of imagining an angry Yahweh responding to human pollution by setting fires that would devour the earth and all its produce, burn the mountains to their foundations, unleash famine, fever and consumption, and grind the people to dust. Yahweh Creator was quite capable of transforming into Yahweh Destroyer, as had been 'demonstrated' during the great flood, the destruction of the Tower of Babel, the destruction of Sodom and Gomorrah, the destruction of the Egyptian first born, the destruction of the Egyptian armies in the Sea of Reeds, and even the destruction of thousands and thousands of Israelite rebels in the wilderness. This ancient

Israelite Yahweh, as opposed to the modern sanitized 'God', was not a deity to mess around with.

The prophets and psalmists also depicted an earth that responded joyfully to the presence of its Creator and with pain and anguish to the abuse of humans. We have encountered in Isaiah the idea of rain and snow coming down from heaven to water the earth, so that it can provide seed for the sower and bread for eating. In the presence of Yahweh mountains and hills break into joyful cries and the trees clap their hands. Cypress grows instead of thorns and myrtle instead of briars. The wilderness and the desert exult and bloom abundantly, and they shall see the glory of Yahweh. But when humans abort the covenant and things go wrong, it is not only the cities of humankind that are smashed to pieces. The earth itself will split into fragments and reel to and fro like a drunkard, and it will fall, warns the prophet, never to rise again. On the great day of wrath, declared Zephaniah, not only humans would be scattered like dust, but all the earth would be consumed, thus making an end of its inhabitants. (Zephaniah 1)

Could the earth really fall, never to rise again? It is hard for any of us to encompass such a bizarre possibility. Every day that we live is another day in an endless existential process. The sun 'rises', bringing daylight, birds sing, life on earth goes about its business. Under these conditions, anything so terminal as a day of wrath seems inconceivable. In six thousand, or six billion, years it hasn't happened yet, at least not in toto; why should we imagine seriously that it might happen tomorrow?

I am reminded of the reaction of a member of the German resistance when he first witnessed, as an army officer on the eastern front, the slaughter by gunfire of thousands of naked Jews. He reported that at that time the comprehension did not exist among him and his colleagues to understand what was going on. He and his fellow officers simply could not get their minds around what they saw with their own eyes. They assumed that orders would come down to stop what was obviously an aberration. But such orders never came. Gradually he and some of his military colleagues came to realize with growing horror that a corruption existed at the very apex of the command system. They made numerous efforts to assassinate Hitler, all of which failed.

This incomprehension was not confined to Germans. When pre-war

German military and civilian resisters tried to communicate to foreign governments their need for assistance in stopping Hitler's march to war, they were advised by British government representatives that their opposition to Hitler was tantamount to treason. Since then historians and ethicists have attempted to probe the virtually worldwide failure of imagination that permitted so many millions of Jews, Poles, Russians and other ethnically oppressed people to be slaughtered by the Nazi war machine, as well as thousands of their survivors to be abused and neglected in the aftermath of the war. We still are far from a satisfactory answer to this catastrophe.

A comparable lack of imaginative understanding appears to underlie the human inability to comprehend the erosion of our biosphere. In the first place, we cannot see this erosion happening on a day-to-day basis. If, on occasion, we do see signs of planetary distress, as the German officer saw signs of Jewish distress, such signs are usually localized and small scale and do not convey the notion of systemic trauma. We may encounter a stretch of burned out mountainside, or a polluted lake (like Lake Erie or the Aral Sea), or see TV images of bulldozers destroying Amazonian or Indonesian rainforest, or read about holes in the ozone layer above the South Pole, or hear about the pollution of Boston Harbor, or the atmospheric pollution resulting from indiscriminate heavy industrialization in parts of Eastern Europe and the former Soviet Union, or the bulldozing of Kentucky mountains to facilitate coal extraction. But all this happens on a here and there basis. Generally, it happens to 'other' people, while 'our' world, as Ecclesiastes said, "stands firm forever." The toxic pollution of Mexico City remains a third world aberration, rather than a portent of a worldwide problem. In particular, the world of governing elites (such as the Reagans, the Bushes, the Trumps, the Marcoses, etc.) generally remains quite pleasant to inhabit, and the Earth continues to maintain an ample, if eco-threatening, lifestyle for millions of people living in Western suburbia. Consequently, we cannot really expect a change in attitude towards the human biosphere until people living towards or at the top of the various command systems and food chains find their own lives personally affected.

It is the problem, once again, of how to turn around the consciousness of an androcentric universe. As lung cancer, heart attacks, emphysema and alcoholism began to take their toll, we have seen some modest turning away from the androcentric lifestyle which made a virtue (in some contexts compulsory) of heavy drinking, eating and smoking. In androcentric environments cigar smoking is no longer considered fashionable. In some major cities, and on some short haul routes, public offices, means of transportation, and parts of restaurants have become smoke-free zones. These are still mere oases in a world encumbered with environmental toxicity, but at least such oases now exist.

However, in describing the physiological effects of androcentric substance abuse we are merely skirting the edges of the problem. Substance abuse is generic to androcentric culture and is symptomatic of androcentric abuse of creation and the natural order, from which such 'substances' are derived. Thus, we must proceed on to the emotional problems arising from human and environmental abuse. The most obvious of these are the problems arising from stress. The development of large human conurbations and megacities, and the assumption that these represent the apex of civilized order, has created a fertile environment for the growth of stress. Stress has become intrinsic to modern urban living. Again, it is easier to observe the effects of stress among underprivileged urbanites, such as the inhabitants of South-Central Los Angeles, or the ghetto areas of any of the major cities of the Western world. No one in their right mind could conclude that these are healthy living environments, or that they represent any kind of covenantal attunement between humankind and the rest of the natural world. Stress in less developed megacities, such as Mumbai, Calcutta, Manila, or Rio de Janeiro, is less well known to people living higher up the hierarchical ladder. Examples of such stress are not regularly featured on network news, as was—for a time—the burning of Los Angeles. Privileged people in their right minds know that the multimillions of humans existing in the slums of 'third world' megacities must cohabit with rats, scorpions and poisonous centipedes, along with malaria-bearing mosquitoes and other intensely toxic organisms. Privileged people could not stand living for long in such environments without getting very stressed out. Dare we assume that those who are forced to live in them can simply make a go of it, without suffering any emotional consequences?

But again, this argument will go nowhere unless we can point to the stress experienced by individuals living in the higher reaches of androcentric culture. We would have to focus our attention on the systemic alcoholism of the Japanese salaryman or the drug and alcohol addictions of privileged Americans. Like rape and domestic violence, this goes on generally behind the scenes and thus has not generally necessitated the attention of public policy. Thus, the 'war on drugs' goes around and around in circles, while the United States continues to be the international drug market of choice.

We must therefore concentrate our attention on the public consequences to the natural world of decisions made in the interests of secular, androcentric power systems. In focusing attention on secular androcentric power, I do not mean to imply the absence of anything corresponding to secular gynocentric power. It is just that since the time of the mythic Amazons it is hard to identify a major gynocentric power system in human history, and certainly impossible to find one operating in our times. Consequently, we must admit to the notion that exploitation of the natural environment is a consequence of androcentrism and an expression of androcentric power priorities. To put this in plainer language: environmental exploitation and pollution result from the exercise of male power, or of power in which male secular values predominate.

Environmental Stewardship in the Kingdom of God

As someone who has attended the church services of several different mainline Christian denominations, I am frankly worried by the frequent absence of adult men from participation in the life of the church. In my limited experience temple congregations do a somewhat better job in getting men to attend their services. This is partly because the temple is not just a focus of Jewish religious and spiritual life but also provides a framework for the expression of cultural and ethnic identity. Some Catholic churches provide a similar focus for ethnically defined sub-communities of French Canadians, Poles, Hispanics, Italians, Irish, etc. Recently hard-up mainstream Protestant congregations have begun to loan their facilities to ethnically defined subgroups of Koreans, Chinese and Haitians. Men also appear to play an active role in the religious life of these subgroups.

But in too many Protestant denominations, particularly those of mainline churches, men are conspicuous by their small numbers. Women provide most of the human power for the community services, while choirs struggle to get by with one tenor or one or two basses. What is going on here? Why have men dropped out to such an extent from the religious life of mainline America? Why are the men who do attend such churches by and large not those to be found providing the leadership of secular institutions? Should we assume that the leading elements of our androcentric world are secretly carrying out spiritual exercises in the privacy of their offices? Probably not. Men bear the burden of maintaining the androcentric power systems that manage our lives, and it is impossible to do that and at the same time commit oneself heart and soul to the life of the kingdom of God. Rather than appear to be hypocritical, it is easier—and in some ways better—for androcentric men to stay out of the life of the church, or to show up only for such obligatory occasions as weddings, baptisms and funerals.

The significant absence of many materially consequential men from the life of the church and from spiritual practice in general points to the gulf that exists between the values of the contemporary secular world and those of the kingdom of God. We could, if we like, hide behind the illusion that these men are simply too busy, or too tired, to be able to attend Sunday services. They need time out from sixty to eighty-hour weeks devoted to making money or to the interests of the corporation, the university, the hospital, the sports franchise, or the government. We should surely be thankful that they are getting some time for rest and recuperation before Monday morning comes around again. We should be particularly grateful for those who manage to get themselves to services one or two Sundays out of fifty. But I am afraid that this kind of thinking is unrealistic. Unless attendance at church serves to reinforce secular responsibilities, we cannot really expect men in search of secular power to regard spiritual practice as a serious option. Church attendance is something for women and children and old people, along with a scattering of well-meaning males, while real men take care of the real world outside the cloister. What use is the church to them?

But conversely, what use are such 'real' men to the ethical and spiritual lives of the rest of us? Why can so few contribute anything to the spiritual life of the modern world, and so little to its ethical life? Why, indeed, are so many of our political and corporate leaders, including those who do attend church, so ethically and behaviorally compromised? Why, for that matter, are 'real' men so silent and incoherent when it comes time to mourn or grieve our troubles?

We have in this silence between the androcentric and the spirit-centered human communities one of the most troublesome existential problems of our times. I used to be worried by the fact that teenagers dropped out of mainline churches in droves, and that young married people simply stayed away. Admittedly, Fundamentalist churches are drawing them in, but this is not helping to solve the problems of androcentrism. But what does that matter, when compared with the absence from mainline churches of decision-making men? It is not the teenagers or the young marrieds who control the policies and choices guiding our lives. It is men in the upper echelons of corporations and political systems who determine these policies. By what criteria and systems of ethics are they making their judgments? How do they listen to our or their inner pain? Through what processes do they examine their own souls?

Is it naive to wonder what happens to the spiritual and material lives of people, many of whom seem never to stop long enough to examine seriously their spiritual existence? Can a large—and by far the most powerful—element of our population live without seriously cultivating the life of the heart and spirit? The Deuteronomists certainly didn't think so, nor did their hero king Josiah. Neither did the brilliant and heroic king David. Can our society really afford to allow so many of our own leading elements to exist in a spiritual vacuum? And do we want a new world order that merely reincorporates and intensifies problems from the old one?

In seeking answers to these questions, I find myself, as someone raised in the Anglican Christian tradition, impressed by the compassion exercised towards 'real' men by Jesus. We could note Jesus' concern for the problems of men in positions of power. Here, for example is a centurion (Roman army captain) whose favorite servant is lying at home paralyzed and in great pain. He comes to Jesus and pleads for help. "I'll come and heal him", says Jesus. "Oh no sir", responds the centurion, "you don't need to come. Just give the word and my servant will be healed. I am under authority myself and have soldiers under me. I say to one 'go' and he goes, to another 'come' and he comes, and to my servant 'do this' and he does it." Astonished, Jesus comments, "not even in Israel have I heard faith like this." And the servant was cured at that moment. (Matthew 8; Luke 7)

There are two versions to this story; the one related here is the simpler version from the Matthew gospel, which focuses on the centurion. Here is a man thoroughly at home in the androcentric world, used to obeying secular power and enforcing it on subordinates. This man understands how power works. But he also perceives the existence of alternative power systems and grasps that they can achieve results that his own can't. The world of power is not confined to Roman militarism. Moreover, Roman militarism, for all its power, cannot heal a sick human being. He comes and pleads with an itinerant healer on behalf of his servant. He demonstrates faith in the power of the healer. During that moment militarism, androcentrism and secular power are set aside so that spiritual power can flow. It is the centurion himself who enables that to happen; and Jesus is there for him.

In another famous story, told in its simplest form in Mark's gospel, a scribe comes up and asks Jesus "which is the first commandment?" Jesus replies not with the opening commandment of the Decalogue but with the text from Deuteronomy known as the shema, which is a regular part of Jewish liturgical service. "Listen, Israel", he says, "the Lord our God is the one Lord, and you must love the Lord your God with all your heart, with all your soul, with all your mind, and with all your strength. The second commandment", he adds, "is this: you must love your neighbor as yourself. There is no commandment greater than these." "Well spoken!", exclaims the scribe. "To love God with all your heart and soul and strength, and to love your neighbor as yourself, is far more important than any burnt offering or sacrifice." Jesus warmly tells him, "you are not far from the kingdom of God." (Mark 12)

What brings the learned scribe to the doorway of the kingdom, and what is needed for other men in power positions to make it that far? First, we can notice the agreement on both sides on the primacy of the Deuteronomic insistence to love the God Yahweh with all one's heart and soul and strength. The Deuteronomic text adds, "you shall repeat these words to your children … you shall fasten them on your hand and your forehead … you shall write them on your doorposts and gates. What you have is from Yahweh. Be thankful and fear and serve Yahweh your God." (Deuteronomy 6) This is the ultimate expression in the Bible of Yahweh-centrism, its locus classicus in both Hebrew and Christian testaments. Jesus and the scribe are both clear about putting Yahweh and Yahweh's creation at the center of their lives. They are also clear about giving primacy to fearing (standing in fear and awe of) and serving Yahweh. There is no ambiguity here between the call of one power system and the call of another. The power of the created order identified with Yahweh-centrism comes first.

Next, from Leviticus, comes love of neighbor as oneself. This also is not part of the Decalogue. It comes as the climax to a series of commandments concerning human relations within the Yahwist covenant. For example, individuals are told they must not steal, rob neighbors, hold back a laborer's wages, curse the dumb or harm the blind, give unjust verdicts or endanger a neighbor's life. They must not hate a neighbor, exact vengeance, or bear a grudge against the neighbor's children. No: "you must love your neighbor as yourself." (Leviticus 19) In Mark's version of this exchange, the scribe agrees wholeheartedly. "This is far more important," he insists, "than any burnt offering or sacrifice." The scribe, in other words, believes in applying the Yahwist covenant not just to his own wellbeing but to that of others. This recognition of the 'other' - which Leviticus expands to include loving the 'alien living in your midst' - indicates the presence of Yahweh consciousness, which cannot be confirmed by practice of rituals. Only if I truly love my neighbor as myself, am I operating from the covenant, practicing Yahweh consciousness, and existing in proximity to Yahweh's kingdom.

We might go further and say that the key to developing respect for our world lies in living life according to these commandments. First of all, we have to understand and practice the consciousness of loving higher power with all our heart and soul and strength—in, let us say, the way that Job did, to such an extent that Yahweh came and opened before his eyes a whole panorama of the beauty and awesomeness of the world, its power, its complexity, and the huge scope of its operation. One might almost say that a Jobian vision of such profound sweep and ardor is worth an attack of boils and all the rest that Job suffered, because it gives us a vision of supra-human power bringing a beautiful and compelling world into being, one which provides the stage for the enactment of our own lives and our consciousness of creation and the joy in its making.

We must also, as the wisdom writers and Deuteronomy insist, learn to fear Yahweh and to recognize that within the power of Yahweh lie forces of destruction as well as creation. In the wisdom literature the human forces of destruction appear to operate in defiance of, or indifference to Yahweh, whereas in the prophetic literature they are seen primarily as expressions of Yahweh's anger towards an idolatrous and polluting humankind. More broadly, the covenantal ethic, as interpreted by the prophets, insists that if we humans pollute the world Yahweh will not stand idly by. According to this ethic, the world is Yahweh's creation, not ours. It was not intended to serve as a dump for our garbage or as grist for our endless self-promotion. We humans are guests and renters, not owners. The earth's biosphere and the universe do not belong to us. If we want to dump our garbage or increase our power, we had better get into the habit of asking Yahweh how to do it, and not just assume that we can go out and dump or control at will. Otherwise our pollution might just kindle Yahweh's wrath.

As I write these words, I am astounded by the notion of how few contemporary mainline Christians there are, including myself, who really understand the idea of Yahweh as wrathful and destructive. If Christians do not comprehend and take on this idea, so insistently repeated in the prophetic texts (not to mention those of other world religions), how could we ever expect androcentric secularists to pay attention to it? The wisdom books repeat again and again that fear of Yahweh is the beginning of wisdom. The prophetic books repeat again and again that failure to respect Yahweh and Yahweh's creation will result in a day or wrath and utter destruction. If one appreciates the vastness of the concept of a Creator-source of our living world and its importance to the preservation of the world, then we need to be increasingly mindful of the challenge of this fundamental wisdom statement. In the androcentric world that we have inherited, fear of the higher order power that is called divine is precisely the beginning of wisdom. Anything that falls short of fear of that which is sacred and divine is in the long run a policy of utter folly.

If the Deuteronomic Shema is the first and fundamental commandment, the second is to love my neighbor as myself. What is meant by this? In Luke's rewriting of this exchange, a lawyer tries to disconcert Jesus by asking "what must I do to inherit eternal life?" What indeed? The Hebrew scriptures do not have a lot to say about inheriting eternal life, as their focus is on life here and now. Jesus replies, "what is written in the law?" The lawyer responds with abbreviated versions of the two commandments.

Very well: if your goal is eternal life, this is as good an answer as any. Jesus laconically comments, "you have answered right. Do this and life is yours."

The lawyer is taken aback by this response. As compared with the dialogue between Jesus and Nicodemus (reported in John 3), Jesus here throws the ball right back into the lawyer's lap. Perhaps the lawyer had been expecting a complicated analysis about how to live in the afterlife (an exchange along these lines is reported in Mark just before the account of the exchange with the scribe). In any case he feels deflated, so he asks defensively, forgetting that the answer is already in text after text of Leviticus, "and who is my neighbor?" This is one of the most famous questions in Christian literature, since it introduces the justly celebrated Lucan story about the travelling Samaritan.

Who indeed is my neighbor? My enemy? A person whom I have spent my life distrusting and reviling? A person whose people have fought with my people, who occupy my former land, and who practice a religion which is a merest echo of mine? A person whom I would rather hate and look down on than love? Yes, as a matter of fact, the Samaritan, or the African American, or the Cambodian, or the Chinese, or the Muslim, or the Mexican, is my neighbor. The boy down the street, or the teenage mother, or the person needing a kidney transplant, or the victim of natural or human calamity, is my neighbor. This is an extension of the original idea in Leviticus, voiced also in the command to "love the alien in your midst." (Leviticus 19) Serbs, Croatians, and Bosnians, are neighbors to each other. So are Blacks and Whites, Catholics and Protestants, Jews and Arabs, Jews and Gentiles, Hispanics and Mayans, Christians and Muslims, rich and poor. Covenantal texts on justice and mercy are quite clear and articulate about this. "You shall love your neighbor as yourself" is what the Bible says. To love one's neighbor as oneself is to love Yahweh's creation and to extend Yahweh's light throughout the world. Or as the Isaiah text put it, "I will make you the light of the nations, so that my salvation may reach to the ends of the earth." (Isaiah 49; see also Acts 13).

I have emphasized in this chapter the basic respect of covenantal thought for divine power and the universe believed to be brought into being by it. One reason for this emphasis is that Christianity (along with Zionism) is sometimes viewed by secularists or non-Christians as a religion condoning exploitation of other people's assets and of other life systems.

As I argued earlier, I believe this expresses a conflation of Biblical thought with religious and secular practice. My intention in this study has been to keep these elements separate, to argue that religious practice results as much from the operation of secular power systems as from Biblical thought. Biblical thought is focused on persuading us to cultivate love and reverence for the divine and the world and its inhabitants with whom and with which we live. It is intended to keep us honest, to remind us that the world and the far-reaching universe do not belong to us. We are only strangers, here for a few moments. We live and die in a blink of eternity.

In short, we do not own this world. If we misuse it, sooner or later, warns the Bible, there will be big, big trouble. We neglect this teaching at our peril.

CHAPTER 17

Covenant as the Key to Justice and Mercy

> He hath shewed thee, O man, what is good;
> And what doth the Lord require of thee
> But to do justly and to love mercy,
> And to walk humbly with thy God?
> Micah 6

We now return to the central question of this book. What is covenant, why does the Bible consider it essential to the establishment of a just society, and what does that mean for us today?

To begin with, a covenantal society is not something that comes into being through a few minor adjustments in legislation or as a result of an election campaign. An entire vision of moral order must be in place, in which the life of human beings is made possible within a shared and pledged continuum. Rules and boundaries need to be established, in such a way that the living order and the life which it incorporates, including our own, is preserved rather than put at risk. If moral breakdown and loss of vision have occurred, new leadership is necessary if such a moral vision is to be recovered. But leadership by itself cannot be effective unless it reveals an understanding of moral and spiritual order and is able to communicate that understanding to human beings. Transformation of self and community is mandatory. Any appearance of self-interest would be enough to challenge the leadership and jeopardize the whole business.

The Hebrew scriptures insist that such transformation is an arduous business. It took "forty years" to transform the Children of Israel from a subservient and oppressed ethnic minority into a morally structured confederation of independent people imbued with a sense of Divine grace. Numerations of forty days or years are used in the Bible to denote critical lengths of time required to achieve a transformation of circumstance or consciousness. Sometimes they denote intervals of peace; in general, they refer to time during which divine power is believed to be in mediation with human. Thus, we might interpret the forty-year time frame as indicating both a long interval of time and a passage of time in which a transformation of consciousness occurs through mediation with supra-human power. The passage of generations is also involved in the Exodus forty-year time frame. The generation leaving Egypt is unable to assume the challenge of the covenant, and that applies even to its leadership. A new generation with new leaders must take over the responsibilities of the covenant developed during the preceding generation.

We should note, too, the spatial wandering that is involved in moral and spiritual transformation. Such transformation, from a Biblical perspective, involves physical and psychological uprooting. Individuals involved in this transformative effort physically leave a safe, familiar environment and voyage out into the unknown, or into a place to which they are called. As wanderers they are uprooted from material security and instead learn to draw on inner, spiritual resources. Although wandering does not necessarily produce transformation, it is no coincidence that the great wanderers of the Bible, such as Abraham and Sarah, Jacob/Israel, Joseph, Moses, Elijah, Ruth, Jesus, or Paul, are also its great innovators and transformative influences. Bereft of material security, they become open to the presence of the divine and conduits for divine communication with earthbound humans. Through this openness and receptivity towards the divine, covenant and moral community are brought into being.

Covenant is the Biblical term for identifying what we mean by moral community. It is applied to the transformation of the wandering Abraham and his entourage into the source of the original Biblical moral community, which defined the descendants of Abraham and Sarah as Yahwists. Similarly, it is applied to the transformation of the wandering Israelites, led by Moses, into a moral community that would prefer freedom and poverty in Canaan to luxury and bondage in Egypt. It was applied to David, another wanderer, as the beloved anointed representative of Yahweh, who would forge warring tribes into a relatively cohesive political union that could sustain the development of the Yahwist cult. After the destruction of the kingdoms of Israel and Judah it was applied, in the Deuteronomic reform, to the reconstituted cultural remnant of survivors of the Babylonian exile, whose loyalty to Yahweh would henceforth be inscribed not just on the outer body and through outer institutions such as kingdoms or temples, but inwardly, on their very hearts and souls. Indeed, in one of the most famous metaphors of the Bible (from Ezekiel 37), even the dead and dry bones of the people of Israel would come alive as the breath of Yahweh's new covenant was breathed into them.

Later, the Jewish sect which opened itself to Jewish and Gentile followers of the way of Jesus, the Galilean wanderer, became transformed by the belief, voiced principally by the community-building missionary Paul, that the death and resurrection of Jesus had achieved the basis for a covenant of redemption available to all believers regardless of ethnic origin. As described in the letter to the Hebrews, the Christic covenant similarly invoked the inner language of the Deuteronomic covenant of the heart. Through the sacrifice of Jesus, it promised to cancel the sins of commission that undid previous covenants and to establish a language of the heart through which humans would be bonded to the Divine and each other. In the Christic covenant, the ten commandments of the Decalogue of Moses were boiled down to two: the quintessential Shema from Deuteronomy, to love God with all one's heart, soul and strength, and to inscribe these words on one's heart; and the injunction from Leviticus to love one's neighbor as oneself. In John's gospel the commandments were distilled down even further to the simple proposition: "love one another, as I have loved you." (John 13) This became the ethic of the Jesus covenant and the basis for Christianity as moral community.

But such a phrase begs the question of what is love, and what is the meaning of the language of the heart on which the Deuteronomic covenant insists? Here again the Bible supplies us with answers, although they are answers more easily talked than walked. For example, John's gospel tells us that God "so loved the world that he gave his only begotten Son, that whosoever believeth in him should not perish but have everlasting life." (John 3) God so loved the world: these words convey the moral and theological essence of this gospel. Here the injunctions about humans loving God—easier said than done—give way to a meditation about God loving the world. It is, to be sure, a human world that the gospel is generally assumed to refer to in this passage, and the intention of God's love is to preserve those humans who reach out to the Gospel's source of life. This intention had been expressed repeatedly through the vocation of prophets, and now through the gift of the one whom the Christic sectarians are coming to call the Son and Servant of God. The expression of love comes through this gift of divine presence, opening the possibility for humans to see the way of life and avoid that death of heart and soul that comes with neglect of the way of life.

Love, in this context, is treated as literally life-saving. It is the difference between life and death of heart and spirit. It is interesting that the text does not simply talk of death, pure and simple, but uses the word "perish" in the sense of extinction of a life form. This is the sense in which the ancient kingdom of Israel and its ten tribes, having fully and finally defaulted on their allegiance to Yahweh and Yahweh's covenant, may be said to have perished. It is also the sense in which Lincoln used the word in his Gettysburg Address, with reference to preserving the heart and soul of democracy from extinction. Thus, it is implied in the gospel passage that God's love may not preserve a human being from individual death of the body but does preserve from extinction of the deeper life of the spirit.

John's gospel is also the source for the statement that "greater love hath no man than this, that a man lay down his life for his friends." (John 15). In other words, first we are told something about God's love; now we are told about human love. This expression of human love was to be the act of Jesus himself, who in Johannine terms assured his followers as he prepared to lay down his own life, "you are my friends." Love here is associated not with personal happiness or carnal pleasure, but with self-sacrifice, risking or losing one's own life in order to preserve the lives of those one loves. To use the Greek terminology, we are talking about agape (selfless love) not eros (romantic love). Willingness to suffer and to lose one's life becomes the measure of greatest love. As a patriarchal text "greater love" has inspired numerous acts of male heroism on and off the battlefield. It became the theme of one of Wilfred Owen's most searing war poems, written by Owen to define the anti-covenantal actions of World War I through its massive slaughter of young men, brought about by ordering them into over four years of trench warfare and murderous frontal assaults. As a non-patriarchal text "greater love" has inspired numerous other acts of personal sacrifice—notably by mothers in life-endangering childbirth—conveying as it does the talk and walk of Jesus as sacrificial lamb and servant-son.

Another demanding text, from the Sermon on the Mount (in both Matthew and Luke versions), adjures the listener to "love your enemies, bless them that curse you, do good to them that hate you, and pray for them which despitefully use you and persecute you." (Matthew 5, Luke 6) The text argues that if you love only those who love you, what reward will you have? "You must therefore set no bounds to your love," demands the sermon, just as God sets no bounds also. (Jerusalem Bible).

What a challenge! Which of us normally loves our enemies or feels like blessing people who despise and oppress us, or who represent values that we despise? Let's get real here. We are, after all, especially if we are male, taught in a thousand explicit or insidious ways the exact opposite. Hate and despise your enemies and get ready to bully or kill them before they kill you. How could wars be fought, if we didn't learn how to hate our enemies? How could I ram my fist into your face or my knife or bayonet into your guts, or slit your throat, or blow you into little bits, if I hadn't first learned how to dehumanize you? How could I shoot you? How could I spray you and your village with napalm? How could I rape you? How, indeed, could we Westerners have dropped an annihilating atomic bomb on Hiroshima, if we hadn't learned how to hate and despise the Japanese people? How could Hitler have brought about the virtual extinction of European Jews and enslavement and killing of Slavic peoples, if there hadn't been a huge reservoir of hatred for Jews and contempt for Slavs to fuel his ambitions and carry out his orders?

This teaching appears to present Jesus at his most contrarian and inexplicable. It's not as if the circumstances of first century Judea were any more favorable to love of enemies than those of occupied Europe or Asia during World War II. Plenty of inhabitants of Palestine and Asia Minor hated the Roman occupiers, with good reason, and were seething with unrest and rebelliousness. Yet the Christic sectarians were asked to drop that kind of hatred and replace it with love, meaning a willingness to go to one's own death in order to preserve the lives and souls of others, including those of one's enemies. Specifically, the beleaguered followers of Jesus were being asked, in effect, to love other sectarians who were publicly cursing them in the synagogues, as well as pray for the wellbeing of the oppressive and lethal Roman soldiery and the indifferent or contemptuous Roman citizenry. They should love and pray for the souls of magistrates who were condemning Christic sectarians to be tortured and executed or sent to public arenas to be torn apart by wild animals.

What is so surprising is that early Christians evidently accepted this teaching of the gospel and grew strong under this kind of oppression. Witnesses confirm that time and again Christic sectarians went to their terrible deaths without bitterness or rage, and on the contrary in a spirit of fraternal love and compassion. How were the Christic martyrs able to manifest this kind of power? As Elaine Pagels has shown, early Christians believed themselves to be engaged in a cosmic war of good against evil, love against hate, the forces of God against the forces of the Devil. The 'reward' of eternal life came through participation in this cosmic struggle. What should be amazing to beneficiaries of democracy, for whom moral community may seem to be a birthright, is how many people threw themselves into this cosmic struggle for redemption versus physical death and gave their lives willingly in the process. Nor were these lives given in vain. Two centuries of martyrs provided the organizational and theological structure, on which Christianity has relied ever since for its moral energy and direction.

If the gospels describe the cosmic struggle waged by Jesus, it is the letters of Paul that so vigorously affirm how every single follower of Jesus, regardless of status, gender, age or ethnicity, could engage in that struggle. With his characteristically ardent assurance Paul proclaimed, "If God is for us, who can be against us?" (Romans 8). Despite endless persecution and slaughter, those guided by the Spirit of God would come through victorious, by the power of "him who loved us." Not a single power on earth, Paul insisted, could come between Christians and the love of God manifested in Jesus. This powerful conviction persuaded the early followers of Jesus to look beyond death to the glory of spiritual victory, in a way that fascinated and shocked those who watched them dying. Paul went so far as to insist that without this power of love all language and speaking, even including the speaking of heavenly powers, was mere empty noise, like the mindless martial clamor of gongs booming and cymbals clashing—or, as Yeats put it in his remarkable poem Byzantium, the "fury and mire of human veins" in a "gong-tormented sea." What is missing in these powerful martial images is any element of moral or spiritual purpose, exactly what Paul focused on in striving to forge groups of disparate followers of Jesus into moral community.

It is as well to keep remembering that these images of love in early Christian texts were associated not with the pleasures of romantic liaison, or having fun in bed, but with conduct acutely affecting how people lived or died. To emphasize the character of the dying that lay ahead for Christians, Paul drew on the words from Psalm 44 that "for your sake we are being massacred all day long, treated as sheep to be slaughtered." (Romans 8, Jerusalem Bible) In the cosmic war of good against evil, the love required by the covenant of the heart is not a commission for the fainthearted. But the stakes were considered so great as to justify pinning faith on this cosmically empowering love of God and neighbor and facing whatever physical death might come. Not only were humans to be spiritually liberated but the "whole of creation itself might be freed from its slavery to corruption and brought into the same glorious freedom as the children of God." (Romans 8)

This vibrant but exacting conception of spiritually liberated community is beyond what most of us are used to or frankly capable of aspiring to. It argues that humans alone cannot achieve such a vision. Left to our own devices we are a prey to moral weakness, or to what theologians call the bondage of fear and sin. We do what we would wish not to do, and do not do what we know we should. Certainly, we are prone to moral cowardice. We would all like to avoid being battered and raped by drunken soldiery, massacred in public arenas, torched or hanged by lynch mobs, or suffocated in gas chambers. Love that puts people in that kind of harm's way is more than tough love; indeed, it could only arise among people who are truly secure in the belief that God loves them and that nothing else matters.

As to our moral misconduct, law, as Paul long ago pointed out, can and should hold us responsible for our wrongdoing. But law by itself cannot get us to do right, nor can fear of punishment achieve that goal. This (as Confucius also long ago pointed out) is the moral vacuum in coercive systems, which ensures that they can never succeed in sustaining moral community. It presents the great dilemma confronting everyone who wishes to participate in the building of moral community. To get anyone to do what is right there must be moral vision and example. Without it we are helpless and rudderless, like the Emperor's drunken soldiery of Yeats' poem, or reduced to making deals with forces of oppression, like Isaiah's drunken priests and false prophets (Isaiah 28), or like those millions of people in modern times who succumbed to tyranny.

In the Biblical tradition moral vision, as the Deuteronomic texts insist, is something that arises from heart and soul. Although it can be constructed by the mind and laid out in rational discourse, it is not a product of the mind. It is the product of the human heart, as the center of feeling and emotional energy, and the human soul, as the center of communication with the divine. It was not rational judgment that prevailed on Abraham to leave the security of the highly civilized city of Ur for an unknown wilderness; and it was not rational judgment that prevailed on Moses to give up his safe-haven as a herdsman in Midian and take on the terrifying task of leading the Israelites out of bondage to the Pharaoh. Rational judgment could not have persuaded the prophets Isaiah or Jeremiah to take up the dangerous vocation of prophecy, or the young David to face the ferocious giant Goliath. Rational judgment alone could not explain the catastrophes that led to the extinction of the kingdom of Israel, the conquest of Judah, the destruction of the temple, or the removal of Jerusalem's leading citizenry into captivity and exile.

In the same way it is impossible to explain contemporary commitments to non-violent civil disobedience in terms of rational criteria. Rational criteria militate against putting one's life voluntarily at risk. Rational calculus did not persuade this century's non-violent martyrs to take to the streets. It is impossible, likewise, for people of the 20th century to come up with satisfying rational explanations for the disdain of created life resulting in the institution of slavery and racism in the supposedly God-fearing United States, or for the bloodbath of World War II and the Nazi Holocaust which destroyed European Jewry, the persecution and enslavement of millions that accompanied Leninist style imperialism, or the subordination of post-World War II resources in both West and East to the development of armaments capable of inflicting planetary destruction. From a Biblical perspective all such behavior is contrary to covenantal ethics, idolatrous, contemptuous of creation, and fundamentally immoral. Since rationalization and defense of immorality is a deep-seated human attribute—one of our most basic defense mechanisms—it is perhaps hard for privileged Westerners to appreciate their own capacity for ethical misconduct or recognize it when they see it. Americans, for example, are now relatively used to the notion that we have been producing more industrialized pollution per capita than any other people on earth. We are only now beginning, as a nation, to contemplate seriously the idea that this behavior may be unacceptable and should be changed; and our political leadership is also slow in bringing us to this realization.

This does not mean that the 20th century was lacking in moral vision. On the contrary, it was full of evidence of spiritually inspired love and self-sacrifice for causes designed to bring peace and renewed joy to human beings. There were heroes everywhere: in the trenches of World War I, in the political prisons and slave camps of tyrannical regimes of left and right, in civil rights movements, in religious missions, in labor movements, in movements of national liberation. Such leaders as Mahatma Gandhi, Martin Luther King, Oscar Romero, Nelson Mandela, Dietrich Bonhoeffer, the Dalai Lama, Thich Nat Hanh, Ai Qing and his son Ai Weiwei, Aleksandr Solzhenitsyn, and Mother Theresa, as well as hundreds of thousands of others following in their footsteps, gave new meaning to the concepts of non-violence and love of neighbor. Voices of protest made themselves heard, even under the most chilling circumstances. The will to prophetic witness remains very much alive in our time.

It does mean, however, that we who are alive today are encumbered with the same capacity to lose moral vision that we see in the Biblical record. The establishment of covenantal law in ancient Israel provided no more guaranty of the preservation of moral vision than the establishment of democracy in modern America or post-war Europe and Japan. Democracy without moral vision becomes unfortunately as much a form of idolatry and abuse of life as any other human perversion. Since this idea runs counter to the prevailing Western view that democracy and market capitalism are better than all other forms of political and economic management, privileged Westerners would naturally have trouble in paying much attention to those, such as the critical voices in Iran or other Middle Eastern countries, who are less than thrilled by our ways of conducting and defining ourselves. What—we might respond—have they to offer, other than dreary ideology, saber-rattling, and oppression and murder of their own dissidents?

But this kind of response is too much like the pot calling the kettle black. Our problem in the West, especially the U.S., is a lack of assurance about the traditional American "dream" and the democracy and will for freedom that is intended to undergird it. More basically, it is a lack of confidence that the Euro-American Enlightenment, which has underwritten the Western concept of human progress over the last three centuries, can withstand the shocks that it has suffered during the 20th century. Industrialization has led us to vastly improved standards of living and life expectancies, but also to vastly increased capacities to kill and destroy. Industrialization produces toothbrushes and soap on the one hand and anti-personnel land mines and napalm on the other. Nationalism and patriotic fervor led us into World War I and again into World War II. Far-sighted Europeans watched in horror as the lights went out over Europe in August 1914 and a reign of atavistic death and hatred replaced civilized discourse. The First World War became in fact the graveyard of the Enlightenment and the progressive science-based story that went with it, although this was barely recognized at the time. As World War II came to an end and the evidence of the Holocaust came to light, people of European stock and inheritance were made brutally aware of the terrifying, numbing racism that infects our souls. Fifty years later we are still groping to understand how our minds and consciences could have become so compromised. In the 1980s Soviet-style Marxist Leninism, once an inspiration to so many oppressed people, met a justly deserved end, leaving in its wake a trail of political repression, murder, impoverishment, and industrial blight. In the post-Cold War 1990s there were still more mad dogs yapping in our back yards, as bloodshed erupted in the Balkans and feuding and killing went on and on in Northern Ireland, Kashmir, Angola, Rwanda and Burundi, The Congo, Colombia, and too many other places as well. Meanwhile chaos has been a way of life in such places as Somalia, Chechnya, South Sudan, Dafur, Haiti, Syria, Yemen, etc. In such nightmare lands the very idea of "development" (the Enlightenment's latest bequest to the non-European world and the ideology that fuels the World

Bank, the World Trade Organization and other such pillars of material progress) is a cruel hoax.

But Americans have their own backyards: in Guatemala, El Salvador and Honduras; or in the Bronx, South Central Los Angeles, or South Boston. The Enlightenment ethic is not working so well in these places either, or in numerous others like them. 'Development' too easily gives way to urban decay. Wherever there are heroes in these places there are also sub-cultures of moral vision; but generally, these are localities where the more fortunate amongst us would prefer not to live. Unless we are very masochistic, we would be likely to conclude that the possibilities of succumbing to drug addiction, unemployment, homelessness, depression, starvation, rape, robbery, AIDs, or death by knife or gunfire, are simply too great to make these places attractive. Their school systems have manifold problems, and some of the schools are disaccredited and little more than armed camps in a no-man's land. Even the prices of basic goods and services are exorbitant relative to income. Who in their right minds would choose to be born or exist in such earthly purgatory?

To point this out is to insist that the search for moral vision must begin with ourselves. Before privileged Americans point fingers at Cubans, Chinese, Iranians, Iraqis, North Koreans, Syrians, or others of whose political behavior we disapprove, we had better first consider our own circumstances. What is the state of our own moral vision, and how are we to make it work in these uncharted times?

Moral Vision and Covenant in the American Tradition

Unlike many countries the United States, as befits a nation of immigrants, is in fact a covenantal society. It has its own faith document in the Declaration of Independence. It has its Constitution and Bill of Rights defining the rights and responsibilities of citizens. It has the Pledge of Allegiance to remind citizenry of their commitment to the national covenant and the covenanting God. It has numerous national anthems to be sung at festive and sacramental occasions, which in the manner of psalms give thanks for the special qualities that bind humans and the divine power to fulfillment of the national covenant. If that were not enough, the Thanksgiving ceremony has been depicted as a creational myth encompassing all inheritors of the American tradition except those whom they displaced.

A reading of these documents is enough to remind us of the moral vision that has permeated the American body politic and enabled it to declare itself a moral community. Although couched in the language of the Enlightenment, the Declaration of Independence draws deeply on Biblical myth and symbolism. It espouses a theory of 'creation', stating that all men are "created equal" (something never explicitly mentioned in the Bible) and endowed by their Creator with certain inalienable rights, including life, liberty, and the pursuit of happiness. The language is narrowly patriarchal, the ideology primarily derived from John Locke and other exponents of natural rights; but the introduction of the Creator and creation reminds us that this is a document drawn up by people grounded in Biblical thought. To use the language of Thomas Berry, it is a framing of a new story drawn out of the old one inherited from the Bible.

Thus, the evocation of British oppression and despotism, to which the Declaration turns its attention, reminds us of the despotism that the Israelites long ago had suffered in Egypt. George III, the latter-day English Pharaoh, who for much of his reign drifted in and out of porphyria-induced insanity, is charged with suppressing rights and instituting an absolute tyranny. Appealing to the "supreme Judge of the world," the signatories declare the independence of the colonies from allegiance to the British Crown. With a "firm reliance on the protection of divine Providence," the signatories then pledge to each other their lives, fortunes, and sacred honor. A figure of Mosaic stature, in the person of George Washington, was found to lead the colonists out of bondage to Egypt-Britain and into freedom. After Washington's death, Jefferson would assume the role of a presidential Joshua, establishing the capital of the new community in Washington, the new Jerusalem of the Anglo-Saxon-French Enlightenment. He would also greatly enlarge the physical domain of the new covenant, although not like Joshua through conquest and massacre but through prudential purchase of the Louisiana territories. Others, who came after him, would do the conquering and killing.

Since then the country revered as "sweet land of liberty", "land of the pilgrim's pride", an empire founded on "brotherly kindness" (depending on one's perspective), where may "all races mingle together as children of God", has been free to put the new covenant adopted in the Bill of Rights into action. No tyrannical British crown or demented sovereign any longer suffices to prevent the pursuit of Jefferson's inalienable rights. A beautiful land of spacious skies, amber waves of grain, and "alabaster cities undimmed by human tears," lies before us. Americans can—indeed must—make the American dream come true. As a matter of fact, for many it has come true. The United States truly is a land of opportunity, and there are many millions of immigrants, myself among them, who would agree wholeheartedly with Irving Berlin in calling on God to bless America, the "land that I love" and "my home sweet home."

Most of us could also agree with the view expressed in a less well-known anthem by William Watson that "dawn is on her forehead still, in her veins youth's arrows thrill, hers are riches, might and fame, all the earth resounds her name." These words present aspects of America that can even today be readily identified by friend or foe. But, as this anthem goes on to remind us, covenant is a two-edged sword. On the one hand is the gift of the land of milk and honey; on the other is the obligation to live according to the covenanted agreement. To quote this under-sung hymn:

> Power Unseen, before whose eyes
> Nations fall and nations rise,
> Grant she not climb to her goal
> All forgetful of the Soul!
> Firm in honor be she found,
> Justice-armed and mercy-crowned,
> Blest in labor, blest in ease,
> Blest in noiseless charities.

Here, too, we find strong echoes of the Biblical covenant. The Power Unseen, before whose immutable eyes human dominion is a transitory thing, can be found on virtually every page of the Hebrew scriptures. The rise and fall of the kingdoms or nations of Israel and Judah is the subject matter of those scriptures, a subject given the most urgent attention in the prophetic writings. What we find in such writings is an unsparing critique of covenantal misconduct, along with an adamant insistence that Yahweh-God is justice-armed as well as mercy-crowned. The covenant, the prophetic writings insist, requires the chosen people to manifest precisely those same qualities in their own moral community. The covenantal nation, in other words, is not just a nation of law and order, for that is a minimum demand for covenantal status. If it is covenanting with the Hebrew God, such a nation had better also be a community that is justice-armed and mercy-crowned, and a community that in pride of its achievement does not forget its soul or its noiseless charities.

Here is where human conduct, alone and unaided, can be seen by history, today as in the past, to fall short in commitment to covenant and moral community. In this respect the Deuteronomic history of the kingdoms of Israel and Judah performs a function comparable to the function of history at its best in our own time: that is, specifically to critique human conduct in terms of the norms and purposes of moral community. History, as the Jewish and Chinese people long ago realized, is the ultimate moral discipline. Its function is to raise moral concerns and warn against moral failure—or, as Chinese historians have done for over 2,000 years, to bestow praise and blame on specific humans according to their fulfillment of moral imperatives. Chinese moral norms, as derived from the Confucian tradition, perform a function comparable to those derived from the Biblical covenantal tradition. Humans are judged in terms of their commitment to moral community, and that judgment is set down in history. Every age, and every historically significant person, is judged in terms of the moral norms.

In short, American history can no more escape judgment than that of any other country. If it is to live by the covenant, it must be judged by the standards of the covenant.

Justice and Mercy in Covenantal Ethics

In the case of Western societies, such as that of the U.S., that derive moral identity from the Biblical covenantal tradition, the two key values that constitute the heart and soul of moral community are justice and mercy. The most pithy and famous statement of those values is given at the head of this chapter. What is meant by justice and mercy? First, we need to differentiate linguistic usage from the cultural tradition underlying it. If someone is torturing me or pointing a gun or knife at my throat, I might very well cry out for mercy, if I still had any voice left to cry out. If I am overcome by a sense of wrongdoing and kneeling in the confessional, I might also beg for mercy. 'Mercy' here means "spare my life" or "please don't hurt me", or it means "forgive me for my wrongdoing." From a covenantal perspective it represents a plea to Yahweh to forgive me for breaching the covenant and abandoning the moral community to which I am sworn. The Kyrie, the basic Christian invocation, is itself an appeal for mercy. "Lord have mercy", it begs, "Christ have mercy, Lord have mercy." Confessional texts address God as "merciful Father" or "merciful Lord". "O Lord have mercy on us" goes the Anglican Episcopal version, "spare thou those who confess their faults." In a more confident tone liturgies assure us that "the Lord (i.e. Yahweh) is full of compassion and mercy." Taking their cue from the psalmists, those in communion with Yahweh claim that "surely goodness and mercy shall follow me all the days of my life." "For thy mercy", they say of Yahweh, "is great above the heavens." "The earth is full of thy mercy."

The appeal to be spared from harm's way is a crucial aspect of the meaning of mercy. It is the ultimate 'cri du coeur 'when moral community weakens or fails. And it is the moral capacity that seems to be least available at that moment of crisis. How many people do we know, whose cries for mercy have been scorned? The history of all nations and ideologies is transfixed by such cries, and the history of the United States is no exception. People in this country are to this day routinely gunned down, kicked, robbed, raped, beaten or tortured by other people, for whom the notion of moral community is a self-defined convenience or a meaningless fiction. The history of the United States, and of all countries drawing their moral compass from the Biblical tradition, is itself a fiction until this record of mercilessness is fully acknowledged. On that point the message of the Biblical prophets and histories is undeviating.

Similarly, in the new Hobbesian world of the global economy the losers in their millions are likewise pushed into the street or the gutter, without mercy of any sort being considered as a factor. How could mercy possibly be relevant in such a winner-takes-all world? In ethnic conflict mercy goes down the drain, to be replaced by rape, torture, and summary execution. Naturally in Stalinist Russia, Maoist China, Nazi Germany, Cambodia under Pol Pot, and all modern tyrannies, mercy for those deemed to be in the wrong is scorned. For such tyrannies the S.S. man in his jet-black uniform becomes the ultimate anti-hero, personification of the merciless hunter-killer-torturer and racist bigot, Satan reincarnated and clothed in human form.

What is happening with all this denial of mercy? Racism, sexism, ageism, classism, religionism, etc., play their part in the denial and rejection of mercy, but mercilessness on such a scale as we have seen in the 20th century constitutes a terrifying contempt for life itself, in whatever form. As such it is an act against the will of creation and an expression of pure nihilism and hatred for what is other than like me. The fact that mercilessness has been so transparent and widespread in our time is something that should greatly concern us. Moral history must, and will, condemn all such vile behavior.

Consequently, those of us living in the United States need to be fully aware that mercy is intrinsic to the covenantal tradition, and that lack of mercy constitutes rejection and betrayal of that tradition. For those of Christian persuasion, mercy is the quality of the good Samaritan traveling from Jerusalem to Jericho. It is love of neighbor in action. Absence of mercy is denial of one of the values most dear to the covenanting God. In Christian terms it means death on the road to Jericho and the endless torture and recrucifixion of Jesus and those he loved.

Thus, it was not by chance that in the wake of the carnage and mass murder of World War II the French organist and composer Maurice Duruflé produced a powerful and elegiac Requiem Mass, in which the plea for mercy is such a paramount theme. Faced with the unfathomable mercilessness characterizing the Nazi occupation of Europe, including France, Duruflé drew heavily on the plainsong accompanying ancient Christian worship to invoke the assurance of divine mercy. This invocation is expressed most fully and majestically in the setting of the Kyrie (Lord have mercy on us, Christ have mercy on us, Lord have mercy on us). But it resonates throughout the entire composition, enabling it to serve as a requiem and remembrance, not just for his father, to whom it is dedicated, but for all those lost souls tortured and killed in that war.

In seeing mercy in its aspect of forgiveness, we should not lose sight of the broader meaning of mercy, which is that quality expressing the love of Yahweh for what is created. So great is our capacity as humans to sin and our propensity to anthropomorphize and romanticize love, that we are apt to lose sight of the notion of Yahweh as lover and the idea of what that kind of love might mean. The Creator-God, in fact, is pictured as loving the life that has been created. "When Israel was a child, I loved him", proclaimed Hosea, the prophet of love, voicing the emotion of Yahweh as Creator:

> I myself taught Ephraim to walk.
> I took them in my arms …
> I led them with reins of kindness,
> With leading strings of love.
> I was like someone who lifts an infant close against his cheek
> Stooping down to him I gave him his food.
> Hosea 11, Jerusalem Bible

Yahweh as lover is a nurturing and cheek-caressing parent. Yahweh is also spouse, and in that capacity an angry because unrequited spouse. "No more love shall the House of Israel have from me in the future" says an angry and dejected Yahweh, observing rulers and people of the kingdom of Israel engaging in merciless bloodshed and idolatry, in complete defiance of the covenant. But Yahweh, speaking through Hosea, looks forward to a reconciliation, when Israel will once again address Yahweh as "my spouse." On that day,

> I will betroth you to myself for ever,
> betroth you with integrity and justice,
> with tenderness and love
> betroth you to myself with faithfulness,
> and you will come to know Yahweh

Or as a later, more prosaic commentator put it, "I will love them with all my heart, for my anger has turned from them." (Hosea 11, 2, 14, from Jerusalem Bible).

Yahweh as unrequited but yearning spouse-lover is an image of God that contemporary America would do well to revive. We would, to be sure, need to revise our understandings of betrothal and love. We would have to rediscover fidelity and tenderness as aspects of love, as these are the qualities which Yahweh as lover embodies, and it is the absence of these qualities in us that makes Yahweh so upset and angry. We would have to imagine—or look around and see—that where these qualities exist the whole of creation, not just humankind, preens itself, dances, and sings songs of joy. Similarly, where and when they have disappeared a country is in mourning, its people pine away, and even the wildlife and the fish are found to be dying off. (Hosea 4) If we Americans and Westerners put aside illusion and look around at our beleaguered urban schools, downsizing companies, inner cities, half empty mainline churches, and consider the pollution of our habitat, the dying off of fisheries, and our obsessions with gasoline, materialism and garbage, we might imagine any Creator of life who valued fidelity and tenderness to feel like a very unrequited spouse, indeed an angry and disappointed spouse, who could very well turn away from us as people who have become tainted and odious. That is the warning that comes to us from the Biblical covenantal tradition—our tradition.

The other value embedded in our tradition is justice. We are sometimes confused about the difference between justice and law, seeing each as an aspect of the other. 'Justice' is often used in this manner by political leaders. The word 'justice' has become a title for our Supreme Court judges; often symbolized as blindfolded, the figure of justice is supposed to embody impartiality as well as strict adherence to the law. But impartiality is a misunderstanding of justice as it is characterized in the Biblical covenantal tradition. Impartiality suggests a rational weighing of competing interests and a search for legal basis and precedent on which to arrive at a prudent decision. From a Biblical, covenantal perspective this kind of process would be better described as jurisprudence rather than justice, because Biblical justice is never impartial. It is concerned not with competing interests but with right and wrong, with what is just and unjust. It is grounded in moral vision and therefore emotionally driven by the heart, rather than based on rational calculus.

Covenantal justice strives to uphold and protect the handiwork and the vision of the Creator-God. It focuses on the needs of less privileged and less powerful people. In the covenantal world there is to be a place for everybody, rich or poor. The rich are in fact responsible for the maintenance of the poor. The prophetic texts and psalms are so driven by this idea that it is impossible to study them seriously without catching on to Yahweh's concern for the poor. Moreover, the covenantal legislation in the Torah is quite explicit on this point. There is to be a safety net to sustain the poor. In the Torah that net is described in terms appropriate to an ancient agrarian culture. In the global economy of today other terms are needed if we are to avert starvation in famine-stricken and war-torn regions or malnutrition, unemployment, despair and homelessness in our own inner cities and decaying industrial regions as well as among millions of refugees. But the principle of establishing ways to sustain poor and disadvantaged people remains the same.

Contemporary society has by and large lost sight of this Yahwist, covenantal equation of justice with provision for those in need. We have allowed ourselves to become sidetracked into the notion that provision for the poor is an act of voluntary charity rather than of covenantal justice. Under our system of charity well-off people, if they so desire, give from their largesse and are rewarded for their virtue with a tax deduction. But such giving is not considered mandatory, otherwise it would not be an act of charity. Nothing obligates the modern rich to keep the poor alive or to give back to them any portion of what has been exacted through means of rents, interest on loans, or payments in minimum wages. If the poor sink into debt, why not let them work like everyone else; or else let them eat cake or go back from whence they came.

The logical consequences of this shift from justice to charity could be obscured so long as charitable giving remained a major focus of well-organized church communities and a policy prescription of modern liberal government. But now we have entered a brave new world in which charitable giving, particularly by the state, is no longer so credible, and due to mounting debt no longer so manageable. The power of the church to induce believers into tithing to help less well-off people has dramatically declined, along with the numbers of believers (at least in so-called mainline churches). There are millions and millions of agnostics and atheists out there for whom tithing is unknown and meaningless. How are they to assess their duties towards the poor, many of whom give the appearance of being freeloading misfits and scavengers? As for modern liberal government, its vitality has been sapped by the decline of popular faith in secular ideologies of progress. Instead of being the measure of the Great Society, the poor have become its nemesis.

Thus, we have entered a brave new world, in which a preference for saving or assisting the poor has been challenged by a preference for disowning or bashing them. Poverty bashing has become good politics, and there are politicians who have become successful bashing so-called illegal (i.e. undocumented) immigrants, welfare queens, social parasites, and squeamish liberals. Hard, tight-lipped men with an eye to budget balancing and tax deductions have taken hold of public life. The poor are being driven out of government institutions and off the government rolls and corporate pension funds and medical insurance policies. Economically marginalized and lacking any perceived social or moral utility, they have become fair game for the accountant's and the executive's axe.

This slow, deliberate discharge of the poor represents a profound reversal of modern progressive ideology. But that does not tell us whether it represents a perversion of covenantal justice. Modern progressive ideology has been losing ground ever since the First and Second World Wars. The claims of the poor on that ideology could not survive the battering that modern progressive ideology in its various forms has taken from the social and military turmoil characterizing the 20th century. A yearning for the ethically neutral market place, or for doctrines of personal salvation, is replacing decades of progressive social engineering. In this respect the U.S. is no different from Russia or China, where the iron rice bowl is disappearing along with the other vestiges of Communist utopia.

What we need to know is whether, in our rush to get rid of secular liberalism, we are reverting to the pristine pathways of the Yahwist covenant or going on to something else. Are the anti-welfare, budget-cutting politicians, who dominate today's state and federal governments, turning back to the pages of Deuteronomy, Isaiah and Amos to find out what belongs to the poor? Is their urge to confine and shackle or get rid of delinquents of all hues driven by Yahwist notions of justice? Certainly, the public record gives little evidence that Yahwism is enjoying a political revival either in the U.S. or elsewhere. To the contrary: the claims of the poor are under assault not only in individual countries but also on a global scale. The 'North', which is the orbit of the richer industrialized countries, has lined up vis-a-vis the 'South', which is the locus of the developing and not so developable countries. Strategies outlined at Rio in 1992 and after, whereby Northern advanced and more developed countries would help to subsidize less advanced and developed Southern countries, have been implemented only in microcosm. The North has shown little interest in truly tithing itself to assist the South.

Indeed, if we look with honest eyes into the pages of 19th and 20th century history, we must conclude that covenantal justice, like covenantal mercy, was never very widely practiced. Its demands would seem to be beyond our scope, just as they were beyond the scope of the ancient Israelites. Apart from a succession of dreary poor laws, which attempted to establish a minimal safety net beneath the 'deserving' poor (forget about the undeserving poor), there has never been much sense among the stakeholders of this world that the poor were a necessary aspect of their wellbeing. Where the Bible speaks of the blessings of sharing bread with the hungry and bringing good news to the poor, as though the souls of the well-off might even be warmed by service to the poor, contemporary society too often has gotten tired of propping up the losers of this world and would rather turn them adrift than send out the lifeboats.

Does this mean that the Yahwist ethic of justice and mercy is too utopian to hold any further claim upon us? Is our Judeo-Christian salvational history, in effect, truly at an end? In the wake of the Holocaust, with its deliberate mass destruction of Jewish life and heritage, Jewish people were forced to face that question. Had Yahweh-God finally abandoned Jews to their tormentors and let loose a firestorm to kill them off? African-Americans, Mayans, and other such oppressed people have also been obliged over several centuries to face the fear of divine abandonment.

But the question really belongs to those who hold the power, since unless they govern according to an ethical mandate there is no ethical government. Do those who enjoy influence and authority in the dominant Western countries still believe in covenantal ethics and salvational history as spelled out in the Bible and at least backhandedly acknowledged in public policy up to our times? If not, can those, who do believe, strive to restore this mandate? And what happens if they can't or won't?

That this is no minor question is exemplified by the domestic and global problems we face today. We all need a vision of moral community to inspire us in our daily lives. Such a vision is spelled out in detail in the Bible, and a modern version of that vision was incorporated into the Declaration of Independence. Americans do not lack documents, visions and stories by which to guide their lives. Nevertheless, we must recognize that we and everyone else have fallen short of those visions, just as did the children of Israel long ago. The Bible is sharply critical of the conduct of the early Israelites. Yet the prophets were there not just to criticize but to restate and re-inspire the Yahwist vision of moral community as conditions of life changed. In their hands and those of their Christian and Jewish successors that story of moral community survived to guide new generations.

The time is ripe for a similar restating of moral community, one that can take us forward better than the versions that prevailed during the twentieth century. The bad news is that there is at present no prevailing agreement in contemporary America on the nature of moral community. The good news, for those who believe in the Biblical covenants, is that we don't have to reinvent the wheel. We just need to apply it to our circumstances and find our own way forward.

CHAPTER 18

Conclusion: The Two Ways

>Where your treasure is
>There will your heart be also
>Matthew 6:21.

One of the earliest Christian handbooks, known as The Teaching of the Lord to the Gentiles through the Twelve Apostles, or more simply as the Didache (teaching), informs its readers that "there are two ways: a way of life and a way of death; and the difference between these two ways is great." The original statement of this idea comes, as we have seen, from the last discourse of Moses in the Book of Deuteronomy, in the course of which the prophet is led to proclaim: "I set before you life or death, blessing or curse. Choose life!" (From Jerusalem Bible). The texts of the Sermon on the Mount, found in the gospels of Matthew and Luke, say much the same thing, and some of their teachings are incorporated into the Didache.

What is interesting about the Didache is that it focuses on the two ways as the most important message to get across to early followers of the way of Jesus. "The way of Life is this," it proclaims. "Thou shalt love first the Lord thy Creator, and secondly thy neighbor as thyself; and thou shalt do nothing to any person that thou wouldst not wish to be done to thyself."[20] Evidently little has changed about the fundamentals of how to live on this earth, as seen in central texts in the Judeo-Christian tradition.

What keeps changing is the capacity of human beings to live up to

---

[20] From Maxwell Staniforth tr., Early Christian Writings. London: Penguin Books, 1968. The translation uses the word "man" rather than 'person'.

these teachings. Some special people do, but many of us try, drift away, try again, and then drift away again. We may start with good intentions. But then too easily we listen to the siren songs of the tempters, or get distracted and tired, or obsess about priorities, or see something we'd like to get a hold of, or get into needless arguments, or compromise about something and end up settling for less. We may suffer a major disappointment or a wound and get taken down by it. As a matter of fact, most if not all of us do suffer wounds, and some of them may affect us for years, or even for a lifetime. Sometimes it is easier to tune out, or to look with a skeptical eye on what other people are saying and doing, especially those who appear to be getting on better than us. Facing one's own wounds and limitations often seems too difficult to handle.

The Deuteronomic histories (the Books of Joshua, Judges, Samuel and Kings) are full of stories about people who got themselves into trouble and fell short. Perhaps the most shocking example is King David, who as a youth was graced by God, who was a musician and poet par excellence in the Book of Psalms, but who died with his credibility shattered. But what do we learn from such case histories? There are times when we seem to be victims of vast forces—even if some of them are nothing more than government policies—that are beyond our capacity as individuals to control or to understand through case studies. Under such circumstances people might reasonably conclude that this is the way life is. As I write these words, I can hear a voice whispering "Look! It never happens the way the idealists would have it. What do you think today's economic crises are all about? You really think people loving their Creator is going to solve everything? Who cares about the two ways, for God's sake? You want me to love my neighbor? Why?"

Yes, we have come through an era in the United States, and indeed in the Global economy, in which getting and taking has been much more on people's minds than giving and letting go. On the U.S. airwaves and in the market place it is customary to hear advertisers refer to human beings as 'consumers'—even in such bizarre contexts as recruitment into the military—because accumulation and consumption, coupled with lack of savings and growing debt, have become a dominant modality of our American economic way of life. In short, we have come to be identifiable as consumers. Admittedly we are needy people, especially when our standard of living is leveling out or going down. We need gasoline, bonuses, gifts, flat screen TVs, computers and cell phones. We need food and drink, shopping malls, sports franchises, bars, movie idols, comfort and luxury, anything that might keep us satisfied or help distract us from our mortality. Although this might sound like a caricature, it is what some of our recent political leaders have even been promoting as the American way, a way that is in their view the duty of our leaders to protect.

Suddenly, however, our world has taken a shift. The once mighty U.S. economy has proved itself vulnerable. In a repeat of the great 1929-30 Crash, the one-time heroes and billionaires of Wall Street are beginning to look less like financial geniuses and more like greedy pillagers of other people's assets. Too many political leaders, for their part, turn out to have feet of clay. Wherever politicians and lobbyists get together, the public trust risks being put up for auction. Too many of us can be sold a line by bankers, mortgage brokers and politicians without sufficiently realizing the risks involved. And lurking behind our own gullibility lies the much greater, and largely unseen, trauma of people across the globe, whose lives have been snuffed out or rendered miserable while we and millions of others pursue our urge to accumulate wealth and security. Those traumatized people are to be found everywhere: not just in Darfur, Afghanistan, Iraq, Palestine, Syria, Yemen, and wherever refugees abound, but on our own streets, and in our own ghettos, shelters and prisons.

"But surely," I can hear myself saying, "you aren't blaming me for all that? How can I do much about refugees or illegal immigrants? I've got my own troubles to deal with!"

Such rationalizations can help calm people who may not know or feel secure about the direction of their lives. That can mean most of us, at one time or another. On the great questions of consequence, such as who am I really, where am I going, why do I exist on this earth, what am I responsible for, what do I really believe in, how do I live in connection with others, or how can I get up every morning feeling alive, joyful and trustworthy, most of our strategies have their limits. So then, what do you do when you have worked hard to accumulate money and buy a nice house, and suddenly neither are there? When your job, your child, your marriage, your engagement, your confidence, your hopes and dreams, disappear or are shafted? When you don't feel safe any longer? When you don't trust your leaders to do the right thing? When public safety nets crumble? Where do you turn for advice and consolation?

Sacred literature has much to tell us about such questions. But it does not provide the usual answers. That is because we cannot have our earthly cake and then proceed to eat it. If we want to learn how to live—in the way that 'live' is defined in sacred literature—we need to ease up on earthly stratagems and learn how to attune ourselves to sacred stratagems: to the covenants, for example, or to what is called here the way of life.

Fortunately, it doesn't take an advanced degree to understand these ways. They are quite simple. The Didache takes only three short pages to lay out the way of life and only half a page to lay out the way of death. The way of life, it says, drawing on the Sermon on the Mount, consists in praying for your enemies. Praying for what? Yes, praying for our enemies. That is to say: we engage in prayer, and the object of our prayer is our enemies—people who may be persecuting and oppressing us; people who may dislike and even hate us; people who may be killing us; people whom we may be resenting, oppressing and killing. Where, it claims, is the merit in loving only those who return your love? Even heathens do that! Love those who hate you, and you will have nobody to be your enemy. (D1)

This is the kind of transfiguring thinking that the Didache and the Bible ask for, so the Didache puts it right up front and asks its readers to take on that challenge. Prayer, it tells us, is a way of loving. The text goes on with some other well-known prescriptions. Give to everyone that asks. Do not covet, do not equivocate. Never give way to anger. (How I wish I had learned that lesson long ago). Refrain from fanaticism. Try to make peace. Judge with justice. Never speak sharply when giving orders to servants … That is the way of life. (D 1, 2, 4).

As to the way of death, "it is evil, and in every way fraught with damnation." In it are murders, adulteries, etc, etc. Here are those who love falsehood … who lie awake planning wickedness … who are bent only on their own advantage … They aid and abet the rich but arbitrarily condemn the poor. They are utterly sunk in iniquity. (D 5) If one has read the Bible, this all sounds familiar.

The Didache doesn't acknowledge that choosing the way of death can be quite beguiling, even in certain ways fun and ego-flattering. The fact that the way of death leads down the road to hell isn't always apparent, and what is worse, may never be apparent to oneself. But what is clear from the Eden myth is that when I choose the way of death, other people end up suffering, not just myself. That is all made quite explicit to people who read the Bible. Life, in short, is about this choice, and this choice is a test of everything we are and have. If you read the gospels of Matthew and Luke, for example, you find the nature of the choice laid out clear as daylight in the dialogue between Jesus and the Satan. One could expect Jesus not to fall for the Satan's blandishments. But what about us ordinary people? Are we so immune to flattering invitations supposedly opening the door to health, wealth and power?

In order to strengthen the reader's resolve, the Didache urges people not to be tempted from the way of life. Pray for your enemies. Start there! But it adds—as if in commiseration—that if all this exhortation is too much to live up to, then do as much as you can. And especially love the Source of your being and your neighbor. (D 6, 1)

The Sermon on the Mount, on which the Didache draws heavily, concludes its teaching with a powerful parable comparing the choice to people who build their houses on rock and on sand. The house built on rock does not fall even when floods rise, and gales hurl themselves against it. But when floods and gales strike the house built on sand, it falls. And what a fall! Of course, floods and gales can rip up most houses, as tsunamis and hurricanes have repeatedly demonstrated. But rock and sand are used here as metaphors to compare people who live according to the way of life with those who hear all about it but don't. The former do not swerve from the path, no matter what happens. The latter are the people who live on sand. When trouble erupts, everything they have gets blown away or swallowed up; and despair and death loom.

The lessons would appear to be simple. All we need to do is to make them our own. And there's the rub. These lessons make demands on us. I need to take responsibility for being who I am, knowing what I know, doing what I do, and letting happen what I let happen. As a unique human being, which is what we all are, I matter, and what I do with my life matters. I need to open my eyes and my heart and listen to what the world is telling me. Above all, I have choices to make. I can choose to honor and love my enemies or to resent and hate them and oppress their friends and children while I'm at it. I can choose the way of life, or I can choose the way of death and listen to the siren songs, the drug dealers, the get rich quick artists, the con men. I can also choose not to choose either way and deny that I have a choice to choose either way; or I can choose a little bit of each way, hoping somehow to stay in balance. But those are default positions, and unfortunately one cannot become fully human by living a life in which one fails to make basic choices about how to live.

That is why the Bible, and sacred handbooks such as the Didache, try to help us make choices about how to live. According to the Bible, everything boils down to choices, right from the word go, beginning with Adam and Eve. According to this all-important myth, Adam and Eve chose a piece of fruit—let us call it a material object—in preference to a sacred agreement, a covenant. They traded a relationship with the sacred world in return for a tiny piece of the material world. How good a deal is that? In so doing they lost their membership in Paradise and woke up in our earthly world, where people (e.g. Cain, and generations of others up to the present day) are willing to kill others to get what they think is theirs.

History and knowledge of current affairs remind us that despite the relevance of the Eden myth, this fall from grace happens again and again. But does it have to be that way? No, it does not. Cain is someone who chooses the way of death; Abraham, Sarah and Moses choose the way of life, as do Ruth and Naomi and all the prophets. Judas chooses the way of death; Paul chooses the way of life, as do Mary Magdalene, Mary the mother of Jesus, and many of his early followers. And for Christians, but not only for Christians, Jesus chooses and sanctifies the wounds of life, and by embodying them shows us the way to heal ourselves and restore our connection to the sacred covenants. All these examples are reminders that the choice to follow such a way and restore that connection—or not to do so—is ours, whether we are inheritors of Judeo Christian traditions or follow some other path.[21] The great Johann Sebastian Bach made his choice clear by writing a wonderful musical meditation for organ on the

---

[21] The Buddha made a critical choice to give up a life of power and privilege for a life of poverty and to confront and overcome the forces of darkness. Gandhi chose life and came to respect his British enemies. Martin Luther King chose to follow Gandhi's example. Dietrich Bonhoeffer chose to return to Nazi Germany and risk death rather than sit out World War Two in comparative safety.

theme "From God I will not depart" (Von Gott will ich nicht lassen). Fortunately, we don't have to be inspired musicians to follow his example.

So, dear reader, take heart. "For where your treasure is, there will your heart be also." If your heart is in the right place, give yourself a star and pray for people you thoroughly dislike. This is what peacemakers do. This is what the Dalai Lama and his colleagues do for their critics in Beijing. Praying for one's opponents frees up one's mind to engage in the work of peacemaking. Once you are on that path you can then, in the words of another of Bach's great choral preludes, "Adorn Thyself, Oh Beloved Soul" (Schmücke dich). For you have chosen life!

Works Consulted and Further Reading

The Bible as Story

If you would like to explore the Bible as story, these sources could be very helpful. Alan Dale and David Kossoff are born story-tellers. Joseph Donders writes like a bard, in poetic form. Henri Nouwen teases layers of meaning out of biblical texts and a famous parable (gospel story). The mystery plays illustrate a form of story-telling popular throughout the Middle Ages, when story-telling was the principal way through which the Bible was conveyed to ordinary people. The libretto of Handel's Messiah is an 18th century work made popular by Handel's brilliant score.

Bullard, Roger A. Messiah: The Gospel According to Handel's Oratorio. London: Hodder and Stoughton, 1995.

Dale, Alan T. New World: The Heart of the New Testament in Plain English. London: Oxford University Press, 1967.

Dale, Alan T. Winding Quest: The Heart of the Old Testament in Plain English. London: Oxford University Press, 1972.

Donders, Joseph G. Jesus the Stranger. Maryknoll, N. Y.: Orbis Books, 1978.

Donders, Joseph G. Beyond Jesus: Reflections on the Gospels for the B-Cycle. Maryknoll, N.Y.: Orbis Books, 1984.

Happé, Peter, Ed. English Mystery Plays. New York: Penguin Books, 1975.

Kossoff, David. Bible Stories. London: Fontana Books, 1971.

Kossoff, David. The Book of Witnesses. London: Fontana Books, 1974.

Nouwen, Henri J. M. Out of Solitude: Three Meditations on the Christian Life. Notre Dame, IN: Ave Maria Press, 1974.

Nouwen, Henri J. M. The Return of the Prodigal Son. New York: Doubleday, 1992.

Stone, Brian, Ed. and Transl. Medieval English Verse. New York: Penguin Books, 1964.

Hebrew Scriptures

The works by Bloom and Rosenberg and Feiler are non-specialist and very readable. Back to the Sources is a wonderful introduction to early Jewish literature. History as Prophecy by Peckham is a detailed and complex study of the textual structure and evolution of the Torah and prophetic texts. It is a huge achievement. Soloveitchik is one of the great Jewish theologians of our time. Congregation illustrates how Jewish intellectuals read the Bible.

Bloom, Harold and David Rosenberg. The Book of J. New York: Vintage Books, 1990.

De Vaux, Roland, O.P. The Bible and the Ancient Near East. Translated by Damian McHugh. New York: Doubleday, 1967.

Feiler, Bruce. Abraham: A Journey Into the Heart of Three Faiths. San Francisco: Harper Perennial, 2002.

Grant, Michael. The History of Ancient Israel. New York: Scribner's, 1984.

Hermisson, Hans-Jürgen and Eduard Lohse. Faith. Translated by Douglas W. Stott. Nashville, TN: Abingdon, 1981.

Holtz, Barry W, ed. Back to the Sources: Reading the Classic Jewish Texts. New York: Summit Books, 1984.

Musaph-Andriesse, R.C. From Torah to Kabbalah: A Basic Introduction to the Writings of Judaism. New York: Oxford University Press, 1982.

Peckham, Brian. History as Prophecy: The Development of Late Judean Literary Traditions. New York: Doubleday, 1993.

Peli, Pinchas H. Soloveitchik On Repentance. New York: Paulist Press, 1984.

Rashi, Commentary on the Torah. The commentary by the great Rabbi Shlomo Yitzhaki (1040-1105 CE) can be consulted online through the Jewish Virtual Library, via Chabad.org. There is no better way to enter into a reading of the Torah or the Hebrew Bible from a rabbinic perspective.

Rosenberg, David, ed. Congregation: Contemporary Jewish Writers Read the Bible. New York: Harcourt, Brace, Jovanovich, 1987

Creation and the Fall

This topic introduces basic themes underlying Judaism and Christianity. Any attempt to understand the Bible has to start from the creation stories. The works by Elaine Pagels are accessible to general readers and are a very good place to begin. Delumeau's book is not an easy read but provides a very illuminating account of the rise of the Western culture of guilt. The work by Sjöö and Mor may be unwelcome to some readers, but it opens up the topic of gender conflict that underlies the Bible; it is a topic with which the Biblical texts are forced to grapple. The commentary by Gibson predates the more complex textual analysis of Peckham (see above), but there is still much of interest in this survey.

Delumeau, Jean. Sin and Fear: The Emergence of a Western Guilt Culture, 13th-18th Centuries. Translated by Eric Nicholson. New York: St. Martin's Press, 1990.

Gibson, John C. L. Genesis. Volumes 1 and 2. Philadelphia: Westminster Press, 1981, 1982.

Pagels, Elaine. Adam, Eve and the Serpent. New York: Vintage Books, 1989.

Pagels, Elaine. The Origin of Satan. New York: Vintage Books, 1996.

Sjöö, Monica and Barbara Mor. The Great Cosmic Mother: Rediscovering the Religion of the Earth. San Francisco: HarperSanFrancisco, 1987.

The Exodus and the Covenant

'Covenant' is the organizing motif of both Judaism and Christianity. Moses, the Egyptian prince who became the Jewish liberator, is its archetypal co-creator. Deuteronomy provides the most impassioned expression of the meaning of covenant. The work by the famous British novelist Anthony Burgess is a splendid poetic discourse on Moses.

Achtemeier, Elizabeth. Deuteronomy, Jeremiah. Philadelphia: Fortress Press, 1978.

Burgess, Anthony. Moses: A Narrative. New York: Stonehill Publishing, 1976.

Davies, G. Henton. Exodus. London: SCM Press, 1967.

Hillers, Delbert R. Covenant: The History of a Biblical Idea. Baltimore: The Johns Hopkins University Press, 1969.

Hoppe, Leslie J. O.F.M. Deuteronomy. Collegeville, MN: The Liturgical Press, 1985

Early Prophecy/Histories

These texts give us the first take on the covenant in action. They record the lives and work of judges such as Gideon, Samson and Deborah, all the kings of Israel and Judah, and archetypal prophets such as Samuel, Nathan, Elijah and Elisha. They also provide a historical context, which judges conduct in terms of adherence to the Biblical covenant. History emerges as a moral discipline by which the actions of those in power are evaluated. In fact history and prophecy are intertwined. The Elijah cycle (I Kings 17-22) and Elisha cycle (II Kings 2-13) give detailed profiles of this interplay.

Bowes, Paula J. First Samuel, Second Samuel. Collegeville, MN: The Liturgical Press, 1985.

Laffey, Alice L., R.S.M. First Kings, Second Kings. Collegeville, MN: The Liturgical Press, 1985.

Rast, Walter E. Joshua, Judges, Samuel, Kings. Philadelphia: Fortress Press, 1978.

Prophetic Literature

Apart from Moses himself, the texts of Isaiah, Jeremiah, and Ezekiel provide the broadest understanding of the prophetic role. But if prophetic literature is unfamiliar to you, it would be easier to start with one of the shorter texts, such as Amos, Hosea or Micah, which have the same vision and power but are less complex as literary documents.

Achtemeier, Elizabeth. Deuteronomy, Jeremiah. Philadelphia: Fortress Press, 1978.

Anderson, Bernhard A. The Eighth Century Prophets: Amos, Hosea, Isaiah, Micah. Philadelphia: Fortress Press, 1978.

Craven, Toni. Ezekiel, Daniel. Collegeville, MN: The Liturgical Press, 1986.

The Psalms

The psalms are texts for singing, meditation and worship. The studies by Alter and Hayes are excellent texts for understanding the Psalms in the context of their times. Lewis provides a guide on how to meditate on the Psalms. The Book of Psalms, with its many beautiful medieval illustrations, reminds one that this is a sacred text, providing expert guidance on how to access the world of the sacred.

Alter, Robert, The Book of Psalms, New York, Norton, 2007.

Hayes, John H. Understanding the Psalms. Valley Forge, PA: Judson Press, 1976.

Lewis, C. S. Reflections on the Psalms. New York: Harcourt, Brace, Jovanovich, 1958.

The Book of Psalms (in the Authorized Version). New York: Henry Holt, 1986.

Job

This text resonates with problems that confront anyone trying to live a powerful and fulfilling life. The translation of the text by Stephen Mitchell is in elegant modern English. There are many modern interpretations of the Job story.

Glatzer, Nahum N. The Dimensions of Job: A Study and Selected Readings. New York: Schocken Books, 1969.

Guinan, Michael D. O.F.M. Job. Collegeville, MN: The Liturgical Press, 1986.

Mitchell, Stephen. The Book of Job. San Francisco: Harper Perennial, 1992.

Christian Testament

This selection provides a smattering of the volumes of scholarship and discourse available for study of the Christian [New] Testament. Over the last century an enormous amount of ground has been covered by scholars in explaining how these texts were put together and what they are able to tell us. Any one of the sources listed here would be a useful guide. Some of the texts of the Christian Testament, such as the Letter to the Romans, or Revelation, are so complex that it is really essential to have a commentary at hand when reading them.

The Complete Gospels, a project of the Fellows of the Jesus Seminar, provides new translations of the canonical and non-canonical gospels, as well as materials incorporated within the four canonical gospels. The New Testament of the New Jerusalem Bible provides detailed notes not available in the basic edition. Who Wrote the New Testament? by Burton L. Mack is a brilliant analysis of the mythmaking that went into the construction of the Christian testament, and the individuals—known and unknown—who prepared and selected the texts.

The study of the Sermon on the Mount by Swami Prabhavananda reflects a devotion to the life and teachings of Jesus that may come as a surprise to Western readers but that is consistent with the highest forms of Vedanta.

Barclay, William. The Acts of the Apostles. Rev. Ed. Philadelphia: Westminster Press, 1976.

Barrett, C. K. Ed. The New Testament Background: Selected Documents. New York: Harper and Row, 1961.

Brown, Raymond E. The Community of the Beloved Disciple: The Life, Loves and Hates of an Individual Church in New Testament Times. New York: Paulist Press, 1979.

Brown, Raymond E. The Churches the Apostles Left Behind. New York: Paulist Press, 1984.

Brown, Schuyler. The Origins of Christianity: A Historical Introduction to the New Testament. New York: Oxford University Press, 1984.

Grant, Michael. Jesus: An Historian's Review of the Gospels. New York: Charles Scribner's Sons, 1977.

Mack, Burton L. Who Wrote the New Testament? The Making of the Christian Myth. San Francisco: HarperSanFrancisco, 1996.

MacRae, George W., S. J. Hebrews. Collegeville, MN: The Liturgical Press, 1982.

Miller, Robert J., Ed. The Complete Gospels: Annotated Scholars Version. Revised and Expanded Edn. San Francisco: HarperSanFrancisco, 1994.

Neill, Stephen and Tom Wright. The Interpretation of the New Testament, 1861-1986. 2nd Edn. New York: Oxford University Press, 1986.

Schüssler Fiorenza, Elisabeth. Revelation: Vision of a Just World. Minneapolis, MN: Fortress Press, 1991.

Spong, John Shelby. Resurrection: Myth or Reality? A Bishop's Search for the Origins of Christianity. San Francisco: HarperSanFrancisco, 1994.

Swami Prabhavananda. The Sermon on the Mount According to Vedanta. New York: Mentor Book, 1963.

John Watt

The New Testament of the New Jerusalem Bible. New York: Doubleday, 1986.

Other Early Christian Writings

The discovery some 50 years ago of the so-called Gnostic gospels has transformed our understanding of the breadth of early Christic literature. It also helps us to understand why the Christian Testament was put together the way it was. Fierce, relentless battles preceded the decisions on what to include and what to leave out. If one only reads the Bible, one cannot appreciate the diversity and complexity of early Christic communities. Proceed with caution, but proceed!

Early Christian Writings: The Apostolic Fathers. Translated by Maxwell Staniforth. New York: Penguin Books, 1968. Contains the text of the Didache and writings by and about early martyrs.

King, Karen L. The Gospel of Mary of Magdala: Jesus and the First Woman Disciple. Santa Rosa, CA: Polebridge Press, 2003.

Leloup, Jean-Yves. The Gospel of Mary Magdalene. Rochester, Vermont: Inner Traditions, 2002.

Pagels, Elaine. The Gnostic Gospels. New York: Vintage, 1981.

Pagels, Elaine. Beyond Belief: The Secret Gospel of Thomas. New York: Random House, 2005.

Pagels, Elaine, and Karen L. King. Reading Judas: The Gospel of Judas and the Shaping of Christianity. New York: Viking, 2007.

Jesus

Studies about Jesus are far more interesting and provocative today than they were when I was young. These citations are just a small sample of the vast literature on Jesus, but they include texts from a variety of cultural and literary perspectives. Try one or two to get a flavor of what is out there.

Borg, Marcus J. Meeting Jesus Again for the First Time. San Francisco: HarperSanFrancisco, 1994.

Borg, Marcus J. Jesus: Uncovering the Life, Teachings and Relevance of a Religious Revolutionary. New York: HarperOne, 2008. Provides a very impressive grasp of the social and political context of the Jesus mission.

Breech, James. The Silence of Jesus: The Authentic Voice of the Historical Man. Philadelphia: Fortress Press, 1983.

Burgess, Anthony. Man of Nazareth. New York: Bantam Books, 1982.

Crossan: John Dominic. The Historical Jesus: The Life of a Mediterranean Jewish Peasant. San Francisco: HarperSanFrancisco, 1992.

Crossan, John Dominic. Who Killed Jesus. San Francisco, HarperSanFrancisco, 1996. An example by a leading Jesus scholar of how to deconstruct the gospel texts and figure how they were put together and with what purposes and what consequences. Provocative and challenging.

Endo, Shusaku. A Life of Jesus. Translated by Richard A. Schuchert, S.J. New York: Paulist Press, 1973.

Meier, John P. A Marginal Jew: Rethinking the Historical Jesus. New York: Doubleday, 1991.

Moltman, Jürgen. The Crucified God: The Cross of Christ as the Foundation and Criticism of Christian Theology. Translated by R. A. Wilson and John Bowden. New York: Harper and Row, 1974.

Moore, Sebastian. The Crucified Jesus Is No Stranger. New York: Crossroad (Seabury Press), 1977.

Pelikan, Jaroslav. Jesus through the Centuries: His Place in the History of Culture. New Haven and London: Yale University Press, 1985.

Riches, John. Jesus and the Transformation of Judaism. New York: The Seabury Press, 1982.

Sandmel, Samuel. We Jews and Jesus. New York: Oxford University Press, 1973.

Sobrino, Jon. Jesus the Liberator: A Historical-Theological View. Translated by Paul Burns and Francis McDonough. Maryknoll, N.Y.: Orbis Books, 1993.

Paul

Scholars of Paul would be appalled by the paucity of sources cited here. But one has to start somewhere, and these commentaries on Paul's famous letters are worth reading. If you are willing to put aside a certain amount of time to read a fascinating reconstructed biography, try The Apostle.

Asch, Sholem. The Apostle. New York: G. P. Putnam's Sons, 1943.

Best, Ernest. The Letter of Paul to the Romans. Cambridge U.K.: Cambridge University Press, 1967.

Scroggs, Robin. Christology in Paul and John. Philadelphia: Fortress Press, 1988.

Mary the Mother

The woman known as the Virgin Mary or The Madonna has been and is the object of intense veneration in the Catholic and Orthodox traditions, as is immediately apparent in their iconography. Mozart, Schubert, Gounod and Rachmaninoff wrote arias in her honor that convey a strong sense of her sacredness. One can read about the aura of the Madonna in the book by China Galland; one can experience her power also in the prose-poetry of Ann Johnson, which is based on gospel texts.

Boff, Leonardo, O. F. M. The Maternal Face of God: The Feminine and Its Religious Expressions. Translated by Robert R. Barr and John W. Diercksmeier. London: Collins, 1979.

Galland, China. Longing for Darkness: Tara and the Black Madonna. New York: Penguin Books, 1990.

Graef, Hilda. The Devotion to Our Lady. New York: Hawthorn Books, 1963.

Johnson, Ann. Miriam of Nazareth: Woman of Strength and Wisdom. Notre Dame, IN: Ave Maria Press, 1984.

Laurentin, René. A Short Treatise on the Virgin Mary. Translated by Charles Neumann Washington, N. J.: Ami Press, 1991.

Mary Magdalene

The recovery of the reputation and standing of Mary Magdalene, and the publication of critical editions of the gospel of Mary, is one of the most significant developments in contemporary Christianity. Brock's scholarly study tells us what went wrong. Women theologians have taken the lead in bringing her out of the darkness and reestablishing the broader claims of women to sacred status that the patriarchs denied to almost all of them for so many centuries. One cannot overemphasize the importance of this development.

Brock, Ann Graham. Mary Magdalene, the First Apostle: The Struggle for Authority. Cambridge, MA: Harvard University Press, 2003.

Calhoun, Flo. I Remember Union: The Story of Mary Magdalena. Bethlehem, CT: All Worlds Publishing, 1992.

Haskins, Susan. *Mary Magdalen: Myth and Metaphor*. New York: Riverhead Books, 1993.

Starbird, Margaret. *The Woman with the Alabaster Jar: Mary Magdalen and the Holy Grail*. Santa Fe, N. M.: Bear and Company, 1993.

[See also two studies of the Gospel of Mary under Other Christian Writings].

Early Christian History

For those who rely on historical analysis, these studies provide the context in which the formation of Christian orthodoxy took place.

Freeman, Charles. *The Closing of the Western Mind: The Rise of Faith and the Fall of Reason*. New York: Vintage Books, 2002.

Frend, W. H. C. *The Early Church*. Philadelphia: Fortress Press, 1982.

Grant, Robert M. *Augustus to Constantine: The Rise and Triumph of Christianity in the Roman World*. San Francisco: Harper and Row, 1990.

Women and Christianity

These studies illuminate the strange and often tragic fate of women in a religion dominated by patriarchal rule. Some of them may make for quite uncomfortable reading. But readers should know that feminist theology is here to stay. If this kind of writing is new to you, I encourage you to get acquainted with it. I started with In Memory of Her and went on from there.

Brock, Rita Nakashima. *Journeys By Heart: A Christology of Erotic Power*. New York: Crossroad, 1992.

Davis, Natalie Zemon and Arlette Farge, ed. A History of Women in the West: III. Renaissance and Enlightenment Paradoxes. Cambridge, MA: Belknap Press, 1993.

Fox, Matthew, O. P. Illuminations of Hildegard of Bingen. Santa Fe, N. M.: Bear and Company, 1985.

Johnson, Elizabeth A. She Who Is: The Mystery of God in Feminist Theological Discourse. New York: Crossroad, 1992.

Miles, Margaret R. Carnal Knowing: Female Nakedness and Religious Meaning in the Christian West. Tunbridge Wells, Kent: Burns and Oates, 1989

Miles, Rosalind. Who Cooked the Last Supper: The Women's History of the World. New York: Three Rivers Press, 1988.

Noble, David F. A World Without Women: The Christian Clerical Culture of Western Science. New York: Knopf, 1993.

Ranke-Heinemann, Ute. Eunuchs for the Kingdom of Heaven: Women, Sexuality, and the Catholic Church. New York: Doubleday, 1990.

Schüssler Fiorenza, Elisabeth. In Memory of Her: A Feminist Theological Reconstruction of Christian Origins. New York: Crossroad, 1992.

Shahar, Shulamith. The Fourth Estate: A History of Women in the Middle Ages. Translated by Chaya Galai. London and New York: Methuen, 1983.

Spong, John Shelby. Born of a Woman: A Bishop Rethinks the Virgin Birth and the Treatment of Woman by a Male-Dominated Church. San Francisco: HarperSanFrancisco, 1992.

Starbird, Margaret. The Goddess in the Gospels: Reclaiming the Sacred Feminine. Santa Fe, N. M.: Bear and Company, 1998.

Witherington, Ben, III. Women in the Ministry of Jesus: A Study of Jesus' Attitudes to Women and Their Roles as Reflected in His Earthly Life. New York: Cambridge University Press, 1987.

Judaism and Christianity

The separation of Christianity from Judaism is one of the most controversial topics in the history of Christianity. Unfortunately the controversy begins even before the writing of the gospels. It is best to accept that this division is part of our cultural background and make the effort to get beyond it. The study by Rosemary Ruether would be a good place to start.

Carroll, James. Constantine's Sword: The Church and the Jews. New York: Houghton Mifflin, 2001.

Grant, Michael. The Jews in the Roman World. New York(?): Dorset Press, 1984.

Ruether, Rosemary. Faith and Fratricide: The Theological Roots of Anti-Semitism. New York: Seabury Press, 1979.

Sandmel, Samuel. Judaism and Christian Beginnings. New York: Oxford University Press, 1978.

Thoma, Clemens. A Christian Theology of Judaism. Translated by Helga Kroner. New York: Paulist Press, 1980.

Poverty and Work

Preference for the poor and respect for poverty are fundamental planks in the Jewish and Christian covenants. My goal has been to make this case from within the Bible texts, but there are many studies that spell out its implications for one's personal life today, such as those noted below.

Brother Lawrence. The Practice of the Presence of God. Grand Rapids, MI: Spire Books, 1958.

Brother Roger of Taizé. Afire with Love: Meditations on Peace and Unity. Translated by Emily Chisholm and the Taizé Community. New York: Crossroad, 1982.

Esquivel, Adolfo Perez. Christ in a Poncho: Witnesses to the Nonviolent Struggles in Latin America. Maryknoll, N. Y.: Orbis Books, 1983.

Foster, Richard J. Freedom of Simplicity. San Francisco: Harper and Row, 1981.

Sider, Ronald J. Ed. Cry Justice: The Bible on Hunger and Poverty. New York: Paulist Press, 1980.

Theologies of Earth and Cosmos

In a time of serious global warming, it is prudent to see what the Bible has to say about the sacredness of the earth and the cosmos. Either of these studies would help you to get started.

Fox, Matthew. The Coming of the Cosmic Christ: The Healing of Mother Earth and the Birth of a Global Renaissance. San Francisco: Harper and Row, 1988.

Ruether, Rosemary Radford. Gaia and God: An Ecofeminist Theology of Earth Healing. San Francisco: HarperSanFrancisco, 1992.

Justice and Mercy

These books enable one to meditate on the meaning and practice of justice and mercy as spelled out in the Bible, well beyond what has been said in this book. Every person who enters down this road is doing the rest of us a huge favor. It would be great if most of us were on it.

The work by Daniel Mendelsohn is a particularly remarkable illustration of the values of justice and mercy, as it explores in excruciating detail how these values were tossed aside, and with what consequences, in the Nazi determination to get rid of Jewish people. While highlighting the lives and deaths of six individuals Mr. Mendelsohn shows us a good deal of additional suffering by other individuals, not all of them Jewish, against a backdrop of basic texts and commentaries from the Torah. In his hands the Bible comes alive in an uncanny way, as do the lives of his protagonists.

I should note here that some scholars prefer to use the word compassion in place of the word mercy. I have stuck to the word mercy because when properly defined it embraces the concept of compassion; but without compassion mercy loses its true meaning.

Boff, Leonardo, O. F. M. Way of the Cross—Way of Justice. Maryknoll, N.Y.: Orbis Books, 1988.

De Vinck, Catherine. A Book of Uncommon Prayers. Allendale, N. J.: Alleluya Press, 1976.

Mendelsohn, Daniel. The Lost: A Search for Six of Six Million. New York: HarperCollinsPublishers, 2006.

Sjögren, Per-Olof. The Jesus Prayer: Lord Jesus Christ, Son of God, Have Mercy on Me. Translated by Sydney Linton. Philadelphia: Fortress Press, 1975.

Fundamentalism

If you want to know what is driving Fundamentalism, and what its take is on the Bible, these sources are all worth reading. Most of them are critical; but this criticism is necessary to get some balance back into the practice of Christianity, especially in the center of our culture. The study by Barbara Rossing on the theology of fundamentalism will be unpleasant reading for fundamentalists; but they should heed it, as should the rest of us.

Armstrong, Karen. The Battle for God. New York: Random House, 2000.

Bawer, Bruce. Stealing Jesus: How Fundamentalism Betrays Christianity. New York: Three Rivers Press, 1997.

Greven, Philip. Spare the Child: The Religious Roots of Punishment and the Psychological Impact of Physical Abuse. New York: Vintage Books, 1990.

Kaplan, Esther. With God on Their Side: George W. Bush and the Christian Right. New York: The New Press, 2005.

Marsden, George M. Fundamentalism and American Culture: The Shaping of Twentieth Century Evangelicalism, 1870-1925. New York: Oxford University Press, 1980.

Rossing, Barbara R. The Rapture Exposed: The Message of Hope in the Book of Revelation. New York: Basic Books, 2004.

Spong, John Shelby. Rescuing the Bible from Fundamentalism: A Bishop Rethinks the Meaning of Scripture. San Francisco: HarperSanFrancisco, 1992.

Understanding The Endtimes: What Can We Know About Bible Prophecy? Grand Rapids, MI: Discovery House Publishers, 2004.

Development of the Bible as Text

If you enjoy knowing how books come into being, these studies help to explain the textual evolution of the Bible. For anyone brought up on the King James Bible, the study by Nicholson is very readable and quite a revelation. The literary analysis by Northrop Frye is a tour de force by a leading literary critic of our times.

Fox, Robin Lane. The Unauthorized Version: Truth and Fiction in the Bible. New York: Knopf, 1992.

Friedman, Richard Elliott. Who Wrote the Bible? New York: Summit Books, 1987.

Frye, Northrop. The Great Code: The Bible and Literature. New York: Harcourt, Brace, Jovanovich, 1981.

Gowan, Donald E. Bridge Between the Testaments: A Reappraisal of Judaism from the Exile to the Birth of Christianity. Pittsburgh, PA: The Pickwick Press, 1980.

Kugel, James L. and Rowan A. Greer. Early Biblical Interpretation. Philadelphia: Westminster Press, 1986.

Nicholson, Adam. God's Secretaries: The Making of the King James Bible. New York: HarperCollins Perennial, 2004.

[See also the study by Peckham under Hebrew Scriptures, above].

AUTHOR DESCRIPTION

John R. Watt, Ph.D, is a historian who has published four books on Chinese history and public health (three in English, one in Chinese). He is also a student of the Bible and a pianist by avocation. His interest in the Bible was inspired by his brother Robin and by the example of his father (an elder of St. Giles Cathedral in Edinburgh, Scotland) and his maternal grandfather (formerly Anglican Bishop of Ontario). With this lineage he decided to find out what the Bible was all about and find a way to put that knowledge to work. It was the decline in public ethics in this country over the last 25 years or more that got him going. Making speeches and giving a few talks didn't seem to be enough. As someone with academic credentials he felt compelled to write a book. The goals of this book have been 1) to identify the key values guiding public and personal life in cultures based on Judeo-Christian traditions, and 2) to make their significance accessible to people not familiar with the Bible. John and his wife Anne also combined with friends to develop a center for K-12 teachers to strengthen teaching on American and global studies. They are fortunate to have three surviving children and four grandchildren, as well as friends from around the world.

Made in the USA
Middletown, DE
08 August 2019